ONLINE PLANNING

Towards

Creative Problem-Solving

Edited by

Harold Sackman

Ronald L. Citrenbaum

Prentice-Hall, Inc., Englewood Cliffs, New Jersey

Library of Congress Cataloging in Publication Data
Main entry under title:

On-line planning: toward creative problem-solving.

  Includes bibliographies.
    1. On-line data processing—Addresses, essays,
lectures. 2. Planning—Addresses, essays, lectures.
I. Sackman, Harold, ed. II. Citrenbaum, Ronald L.,
ed.
HF5548.3.05   658'.05'44   72-543
ISBN 0-13-634295-7

© 1972 by
PRENTICE-HALL, INC.
Englewood Cliffs, New Jersey

Current printing
10 9 8 7 6 5 4 3 2 1

Printed in the United States of America

CONTENTS

PREFACE

This book is concerned with the advent of interactive, online planning, a technological advance that is expected to revolutionize planning theory and practice as it is understood today. The concepts for online planning grew out of research with pioneering time-sharing systems and online problem-solving studies at System Development Corporation. The senior editor, Harold Sackman, was leader of the online planning activity at SDC for work sponsored by the Advanced Research Projects Agency of the Department of Defense. The associate editor and contributors were senior staff members. This project was conceived and designed with ultimate publication for the planning community in mind. The widespread interest evoked by our efforts in leading planning quarters, and increasingly urgent needs for improved planning to meet mounting social problems, prompted us to consider publication in book form for wider distribution.

Our project was motivated by four basic objectives: improved planning, diversified planning, creative impact, and advanced research. Improved planning refers to faster planning, higher quality plans, and comprehensive planning capability throughout all stages of the planning process. Diversified planning, in many respects, is an extension and elaboration of comprehensive planning. It includes the exploitation of promising and powerful online techniques such as interactive simulation, online graphics, and natural language processing. On the application side, it involves individual and team planning, network allocation procedures, and new forms of online teleconference planning. With creative impact we are concerned with problem solving, educational and learning effects, computer-aided insight, and the development of planning consensus among competing and conflicting alternatives. Finally, in working toward a framework for advanced research in online planning, we inquired into planning theory, online experimental methodology, and empirical planning performance evaluation. These four objectives are manifest in the organization of this book.

The text is divided into three parts. Part I explores the principles and techniques of computer-aided planning with special emphasis on theory and method of interactive man-computer problem solving. Part II develops new management approaches to project planning with the aid of powerful online techniques, including interactive graphics, resource allocation procedures, and online simulation. Part III focuses on experimental analysis of online planning in terms of human factors and advanced recording and reduction techniques. Thus, the three parts are designed to explain the nature and principles of online planning, its application in planning projects, and empirical validation through advanced scientific techniques.

To our knowledge, this is the first book devoted to online planning, a pioneering pacesetter. Online computer systems have only recently achieved sufficient technological maturity to displace many of the more conventional batch techniques for improved, interactive man-computer problem solving in planning. This book is designed to provide an authoritative review of the imminent transition from offline to online planning as the circle of computer users expands rapidly with increasing computer power at decreasing machine costs

Since online planning is only in an embryonic, formative stage, special stress needs to be placed on scientific development, test, and evaluation of leading planning hypotheses. There are no ready-made, cookbook rules that can be routinely applied in this swiftly changing technology. Only long-term evolutionary test and evaluation with continuing empirical feedback can materialize the powerful potential of online planning. Thus, the theory of planning, the scientific status of man-computer problem solving, the design of online experiments, and the tools for recording, reduction, and analysis of planning are strongly emphasized.

A unique feature is the application of advanced online technology. Examples include online simulation, artificial intelligence and computer-aided heuristics, graphic networks, online polling, and regenerative recording. These techniques and their expected utility are described with extensive references for further study.

This book is not narrowly concerned with planning and computer technology as such. It is more broadly oriented toward the human use of online planning technology, toward individual creativity and team problem solving, toward management and control of planning, and toward ultimate social effectiveness in a world that desperately needs order of magnitude advances in social planning.

The focal audience is the planning world: managers, planners, systems analysts, and general users of computer-aided planning in government, educational, scientific, engineering, and business applications. With the steady extension of computers throughout society, and with the imminent appearance of mass, online information utilities, social planning will eventually spread to all levels of society, at least in democratic states.

The scientific context of this book is oriented toward the various scientific disciplines that have some stake in planning procedures and applications. These include the computer and information sciences, engineering, operations research, management science, and, for human creativity and problem-solving in a computerized milieu, the social sciences. Since the broad interdisciplinary nature of planning involves multiple skills and diverse technologies, the text has been written in an introductory vein. More technical aspects are described for the lay reader as they occur.

The editors are personally indebted to each of the contributors, not only for their individual chapters, but also for the continuing discussion, debate, and intellectual confrontation that they triggered throughout the course of our joint effort. And we are especially grateful to Catherine E. Perrone, who was tireless in outstanding secretarial support throughout all phases of the manuscript up to final publication.

"The formulation of the problem is often more essential than its solution, which might be merely a matter of mathematical or experimental skill. To raise new questions, new possibilities, to regard old problems from a new angle requires creative imagination and marks real advance in science."

ALBERT EINSTEIN and LEOPOLD INFELD,
The Evolution of Physics, 1938.

I

Theory and Method of

Man-Computer Planning

Part I is oriented to set the basic framework for comprehensive online planning, and to set the pace for the rest of the book. All three chapters by Sackman, Hormann, and Citrenbaum are concerned with the definition and nature of planning. The essence of planning is interpreted by these authors as a variant of human problem solving. Computers are seen to enhance the problem-solving process, and online systems emerge as the method of choice for creative advances in socially effective planning.

Theoretical frameworks for planning are developed from three approaches. Sackman emphasizes plans as hypotheses subject to empirical test and evaluation; Hormann stresses the division of labor in the partnership between man and the computer in the planning process; Citrenbaum critically evaluates the potential of artificial intelligence to improve planning. Recommendations are made to move from the current predisciplinary status of planning to planning as an interdisciplinary science catalyzed by computerized experimental method. Various additional research recommendations are put

1

forth for testing specific behavioral hypotheses and for further developments in man-computer planning techniques that may lead to planning breakthroughs.

1

ADVANCED RESEARCH
IN ONLINE PLANNING

H. Sackman

Abstract

This chapter is an initial, exploratory effort concerned with the problem of selecting a fruitful line of research in the virgin field of online planning. To help cast the problem in perspective, the status of planning and online problem solving are reviewed for useful leads. Planning is seen to be in an early predisciplinary stage, undergoing rapid change and remarkable growth. Although online problem solving is also in an inchoate stage, available experimental evidence indicates that the online mode is probably better suited for relatively unstructured, open-end problems requiring much exploration and creative insight.

Planning theory is reviewed and found wanting. A provisional definition and a theory of planning are developed to make planning more amenable to scientific method. The crux of the proposed approach is to conceive of plans as operationally defined hypotheses subject to empirical test and evaluation. Building on individual and group expectation theory and findings in the social science literature, a mutual expectation theory is suggested. This theory is derived from an

5

analysis of conditions that lead toward a working consensus of cognizant individuals in object plans.

A proposal for "Participatory Online Planning" is outlined, stemming from initial considerations of mutual expectation theory for planning. In essence, participatory online planning refers to online implementation of problem-solving, tutorial, and adversary processes among planning alternatives that culminates in consensus, particularly among dispersed participants. The chapter closes with an extensive listing of arguments for and against advanced research in participatory online planning.

This chapter is concerned with assessing the state of the art in planning, surveying the possibilities for productive research within an online planning framework, and working toward a preliminary recommendation for such research within current constraints. Accordingly, the chapter follows five steps: formulation of the problem, a review of the state of the art, a theoretical framework for planning, a comparison of alternative methods in planning, and a provisional recommendation.

1-1 FORMULATION OF THE PROBLEM

Social organizations, in and out of government, are encountering mounting problems in planning effectively to meet the accelerating tempo of contemporary change. The general problem, simply stated, is: how can the planning process be accelerated in time, reduced in cost, and improved in quality? More specifically, can improvements in planning be scientifically advanced within the framework of online computing systems?

No attempt is made at this point to develop criteria for acceptable solutions of the problem; these are developed in the course of the discussion and are brought together when cross comparisons are made among competing approaches to research in online planning.

1-2 RETROSPECT AND PROSPECT IN PLANNING

The first step is to take a critical look at the scientific status of planning, take a similar look at the scientific status of online problem solving, and then determine the locus of an optimal intersection between the two domains. Since the leading mission of the eventual program of advanced research is improvement of planning, research needs in planning are reviewed first, and the relevant online problem-solving literature is subsequently reviewed in relation to potential cross-fertilization with planning.

1-2-1 The Predisciplinary Status of Planning

The general literature on planning reveals some noteworthy trends. Although most of the literature is of the anecdotal, case-history variety, full of platitudes and maxims on how to plan, there is, nevertheless, a growing awareness of the need for establishing an applied scientific discipline in planning. The United Nations has well-established standing committees on national and international planning; The Institute of Management Science (TIMS) conducts an on-going "College on Planning"; the Federal Government continues to endorse the "Planning-Programming-Budgeting" concept originally developed in the Department of Defense under McNamara's aegis (Novick, 1965); voluntary international leagues for advancing the techniques of socio-economic planning are being formed by private groups such as "Futuribles" (DeJouvenel, 1967), and a growing number of universities are recognizing planning as a unique discipline and are offering graduate programs in planning (Branch, 1966). In 1967, the World Future Society was formed, with over 1000 members from 18 countries. The Office of Education and DOD in the United States have funded a growing number of future-oriented research centers. The American Academy of Arts and Sciences appointed a Commission on the Year 2000 (*Daedalus*, Summer 1967). The Third International Conference on Science and Society, held in Yugoslavia in 1969, focused on scientific planning and futurology. These quickening trends in planning for the economy, government, education, and international affairs are being matched by increased corporate and group planning, a trend that is extending rapidly to all levels of society.

The general literature on planning is useful in the present context for the light it casts on the method of planning, as distinguished from the content of planning which already has a vast literature in business, government, and social science. Branch is one of the leaders in this field; the following comments are derived from his text on planning (1966), which is oriented toward establishing planning as an interdisciplinary, applied science. He points out that the first significantly organized approach to planning occurred in 1909 in the United States to meet the needs of city planning. While city planning has the longest tradition and has become highly specialized, the more recent outgrowth of planning in the Federal Government has shown the most sophisticated developments, particularly in military contingency planning. He specially singles out cost-effectiveness techniques, such as program evaluation and review technique (PERT), and contingency modeling as indicative of quantitative and empirical trends in planning. Branch stresses psychological factors in planning and how little we know of such factors. His goal is that of "comprehensive planning," which he views as a distinct discipline in its own right, drawing freely from pure and applied sciences, and aimed at securing greater human control over changes in the physical and social world. Branch's claim for the scientific status of planning requires greater emphasis on empirical verification and corrective feedback. While he recognizes the need for checking predictions against outcomes, he does not formalize the verification of planning to the extent possible with modern experimental procedure. This criticism applies generally to the field of planning—planning will not become an applied science until plans are viewed as evolving hypotheses, subject to iterative formulation, test, and verification in the course of changing conditions.

Jouvenel (1965 and 1967) disputes the claim that planning can become an applied science. He believes that planning is not concerned with "true or false," but with the "realm of the possible." His approach is to use "reasoned conjecture" by pooling the best techniques through organizations devoted exclusively to planning, through "look-out institutions." A major objection to Jouvenel's approach is that he views the present, largely intuitive status of planning as a permanent condition of planning. In this respect he seems to echo Henri Bergson's intuitive philosophy of "creative evolution." Jouvenel espouses a planning aristocracy to handle human planning rather than a more democratic interpretation which holds that planning, in its broadest aspects, is everybody's business. Jouvenel does capture the contemporary mood of planning, however, when he insists that the increasing tempo of change implies a decreasing life expectancy of present knowledge, which, in turn, requires more intensive planning at more frequent intervals. Increased planning can compensate, at least in part, for growing uncertainty.

Helmer (1967) stresses the value of structured expert opinion in planning and has attempted to formalize rating procedures in fore-casting scientific and technological events. He describes an iterative rating scheme in which the experts do not interact directly, which he calls the "Delphi" technique, after the celebrated oracle of ancient Greece. The original rating procedures were rather crude by modern standards in the construction and analysis of rating forms. Helmer originally applied such standardized techniques to a large (82) and impressive panel of experts.

The results of a 1968 Delphi study in the area of computer applications by Parsons and Williams are illustrated in Fig. 1–1, which shows the median expectation for the given event at the highest point, the quartile expectation at the left end, and the third quartile (or 75th percentile) at the right end. These graphs have the advantage of showing dispersion of ratings as well as central trends. The results provide interesting forecasting material for long-range planning. A significant literature on Delphi studies has subsequently emerged, nationally and internationally, based on variations of Helmer's original techniques.

In connection with the possibility of evolving toward online Delphi, Helmer (1967) has offered the following general picture:

> As for automating part of the Delphi process, I may mention that we have begun to experiment with the use of JOSS on-line computer consoles. By having each participating expert in a Delphi inquiry give his responses on a JOSS console, we can process a group's responses automatically and immediately feed back the information and instructions that make up the next questionnaire. Thus an effort which might otherwise take weeks or months can be carried through in an hour or less. Moreover, once the interaction among the respondents is via machine, it would be relatively easy to enrich the process by providing on demand automated access to existing data banks and eventually even to banks of mathematical models that might aid the expert in the analysis of the situation under consideration. Once this process has been perfected, it is easy to imagine that for important decisions simultaneous consultation with experts in geographically distinct locations via a nation-wide or even a world-wide computer network may become a matter of routine.

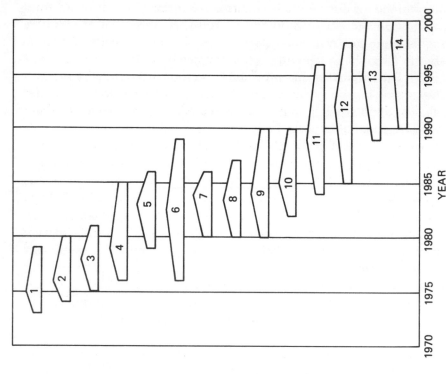

(1) Direction of large urban traffic flow by computer

(2) Control of patients in major hospitals by computer

(3) Widespread use of Computer-Aided Instruction (CAI) in schools

(4) Computer controlled commercial airplanes, including takeoffs and landings

(5) Recording of scientific and other advances so that constantly updated status is maintained in central files

(6) Computer as diagnostician (giving reliable results)

(7) Policing of individual vehicles by combined radar detection and computer record of violation (license number, excessive speed, etc.)

(8) Majority of doctors having a terminal for consultation

(9) 50% reduction of labor force in major industries because of EDP automation

(10) Recording of all income by majority of employers on terminals and automatic transfer of this information to various tax authorities

(11) Instruction at home through computers

(12) Obsolescence of book libraries as known today for general factual information

(13) Widespread use of automobile autopilots

(14) Computers as common as telephone or television in private homes

Figure 1-1. Predictions of computer applications (from Parsons-Williams, 1968).

Emery (1965) is among the theorists in the field who have attempted to formalize the planning process and relate such formalizations to computer models. Emery operates from a management context in virtually identifying planning with management. If this identification of management with planning sounds extreme, consider Willmorth's (1965) classification and description of organizational planning shown in Table 1–1. Willmorth's functional analysis of planning amply demonstrates the pervasiveness of planning in organizational management.

Emery's central notion of hierarchical planning is essentially isomorphic with the organizational hierarchy; that is, broad planning policy is generated at the top, more detailed policy at middle-management levels, with fine details worked out and implemented at the operational levels. In his hierarchical model Emery poses a means/ ends nesting of tasks within tasks where higher-level planning imposes constraints on lower-level planning. His models, unfortunately, are descriptive and highly general.

Emery views planning as "deciding in advance what is to be done." He distinguishes between formal and informal planning, but does not follow up on the implications of this useful distinction. The key steps in the planning process, according to Emery, are: assembling data; constructing a model; developing alternative plans; evaluating consequences of the alternatives; selecting the best plan; implementing the plan; and controlling the plan in operation. Although Emery sees the educational potential of planning, he pays virtually no attention to the contribution of human elements, such as problem formulation, consensus, creativity and problem solving, or negotiation and compromise.

In describing computer-aided planning, Emery cites potential advantages of computers:

Cut planning costs
Decrease planning time
Explore a wider variety of planning alternatives
Generate more comprehensive plans
Standardize planning procedures and planning control
Generate detailed consequences of planning alternatives
Provide more rapid convergence toward the few best alternatives

Emery does not distinguish between online and offline computer-aided planning, nor does he go beyond his notion of the isomorphism

Table 1-1.   Factors in Organizational Planning (from Willmorth, 1965)

Influencing Factors	Product Plans	Process Plans	Organizational Plans
Objectives and Policies	Is the product commensurate with the stated objectives of the enterprise? What are the mission and objectives of the product? What needs does it satisfy? How will it be employed?	What is the policy toward standardization? What is the desirability of expanding capacity or technology? What are the objectives of this process? What will it do?	What are the growth possibilities, operating environment, and customer desirability of the area? What objectives must the organization serve?
Resources	What resources (personnel, machines, materials, information) are required? Are these available? Where? Does anyone have special knowledge or experience with this product?	What resources (men, machines, tools, materials) are required? Will men have to be trained to do this job? Machines acquired? Tools developed? Who knows the process and can show others?	Should an existing organization assume the project, or should a new project be created? What are the skills, jobs, and positions to be filled? The tasks to be accomplished? Are there organizations that can serve as sources of supply of expertise? How many people will have to be acquired, transferred, trained? When must they be available? When can they?
Technology	Is the product within the state-of-the-art? Are any innovations required? Is the application a well-known one? Have we produced one like it before?	Is this process within the state-of-the-art? Is this an existing, tried procedure or is it a new one? Will any methods have to be developed?	What organizational strategies are possible? What kinds of units are needed? Will new jobs have to be created? New kinds of organizational units?

Table 1-1 (Continued) Factors in Organizational Planning (from Willmorth, 1965)

Facility Plans	Personnel Plans	Developmental Plans	Production Plans
What is the relation of facility plans to the growth and expansion plans of the organization? What policy should be adopted regarding construction methods and space requirements? What objectives are sought in housing men and machines?	What are the policies toward recruitment, transfers, career guidance, compensation, fringe benefits, and personnel practices and procedures?	What developments will advance the objectives of the enterprise (a) in the main area of interest, (b) diversification goals, (c) toward markets and customers, (d) methods of solicitation and marketing?	What are the policies of the enterprise in relation to standard procedures and methods, costs, cost accounting, efficiency, and close control of operations?
How much space and of what kind is needed? Are adequate facilities available? Are special environmental control measures necessary (air conditioning, heating, noise abatement)?	What are the numbers and types of personnel skills needed? What kind and degree of training is required? What is the labor market, state of competition?	What capabilities does the enterprise have in supporting development: financial, personnel, methodology, technology?	What present production planning and control procedures are used? Are there enterprise operations for methods for procedures, PERT, and other schedule control? Quality control?
What structures and layouts would be best to satisfy the needs? Are special facilities (security, environmental control) necessary? Must they be built? What is the relation of the facility to customers, information sources, personnel supplies?	What is the state of educational practices and plans for these skills? Are other enterprises developing experienced personnel in these areas?	What are the future possible areas of application? What must be done to prepare for these and for future developments?	How does the enterprise stand in relation to other organizations in the area of emphasis upon production planning and control? Cost control? Quality control?

Table 1-1. Factors in Organizational Planning (from Willmorth, 1965) (Continued)

Influencing Factors	Product Plans	Process Plans	Organizational Plans
Change	Are frequent changes in the product expected? Is it a new application? Are any promised innovations likely to fail? Is an evolutionary plan adopted? What major additions or changes are expected?	Are there any processing changes planned or expected? When? What will their impact be? Is this a stable area of applications or is it a rapidly developing one? If new tools are being developed or machines acquired, when will they be available? What will be the expected life of tools and techniques developed here?	When will major organizational changes occur? What will be the rates of build up and phase down of various activities? How may individuals and responsibilities be shifted to meet varying conditions?
Performance and Quality Requirement	Are performance requirements realistic? Can they be met? Are criteria of successful performance given? What are they? Are test methods available and feasible? Who is the final arbiter of quality? What are the product acceptance procedures?	What productivity rates are expected from the process? Men? Machines? What are the criteria of good or successful performance? Are any substandard tools or techniques being used? Who will evaluate the process? How?	What evidence is needed to tell whether an organizational arrangement is working out appropriately? What are the responsibilities, duties, authority of each job position? Relations to other positions? Organizations? What are the personal qualifications needed for the job?
Contingencies	What is to be done if the product fails or proves infeasible? Are there other items that could be substituted? Should a back-up program be undertaken?	What is to be done if a process or approach proves infeasible or uneconomic? How soon, or at what points, must decisions be made to change or go ahead?	What shall be the direction of organizational shift if the various inefficiencies appear? Are there persons designated to assure positions of Leadership if supervisors or key personnel separate? What is the order of succession? Are all jobs covered?

Table 1-1.   Factors in Organizational Planning (from Willmorth, 1965) (Continued)

Influencing Factors	Product Plans	Process Plans	Organizational Plans
Are there plans for future expansion and change? How fast will the organization grow? Decline? Is there room for expansion?	What are the plans for growth, opportunities for promotion and careers?	What are the likely areas of technological innovation and advance? What are the likely future trends in social, economic and political conditions as well as technological? What are the likely areas of decline?	What is the industry trend in regard to production control? More or less? Automation or manual? What is the trend within the enterprise toward more formal production control techniques?
How adequate are existing facilities? Does the layout foster efficient flow of work? Can related activities be located contiguously? Are adequate power, transportation, supplies, available? Are maintenance costs satisfactory?	What are the requirements for performance evaluations? Are there precisely stated criteria of required performance levels for all jobs?	What factors influence development and how does the enterprise stand in relation to these? How effectively is its present plan for development being carried out?	How well does the enterprise do in meeting schedules and budgets? Is its performance improving? Is it meeting competition?
If facilities prove too small, is there room for expansion? If facilities prove unsatisfactory, where will the activity move or how will the facility be improved? If the project folds, what disposition will be made of the facility?	Are there contingency plans for personnel budgets, turnover rates, growth rates, training plans and curricula, personnel policy and procedures, employee benefits, compensations, job descriptions, etc?	If developments fail, or prove unsatisfactory, what shall be done?	Are there contingency plans for schedules, operations plans, procedures for receiving, shipping, ordering, routing, inspecting, servicing, expediting, monitoring, reporting, inventory control and trouble shooting?

between planning space and organizational space in discussing computerized planning formalisms. The disadvantages and pitfalls of computer-aided planning are not developed. This broad-brush treatment is typical of the predisciplinary status of computer-aided planning in the literature.

For example, in his recent text on forecasting and planning, Ayres (1969) does not list computers in the appendix nor does he treat computer-aided planning (let alone online planning) as a methodology in its own right. To take another example, while Kahn and Wiener (1967) expatiate upon the impact of computers on society in "The Year 2000," they do not pursue the impact of computers in their own domain of methodology in planning and forecasting.

A potentially revolutionary trend in planning is the involvement of an ever increasing circle of individuals in planning, both qualitatively in terms of diversity of contributing disciplines, and quantitatively in terms of sheer numbers of planning participants. Jungk (1969) has epitomized the democratization of planning:

> The democratization of future research will really have to start at school level. Lessons devoted to the probable, possible and desirable futures should gain at least as much importance as the teaching of past history.
>
> A democratization of forecasting, future studies and future research will probably have to contend with the reproach that it will be time consuming. In fact, fast decision making is easier in autocratic types of societies. But in the next phase of humanity, there will be even less people willing to accept orders and directions coming 'from above'. They will want to participate actively in the shaping of their future destiny. The future belongs to all of us, not just a small elite of ruling experts and decision makers.

The trend toward democratization of planning is occurring in the midst of growing dissatisfaction with the methods and effectiveness of planning at all social levels. The United Nations finds national planning, particularly for developing countries, in a state of disarray. Political instability, poorly trained planners, unrealistic goals, inadequate resources, lack of planning controls, and indifference toward planning plague many countries. National planning has been criticized as aimless, misanthropic, and destructive of cultural values in advanced countries on both sides of the Iron Curtain. Corporate planning is under continuing attack by planners who claim that management has yet to understand the scope and role of planning and the disciplined support it needs. Individuals find personal planning increasingly unstable as the rate of social change spirals upward, and as personal obsolescence is accelerated. Problems are mounting faster than they can be solved, and some, such as Platt (1969), claim that "Every problem may escalate because those involved no longer have time to think straight." There is a gloomy cloud of impatience and impotence that hangs over contemporary planning as the circle of participants widens.

1-2-2 Alternative Methods in Planning

Although the planning literature is immense, spilling over into almost every imaginable field of social endeavor, the literature on planning methodology, as indicated above, is conspicuous by its absence. One reason is the newness of planning as a discipline. In a recent review of the theory and practice of planning, Mockler (1970) points out that there were virtually no books on planning prior to 1960, followed by 25 book-length studies in the 1960's. Perhaps the key reason for this embarrassing state of affairs is that planning has not made an organic link with scientific method in the fundamental sense of tying planning hypotheses to experimentally controlled empirical verification of such hypotheses. There are many factors contributing to this unfortunate situation. A leading factor is the lack of a tradition of real-world experimentation; experimental method is still confined primarily to the antiseptic confines of the laboratory while planning must prove itself in the crucible of the real world. A show of scientism is put on by many practitioners through the use of esoteric mathematical, statistical, and logical techniques; but without the acid test of empirical verification in a credible experimental setting, the most elaborate mathematical and verbal posturing on the planning stage, while full of sound and fury, does not signify science. A central requirement of proposed online research in planning, as far as this study is concerned, is amenability to empirically verified scientific method.

A set of factors for the failure of planning to achieve scientific status is human culpability. Free-wheeling armchair speculation is safer, faster, easier, and, for many, more fun than careful experimentation. Esoteric models of planning provide excellent insulation from the outside world against invasions of the modeler's privacy. And neither do managers like their planning estimates and predictions to be compared with actual outcomes—a gentlemen's agreement not to pursue seriously such comparisons seems to be an article of faith in the planning management establishment for mutual privacy, protection, and security.

Finally, there is a lack of scientifically based planning theory to guide research. Tools, models and techniques are not theories, no matter how elaborate they may be; simplistic or fanciful analogies are not theories unless they are systematically linked to experimental method. In a later section an attempt is made to develop a theory of planning amenable to experimental test and evaluation in an online planning context.

The immediate goal of this section is to present an introduction to the variety and scope of planning techniques, and to some preliminary comparisons among them. We are fortunate that this task has been initiated by Rosove (1967) in a project concerned with educational planning. Building upon techniques described by Bell (1964) and others, Rosove lists 21 planning and forecasting methods, to which I have added five additional categories: dialectical planning (Mason, 1969), PERT/CPM, PPB (Bureau of the Budget, 1965), normative planning (Ayers, 1969), and confrontation techniques. The 26 "methods" are briefly described below, adapted from Rosove.

Definitions:

> *Brainstorming:* A form of group dynamics designed to encourage creative and imaginative thinking about the future via an uninhibited exchange of ideas.
>
> *Delphi Technique:* A procedure for systematically soliciting and collating the opinions of experts on the future of a preselected subject by sequential individual interrogations, usually by questionnaires. An effort is made to achieve consensus or convergence of opinion by the feedback of results to the participants.
>
> *Expert Opinion:* The opinions of qualified specialists about the future of the phenomena within the field in which they have renown or the recognition of their peers.
>
> *Literary Fiction:* Novels or other forms of literature which

imaginatively or creatively construct future social systems or conditions.

Scenarios: The imaginative construction into the future of a logical sequence of events based on specified assumptions and initial conditions in a given problem area.

Historical Analogy: Inferring the similarity between attributes or processes of two or more different historical developments, social conditions, or societies on the basis of other presumed similarities.

Historical Sequences: Formulations of the independent recurrence of similar sequential social, economic, and cultural processes and conditions in different societies or nations; or the treatment of socio-cultural phenomena, in general, in terms of logico-historical sequential phases or stages of development.

Content Analysis: Abstracting from content—speeches, novels, art forms—generalizations or trends pertaining to a wide range of phenomena such as public attitudes, values, political ideology, national style, etc.

Social Accounting: An effort to conjecture about the future of a nation, social system, or institution by determining the "sum" of a series of independent factors, $a, b, c, \dots n$ which comprise it at time t, resulting in profile A, and then progressing to series a', $b', c', \dots n'$ at time t', resulting in profile B.

Primary Determinant: The interpretation of sociocultural events, conditions, and processes in the past, present, and future in terms of the consequences of a single major factor or primary determinant such as Marx's mode of production or McLuhan's media.

Time-Series Extrapolation: The extension of a series of measurements of a variable over a period of time from the past into the future.

Contextual Mapping: The extrapolation in graphic form of the interrelationships of functionally related developments. A "map" shows logical and causal interdependencies.

Morphological Analysis: A systematic procedure for exploring the totality of all possible solutions to a given large-scale problem; e.g., all possible ways of propelling rockets. The definition of the problem provides an initial set of parameters, and the full range of possible answers to the problems inherent in each initial parameter represent another set of parameters, and this set is then explored, and so on, until all the parameters have been exhausted. A possible solution to the problem of propelling rockets may then be any combination of the dependent parameters within the sets of parameters at different levels of the analysis.

Relevance Trees: A procedure for determining the objective means or techniques required to implement an explicit qualitative goal; e.g., to permit all students to proceed through educational programs at their own pace. Each branch point of the tree, moving downward from the stated objective, represents a potential decision to follow a particular implementation direction. Either qualitative or quantitative criteria, or both, may be used to aid the selection process. Each subsequent branch level is considered, in turn, as a possible set of alternative goals, and each alternative is analyzed to determine the objective means required to implement it.

Decision Matrices: A method for allocating resources, determining priorities, or selecting goals by graphically displaying the relationships or multiple interdependent variables in two or three dimensions. For example, one dimension of a decision matrix in education might be available funds while the other dimension might be faculty and administrators' salaries, maintenance costs, library costs, etc.

Deterministic Models: A deterministic model is a mathematical abstraction of real-world phenomena. It is a set of relationships among quantitative elements of the following types: parameters, variable inputs, and variable outputs. The development of computer technology has made possible the implementation of models which are too complex for noncomputerized solutions.

Probabilistic Models: A probabilistic model is a mathematical representation of the interactions among a number of variables in which the value of at least one variable is assigned by a random process. The numerical results of repeated exercises of the model will yield different numerical values. The values of variables may be based on estimates of future conditions. A computer facilitates running many exercises with the model.

Gaming: (Not to be confused with game theory.) Provides a simulated operational present or future environment structured so as to make possible multiple simultaneous interactions among competing or cooperating players. Games may be entirely manual in nature, or a computer may be used in some types of games to provide inputs to players, and to record their performances.

Operational Simulation: The exercising of operators of a system in their actual environment by the use of selected simulated inputs to provide education and training to the system's operators and/or to facilitate analysis and understanding of the system's operations for evolutionary design and development. The inputs may represent the world of the future.

Benefit-Cost Analysis: A quantitative method designed to assist decision makers to make the most efficient tradeoffs between financial resources and competing programs. The total cost of each program, both direct and indirect, is estimated and the programs may be evaluated in terms of the advantages, outputs, or results (benefits), both short-run and long-run, which each is estimated to have. These estimates are expressed quantitatively. Since both program costs and their benefits have specific values, several alternative courses of action may be systematically compared and evaluated.

Input/Output Tables: Models of an economy which is disaggregated into sectors and in which explicit account is taken of sales and purchases between sectors. One set of parameters which is common to all such models is technical coefficients; the technical coefficients of an industry are the numbers of units of input of each industry which are required in order to produce one unit of output of the given industry.

Dialectical Planning: Generation of an opposing set of "best" plans representing conflicting values and views, followed by structured debate, using the same data base until the data bank is exhausted, performed by opposing advocates for management.

PERT/CPM: Program Evaluation and Review Technique using Critical Path Method analyses; the analytic portrayal of costs, manpower, and schedules in graphic form in terms of activities and milestones for an object system to achieve planning objectives within specified resource levels.

PPB: Planning, Programming, and Budgeting; technique introduced by DOD and used extensively in other government agencies since 1965; requires systems analyses of agency objectives, definition of a five-year plan, cost-effectiveness analyses of proposed programs, with annual updating of plans and budgets for the five-year projection, and continuing assessment of programs.

Normative Planning: Also referred to as teleological planning;

deliberate and critical examination of the fundamental value judgments underlying planning goals, prior to and distinguished from strategic planning for working toward specified goals, and tactical planning to achieve defined goals.

Confrontation Techniques: This category includes a broad class of techniques involving some element of involuntary external coercion of individuals or groups to change individual traits, group policies, or plans by some form of social confrontation; e.g., psychodrama, T-groups, sensitivity training, Synanon game, intervention in professional meetings, marches, strikes, and "sit-ins."

Rosove rated each of the initial 21 techniques on a common scale for seven criteria, including:

1.   Generation of alternatives
2.   Exploration of alternative futures
3.   Exploration of consequences of decisions
4.   Potential for informed public dialog
5.   Training potential
6.   Amenability to research
7.   Identification of research needs

Rosove weighted each of the above criteria equally and arrived at a composite rating for each of the 21 "futures-creating" techniques. The author went through a similar exercise with the five additional techniques that were added to Rosove's list without changing the

Table 1-2.   Suggestive Rank Order of Futures-Creating Methods

Rank	Methods	Rank	Methods
1	Gaming	14	Relevance Trees
2	Operational Simulation	15	Confrontation Techniques
3	Delphi Technique	16	Brainstorming
4	Deterministic Models	17	Benefit-Cost Analysis
5	PERT/CPM	18	Input-Output Tables
6	Probabilistic Models	19	Time-Series Extrapolation
7	PPB	20	Morphological Analysis
8	Scenarios	21	Contextual Analysis
9	Dialectical Planning	22	Content Analysis
10	Social Accounting	23	Primary Determinant
11	Expert Opinion	24	Historical Analogy
12	Normative Planning	25	Historical Sequences
13	Decision Matrices	26	Literary Fiction

Basic, Long-term Trends	Major Sub-Trends	Social and Techni-cal Implications	Implications for Education	Educational Functions	Possible Future Roles	Major issues
(Cultural Sector) Increasingly sensate, empirical, humanistic, pragmatic, utilitarian culture.	1A	2A	3A	4A	5A	6A
(Socio-cultural Sector) Increasingly sensate, empirical, humanistic, pragmatic, utilitarian culture.	1B	2B	3B	4B	5B	6B
(Economic Sector—National) Transitional, mass-consumption society characterized by higher GNP and personal incomes, affluence (among better educated).	1C	2C	3C	4C	5C	6C
(Economic Sector—International) World-wide industrialization and modernization.	1D	2D	3D	4D	5D	6D
(Science & Technology Sector) (I Organization) Institutionalization of change, especially through research, development, innovation & organized diffusion.	1E	2E	3E	4E	5E	6E
(Science & Technology Sector) (II Information) Accumulation of scientific and technological knowledge.	1F	2F	3F	4F	5F	6F

Figure 1-2. Educational context map (from Rosove, 1967).

original ordering. The rank-order rating of the combined results for the 26 techniques is shown in Table 1–2.

No claims are made for the reliability or validity of the rating scales or the evaluation technique. The ordering is strictly suggestive. The exercise is useful in introducing and comparing a wide range of alternative methodological approaches to planning. Although educational and research criteria are pertinent to this chapter, Rosove's evaluation criteria did not include amenability to online computing techniques, which is of major concern in this inquiry. Rosove finally selected contextual mapping technique for his educational forecasting problem. A portrayal of key steps in contextual mapping is shown in Figs. 1–2 and 1–3 for Rosove's application; long-term trends in Fig. 1–2 were derived from Kahn and Wiener (1967).

1-3 AN EXPERIMENTAL CRITIQUE OF ONLINE PROBLEM SOLVING

It is all too easy, even for professionals who should know better, to become very fond of online, interactive, real-time, conversational, symbiotic, man-computer problem solving. There is a perverse and pervasive ethos in the computer world, almost at an unconscious level, that looks at "manual" activities as the lowest form of life in the

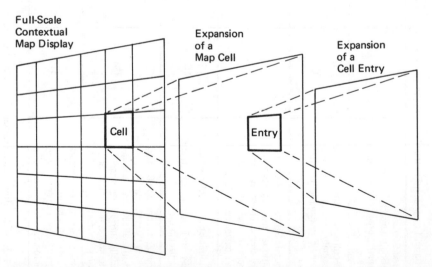

Figure 1-3.   Progressive analysis in contextual mapping (from Rosove, 1967).

universe, batch or offline activities as an enlightened step upward, time-sharing or online functions as a giant leap forward, and, on Mount Olympus, artificial intelligence as the *summum bonum*. This idolatry of the computer is based on insinuating "manual" at the start of the series instead of "cranial"; for once the human brain enters the picture, the pyramid is seen for what it is—standing on its head.

Undoubtedly, over the long run, some computer-aided planning techniques will prove more effective than similar planning without computers. Also undoubtedly, over the long run, some online planning techniques will prove superior to comparable offline planning. The greatest mistakes in deciding whether planning functions should be computerized, and whether such functions should be done online or offline, are most likely to occur in the pioneering era when such paths are charted in unknown wilderness. Pioneers are the guys who get the arrows in their backs. A continuing major hypothesis for any early venture into online planning is: "Does it make any difference whether a planning function is handled without the benefit of computers, offline or online?"

A central question in arriving at the ultimate goal of a desirable online planning vehicle for advanced research is: "What are the advantages and limitations of online systems for human problem solving?" If such advantages and limitations could be identified, we would have useful guidelines for reaching our goal. Fortunately, some significant experimental work has been done over the last four years in comparing time-sharing and batch-processing systems. The author has written a book concerned with this area (1970). The results of this and related work are summarized in this section to arrive at empirical guidelines for online planning.

1-3-1   Online User Statistics

The pioneering time-sharing systems, in breaking new ground, had to develop empirical statistics for user traffic, scheduling efficiency, and central system accounting procedures. This effort led to various simulation and recording procedures to enable the various characteristics of users and the central system to be timed and measured. These procedures led to preliminary descriptive data on users, problem tasks, and man-computer effectiveness in system timing and system capacity. The leading studies from which these data were gathered include Scherr (1967) and Raynaud (1967) at MIT using the Compatible

Table 1–3.   Online User Characteristics from Statistical Studies

Timing and Pacing

1. More often than not, the time-sharing user will employ a terminal only once a day, and not every day; this rule is subject, however, to numerous exceptions for individual users and between different users.
2. The typical user spends between half an hour to an hour at his console at each session; this rule is also subject to great intra- and inter-subject variability.
3. Approximately 10 percent of the typical user's total working time is spent in man-computer communication at his console, whereas 90 percent of his working time is spent away from the console.
4. His median input rate is at the general order of one request every half-minute, whereas his average input is roughly one per minute at the terminal.
5. Half of the time he will insert a new command some 10 seconds after he has received a complete output from the computer; only on comparatively rare occasions will he wait as long as a minute before making a new request after receiving an output.
6. The ratio of human time to central processor time is at the general order of magnitude of 50:1; that is, approximately 50 seconds of elapsed human time is associated with one second of computer operating time on the user's program.

System Effectiveness

7. Users with tasks requiring relatively small computations become increasingly uncomfortable as computer response time to their requests extends beyond ten seconds, and as irregularity and uncertainty of computer response time increases. Users with problems requiring much computation tolerate longer intervals, up to as much as 10 minutes for the largest jobs.
8. As system load rises with increasing numbers of users, system response time increases, and, at high-load levels, both central system effectiveness and user performance tend to deteriorate.

Individual Differences

9. The computer is generally more verbose than the human; each line of human input tends to be accompanied, roughly speaking, by about two lines of computer output. New users tend to be more verbose; more terse responses occur with increasing experience.
10. Programmers seem to use, on the average, larger object programs and more computer time than non-programmers.
11. As the central system matures, and as users become more experienced, there is a tendency for object programs to grow in size and complexity, and for experienced users to require more computing time and a larger share of system capacity. Experienced users are more adept in exploiting central system resources.

Time-Sharing System; Totscheck (1965) and McIsaac (1966) using the SDC Time-Sharing System; and Shaw (1965) and Bryan (1967) at RAND with the JOSS system. A summary of user findings is found in Table 1–3.

Some of the more striking aspects of user behavior in time-sharing from Table 1–3 should be stressed. First, most of the user's time is spent away from the terminal. This means that man-computer problem solving is predominantly a human-directed process, involving mostly introspection or man-to-man communication—a central fact of life for the design of online planning systems. These descriptive data suggest that the user formulates and imaginatively rehearses solutions to problems at his desk, and that the computer is primarily used for follow-up implementation, test, and verification of human ideas. The computer and its information services accordingly represent a tactical tool in human problem solving, with the user as the directive source of strategic intelligence.

Further confirmation for this interpretation of man-computer problem solving is found in the striking uniformity of user interarrival times in independent studies. Table 1–4 shows mean and median figures for user interarrival times for large samples of user traffic in five independent investigations. The combined pool of man-computer messages in these five studies is on the order of one million commands. The interarrival time is the interval between the completion of the last computer output and the insertion of the user's next input. The remarkable uniformity of the observed medians, ranging from 9 to 13

Table 1–4.   Comparison of Online Interarrival Statistics

Author	Totschek (1965)	McIsaac (1966)	IBM Memo (1966)	Scherr (1967)	Bryan (1967)
Time-Sharing System	SDC Q-32 System 1965 Study	SDC Q-32 System 1966 Study	IBM 7090 System	MIT Project MAC System	RAND JOSS System
Mean (sec.)	27.7	70.7 (35.3)*	20.0	35.2	34
Median	12.8	9.0	10.0	11.0	11

*Adjusted by removing all interarrival times greater than 30 minutes (1.55% of total).

seconds, shows that most user interactions occur at essentially a fast conversational clip. The user is apparently following well-structured behavioral sequences that have been thought through previously.

The other data on user pacing seem to fit into the suggested human problem-solving scheme. The single day seems to be the basic unit for user self-scheduling. Most of the day is apparently employed in figuring out new or revised problem strategy and tactics, coupled with a single session at the terminal to try out new variations to see if they work. The single day seems to emerge as the basic working unit for human turnaround time.

Another noteworthy feature of these early statistical and accounting studies is the striking learning and adaptation that takes place with users with increasing online experience. More experienced users—programmers and non-programmers—learn how to exploit the central system more effectively. Unless constrained by the system, more experienced users tend to use larger programs, more primary and secondary storage, and more central processor time. Online planning systems should have a built-in evolutionary capability to expand and adapt to more sophisticated information services with increasing user experience.

1-3-2 Comparative Online/Offline Studies

Table 1–5 lists the composite results of the ten available studies comparing time-sharing and batch processing with respect to four performance measures: man-hours, computer time, costs, and user preference. Median results are shown for each performance measure as a crude indication of central tendency. The overall results deflate exaggerated claims for unqualified online superiority over batch for man-computer problem solving. The online mode is indeed faster, but only 20 percent faster in terms of man-hours. But batch uses much less computer time, and is consequently less costly than time-sharing as far as immediate man-machine costs are concerned. On the other hand, users show a definite preference for the online mode. Thus, the gross results indicate that the online mode is preferable if human time is at a premium and if user attitudes toward the computer system are critical.

The criterion problems in these studies included puzzles, simulations, mathematical problems, language conversion, and sorting procedures. Practically all had fixed, correct solutions, except in one notable case, Gold's study where an open-end simulation vehicle

Table 1–5. Composite Results: Online Versus Offline Performance
for Ten Studies

Study	Man-Hours	Computer Time	Costs	User Preference
Air Force Academy (1968 Pilot Study)	Time-Sharing* 1.2:1	Batch 1.7:1	Approx. Same	Approx. Same
Air Force (1969 Pilot Study)	Batch 1.2:1	Batch 1.8:1	Batch	Approx. Same
Air Force Academy (Main Study, 1969)	Batch 1.1:1	Batch 1.9:1	Batch	Time-Sharing
Adams and Cohen (1969)	Approx. Same (1:1)	Batch 3.8:1	Batch 6.7:1	Batch
Erikson (1966)	Time-Sharing 1.9:1	Time-Sharing 3.4:1	Time-Sharing	Time-Sharing
Frye and Pack (1969)	Not Reported	Batch 3.8:1	Batch 3.3:1	Time-Sharing
Gold (1967)	Time-Sharing 1.2:1	Batch 5.7:1	Approx. Same	Time-Sharing
Grant and Sackman (1967)	Time-Sharing 1.6:1	Batch 1.4:1	Approx. Same	Time-Sharing
Schatzoff, Tsao and Wiig (1967)	Batch 2.1:1	Time-Sharing 1.1:1	Batch 1.5:1	Not Reported
Smith (1967)	Instant** 1.2:1	Batch 1.5:1	Approx. Same	Instant
Median for All Studies	Time-Sharing 1.2:1	Batch 1.8:1	Batch Costs	Time-Sharing Preferred

*The mode showing a reported *advantage* appears in each box together with its favorable ratio; e.g., this entry shows less man-hours for time-sharing at a 1.2:1 ratio.
**"Instant" batch is treated in this table as a simulated version of time-sharing.

allowed the user to keep improving his profit score. Planning problems run the gamut from well-structured situations admitting unambiguous solutions to highly exploratory, open-end situations. Although planning involves both kinds of problems, a stronger case can probably be made for the desirability of open-end planning problems as the area of greatest need for advanced research. A great many quantitative techniques, both deterministic and probabilistic, already exist for the solution of many types of well-defined problems which intersect the planning domain. However, relatively few quantitative techniques have been developed for problem formulation and problem exploration.

The most significant findings in the online/offline experimental literature lie in individual differences and the dynamics of human problem solving. Some of the leading findings in these areas are briefly reviewed. Time-sharing embodies the advantages of massed learning, whereas batch benefits from the advantage of spaced or distributed learning. For example, massed learning is better for more complex tasks, requires less warmup time, is better for short tasks learned directly to completion, facilitates extensive exploration, and involves less forgetting between successive work sessions. Spaced learning minimizes fatigue and boredom, works better for long routine tasks, involves fewer interference effects and mental ruts, involves fewer trials or less effort to reach the performance criterion, and places more dependence on long-term as opposed to short-term memory.

A related area is part versus whole learning. Behavioral studies have generally shown that optimal learning occurs when subjects attack the largest piece of the problem that they can handle, and progressively work up to the total problem. The online mode tends to have the edge over batch in this respect since it is usually easier for an online user to split the problem into manageable pieces, and work up to the entire problem than it is for the batch user. This is particularly crucial for the marginal performer who must start with small portions of the overall problem. An online mistake is easily recoverable at the console. An offline mistake can abort an entire computer run and force the user to wait the full turnaround time to get his next pass at the computer.

Another major area in man-computer problem solving lies in the distinction between trial-and-error learning and insightful learning. Both types of learning occur under online and offline conditions. Insight was found by most subjects to occur when they concentrated intensively upon their problem when they were alone. The online mode favored greater creativity and insight for open-end tasks, provided that the terminal was accessible and the service satisfactory. Under such conditions, the online mode permitted subjects to explore their problems more extensively, try out more hypotheses, and

Table 1-6.   Stages in Creativity and Problem Solving

HELMHOLTZ (1896)	*WALLAS (1926)*
• Preparation • Incubation • Illumination	• Preparation • Incubation • Illumination • Verification

ROSSMAN (1931)

- Observation of a need or difficulty
- Analysis of the need
- Survey of the available information
- Critical analysis of the proposed solutions for advantages and disadvantages
- Birth of the new idea, the invention
- Experimentation to test the most promising solution; perfection of the final embodiment by repeating some or all of the previous steps

DEWEY (1938)

- Disturbed equilibrium, initiation of inquiry
- Problem formulation
- Hypothesis formulation
- Experimental testing
- Settled outcome, termination of inquiry

YOUNG (1940)

- Assembly of material
- Assimilation of material in our mind
- Incubation
- Birth of the idea
- Development to practical usefulness

OSBORN (1957)

- Orientation: pointing up the problem
- Preparation: gathering pertinent data
- Analysis: breaking down the relevant material
- Hypothesis: piling up alternatives by way of ideas
- Incubation: letting up, to invite illumination
- Synthesis: putting the pieces together
- Verification: judging the resultant ideas

(Adapted and modified from Haefele, 1962)

generally build a richer cranial data base to work toward the critical apperceptive mass that led to reported insight. But it should be emphasized that such insight was more frequently a private experience, not an interactive man-computer experience, at least according to the testimony of 415 experimental subjects (Sackman, 1969).

The fundamental stages of man-computer problem solving were found to be essentially the same as the classical problem-solving stages observed without computers. These stages, as hypothesized by various investigators, are shown in Table 1-6.

A more recent model of problem solving is shown in Fig. 1-4, derived from Guilford's theory of the structure of the intellect (1967). A noteworthy feature in Guilford's scheme, as shown in Fig. 1-4,

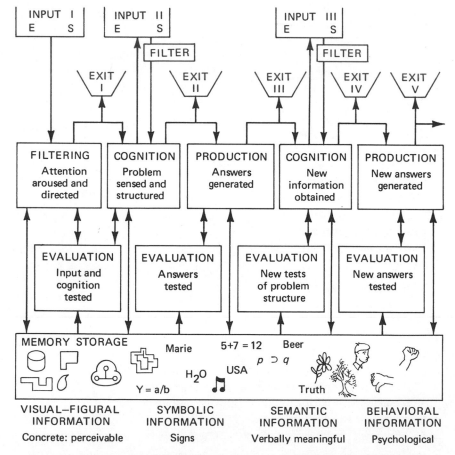

Figure 1-4. The structure-of-intellect model of problem solving (from *The Nature of Human Intelligence* by J. P. Guilford, 1967, McGraw-Hill Book Co. Used with permission of McGraw-Hill Book Co.)

which is not emphasized in other approaches, is the repeated sub-process of evaluation at each sub-stage of problem-solving, culminating in final evaluation of the accepted solution. Guilford's approach stresses the dynamic role of evaluation in the evolution of the problem-solving process. Special emphasis is placed on individual and group evaluation in planning which is developed later in this chapter.

The four stages posed by Wallas (1926) remain, more or less, as the basic paradigm for creativity: preparation, incubation, illumination, and verification. While there is some doubt over the nature and conditions of the incubation stage (see, for example, Woodworth and Schlosberg, 1954), the other stages are experimentally well established. A key problem in all the problem-solving literature, with or without computers, is a reliable and valid taxonomy of problems linked to the dynamics of problem solving. For example, lower-order tasks such as rote memorization, nonsense syllables, mazes, and simple conditioning situations seem to be better interpreted by trial and error classical learning curves espoused by behaviorists and associationists; more novel situations and more creative tasks, for man and animal, seem to be characterized by insightful learning as depicted in gestalt and functionalist theories. The author has demonstrated a combination of trial-and-error and insight learning in solving computer program tasks in which insight corresponds to new or substantially improved logical solutions, with trial-and-error characterizing lower-order syntactical solutions as in the debugging process. In any case, a working taxonomy of human problems persists as a major theoretical challenge in the literature on creativity and problem solving, and remains as a particular challenge in any attempt to compass planning problems.

Another fundamental methodological problem in the general area of human creativity with computers lies in the distinction between problem formulation and problem solution. The online/offline literature and most of the behavioral literature are primarily concerned with solutions for well-defined problems. Except for case histories and biographical studies, we have not yet made much experimental headway into the analysis of creativity in the formulation of significant problems. Mackworth (1965) has stated the general case for problem finding as opposed to problem solving. In the computer milieu, except for sporadic anecdotal reports, significant work has not been done on the potential impact of computers in enhancing the exploratory behaviors that enter into the creation of significant new problems. In online planning, the analog lies in finding and formulating creative plans as opposed to solving well-structured plans.

1-3-3 The Structure of Human Skills in Man-Computer Problem Solving

In this section, the intent is to portray available evidence on individual differences in man-computer problem solving in a coherent conceptual framework. Factor analysis has been a leading tool in behavioral studies concerned with the structure of the intellect, personality, and various skills. Major controversies have developed in the last few decades over competing theories of intelligence, personality, occupational skills, and traits. Computers are now entering the scene in force and they are bound to influence such theories.

The author has developed a hypothesis, a Progressive Differentiation Hypothesis, which offers certain advantages in explaining initial findings on individual differences in man-computer problem solving. This hypothesis was motivated by several considerations. First, computers, viewed as an extension of the human intellect or as an aid to effective human intelligence, seem to expand individual differences. There is no need to enlarge on the ubiquitous presence of very large individual differences in man-computer effectiveness; it is everywhere in the available literature. The proposed hypothesis, as we shall see, goes a step further and asserts that computer developments are likely to continue to enhance effective human intelligence, perhaps almost indefinitely, which would continue to expand individual differences over a growing spectrum of human capabilities.

A second motivation lies in the apparently limitless number and diversity of problems to which computers can be applied in a man-computer context. This diversity requires a pluralistic conceptual framework to allow elbow room for new and perhaps radically different computer applications that could arise in the future. Here is one potential solution to the taxonomy problem mentioned earlier— a pluralistic, open-end, evolutionary framework changing with the changing ecology of human needs, skills, and technology.

A third motivation lies in the need to systematically chart the genetic growth of computer knowledge and skills in individuals from their first encounter with computers through the most advanced stages of computer skill and expertise.

A fourth motivation lies in the need for more effective teaching of computer knowledge and skills, and in systematic test and measurement of such attributes in a practical manner.

A fifth motivation lies in the desirability of linking computer-related skills to the mainstream of behavioral experimentation on the structure and dynamics of skills and traits in the areas of intellect, personality, and occupation.

With these various considerations in mind, the Progressive Differentiation Hypothesis is defined in two parts:

1. Progressive advances in computer tools and information services tend to extend the range of individual differences in man-computer performance, and such advances will continue to expand effective human differences in a freely competitive and open environment.

2. The pattern of expanding individual differences assumes the following general form: when individuals are first exposed to and indoctrinated in the use of computers, either a general factor, or a small number of well-defined group factors in man-computer communication proficiency, or a combination of both, are held to account for a substantial portion of observed individual differences; however, with the advent of diversified tasks and increasing experience, this relatively small set of general proficiency factors for beginners tends to differentiate progressively into numerous separate and independent factors associated with increasing specialized experience.

The pattern of progressive differentiation of man-computer skills was suggested to the author from the factor findings in the literature on intelligence testing. In essence, at early ages a general verbal factor was found in various test scores of children, that is, children scoring high in one type of test tended to score high in most of the other types of tests. At later ages, particularly at the college level, the factor structure progressively changed to differential, specialized skills that were relatively independent of each other, such as numerical, spatial, motor, and logical skills. The analogy in the computer milieu is that computers are becoming a powerful force in helping to accelerate the further differentiation of human skills and traits in man-computer tasks, including extensions into online planning.

In closing this section, a brief mention should be made concerning the structure of planning skills derived from the factor-analytic literature. The work of Berger, Guilford, and Christensen (1957) probably remains as the most ambitious attempt to scale the dimensions of planning skills and traits. They found 14 identifiable planning factors in a battery of 52 tests administered to 364 USAF air-crew trainees which included one test representing a general planning activity. The orthogonal factors included 10 found previously: verbal comprehension, numerical facility, visualization, general reasoning, logical evaluation, ideational fluency, eduction of conceptual relations, judgment, originality, and adaptive flexibility. Four new factors were interpreted as: ordering, elaboration, perceptual foresight, and conceptual foresight. In the planning test, the greatest proportions of common factor variance were contributed by: elaboration, originality, judgment, and ideational fluency. Although the planning test did elicit some new factors, it was apparent that the factor structure for this measure of planning was largely comprised of primary mental abilities. Guilford (1967) integrates these findings on planning into his structure-of-intellect theory. These results tend to support a fundamental assumption of the present review of man-computer problem solving; that is, findings generally applicable to man-computer problem solving are also likely to be relevant to computer-aided planning.

1-3-4 Provisional Characteristics for Online Planning from the Man-Computer Problem-Solving Literature

A composite portrait may be drawn for provisional recommendations taken from the experimental literature and extrapolated to online planning. Such extrapolation is risky in view of: the relatively small number of experimental studies to date; the pilot nature of most of these studies; the lack of experimental controls in many studies for such factors as computer languages, adequacy of computer system service, and controlled experience level of subjects; the lack of any studies on online team problem solving; and, with the marginal exception of Gold's study (1967), the lack of experimental problems on planning. With these kinds of provisos in mind, the following sketch emerges in comparing online and offline problem solving for three broad areas: costs, problem-solving conditions, and user effectiveness.

In cost, the offline mode tends to be less expensive for immediate man and machine expense. The slight advantage in fewer man-hours to solve standard problems in the online mode (about 20 percent) is neutralized by considerably less computer time for such solutions under the offline mode (only about half as much computer time under batch). Any claims for greatly speeding up the planning process, or significantly reducing planning costs, under these results, would have to be based on the argument of computerizing slow and costly manual planning functions, rather than going from batch to an online mode.

Generally speaking, online planning cannot be justified on the grounds of greater speed and lower cost against offline planning. The justification for online planning has to be sought in other factors.

There are other myths concerning online problem solving that need to be exploded. For virtually all experimental studies, online subjects spent only a small proportion of their problem-solving time at the console (on the order of about 10 percent), and spent most of their time at their desks in formulating the problem, checking results, and developing alternative solutions. Typically, a subject would spend less than an hour at the console, with the rest of the day on non-interactive tasks. Problem-solving progress occurred in the user's head when he was away from the console. Accordingly, the justification for online planning is to expedite and improve the natural progression of problem solving as it shapes up in the mind of the user while he struggles with his problem. This occurs under offline as well as online conditions.

The myth that needs to be exploded lies in the fundamental philosophy of the relation between man and the computer. The myth holds that the ultimate objective of online systems is to improve man-computer communication. The experimental data, on the other hand, make it clear that improved man-computer communication is merely the means to achieve the more fundamental end of improved human communication, including self-communication and man-to-man communication. Creative insight, and the concurrent attainment of correct and satisfactory solutions to problems, whether planning problems or other kinds of problems, is ultimately a human, not a machine process.

The experimental literature also indicates that user system service must be satisfactorily reliable, and terminals must be accessible to the users to sustain online advantages. Otherwise, the offline mode proves superior as demonstrated in several studies. In addition, the overhead of user time and effort in learning how to use the online system should not be prohibitive.

The fundamental justification for going to online planning, as far as the available experimental literature is concerned, lies in the quality of the problem-solving experience and the excellence of the solution. Several key elements contribute to the potential for online systems to lead to a more satisfying and more effective problem-solving experience. First, online systems are apparently more universally preferred by users over offline systems. For various reasons, the online mode is generally more enjoyable, more challenging, more permissive, and more responsive. For example, even when online users received less reliable service than batch users, time-sharing was still preferred over batch in the Air Force Academy study. In view of the long and sorrowful history of prototype computer services that failed, it is crucial to have positive user preference working with the proposed system, and the online system represents a major evolutionary mutation toward greater user acceptance.

Although positive user acceptance is necessary for the survival and growth of online systems, it is not sufficient. The sufficient condition lies in the achievement of excellence in problem solution. The experimental literature gives us some indication of conditions favorable for the achievement of excellence under the online mode. First, the open-end task, which admits many levels and degrees of correct solutions (as in the Gold study, 1967), is apparently more conducive to the achievement of excellence in the online mode than the closed, well-structured problem that requires an all-or-none, correct or incorrect solution. Thus, the least structured problems—which are the more creative problems—are more desirable candidates for online planning. Further, the earlier stages of the creative process, such as problem finding and problem formulation, are also better candidates for online planning than the later stages, such as construction of problem solutions. The main exception to this rule, and an economically important one, is program debugging where immediate knowledge of results gives the online user a major advantage.

Looking at key dynamics of the problem-solving experience, the online mode is more effective for situations requiring massed learning, easy movement from part to whole learning, insightful learning, individualized problem-solving styles, and immediate knowledge of results. Summarizing, the online mode is the method of choice for exploratory problems requiring intensive, highly individualized human efforts aimed at creative insight in open-end environments. Such problem situations are more likely to enhance the quality of the online problem-solving experience, and they are more conducive to the achievement of excellence in solution.

1-4 TOWARD A THEORY OF PLANNING

1-4-1 The Vacuum in Planning Theory

Advanced research in online planning presupposes a theoretical framework for planning. We look in vain for a substantive planning theory in the literature. For example, Branch (1966) speaks about a "comprehensive planning process," but not a planning theory. Ayres (1969) discusses the "epistemology of forecasting," but does not come up with any theory of planning. Emery (1965) describes a "formalization of the planning process," but does not venture into planning theory. The record of the Commission on the Year 2000 (*Daedalus,* Summer 1967) does not lead to any planning theories among its numerous articles.

LeBreton and Henning (1961) wrote a book entitled *Planning Theory.* Their "theory" turns out to be an amalgam of activities and disciplines that contribute to the planning process, consisting of seven sub-theories; theory of need determination, theory of choice, theory of data collection and processing, testing theory, theory of organizing for planning, communication theory in planning, and persuasion theory. What LeBreton and Henning put forth is not a theory, but a description of planning, arguing that all and any disciplines that contribute to such activities are part of planning theory. Their effort at theorizing is valuable in highlighting the eclectic and pluralistic nature of planning.

In an extensive and thoughtful compendium on management planning, Steiner (1969) puts forth fundamental requirements for a theory of planning (p. 715):

> "This is an aggregate body of theory that has a number of characteristics. First, it should have a set of principles and laws with broad applicability. Second, these should have predictive value. Third, the detailed theories should be tested and found to be valid. Fourth, the theory must explain and describe the phenomenon of planning in total and in its parts. Fifth, it must be useful in actual practice. Sixth, the theory must organize effectively and classify properly the relevant knowledge and experience. Finally, it should give direction to research and teaching of the subject."

In his assessment of the status of planning, Steiner asserts that planning theory is rapidly approaching maturity, but has not yet arrived. He bases his overall conclusion on several generalizations: a variety of planning models have been tested and found to be usefully valid; description and classification of planning are advanced in important areas (e.g., the system-development cycle is well understood); prescriptive statements—such as the proposition that top-management involvement and support is essential for successful planning—have been generally validated, even though such statements are scientifically imprecise; and quantitative methods and tools in planning reflect a high degree of precision, sophistication, and diversification.

Steiner has demonstrated, by and large, that an eclectic methodology has been recruited from many disciplines and has been pressed into service for planning, and that fragmented findings are scattered unevenly in the planning arena. His assertion that planning theory is approaching maturity may itself be criticized as premature. Although, like Branch, Steiner speaks of comprehensive planning as a framework for planning theory, nowhere can a theory of comprehensive planning be found in his book in the sense and spirit of his own criteria quoted above. Much as all of us would like to wish otherwise, planning theory is not premature, it is immature.

The planning literature presents a problematic pyramidal structure. At the bottom is a vast literature on planning applications for almost every endeavor known to man. The massive five-year plans of the USSR are a case in point. In the middle is a much smaller and limited literature on planning methodology (e.g., the 25 books on planning techniques produced in the 1960's, as mentioned by Mockler, 1970). At the apex is the virtual nonexistence of any substantive literature on planning theory. What are some of the reasons for this state of affairs?

Some have already been discussed. Planning is in a fast-moving predisciplinary stage. Planning is everywhere at individual, group, national, and international levels. Planning begs, borrows, and steals from all disciplines and is applied to virtually every social endeavor. In its broadest sense, planning is almost coextensive with human behavior which invariably contains an anticipatory element. Planning is like a vast, amorphous inkblot into which we can project any type of human or social behavior that can be linked to some aspect of the future. If planning is to be a fruitful concept, it needs to be defined in a scientifically useful manner, and embedded in a constructive theoretical context.

1-4-2 Current Definitions of Planning

The definitions of planning are legion. Illustrative examples are shown, leading toward a definition suitable for a scientific discipline of planning.

At a general level, Meyerson and Banfield (1955) define *planning* as "a method for delineating goals and ways of achieving them"; and they define a *plan* as "a course of action which can be carried into effect, which can be expected to lead to the attainment of ends sought, and which someone intends to carry into effect."

At the individual level, Miller, Galanter, and Pribram (1960) define a plan as "any hierarchical process in the organism that can control the order in which a sequence of operations is to be performed."

Branch (1966) defines comprehensive planning as "the ultimate in man's endeavor to perform a major achievement, shape his environment or affect the future. . . . What we are concerned with in comprehensive planning is the spectrum of human awareness, knowledge, and capacity to consider and act."

Steiner (1969) defines planning as a process coextensive with management in its broad sense. "Planning is a process which begins with objectives; defines strategies, policies, and detailed plans to achieve them; establishes an organization to implement decisions; and includes a review of performance and feedback to introduce a new planning cycle."

In economics, Clay (1950) defines planning as "the opposite of reliance on a market economy." In a more positive vein, Florence (1953) defines national planning as the "intention to promote the public interests by the more or less visible hand of the state."

For Mannheim (1940) planning is "a mode of thought which not only changes individual links in the causal chain and adds new ones, but also tries to grasp the whole complex of events from the *key position* which exists in every situation."

In another attempt to reach the essence of planning, Millett (1947) says "the job of planning, reduced perhaps to its most elementary aspect, is the constant task of defining and sharpening the objectives."

Along similar lines, Bell (1964) emphasizes that "The true function of the planning process is not to designate the most appropriate means for given ends, but to predict the possible consequences to explicate the values of a society and make people aware of the costs of achieving these." In the same paper, Bell also states that "the function of prediction is not, as often stated, to aid social control, but to widen the spheres of moral choice."

Ayres (1969) does not offer any general definition of planning, but distinguishes between three main types:

- *Policy Planning:* Formulation of alternative goal patterns or functional objectives for the future—based on alternative future environments or scenarios—in a (continuous) comparison, selection, and feedback process.
- *Strategic Planning:* Formulation of a set of alternative routes or options for achieving the chosen set of goals, together with a procedure for systematic comparison and assessment.
- *Tactical Planning:* Delineating the sequence of actions necessary to implement a particular strategy. The technological aspects of tactical planning would be concerned with reaching well-defined technological (as opposed to functional) objectives generally in terms of specified systems or subsystems.

In anticipation of the definition of planning linked to scientific method that is developed later, note the approach of Nadel (1951) which points to the analogy between means and ends in relation to cause and effect: ". . . we can readily visualize the double relationship of means-and-ends and cause-and-effect as a gradual process in which, step by step, one becomes adjusted to the other; that is, an end is anticipated, however vaguely; causal effects are observed which suggest a suitable means, until the means has been fully tested and fitted to the desired end."

The above definitions underscore the diffuse, predisciplinary status of planning, and the need for a rigorous approach more amenable to scientific method. The following approach to planning is offered as an initial step toward a scientific theory of planning. The proposed approach is an outgrowth of ideas on experimentally regulated system development found in the author's book (1967).

1-4-3 Prolegomena to a Theory of Planning

The foundation stone is disarmingly simple, but crucial: plans may be conceived as hypotheses, subject to empirical test and evaluation in a scientific manner. Given certain conditions, hypotheses predict consequences in accordance with specified relations among operationally defined variables. Why shouldn't we construct plans in the form of hypotheses so that we can rigorously test plans and the planning process?

Hypotheses are embedded in the context of an overarching theory.

How can theory be linked with plans? The necessary step is to embed plans in the context of an object system such that the system serves as an operational definition of a plan in a concrete working context. Thus, plans could be working hypotheses concerning system performance subject to continual test and evaluation throughout the life cycle of the object system. The plan is essentially a blueprint of evolving hypotheses concerning system performance, and system development is the embodiment or actualization of the plan, which permits empirical measurement of the validity and internal reliability of the plan. An overriding advantage of the proposed approach is that the real-world system serves as the source of its own planning hypotheses, and also provides the means for testing such hypotheses.

The scientific confrontation between general abstractions and concrete systems is a new version of the age-old controversy of pure versus applied science. This controversy is taking on a significant new twist with the advent of formally planned systems, particularly with computer-aided systems. In the past, scientific man-machine experimentation was conducted in a laboratory setting in which dependent and independent variables in object system behaviors were relatively isolated, while other factors were controlled or held constant, in an idealized and simplified model or representation of the system. This approach may be described as experimental idealism. At present, particularly in computer-serviced systems, it is becoming increasingly possible to tap real-world and real-time system behaviors in a credible test setting involving an adequately representative complex of the elements of the object system and its environment, with results that have useful predictive value in extrapolating and assessing system performance. This approach may be described as experimental realism in contrast to experimental idealism. To state the case bluntly, why test abstract surrogates when we can test the real thing? Why play with laboratory esoterica when we can go where the action is?

The philosophy that can be only briefly summarized here is, in essence, the extension of experimental method to real-world planning— the extension of system test and evaluation to total system planning and associated system development. The basic starting point is that system plans and derived system design can be viewed as a set of evolving hypotheses concerning system performance—hypotheses that are continually subject to system test, evaluation, and reformulation in the light of new findings and changing conditions. This means that planning objectives, planning requirements, system design, and system specifications should be conceived and written as operationally defined procedures subject to empirical testing. It also means that resources and facilities for system test and evaluation have to be anticipated in early planning at the system definition phase.

Planned system development, viewed as a scientific activity, implies a number of far-reaching differences from traditional scientific endeavor. One of the most striking differences is that there are as many applied sciences as there are concrete systems. The planned system spells out its own framework of hypotheses concerning its own development and its own performance, with respect to its own resources and objectives. As plans for systems are plastic creations of men and are virtually unlimited in the imagination of men, so is the domain of planned system sciences also unlimited. Whereas traditional sciences tend to be compartmentalized into classical Aristotelian subject areas, such as the mathematical, physical, biological, and social sciences, planned system sciences, in contrast, are freely interdisciplinary as required for the accomplishment of system goals.

Traditional science has as many competitive sets of theories for a given subject area as there are recognized experts in the field who can attract a following. In the proposed approach to scientifically planned systems, there is usually just one set of authorized, official plans and system specifications that describe the system and its leading performance hypotheses. In traditional science, the logical classification of subject matter is relatively abstract, whereas in systems the detailed plans, including the men, machines, and communications of an object system, provide a tangible, coherent framework for operational performance hypotheses that does not exist in generalized scientific domains. In particular, real-world experimentation lends itself naturally to a concrete systems setting, whereas generalized scientific models are designed to be temporally and situationally invariant.

There are basic behavioral differences between conventional science and planned-systems science in the proposed approach. In the systems approach, those significantly involved in system development and operations—such as planners, managers, designers, analysts, users, operators, and technicians—constitute the potential planning community of the object system. The associated technical literature, including evolving system plans, design specifications, and published test findings, can serve as the equivalent of a public forum for this community, open to criticism from peers and subject to continual reformulation in response to changing conditions. The system community can thus provide many of the checks and balances on method and findings in system planning that are provided by the scientific community in its own specialties in scientific matters.

In this view, experimental method is not restricted to the scientific elite who have been professionally trained in a specialized subject area. It is widely dispersed to all who can participate and contribute significantly to system planning and associated system development, with experimental techniques and aids designed specifically for the role and skill level of the user. With this approach, experimental method could evolve into more humanized and approachable forms that would facilitate user planning and user self-service from grass-roots to managerial levels. If planned systems are conceived as forms of applied science, each unique to the object system, what sort of science will this constitute? Systematic eclecticism, a term suggested by Allport (1963) in another context, seems well suited to character-ize, at the same time, the diversity and unity of the proposed approach. As plastic human plans, each system extracts what is useful from available science and technology. Planning is eclectic and justification is pragmatic—will the planned pieces fit together and do the job? This kind of planned eclecticism is not arbitrary or capricious; it must prove its worth in successful system operations.

The proposed philosophy of scientifically planned system develop-ment is admittedly sketchy and incomplete. The limitations stem from the youthful status of planning and system science. Fundamentally, this philosophy is an appeal for excellence in system planning through the extension of experimental method in system development.

1-4-4   Definition of Planning

In accordance with the above philosophy of planning, the follow-ing definition of planning is offered: *Planning refers to plastic evolving hypotheses concerning system objectives and performance in specified environments, including embedding ecosystems, to achieve desired levels of operationally defined effectiveness, within stated resources, throughout the life-cycle of object system and successor systems.*

This definition is not easy to digest when swallowed for the first time. But a closer examination will reveal that it meets key criteria for the philosophy of planning outlined above:

- It states that plans are hypotheses.
- It places planning in an evolutionary system context.

- It requires that plans be operationally defined so that they can be tested in the system setting.
- The environment of the object system also includes the ecosystem in which it is embedded.
- It emphasizes that plans are plastic human creations of desired features within time and resource constraints.
- Plans are placed squarely in the middle of the real world.
- The definition underscores the fallibility of the "best laid plans of mice and men" by insisting on the need for accountability through continual testing in an uncertain world.

Other definitions of planning have anticipated various aspects of the proposed definition, as indicated earlier, but apparently none have encompassed all of the above attributes in a single definition that uncompromisingly weds planning to scientific method.

There are further implications of the above definition of planning, the proposed theory of planning, and the intersection of the above approach to planning with online problem solving. These are treated next in working toward a specific recommendation for research in online planning.

1-5   PARTICIPATORY ONLINE PLANNING (POP)

In this section, previous considerations on planning are joined with the disiderata of online problem solving, and with various additional considerations and constraints not mentioned earlier—culminating in an initial proposal for research in online planning. The first step is to take a closer look at where the greatest research potential for planning lies.

1-5-1   Planning Techniques and Planning Research

As an aid to determine where research needs in planning are greatest, Fig. 1–5 portrays the planning techniques mentioned earlier. The context incorporates planning stages (x-axis) and system development (y-axis). Planning stages, from earliest to final stages, as shown in Fig. 1–5, are: normative, strategic, tactical, and operational. The system development steps are self-explanatory. Both scales show a time dimension from the present as the origin reference point, to the future, in rank-order of stages in planning and system development. The planning/system development space has a significant property, probably not obvious at first glance. In essence, it indicates that all levels of planning occur at all points throughout the system development process. That is, normative, strategic, tactical, and operational planning occur not only when the system is still a gleam in someone's eye, but also throughout the definition, design, operation, and obsolescence of the system. This portrayal thus emphasizes both the gestalt nature of planning and its evolutionary thrust. It also provides a backdrop for scientific test and evaluation of planning in a systems context.

Note that planning techniques are distributed in the system development/planning stage space in Fig. 1–5 in six groups. Starting from earliest planning and earliest system development stages, the first group of techniques consists of brainstorming, Delphi, expert opinion, scenarios, dialectical planning, confrontation, contextual analysis,

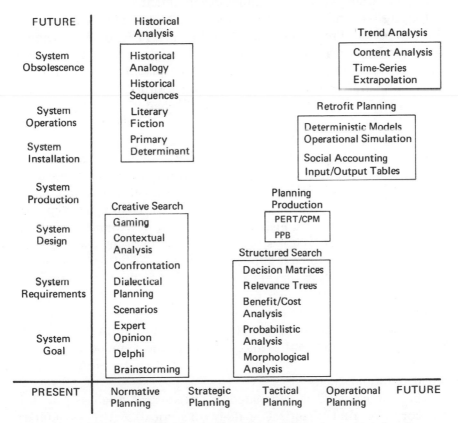

Figure 1-5. Temporal distribution of planning techniques in system planning and system development.

and gaming. This group of techniques represents the earliest, most creative, most controversial, and most open-end aspects of planning and system development; they may be characterized as creative search techniques. These techniques represent the more formative aspects of planning where, probably, the least research has been accomplished, the greatest need exists, and the greatest research break-throughs might be expected to occur.

The "Structured Search" grouping in Fig. 1–5 includes decision matrices, relevance trees, benefit/cost analysis, probabilistic analysis, and morphological analysis. These techniques are characteristically employed further down the line in planning and system development—in early system design and at the junction of strategic and tactical planning where the end in view is well structured and where the problem is to determine the most effective means to achieve the desired ends. Although this area is fairly well researched, there are still many leads open for planning development.

Closely related to the "Structured Search" techniques are the two listed "Planning Production" methods, PPB and PERT/CPM. Although these techniques cut across the entire planning cycle, they generally focus on system implementation, when the planning problem is well structured and when most of the searching for alternative means has been completed. Detailed budgeting and scheduling at this level are indicative of the planning production process. This area has been fairly extensively researched.

The next category, "Retrofit Planning," refers to ongoing evo-lutionary modications of relatively well-established plans based on feedback from deterministic models, operational simulation, social accounting, and input/output tables. These techniques typically occur further down the planning and system development pipeline. Although much research has been done in some of these areas, a vast area is opening up in newer applications such as social accounting.

The "Trend Analysis" techniques occur last in the planning/system development cycle since they require historical perspective to demon-strate trends, as in content analysis and time-series extrapolation. This area has been heavily researched; significant improvements could occur in the development of more accurate and more powerful tech-niques for data collection and analysis leading to more effective trend determination.

The last category is designated as "Historical Analysis." In this category we find historical analogy, historical sequences, literary fiction, and primary determinant approaches to planning. Note that these techniques are located at the normative stage of planning and at the obsolescence point in system development in Fig. 1–5. The reason for this juxtaposition is that historical techniques provide one of the most powerful methods available for evaluating the normative assumptions in planning. Historical perspective is probably the broadest perspective of all, but under current conditions, it suffers from entering into planning too late with too little. What is needed is a real-time acceleration of historical data collection and analysis so that credible historical evaluations can be more timely and more relevant. The discipline of the history of science and technology is still very new; we still do not know how to design useful data collection and reduction techniques for effective historical analyses in the fast-moving technological arena. There are many unprecedented opportunities for planning research in this area that have hardly been tapped.

1-5-2   Rudiments of a Mutual Expectation Theory of Planning

Earlier discussion of a theory of planning was primarily concerned with the application of scientific method to planning. The emphasis in this context is more on an interpretation of the problem-solving process in planning. An early statement of a mutual expectation theory of planning is presented at this point to identify a crucial research area in planning and to provide additional theoretical support for the proposal for online planning that follows in the next section.

Planning may be viewed as the institutionalization of concurred social change for individuals and groups. As such, planning is the vehicle for directed social change. The accelerating tempo of contemporary change, and the growing complexity and ecological interdependence of social problems—and this assertion is central to the proposed theory—require an increasingly broader social consensus, qualitatively and quantitatively, to create a working mandate for viable plans. That is, plans effectively undergo a process of birth contingent on a prior mandate from cognizant social interests. The political process and the corporate process, to cite only two examples, have well-established channels for the institutionalization of change in the form of authorized plans. Accordingly, plans are the overt embodiment of the mutual expectations of concerned individuals and groups. The genetic structures of embryonic plans are embedded in such mutual expectations.

The general hypothesis put forth is that the planning process—

viewed as authorized and directed social change—is initially triggered and sustained by an effective consensus in the concerned community which is shaped by mutual expectations concerning social values, goals, resources, alternative courses of action, and priorities. This hypothesis further states that such consensus is increasingly reaching into more diverse levels of society and to more individuals as social problems grow in size, scope, and urgency, leading to increasing need for participatory planning in all walks of life.

The proposed mutual expectation theory of planning holds that the initial stage of planning—normative consensus—is undergoing a profound process of democratization, by evolutionary and revolutionary methods of social participation throughout the world. Perhaps the most crucial challenge to research in planning lies in systematic and rational extension of participatory planning, particularly in the earliest stages of planning.

The mutual expectation theory of planning does not maintain the untenable position that everyone and his brother should or could participate in all stages of planning; this would undermine the rational division of labor in planning and lead to chaos. The proposed theory applies primarily to the germination stage of planning, the point at which social sanction occurs in some form of consensus. As such, it is put forth as a partial rather than a comprehensive theory of planning. Subsequent to the initial mandate, the design and implementation of a plan follows the characteristic division of labor in the system development process. The planning mandate, which is the point at which a plan is overtly institutionalized, involves a broader set of individuals than those engaged in the immediate design and implementation of the plan, a consensus set that might be called a planning community or a planning public. It is this planning community that is the object population in the proposed mutual expectation theory.

Expectation theory is not something new under the sun. Stogdill (1959) provided a useful, early review of group expectation theory. Although still a loosely aggregated body of theory and experimentation, expectation concepts have a long and fairly extensive history in the social sciences (e.g., Mead, 1934; Barnard, 1948; Mayo, 1933; and Roethlisberger and Dickson, 1941). These authors have posited expectation as a basic dimension of group behavior and they have variously suggested that stable expectations render predictable behavior; socialized individuals are those who act in accordance with the expectations of others; and systematic changes in expectations are correlated with systematic changes in group performance. Learning theorists, such as Tolman (1932), Mowrer (1950), MacCorquodale and Meehl (1953), and Rotter (1954), have accumulated substantial experimental data demonstrating systematic relationships between the reinforcement of expectations and the rate of learning. Kelly (1955) based his theory of personality on the fundamental premise that "a person's processes are psychologically channelized by the ways in which he anticipates events."

Stogdill (1959) believes that expectation theory is the most promising avenue in learning theory to unravel the problems of social learning. He develops expectation theory as one of the keystones of his theory of group achievement. Expectation is defined as ". . . readiness for reinforcement, a function of drive, the estimated probability of occurrence of a possible outcome, and the estimated desirability of the outcome." It remains to be demonstrated that this nexus of psychological elements in expectation is intrinsic to the human dynamics of planning.

Although an extensive review of expectation research is beyond the scope of this chapter, a few illustrative findings may help to suggest the value of expectation theory for understanding the dynamics of planning. As a starter, Stogdill puts forth the general hypothesis that much of what is known of reinforcement theory in learning can be transferred to the reinforcement of expectation.

- Some studies have shown that prediction of social events may be strongly influenced by the desirability of alternative outcomes, and that attitudes toward events tend to dominate predictions when little information is available on such events.
- Unrealistic expectations tend to be more highly generalized in predicting events than realistic expectations; that is, unrealistic expectations exhibit a more extensive "halo effect" in predictions of related classes of events.
- Individuals tend to shift their expectations to conform with overt group norms, particularly in cohesive groups.
- Expectations are systematically linked to individual value systems in a manner that tends toward selective perception to reinforce well-established values.
- Deviant individuals tend to demonstrate greater certainty in their value systems and greater rigidity in their expectations.

- Group and individual expectations vary with the perceived effectiveness of the group.
- Individuals with similar expectations tend to seek each other out and to reinforce mutual values.
- Public expression of expectations tends to be more powerful in changing expectations than private expression.
- Under certain conditions, anonymous feedback of individual expectations is more accurate and more efficient than face-to-face confrontation.

As mentioned in the title of this section, only the rudiments of a mutual expectation theory of planning are presented. Some of the methodological and research implications of this theory of planning are worked out in the proposal for research in online planning in the concluding section, in which various advantages and disadvantages to the proposed approach are cited. Beyond this introductory and cursory treatment, the reader is left to his own devices in assessing the value of the proposed mutual expectation framework for planning.

1-5-3 Initial Framework for Participatory Online Planning

Participatory planning refers to mutual expectations in social creation of a plan—the attitudes, beliefs, values, goals, priorities, judgments, and supporting rationalizations that enter into social consensus for defining and initiating an authorized plan. Research in participatory online planning (POP) refers to systematic experimentation in the creation of plans as expressed in planning consensus in an online computing environment.

What do these general statements imply for a program of research in participatory online planning? First, the emphasis is not evenly distributed over the entire planning process from the gleam in someone's eye to the completed final plan. The focus is primarily on the early normative stage of planning—the creation of a concurred and accepted mandate for planning in a specified planning community. Thus, the planning techniques for the earliest stages of planning (normative planning) and the earliest stages of system development (system goals), as shown earlier in Fig. 1–5, are the starting point for participatory online planning. It was previously seen that these earlier and more creative stages in planning were most in need of research and development, and probably represented the best possibilities for planning breakthroughs. They include gaming, brainstorming, dialectical planning, Delphi, expert opinion, scenarios, contextual analysis, and confrontation techniques. This proposal does not necessarily exclude other techniques. Nor does this proposal exclude later stages of planning. In principle, POP can be applied wherever human evaluation is invoked, and wherever there is a difference of opinion on explicit issues, which can occur at any point throughout the entire planning cycle.

Not all planning techniques are suitable or desirable for online implementation. A subset of a few of these techniques or improved variations should be selected. Criteria for such selection include:

- Ease and objectivity in formalization for online implementation.
- Amenability to quantification and experimental investigation.
- Capitalization on the leading advantages of online problem solving.
- Flexible application to a wide variety of planning problems.
- Amenability to available natural language and natural I/O techniques.
- Rapid and valid experimentation on significant hypotheses in participatory planning.
- Feasibility within available resources and timetables.
- Ease and utility of supporting user languages and data bases.
- Ease of manual and offline experimentation while online computerized tools are being designed and developed.
- Research potential for making original and substantive contributions to the theory and methodology of planning.

With these criteria in mind, gaming, Delphi, scenarios, expert opinion, and contextual analysis are probably more fruitful techniques for initial work in participatory online planning. It is not recommended that one or more of these techniques be grafted onto an online system. The issue in point is to develop a new generation of online planning capability, using the best characteristics of manual and offline percursors and rearranging them in an improved online configuration for the initial version of participatory online planning— POP—which is father to this generation.

The heart of the required evolutionary mutation to an online configuration lies in adaptive generalization in man-computer communication and in the interactive data base. Adaptive generalization refers to an evolutionary advance that enables the organism to cope with and adapt to a wider range of problems and situations. The human brain is the ultimate example of adaptive generalization. In this context, the four major evolutionary steps are the advent of natural I/O, the development of adversary information systems, the inclusion of educational features, and the application of teleconference procedures for remote planning.

Natural I/O refers to the use of natural language as it is spontaneously written, spoken, or otherwise expressively used in man-to-man communication, transferred to an online setting as in typewriter, voice, graphic, pointing, or pushbutton input. The advantages of natural I/O are obvious, and significant breakthroughs in this area would lead toward adaptive generalization.

The adversary information system is a newer and less well-understood concept. Adversary information systems refer to the organization of information on opposing sides of contested issues such that reasons for and against each position are solicited, stored, and tracked in a realtime transaction that converges toward an operationally defined resolution. Statistical hypothesis-testing is one objective form of simple adversary decision in the sense that a hypothesis, such as the null hypothesis on the significance of the difference between two means, is accepted or rejected by a precise quantitative test.

The proposed concept of adversary information systems goes further than isolated hypothesis testing in also including reasons for and against the position taken on contested issues. In matters of opinion, the proposed adversary information system would not only poll participants, but would also record and organize the reasons put forth for the positions taken. This process of querying participants generates a dialectical data base. As the dialectical data base grows and changes in real time in an online context, an adversary dialogue develops in which participants can exchange views, take sides, and follow the course of consensus, deadlock, or polarization.

The adversary information system has several notable properties not found in conventional information systems and data bases. The conventional data base is comprehensively organized *a priori* to encompass all queries of users in the data domain. It is encyclopedic and deductive and may be described as Aristotelian. The dialectical data base, after the originator of dialectics, is organized along Socratic lines. There is always a point or issue that is being contested. Statements are oriented for or against specified positions. The dialectical data base virtually starts from scratch, develops inductively as the argument progresses, and is completed when the argument is terminated by some specified criterion or reaches a point of diminishing returns.

Dialectical data bases need to be tied to natural language to encourage active participation, credibility, and high motivation on the part of the user. They should be concise and highly relevant data bases that can be easily generated and easily disposed of as overriding inquiry takes new turns. The ideal dialectical data base is a boiled-down, agreed-upon list of key reasons for and against a contested issue with such reasons ranked in order of importance. Throwaway data bases, or easy-come/easy-go data bases, are needed to permit the adversary information system to adapt in real time to online users.

The proposed adversary information system combines available advances of natural I/O with the requirements of searching mutual expectations in initial planning. Primitive forms of adversary information systems are possible now within the current state of the art, such as online opinion polling, accompanied by one-word or one-phrase reasons or justifications in English. The aim of such systems would be interactive convergence toward rationalized consensus in planning.

The third evolutionary feature of POP may be described as online education. Among other characteristics, planning is, in large part, an educational experience. The planner emerges from the planning process better informed and hopefully wiser in the trials and tribulations of his planning problem and in planning skills. If planning is in fact a type of learning experience, it should be explicitly supported and designed as an educational tool. Since POP is an online planning system, it should have available an online facility to support interactive construction of plans, selective presentation of textual material, tutorial support, and real-time tracking and measurement of planning performance against specified criteria. The educational aspects of planning should be systematically exploited to improve planning skills and the quality of end-item plans.

An interactive educational computer language such as PLANIT (Feingold, 1967) would meet the above general requirements. PLANIT (Programming Language for Interaction and Teaching), or an equivalent tool, could be used for the design of any instructional, questionnaire, or itemized planning sequence that can be broken down into frames, for rating or classifying user responses, for tracking the course of consensus, for tutorial branching, and for measurement of man-computer performance.

There has been no tradition in the planning literature to define, measure, and track the proficiency of planners in the performance of their task. An educational vehicle for POP could make such experimentation possible, and open up a new area of study in real-time planning effectiveness.

The fourth evolutionary feature of POP is to work with planning communities in which individuals and groups are physically remote from each other. Since more and more planning problems require more diverse skills and more extensive opinions, it becomes virtually impossible to get all concerned individuals together to work out a common approach for a planning mandate. In public issues large numbers of people may be involved. The wide-ranging problems of large organizations, such as DOD, often involve many people and require a great variety of experts from different disciplines. Computer networks—such as the ARPA prototype with approximately 20 "host" computers throughout the United States—are needed to distribute such issues to "planning publics," to collect and organize responses, and to mediate rationalized consensus in planning. Thus, POP is advocated as a plausible approach to dispersed community participation in developing rationalized consensus for planning.

Computerization of planning consensus, as embodied in POP, offers several fundamental advantages for online planning. First, POP is an ideal way to very rapidly collect and disseminate diverse opinions and the rationale behind such opinions to and from individuals in different locations. Second, there is a case to be made for greater efficiency in arriving at group consensus in a distributed arrangement of participants as opposed to face-to-face groups which become unwieldly in large numbers. Helmer (1964) and Dalkey (1969) have presented extensive experimental evidence in connection with Delphi studies to the effect that more accurate and more useful consensus can often be achieved in distributed groups, under certain conditions, as compared to face-to-face groups for many types of problems. In fact, POP can pick up where Delphi and related techniques have left off. Third, work with POP *now* will permit an extensively tested technique for polling, adversary presentation, and consensus to be available for use *later* when extensive computer networks and mass information utilities become commonplace. Fourth, adversary information systems, as sketched for POP, represent a powerful vehicle for exploiting the vast potential of natural-language

I/O for natural solutions to a virtually unlimited number of decision-making applications. Fifth, the relatively simple and straightforward requirements of polling and examining both sides of a contested issue in natural language make a technique like POP an eminently painless and attractive way to introduce a vast user audience (the silent majority) to online information services—a popularizing break-through that no computer service or application has achieved to date. Finally, POP could exploit the great educational potential of planning, objectively testing for improved planning skills and better plans.

The fundamental problem is a basic problem in society; face-to-face communication is inadequate to resolve numerous wide-ranging issues involving dispersed individuals and groups. The computer can help in catalyzing man-to-man communication to clarify issues and resolve differences to the point where working consensus may be reached, or at least to the point where polarizing issues are explicitly identified and understood. Planning can be designed to catalyze consensus via computers.

1-5-4 Experimentation with POP

Although the scope of this chapter precludes any detailed consideration of the design and application of POP, an attempt is made in this section to demonstrate the functional rudiments of POP in applied experimentation. Table 1–7 shows a sequential task analysis of a prototype POP experiment. Ten tasks are listed; the initial task is formulation of the experiment, which leads to various steps in implementation and analysis. For each experimental task, Table 1–7 lists suggested computer languages and associated techniques and products. For illustrative purposes, various SDC languages and tools are mentioned under the "Language" column in Table 1–7, including: PLANIT (Feingold, 1967) for computer-aided instructional tasks, CONVERSE (Kellogg, 1970) for natural-language processing, Display-70 (Lickhalter, 1969) for online graphic display manipulation, Graphic I/O (Bernstein, 1970), and regenerative recording (Sackman, 1967, and Karush, 1970) for complete capture and reconstruction of the real-time exchange between the user and the computer system. Table 1–7 is only suggestive; it illustrates the kinds of tasks and procedures that could occur in POP experimentation—particular applications could vary widely from this prototype, contingent upon the developmental stage of online procedures and the unique requirements of each experiment.

Table 1-7.   Prototype Task Analysis for POP Experiments

Task	Languages	Techniques and Products
1. Formulation of Experiment	Natural Language	Theory, literature, conferences, application areas.
2. Construction of Experiment	PLANIT, assembly macros	Plan requirements, data base design, experimental design, questionnaire construction.
3. Initial Conditions	PLANIT	Subject preparation and training, scenarios, gaming, Delphi, contextual analysis, etc., starting points.
4. Pretest Comprehension	PLANIT	Online test administration, scoring and analysis.
5. Online Polling	PLANIT, Display-70	Questionnaire administration, item analysis, diagnostics, branching, tutorial, initial consensus level.
6. Generation of Adversary Data Bases	CONVERSE	Natural I/O, ad hoc data bases, man-computer umpiring, response classification, dialectical display.
7. Online Search, Query, and Planning Analyses	Display-70, CONVERSE, PLANIT, Graphic I/O	Gaming, simulation, resource allocation, optimization techniques, data base analyses.
8. Iterative Polling– Consensus Convergence	Display-70, PLANIT, CONVERSE	Sequential analysis, summary adversary displays, final plan.
9. Posttest Comprehension	PLANIT	Online testing, scoring, and analysis.
10. Experimental Analysis	Regenerative recording, selective recording, Display-70, statistical routines	Hypothesis exploration, hypothesis testing, result generation and display, report assembly, analysis of final plan.

1-5-5   The Case for and Against Participatory Online Planning

As the physician is enjoined to "heal thyself" before plying his trade on others, the author will try to take some of his own adversary medicine. In Table 1–8 a list of 25 pros and cons are presented for the proposed research in participatory online planning. Included are points raised throughout the paper and some new considerations.

Table 1-8.   Adversary Views of Participatory Online Planning

Arguments for Research in Participatory Online Planning	Arguments Against Research in Participatory Online Planning
1. Research in the earliest phases of planning is urgently needed.	Research in other phases in overall planning is needed, particularly for professional planners.
2. POP is primarily concerned with planning consensus, and, as such, is well-focused.	Does not lead to complete plans.
3. POP is based on a theory of planning-mutual expectation theory.	The mutual expectation theory is very provisional and sketchy at this point, and has not been tested in a planning context.
4. Capitalizes on key advantages of online man-computer communication for open-end exploratory, insightful problems.	Many planning problems may be better handled batch or offline.
5. Capitalizes on advantages of natural I/O, and can take advantage of human aid in interpretive problems until sufficiently powerful computerized techniques become available.	Only a very simple and crude form of natural I/O could be used at this point, and perhaps for several years to come.
6. Requires adversary information systems, which is a major development in its own right in computer technology.	Adversary information systems may not progress beyond a primitive stage.
7. Enables more people to participate in early planning more effectively.	Too many cooks spoil the broth.
8. Controversial planning issues can be rapidly set up and run under controlled experimental conditions with quick results.	Opinion is subject to many well-known pitfalls and limitations.
9. Normative planning has been grossly neglected; POP can open up this critical area.	Normative planning is too diffuse for credible research.
10. Consensus is easily quantifiable and lends itself to rigorous statistical testing.	Consensus is subject to the vagaries of questionnaire techniques.
11. A great variety of planning issues in almost any domain can be rapidly tackled with POP.	Diversified experimentation may not be as convincing as an investigation of one area in depth.
12. Many different types of subjects, from expert to naive, may be used in POP.	Consensus testing often requires large samples which may be prohibitively costly.

Table 1-8.   Adversary Views of Participatory Online Planning (Cont'd.)

Arguments for Research in Participatory Online Planning	*Arguments Against Research in Participatory Online Planning*
13. Case histories of individuals may be studied in consensus formation.	Many case histories would be required to warrant useful generalizations.
14. Manual and offline versions of POP can be implemented immediately to improve method and theory and guide online design.	Manual and offline versions may possibly prove more fruitful than online versions.
15. POP lends itself to advances in online collection, reduction and analysis of data for online experimentation.	Offline data collection and analysis may be almost as fast and cheaper.
16. POP would attract the interest and cooperation of planning professionals because of its simplicity, novel features, advances, and utility.	Planning professionals may be more interested in objective analytic techniques than in policy formulation and planning consensus.
17. POP would provide the first computer-aided vehicle to systematically study the most creative stages of planning.	POP findings may not progress beyond available evidence on creativity in problem formulation.
18. POP would significantly extend available research findings in Delphi, gaming, scenarios, expert opinion and related areas.	POP may not develop significantly beyond a simple online version of these techniques because of unexpected developmental and research problems.
19. POP would provide an excellent vehicle for demonstrating cooperative interaction for dispersed users in a distributed computer network, such as the ARPA prototype.	Available prototype computer networks may not be able to handle complex host-to-host problem-solving in the near future.
20. A system such as POP would enable large government agencies to query a wide range of distributed experts and cognizant groups on major policy and planning issues over computer networks.	There are many political issues to resolve before large-scale query and consensus systems can be implemented and tested.
21. POP would allow advanced techniques in test construction and item analysis, as developed in psychological testing and in polling procedures, to be implemented online to improve the rigor of experimentation in planning and to cross-fertilize behavioral findings with the planning domain.	While cross-fertilization of POP with advanced psychological and behavioral methodology is admirable, the effort may dilute the resources necessary to develop a significant version of POP.

Table 1–8.   Adversary Views of Participatory Online Planning (Cont'd.)

Arguments for Research in Participatory Online Planning	Arguments Against Research in Participatory Online Planning
22. POP is based on the concept of plans as hypotheses and would advance the scientific status of planning.	The attempt to experimentalize planning may be premature in this rapidly changing field.
23. The online adversary process in POP would facilitate user motivation and user learning in mastering controversial issues.	The POP adversary process may be less effective than face-to-face interaction without online support.
24. The POP vehicle may lead to a powerful semimechanized persuasion technique for complex issues, opening up new fields of computer-aided persuasion research.	POP may possibly help to accelerate critical appraisals of controversial issues, but it does not follow that it would necessarily lead to systematic alteration of initial opinions.
25. POP explicitly recognizes the educational benefits of planning, which would make it useful as a demonstration vehicle for policy-makers and as a training vehicle for planners.	Online training for planning may not prove to be as cost-effective as conventional training techniques.

1-6 SUMMARY AND CONCLUSIONS

Statement of the Problem: How can improvements in planning be scientifically advanced within the framework of online computing systems?

Growth of Planning: Formal and informal efforts in planning are growing by leaps and bounds in national and international affairs and in education and industry at state and local levels, and are spreading to virtually all walks of life.

Predisciplinary Status of Planning: Although planning borrows liberally from many fields and operates as an eclectic enterprise, and although the applications literature in planning is immense, there is surprisingly little work on the theory and methodology of planning, and virtually no scientific work in this field.

Varieties of Planning and Forecasting Techniques: Some 26 methods used in planning and forecasting were extracted from the literature, covering a broad spectrum of approaches, ranging from operations research techniques to accounting practice, to expert opinion, to statistical trend analysis, to historical and fictional approaches. These were later aggregated into five functional areas: creative search, structured search, planning production, retrofit planning, trend analysis, and historical analysis.

Online Problem Solving: The experimental literature indicates that online techniques are generally more expensive, and are not substantially faster than offline problem solving. The advantages in online problem solving seem to lie in greater user motivation and acceptance, and in higher quality problem solutions for creative, open-end tasks, requiring extensive exploration.

Individual Differences in Man-Computer Problem Solving: The experimental data supports the contention that computer-aided techniques tend to expand individual differences. Adapting to large individual differences in online planning, behavior will be a major challenge in system design and in planning research. Educational operating features are needed to meet the vagaries of human error, differential learning rates, self-tutoring, variable personal style, and differential reinforcement.

Planning Skills and Primary Mental Abilities: Initial research in the structure of human planning skills indicates that such skills overlap extensively with general intellectual skills, even though some skills seem to be unique to planning. This finding supports the contention that experimental results generally applicable to man-computer problem solving are likely to be relevant to computer-aided planning.

Scientific Planning Theory: In working toward a scientific theory of planning, it was maintained that plans should be conceived as hypotheses subject to empirical test and evaluation in an operationally defined environment. It was argued that plans may be interpreted as a set of evolving hypotheses concerning system performance throughout the life cycle of object systems. According to this view, the theory of planning is the theory of correspondence between hypothesized system planning and actualized system development.

Definition of Planning: Planning refers to plastic evolving hypotheses concerning system objectives and system performance in specified environments, including embedding ecosystems, to achieve desired levels of operationally defined effectiveness, within stated resources, throughout the life cycle of the object system and successor systems.

Research Needs in Planning and Online Problem Solving: Research in both planning and problem solving is urgently needed at the early and creative stages of these processes—in normative planning and in problem formulation. The least amount of research has been performed in these creative stages in both domains where the greatest research breakthroughs may be expected to occur. Online problem solving was previously seen to indicate major potential for problem exploration and insightful problem formulation. The fundamental challenge to online planning seems to lie in the more creative aspects of planning.

The Mutual-Expectation Theory of Planning: The mutual-expectation theory maintains that the planning process is initially triggered and created by an effective consensus in the concerned community, a consensus which is shaped by mutual expectations concerning social values, group goals, resources, and priorities. The planning mandate, which is the point at which a plan is overtly institutionalized, involves a broader set of individuals than those normally engaged in design and implementation of a plan. This broader "consensus" set might be called a planning community or planning public, and it is this planning community that is the primary population in the proposed mutual-expectation theory. According to this theory, the crux for advanced research in planning lies in systematic and rational extension of participatory planning. Expectation theory should build on related experimental knowledge in the areas of human learning and group dynamics.

Participatory Online Planning: Participatory planning refers to mutual human expectations that enter into the consensus that leads to social creation of a plan. Research in participatory online planning (POP) refers to systematic experimentation in the creation of plans in the form of planning consensus in an online computing environment. The research focus is primarily, although not necessarily, at the early, normative stage of planning—the creation of a concurred and accepted mandate for planning in a specified planning community. The research objective is to develop a new generation of online planning capability to advance and catalyze rational planning consensus, particularly in a dispersed planning community.

Computerization of POP: There are four novel design features of the proposed planning research vehicle in the online computing environment. One is the inclusion of natural I/O, primarily typewriter, voice, and graphic communication.

The second is the development of adversary information systems. Such systems refer to the organization of information on opposing sides of contested issues such that reasons for and against each position are solicited, stored in a "dialectical" data base, and tracked in a real-time man-computer transaction that converges toward an operationally defined resolution.

Third, POP is envisaged as a vehicle for distributed planning communities in which individuals and groups who are physically remote from each other work toward common planning goals, particularly for planning problems requiring diverse skills and extensive opinion to arrive at a planning mandate. Large-scale time-sharing systems and distributed computer networks could provide the appropriate setting for such participatory online planning.

Fourth, POP is conceived, in large part, as an educational process. Planning is fundamentally a problem-solving, learning experience. Educational design features are mandatory for accommodating large individual differences, human error, self-tutoring, differential reinforcement, and performance evaluation.

All four features—natural I/O, adversary information systems, distributed computer services, and educational monitoring—require extensive new development. True to the adversary spirit of participatory online planning, this chapter concludes with a list of 25 arguments for and against advanced research with POP, as presented in Table 1–8.

REFERENCES

Adams, Jeanne, and Leonard Cohen, "Time-Sharing Vs. Instant Batch Processing," *Computers and Automation,* March (1969) 30–34.

Allport, Gordon W., "The Fruits of Eclecticism—Bitter or Sweet?" *Proceedings of the XVIIth International Congress of Psychology, August 20-26, 1963, Washington, D. C.,* Amsterdam, North Holland Publishing Company, 1964.

Ayres, Robert U., *Technological Forecasting and Long-Range Planning,* New York, McGraw-Hill Book Co., 1969.

Barnard, D. J., *Organization and Management,* Cambridge, Mass., Harvard University Press, 1948.

Bell, Daniel, "Twelve Modes of Prediction—A Preliminary Sorting of Approaches in the Social Sciences," *Daedalus,* Summer (1964) 845–880.

Berger, R. M., J. P. Guilford, and P. R. Christensen, "A Factor-Analytic Study of Planning," *Psychological Monogram.,* 71, No. 6, 1957.

Bernstein, M. I., "The Design for an Interactive Flowchart Programming System," *Proceedings of the Third Hawaii International Conference on System Sciences,* Part 2, 1970, 894–897.

Branch, Melville C., *Planning: Aspects and Applications,* New York, John Wiley & Sons, Inc., 1966.

Bryan, D. G., "JOSS: 20,000 Hours at a Console—A Statistical Summary," *AFIPS Conference Proceedings,* Vol. 31, 1967 Fall Joint Computer Conference, 769–77.

Bureau of the Budget, "Planning-Programming-Budgeting," *Bulletin No. 66-3,* Washington, October 12, 1965.

Clay, Sir Henry, "Planning and Market Economy," *American Economics Review,* Vol. XL, 1950.

Dalkey, Norman D., "The Delphi Method: An Experimental Study of Group Opinion," AD-60-498, The RAND Corporation, Santa Monica, Calif., June 1969.

Dewey, John, *Logic: The Theory of Inquiry,* New York, Holt, Rinehart and Winston, 1938.

DeJouvenel, Bertrand, *The Art of Conjecture,* New York, Basic Books, Inc., Publishers, 1967.

_____, "Utopia for Practical Purposes," *Daedalus,* Vol. 95, No. 2, Spring 1965, 437–453.

Einstein, Albert, and Leopold Infeld, *The Evolution of Physics,* New York, Simon & Schuster, 1938.

Emery, James, "The Planning Process and Its Formalization in Computer Models," *Proceedings of the 2nd Congress of Information System Science,* 1964.

Erikson, W. J., *A Pilot Study of Interactive Versus Noninteractive Debugging,* TM-3296, System Development Corporation, Santa Monica, Calif., December 1966.

Feingold, Samuel L., "PLANIT—A Flexible Language Designed for Computer-Human Interaction," *Proceedings of the Fall Joint Computer Conference,* 1967.

Florence, P. S., *The Logic of British and American Industry,* London, Routledge & Kegan Paul Ltd., 1953.

Frye, Charles H., and Elbert C. Pack, "A Comparison of Three Computer Operating Modes for High School Problem-Solving," TM-4356/001/00, System Development Corporation, Santa Monica, Calif., 1969.

Gold, M., Methodology for Evaluating Time-Shared Computer Usage, Doctoral Dissertation, Massachusetts Institute of Technology, Alfred P. Sloan School of Management, 1967.

Grant, E. E., and H. Sackman, "An Exploratory Investigation of Programer Performance Under On-Line and Off-Line Conditions," *IEEE Transactions on Human Factors in Electronics,* HFE-8, (1), March 1967, 33–48.

Guilford, J. P., *The Nature of Human Intelligence,* New York, McGraw-Hill Book Co., 1967.

Haefele, John W., *Creativity and Innovation,* New York, Reinhold Publishing Corp., 1962.

Helmer, Olaf, "Systematic Use of Expert Opinions," P-3721, The RAND Corporation, Santa Monica, Calif., November 1967.

Helmholtz, H.L.F., von, *Vortrage and Reden,* 1896.

Jungk, R., "Forecasting as an Instrument of Social and Political Power," Third International Conference on Science and Society, Herceg-Novi, Yugoslavia, 1969.

Kahn, Herman, and Anthony J. Wiener, *The Year 2000,* New York, The Macmillan Company, 1967.

Karush, Arnold D., "Regenerative Recording," Master's Thesis, University of California at Los Angeles, 1970. Unpublished.

Kellogg, C., and J. Burger, "Progress in Natural Language Data Management," *Proceedings of the Third Hawaii International Conference on System Sciences,* Part 2, 1970, 846–849.

Kelly, G. A., *The Psychology of Personal Constructs,* New York, W. W. Norton & Company, Inc., 1955.

LeBreton, Preston P., and Dale A. Henning, *Planning Theory,* Englewood Cliffs, N.J., Prentice-Hall, Inc., 1961.

Lickhalter, R. A., "Display 70—An Interactive Data Analysis System for Management Decision," SP-3457, System Development Corporation, Santa Monica, Calif., 1969.

MacCorquodale, K., and P. E. Meehl, "Preliminary Suggestions as to Formalization of Expectancy Theory," *Psychological Review,* **60**, 1953, 55–63.

Mackworth, Norman H., "Originality," *American Psychologist,* Vol. 20, January 1965.

Mannheim, K., *Man and Society in an Age of Reconstruction,* London, Kegan Paul, Trench, Trubner, 1940.

Mason, Richard O., "A Dialectical Approach to Strategic Planning," *Management Science,* Vol. 15, No. 8, April 1969, B-403-414.

Mayo, E., *The Human Problems of an Industrial Civilization,* New York, The Macmillan Co., 1933.

McIsaac, Paul V., Job Descriptions and Scheduling in the SDC Q-32 Time-Sharing System, TM-2996, System Development Corporation, Santa Monica Calif., June 1966.

Mead, G. H., *Mind, Self and Society,* Chicago, University of Chicago Press, 1934.

Millett, J., *The Process and Organization of Government Planning,* New York, Columbia University Press, 1947.

Miller, George A., Eugene Galanter, and Karl H. Pribram, *Plans and the Structure of Behavior,* New York, Holt, Rinehart and Winston, 1960.

Mockler, Robert J., "Theory and Practice of Planning," *Harvard Business Review,* March-April 1970, 148–159.

Mowrer, O. H., *Learning Theory and Personality Dynamics,* New York, The Ronald Press Co., 1950.

Myerson, M., and E. C. Banfield, *Politics, Planning and the Public Interest,* Glencoe, Ill., The Free Press, 1955.

Nadel, S. F., *Foundations of Social Anthropology,* London, Cohen & West, 1951, 286–7.

Novick, David, (ed.), *Program Budgeting,* Cambridge, Mass., Harvard University Press, 1965.

Osborn, Alex, *Applied Imagination,* New York, Charles Scribner's Sons, 1957.

Parsons-Williams, "Forecast of 1868-2000 of Computer Development and Application," Copenhagen, Denmark, 1968.

Platt, John, "What We Must Do," *Science,* Vol. 166, 1969, 1115–1121.

Raynaud, Thierry G., Operational Analysis of a Computer Center, Technical Report No. 32, Operations Research Center, Massachusetts Institute of Technology, July 1967.

Roethlisberger, F. J., and W. J. Dickson, *Management and the Worker,* Cambridge, Mass., Harvard University Press, 1941.

Rosove, Perry E., The Use of Contextual Mapping to Support Long-Range Educational Policy Making, SP-3026, Santa Monica, Calif., System Development Corporation, December 1967.

Rossman, Joseph, *The Psychology of the Inventor,* Washington, D. C., Inventor's Publishing Company, 1931.

Rotter, J. B., *Social Learning and Clinical Psychology,* New York, Prentice-Hall, Inc., 1954.

Sackman, H., *Computers, System Science, and Evolving Society,* New York, John Wiley & Sons, Inc., 1967.

____, Experimental Evaluation of Time-Sharing and Batch Processing in Teaching Computer Science, SP-3411, System Development Corporation, Santa Monica, Calif., October 1969.

____, *Man-Computer Problem Solving,* Princeton, N.J., Auerbach 1970.

Schatzoff, M., R. Tsao, and R. Wiig, "An Experimental Comparison of Time Sharing and Batch Processing," *Communications of the ACM,* Vol. 10, No. 5, May 1967, 261–265.

Scherr, Allan L., Analysis of Time-Shared Computer Systems, *Research Monograph No. 36,* Cambridge, Mass., The M.I.T. Press, 1967.

Shaw, J. W., "JOSS: Experience With an Experimental Computing Service for Users at Remote Typewriter Consoles," P-3149, Santa Monica, Calif., The RAND Corporation, May 1965.

Smith, Lyle B., "A Comparison of Batch Processing and Instant Turnaround," *Communications of the ACM,* Vol. 10, No. 8, August 1967, 495–500.

Steiner, George A., *Top Management Planning,* London, The Macmillan Company, 1969.

Stogdill, Ralph M., *Individual Behavior and Group Achievement,* New York, Oxford University Press, 1969.

Tolman, E. C., *Purposive Behavior in Animals and Men,* New York, Appleton-Century, 1932.

Totschek, Robert A., An Empirical Investigation into the Behavior of the SDC Time-Sharing System, SP-2191, System Development Corporation, Santa Monica, Calif., July 1966.

"Toward the Year 2000: Work in Progress," *Daedalus,* Summer 1967.

Wallas, Graham, *Art of Thought,* New York, Harcourt, Brace, 1926.

Willmorth, N. E., System Programming Management, TM-L-2222,* System Development Corporation, Santa Monica, Calif., 1965.

Woodworth, Robert S., and Harold Schlosberg, *Experimental Psychology,* New York, Holt, Rinehart and Winston, 1954.

Young, J. W., *Technique for Producing Ideas,* Chicago, Advertising Publications, Inc., 1940.

*This document is an internal, unpublished SDC communication and is not appropriate for release outside the Corporation.

2

PLANNING BY MAN-MACHINE SYNERGISM

Aiko N. Hormann

69

Abstract

This chapter describes an attempt to couple the complementary capabilities of man and machine in the context of planning and creative problem solving.

Some real-world problems to which man-machine techniques can be fruitfully applied are characterized, and the types of decision dynamics influenced by these characteristics are identified. Then, how man tends to handle complexity and uncertainty is discussed in terms of the concept of "cognitive economy." An attempt is made to identify the interdependencies of man's capabilities and limitations and the machine's potential capabilities and limitations. Several guidelines and techniques for developing a man-machine system that promotes effective intermeshing of these capabilities are described.

Next, characteristics of planning processes are discussed in terms of (a) the levels of planning (conceptual, definitional, developmental, and operational) and (b) the stages of problem solving (goal setting, alternative generation, consequence estimation, and evaluation and alternative selection). Structural attributes extracted from such characterization constitute the basic framework and guiding mechanism for inter-

*action in Gaku, a system of computer programs
designed as a step toward man-machine synergism.*

*An example of man-machine interaction is presented,
suggesting desirable capabilities of Gaku. Features
of Gaku are then described in terms of both built-
in capabilities that are relatively problem independent,
and man-machine actions for dynamic extension of
these capabilities that are problem dependent and
user oriented. The latter can be seen to make the
system increasingly useful and powerful as a "co-
evolving" man-machine team. Next, justifications for
promoting man-machine synergism are presented in
terms of serious or important consequences of decisions in real-world problem situations.*

*The necessity of allowing imprecise and subjective
value judgments to be expressed and manipulated, especially at higher-level planning stages, is stressed. A
way to handle this is suggested by the use of a "fuzzy-
set" concept and techniques, but the details are delegated to Appendix B. Two useful areas of application,
the handling of implicit trade-off concepts and the
handling of planners' diverse value orientations in team
planning, are described, and a few other areas are
suggested.*

2-1 INTRODUCTION

Planning is an integral part of problem solving, whether it is done
vaguely in an individual's head or within an elaborate organizational
structure. Planning processes employ a wide range of intellectual
functions and permeate through problem-solving activities from the
very nascent stage of problem identification and conceptualization
to the implementation of detailed decision steps.

This chapter describes an attempt to couple the complementary
capabilities of man and machine for cooperative planning. Man is
accredited with imaginative and innovative mental functions, which
in turn depend on his capabilities for making plausible inferences in
the face of incomplete information, for recognizing patterns and re-

lationships and inventing categories, and for taking differing points of view and restructuring the original problem.

Remarkably ill-defined as these functions might seem, they contain and depend on subprocesses that can be clearly specified for the machine. These include generating combinations of conditions and attributes from assigned relations and conditional features, keeping track of detailed changes and evaluating and classifying them with differing sets of criteria, extracting pieces of data from diverse files of stored information and rearranging these with a specific set of rules, making some limited deductive inferences with a given set of inference rules, and making detailed calculations on data. In these subprocesses, man is the specifier of rules and criteria which he can change in different contexts and at different levels of abstraction, and the formulator of relevant questions in the light of new findings and insights gained with the aid of the machine.

The machine can be increasingly helpful when man is able to (a) guide the machine's processes for selective exploration of the problem situation rapidly at varying levels of detail to gain insights and test new ideas and hunches as they come to him; (b) instruct the machine to summarize results in various ways and display them for visual inspection in a variety of formats; (c) request machine assistance in choosing and using certain decision-aiding tools and techniques or in devising new aids to suit his unique needs and situations; (d) delegate more and more detailed functions to the machine, as these become identified as useful and delineable, so that his own efforts can be directed toward strategic-level decisions and creative ideas; (e) ask the machine to remind him with a checklist at an important decision point regarding crucial issues or factors that could not have been known at the outset; and (f) give rules for handling a certain set of subprocesses semiautomatically, receiving notices only when something wrong or unusual is detected.

With these possibilities in mind, this chapter starts with an investigation of some types of problem situations that cannot be handled adequately by man alone or machine alone. Characterization of real-world problems from which substantial payoffs can be expected by applying man-machine synergistic techniques are then presented.

2-2 CHARACTERIZATION OF REAL-WORLD PROBLEMS

Accelerated changes in the environment, technology, and human attitudes and values of our society require frequent reassessment and

planning. The faster and wider interactions now possible throughout the world also force planners to examine the deeper and
more far-reaching ramifications of the effects produced. With
these considerations, the following interrelated characteristics are
identified.

Unbounded problem environment.   A problem with this characteristic has a poorly defined domain in that it is difficult to isolate the
problem clearly from the rest of the world. A seemingly simple
decision or action intended for a well-circumscribed problem area can
create unexpected side effects or "ripple effects" in other areas.
Conversely, a certain factor that has been considered irrelevant
in a given problem area may turn out to have a subtle but important
effect, or a new factor, heretofore unknown, may crop up un-
expectedly. Whenever such outside influences enter into the picture,
assumptions and constraints stated within the initial problem definition must be modified, thus often changing the nature of the
problem itself.

Dynamic and nondeterministic environment.   Dynamic problems
are never solved once and for all. When alternative courses of action
are formulated as stated strategies over time, uncertainties associated
with possible changes in the environment must be taken into account.
Changes in the environment may be caused by the planner himself
(by the implementation of the planned course of action, or even
"leaked" information about the plan before implementation); by
possible opponents or competitors; and/or by impersonal forces,
such as technological innovations, weather, and consumer demands.
During the implementation period, changes in the environment,
technology, and human value orientation may force conceptions of
the problem task to be changed.

Unlike the environment of a chess game, in which each action
leads invariably to a set of specific outcomes, outcomes in a nondeterministic environment cannot be determined with certainty.
Some variables may have to be treated as random, either intrinsically
or because of the ignorance of the observer, or some outcomes may
be assumed to occur with known probabilities. Assigning a "probability," however, often involves subjective and even arbitrary judgment.
Therefore, the planner should be aware that using such probability
measures in calculating other considerations can have a decisive in-

fluence in making inferences and can be misleading to himself and others on the planning team.

Because of changing conditions in the environment, conclusions made on observed phenomena—their periodicity, regularity, and relations—are subject to change. Therefore, adaptive planning is necessary for both short-range and long-range planning; the longer the planning range, the wider the propagation of the decision effects and the greater the uncertainty.

Complexity. Complexity can be defined intuitively in terms of the number of interrelated factors and the number of interdependence relations in the problem environment. If the problem is unbounded and nondeterministic, the complexity will be increased. However, these characteristics are not necessary to make the problem complex. A chess environment is very complex, but it is deterministic, finite, and well defined. The term "complexity and uncertainty" is often used to describe a problem environment possessed of all three characteristics described here.

2-3 CHARACTERIZATION OF DECISION DYNAMICS

Let us now consider how these three environmental characteristics affect the nature of decision making. A "prescription for the systems approach to planning" is usually stated in terms of four (or more) basic steps, which may be phrased differently but are essentially as follows:

- Define the objectives and formulate a utility function.
- Enumerate possible alternative courses of action.
- Identify the consequences of each alternative.
- Evaluate the consequences in terms of the objectives via the utility function and choose the alternative which best achieves the objectives.

Usually a statement or two to indicate the iterative nature of these steps is then made.

Let us recast the above four steps in a problem environment with the three characteristics just described. It will be seen that all of the steps are difficult to follow in the clearly specifiable ways presented in the above "prescription," and that the order in which the four steps appear is often irregular (see Amarel, 1968; Eastman, 1969; Emery, 1964; Manheim, 1966, 1967; Newell, 1966).

The multiplicity and changing nature of objectives and criteria.
Many complex problem formulations contain multiple objectives,
both stated and unstated, along with many unstated assumptions and
constraints, some of which may be in conflict. Furthermore, these
objectives and criteria, including their associated utility values, tend
to change in different contexts and in time.

When a group of planners is involved, individual differences in
value orientation also cause subtle differences in the interpretation
of goals and objectives. Extra care must be taken to provide an effective communication means among planners to disseminate timely
information, including any changes made in objectives, assumed conditions, and constraints. Inconsistencies and conflicts are often
caused by "side" objectives and constraints that are assumed but
not explicitly stated.

In some cases, alternatives may be proposed first, the "rationale"
given later, and a set of goals and objectives gradually formed. Objectives, which are difficult to formulate in the abstract in advance,
can be clarified after examining the consequences of specific alternatives. In fact, there are instances in which people agree readily on
alternatives, while widely disagreeing on objectives.

Incompletely known alternatives. Alternatives are often discovered. All are seldom known at the outset. It is likely that analysis
and evaluation of initially proposed alternatives A, B, and C will lead
to the discovery or invention of alternatives D and E, which may be
preferable. In both business and military situations, a novel approach
to a problem may open up a new range of possibilities; human in-
genuity and imagination may lead to handsome rewards in a competitive field.

Having "ideation sessions" with Gaku and with other participants,
who may be located at different places but connected through a
time-shared, man-machine system for generating new ideas, may be
fruitful here. Postponement of judgment and criticism is emphasized
to encourage free, uninhibited expression of thoughts and ideas. Each
person would receive typed or displayed statements of ideas generated
by others, expressed in a few words or a simple phrase. Each could
add his own ideas by typing them in or speaking into a speech-
recognizing device (when available). Simultaneous expression could
go on without interference, at the same time allowing everything that
each person has to say to be available to the whole group (thus
stimulating even further ideation). Such ideation sessions can be

fruitful in the many stages of problem solving where new ideas are needed. For more details on ideation, especially on the role of the machine in assisting man, see Hormann, 1965.

Difficulty of estimating consequences. A useful technique in problem solving is asking "what if" questions, i.e., examining possible consequences of alternative courses of action before commitment to a particular course. However, consideration of future events and actions brings uncertainty into the picture, and the complexity of the problem makes it difficult to trace effects of decisions that propagate through interrelated subsystems. In addition, many relevant consequences and indirect effects may be left out because of the unbounded nature of the problem.

Simulation techniques are often fruitful in answering "what if" questions. If the problem is unbounded, however, answers coming from the simulated model may become unreliable. In man-machine cooperative planning, man's background knowledge and experience can supplement such a deficiency. Man seems to have a cognitive map* or internal model of the external world which is continually being built and modified throughout his lifetime. New experiences, formal education, informal acquisition of information, and similar circumstances contribute toward understanding of the environment in general, of himself, and of the interactions between the two. He is thus an actor and an observer simultaneously.

A computer model of any system or phenomenon is a small and often grossly simplified portion of such an internal model, but man can repeatedly fall back on his internal model for missing information or contextual orientation not known at the outset. Man's knowledge of "gray areas," where subtle effects of decisions may be discerned but cannot be made explicit, can guide the model system in a direction that "makes sense" when no explicit criteria for validation can be given.

For long-range planning, it may be fruitful to apply some forecasting techniques such as the "Delphi" technique of soliciting and collating experts' opinions (Dalkey, 1969; Helmer, 1966) or the technique of "scenario writing" the future (Kahn and Wiener, 1967) by imaginative construction based on specified initial conditions and using a logical sequence of events under varied sets of assumptions.

---

*The term was first introduced by E. C. Tolman (1958).

If the projected future by these methods shows some critically undesirable conditions, then the desired conditions can be stated and the events and steps retraced to examine what must be done at what point in time to avoid the undesired and arrive at a more desirable future.

Difficulty in evaluating alternatives. Some objectives may provide a natural means of measuring progress toward goals with a clear-cut numerical assignment, but those that require subjective and qualitative judgment defy full quantification. Furthermore, it is usually difficult or impossible to completely identify the relative values of all possible combinations of the various objectives—that is, to formulate a fully defined utility function. Complex trade-off implications are often ill-defined when attributes to be traded are not comparable as in trading off personality qualities and professional capabilities in comparing employees.

A way to assist planners to become aware of such trade-off implications and progressively articulate their preferential judgments is suggested in Appendix B and also in Hormann (1971a). Such techniques are especially useful in time-staged planning with a number of planners who have diverse value orientations for evaluating alternatives toward the common goal. By allowing each planner to adjust his preference function while interacting with other planners and with the machine, and by making trade-off implications clear, an agreement regarding "rational" choice of an alternative may be reached.

Difficulty in cvaluating alternatives in terms of objectives is typical of ill-defined problems. Minsky (1961) states that a problem is well defined if there is some systematic way to decide when a proposed solution is acceptable. By this definition, most of the real-world problems are in the ill-defined category. We must realize that no solution to an ill-defined problem can count on universal acceptance (Reitman, 1965).

Another useful concept is that of ill-structuredness. Typically, there is no systematic method for detecting improvement in an ill-structured problem. This is to be contrasted with optimizing a function of continuous real variables, where a "gradient" is available to point the direction to an improved alternative. Chess is a well-defined problem but has an ill-structured solution space. Many discrete combinatorial problems are ill-structured.

Ill-structuredness, however, is not necessarily an intrinsic characteristic of the given problem (nor ill-definedness, for that matter); it
depends on a particular problem solver at a particular time. Depending
on the understanding of the problem at hand, decomposing and
restructuring the original problem into a new "map" might reveal a
kind of structure in which a solution becomes "transparent" or at
least some measure of progress is possible.

Man-machine techniques, with which man can try different ways
of decomposing and restructuring the problem, can open up an exciting area of possibilities for enhancing man's creativity. With these
man can seek quick answers to various probing questions and try out
new ideas of restructuring, or he can explore new avenues of possibilities in the light of new findings and the changing environment.
The power of the computer to search through a large number and a
great variety of cases (and present the results in various formats on
a display scope) as specified by the man can be coupled with the
intuition and pattern recognition capability of the man in a cooperative attempt to gain deeper insights into the problem situation.

Let us summarize what we have discussed so far. We have found
that many real-world problems are complex, unbounded, dynamic,
and nondeterministic. Next, we have found that these characteristics
can have far-reaching effects throughout human planning, decision
making, and problem solving. Notions of ill-definedness and ill-
structuredness have been introduced.

The complexity and uncertainty of our environment are increasing.
Man's capacity to handle them are also increasing with new techniques
and devices, but increasing the capacity by using more of the same
(more men, more devices—even faster and bigger computers) will
eventually reach the point of diminishing returns because of the
complexity of coordination required When the complexity of the
problem exceeds the capacity of man to cope with it, something will
have to give. Licklider and Taylor's (1968) statement, although made
in a different context, applies: "It is frightening to realize how early
and drastically one does simplify, how prematurely one does conclude,
even when the stakes are high . . . ."

In the following section, the concept of cognitive economy is introduced and what man tends to do for cognitive economy is
described. This is followed by a description of how man-machine
synergistic teams may help overcome runaway complexity.

2-4 COGNITIVE ECONOMY

*One basic pattern of thinking is a combination of both a conscious and unconscious effort toward "cognitive economy."**

> Cognitive economy is the tendency of an individual to try to reduce his effort in transforming his unprepared state of mind about himself and parts of his environment into a prepared state of mind, using whatever means are available in a given situation and time, conditioned by his current orientation. Cognitive economy can be applied for either a short-term or a long-term benefit and can have both desirable and undesirable effects.

This reduction of effort can be achieved in a number of ways, including the use of the decision-aiding tools and techniques embodied in computer programs. However, man's natural tendency to promote cognitive economy and the outside forces or conditions that influence this tendency must first be understood. Effective coupling of man-machine talents must draw on this understanding.

2-4-1 Prepared and Unprepared Conditions

All conditions for which a need for decisions or actions are initially detected are considered to be in the unprepared category until prepared decisions are found or devised. For familiar situations in which the individual is highly skilled, matching the given condition to one of the prepared conditions (for which prepared decisions or behavior patterns are already available) is instantaneous, precise, and even semiautomatic in matching and executing the whole sequence of actions.

Since preparedness is a relative concept, this matching of a given condition to a prepared condition may be imprecise through oversimplification and distortion, but it can still be considered prepared

*The term "cognitive economy" is used in "A Study of Thinking" by Bruner, et al. (1956), but no definition is given. The basic need for cognitive economy may be the need for order and simplicity. Search for invariance, i.e., search for unchanging conditions and relations in a changing environment, seems even more basic. However, our search is not for *the* most basic elements in cognition but for a convenient starting point from which "theory" of man-machine synergism may be developed. Therefore, issues related to philosophical and epistemological questions are beyond the scope of this chapter.

as long as the consequences are within the range of satisfactory behavior. When the stakes are high, more careful preparation is usually
attempted. However, as soon as the complexity of the problem exceeds the cognitive capacity of man (cognitive overload), cognitive
economy must be applied. When time constraints are placed simultaneously with complexity, a drastic simplification may result. It
appears that cognitive economy operates all of the time, but its effects
become noticeable only when there is a cognitive overload. Section
5 describes those types of impacts that are serious enough to warrant
extra efforts by man-machine teams, beyond current or conventional
practices.

A prepared decision is that portion of thinking or decision making
that is done in advance so that the analyses and reasoning do not have
to be repeated. Although execution of such prepared decisions may
appear to be decision making, execution itself is not decision making
but decision following. However, given a decision-making situation,
the steps of (a) understanding the situation and recognizing the need
for decisions, (b) searching for and identifying a suitable prepared
decision (if there is any), and (c) executing the decision steps (with
possible last-minute adjustments) may involve complex pattern recognition and reasoning, some of which must be done on the spot. These
steps are also considered decision making.

A major benefit gained by having a set of prepared decisions is that
decisions, once prepared, can be manipulated conceptually as a single
action, thus achieving cognitive economy. Higher-level decisions are
composites of many such prepared decisions; thus, building blocks of
various sizes and complexity are formed. When we need to construct
a new composite, we can use these building blocks as single actions,
paying special attention to the way they fit together to form the total
function, rather than to the detailed steps within each block. Each
building block is manipulated in terms of what it does, rather than
how it does it.

Effective as this may be for cognitive economy, there are also
problems. Some of the building blocks stored in man's memory may
get lost from lack of use or from interference. Identification mechanisms may confuse categories and cause faulty associations to be
formed. Although details may be forgotten, the whole process may
still be treated as prepared because, at the higher level, the feeling of
familiarity is still connected with it. Only at the time of execution
will the loss of details be recognized. Identification of a prepared con-

dition that is embedded in complex surroundings may be missed; thus, the same decision may have to be prepared over and over again. Further, an increased rate of change in the environment may require frequent modification of prepared decisions and associated identification rules.

A major influencing factor in successful identification and matching and in construction of useful building blocks is categorizing. Since events and processes can be categorized in many different ways, the proper choice of categorizing criteria is important for a specific purpose. For example, process categorization will generally be more useful if it is based on the resulting conditions the process produces than if it is based on a physical description of the process. Many influencing aspects of categorization are discussed in the next section.

2-4-2 Categorization

Categorizing is one of the basic processes contributing to cognitive economy. By categorizing things and events into a set of equivalence classes, man can respond to discriminably different things as the same kind of thing (Bruner, et al., 1956). Categories such as "chairs," "houses," and animals" are examples. At first, the learning and utilization of categories requires "cognitive exercise," but it leads to significant cognitive economy. By categorizing discriminably different events as equivalent, we can reduce the complexity of our environment and the necessity of constant relearning. By categorizing, we can map and give meaning to our world by relating classes of events rather than individual events. It should be noted, however, that this simplification of the environment by categorizing achieves cognitive economy but can also force stereotyped identification and reactions.

Let us restate the above as follows. After a decision P is made for a problem condition x, and confirmation is made that the result of executing P produces a desired condition, $y = P(x)$, many other conditions "similar" to x may be discovered to be adequately taken care of by the same decision P. Then P becomes a prepared decision for a class of conditions $X = \{ x_1, x_2, x_3, \ldots \}$. Causal relations by category are especially relevant here. A set of conditions X called "a child playing with matches" and a set of events Y called "fire accident" create a likely causal relation in our mind that permits us to utilize cues ("cause" patterns) to prepare outselves in advance, by searching for an appropriate prepared decision, and reach decision P_1 "substitute a toy for the matches" in time to avoid an undesirable effect before it happens. It is this future-oriented, anticipatory nature of category utilization that is especially useful when we interweave prepared and unprepared decision making in accordance with the level of our experience and our knowledge of the situation.

Later, a generalized decision "substitute something harmless for the matches" may be recognized, or a further generalization "substitute something harmless for anything potentially harmful" may be established. Thus, a class of prepared decisions can now accommodate a large class of conditions such as "a child playing with something that could be harmful." This is categorical control over categorical cause-and-effect relations. In more complex situations, many of the concepts about conditions and events are composite concepts to start with, and we generate many classes of objects, events, actions, and relations around them.

Generating and manipulating such sets of sets can be done by a computer once criteria for forming sets are given and rules for manipulating them are specified, as can the previously described handling of prepared decisions as building blocks in preparing complex decisions. An important distinction between man and machine which must be realized is that many of what humans consider "prepared" decisions (with minor adjustments to variations) defy the precise and complete specification needed for a computer. For example, an air-traffic controller may have a set of prepared decisions about proper safety distances between two planes according to categorized conditions such as speed, altitude, type of plane, weather conditions, a particular region, and air traffic congestion. But assessing the "here and now" conditions against combinations of these considerations requires both machine capabilities and human judgmental capabilities that include fast and accurate calculations, value orientations, complex pattern recognition, and imprecise trade-off considerations, many of which are unprepared, on-the-spot decisions intermeshed with prepared decisions and concepts. A major difficulty is that these judgmental decisions cannot be made explicit because of their fuzzy qualities.

Humans seem to group their life experiences into indeterminate collections of sets and manipulate these as concepts and rough rules of action. Boundaries are not clear, and many categorizations produce overlapping sets rather than clear-cut, mutually exclusive sets. In some respects, however, this fuzziness may be one of the very reasons why humans can handle some tasks much better than machines.

2-4-3 Adaptive Planning

So far, relatively simple situations have been considered. Let us now consider prepared-unprepared conditions in a larger, more complex situation.

Clearly, a problem of any complexity for which planning is required is in the unprepared category, and no ready-made decisions are available. However, after examination and analysis, there are usually some portions of the total picture that are recognizable as prepared (perhaps vaguely familiar or similar to some prepared conditions). Decomposing and restructuring often reveals new patterns that can be used in identifying some relevant elements toward synthesizing prepared decisions.

The initial conceptual stage of planning is a typically vague and aggregated consideration of possible alternatives. Broad-brush description of actions or guideposts may be given. Later, more details are added, and vague and hazy concepts are made more clear. In addition, long-range planning is necessarily adaptive in a form of anticipatory decision making and progressive adjustment to changing conditions.

Adaptive planning processes can now be defined.

> Adaptive planning is an evolutionary process which starts with partial and aggregate specifications, but which adapts, by progressive articulation, substantiation, and adjustment, to changing conditions in the environment and to new knowledge and techniques as they become available.

Note that this definition recognizes the necessity of planning processes to anticipate uncertainties in the environment and also to allow for incompleteness in the planner's knowledge and understanding of the problem situation.

2-4-4 Partial and Aggregate Specification

Let us now examine the nature of partial and aggregate specifications separately, although they are usually intermixed in practice.

Partial specification leaves some open, unspecified portions to be filled in later. The reasons for these unspecified portions may be that the planner (a) does not know what to do, (b) knows vaguely what to do but cannot formulate this knowledge explicitly, and/or (c) deliberately leaves certain portions unspecified to maintain degrees of freedom.

Judicious uses of (c) achieve cognitive economy. For example, rules and conditions that are relatively invariant in time and context are specified initially to place them in the prepared category. Parameters are assigned for those features that are transient in nature or have highly specific or localized peculiarities. Other features are left unspecified until the time of plan implementation.

Flexibility and generality can be achieved by this method, but a proper balance between the specified and the unspecified should be maintained. Too many unspecified portions in the plan may cause last-minute preparations to be too complex to handle, causing a cognitive overload. A standard method of handling (c) is to supply an operational description of the known patterns of behavior in terms of parameters that can subsume a number of values. Specifying the parameter values at the time of execution specifies the behavior. Too detailed specifications or too little freedom may make the plan inflexible, although implementation of the plan may be more efficient. A way of avoiding either extreme is to use time-staged contingency specifications, along with a mixture of both partial and aggregate specifications of the planning process, until the time of implementation.

Cases of (a) and (b) are difficult and require additional information gathering and analysis. The problem may be conceptual and technical, rather than simply a lack of information. Cost and time required to do the analysis and exploration must be weighed against the gain in generating better plans. Conditions (a) and (b) both create new subproblems that are unprepared, and the whole process may have to be repeated. General planning and problem-solving techniques are discussed later.

In some instances (a) and (b) can be broken down to the level of parameter specification. This will allow random choice of values within a specified boundary condition or within a given set of values, or it will allow a probability distribution function, depending on the degree of ignorance or haziness.

Aggregate specification is done by abstracting and generalizing the conditions and processes. Conditions and processes with some common properties are grouped together by an operational principle or a rule which, when processed, produces the original set of conditions and processes. There are many ways of forming aggregate specification. Choosing an appropriate method of aggregation and representation suitable for a particular problem may be the mark of a seasoned planner.

Let us examine a simple, abstract example of aggregation. Suppose a sequence of conditions $a\alpha_1\beta_1$, $a\alpha_2\beta_2$, $a\alpha_3\beta_3$, . . . is observed. They can be represented by the single expression axy, where a is identified as a constant and x and y are lists containing α_i's and β_i's, respectively. Or, x and y can be expressed as formulas or functional expressions which generate α_i's and β_i's, rather than by enumerating them. Functional abstraction can be expressed on more than one level, e.g., the first level can contain formulas, the second level, derivation rules to generate formulas, etc.

Since all aggregate specifications require some processing to get to the desired level of specification, trade-off considerations between generality and specificity should be noted. For example, finding the "present" value of annuity P, given the amount of each payment p, the number of payments n, and the interest rate r, can be made by

    (a)   a table look-up,

    (b)   calculating P from the formula $P = p[1-(1+r)^{-n}]/r$, or

    (c)   deriving the formula from the basic understanding of annuity and what the compounding interest entails.

The choice of a particular method depends on the availability of the methods and the frequency of using such values.

Human memory has limitations in storing many pieces of data accurately. Therefore, aggregation contributes to cognitive economy, especially in conceptual manipulation of ideas. In the above example, annuity is a single concept even though it potentially subsumes many pieces of data.

This is one of the reasons why early stages of planning always contain aggregate specifications. It should be realized, however, that aggregate concepts in the human mind tend to lose preciseness in that the rules for generating particulars may become hazy and inaccurate in time (or they may not have been precise to start with). Note that portions of aggregate specifications can be partial specifications, in which case haziness will be greater. In man-machine cooperative efforts, these generating principles, once known or developed, can be stored away for later use. Humans need only to retain these general concepts. In fact, man has developed many complex tools and techniques so that once the details have been worked out, they can be used any number of times without redeveloping them each time.

The techniques of partial and aggregate specifications are not new. We have been using them all along for cognitive economy for such relatively simple planning situations as meal planning to such highly complex ones as military, business, and urban planning. These simple techniques can be exploited more fully when they are used in conjunction with man-machine cooperative techniques.

In the man-machine context, these techniques can be used to bridge the gap between the impreciseness of human thinking and the preciseness and completeness required by the computer. Complete formalization is not necessary at the outset. Man can finesse the computer restrictions by partial and aggregate specifications and supply details later as they become available and/or clarified. For the exploratory and conceptual phases of problem solving, discerning "interesting" avenues of possibilities and "relevant" criteria for evaluation is in man's province, but the exploration and evaluation phases can be done more efficiently by the machine once they are specified. This intermeshing of the two capabilities can be promoted to the fullest when we understand the many-faceted aspects of cognitive economy and partial and aggregate specifications. An attempt to utilize our current understanding can be seen more clearly in Section 6 in which the design philosophy underlying Gaku's framework and features is discussed.

2-5 COMPELLING REASONS FOR PROMOTING MAN-MACHINE SYNERGISM

The unbounded, complex characteristics of real-world problems suggest to us why planning and decision making are difficult, but they do not tell us anything about the importance or seriousness of the decision impacts on our lives and the environment. Clearly, the consequences of wrong decisions are more serious in some problem situations than in others. Those types that are serious enough to warrant extra effort in developing adaptive planning by man-machine teams, beyond current or conventional practice, are now presented.

● *The consequences of some decisions are vital or of ultra-high cost.* If the plan adopted for implementation, including the decision "not to do anything," will cost human lives or an extraordinary amount of funds, extra efforts in contingency planning are justified. Some emergency situations can be avoided or minimized by careful consideration of contingent events before they arise.

Time constraints coupled with complexity and uncertainty are among the major causes of difficulty in making good decisions. Therefore, one of the purposes of planning is to prepare a large number of contributing decisions in advance so that last-minute decisions require only adjustments of details that are relatively minor in importance and scope.

Judicious use of planning techniques by man-machine teams might improve the quality of plans, increase the speed of plan generation, and reduce the cost in the long run.

● *Some decisions, once made, cannot be stopped, changed, or reversed.* Decisions with such characteristics appear in political, military, social, and economic affairs, and range from decisions involved in push-button warfare to those in dropping a letter in a mailbox. Between these two extremes are decisions for long-range construction projects such as dams, freeways, and large buildings, in that resources committed initially and at various subsequent stages cannot be withdrawn in any large scale. These characteristics, when combined with vital or ultra-high cost features, justify spending extra planning effort.

● *Some decisions have important long-term effects.* Decisions on use of new methods and products—defoliants, for example—may continue to have effects on people and the environment long after their use has been discontinued. In such cases, original actions can trigger secondary actions, and the resulting "shock waves" can have an impact on the entire ecosystem. Such indirect, far-reaching effects, if undesirable in nature, can effectively nullify or overpower the direct, desired results intended at the time of planning.

Although the effectiveness and accuracy of available long-range forecasting techniques can always be questioned, they can provide a tentative future "map" to serve as an "early warning system" in contingency planning, drawing our attention to where undesirable conditions and events could appear.

● *Many complex decisions are used repeatedly.* Many decisions in the prepared category for man's everyday affairs are not optimal. When a situation tends to repeat itself with minor variations, and if the repetitive part of the total operation is costly, the saving made by preparing an optimal handling of the operations could be very significant. However, if the problem is complex, ill-defined, and nondeterministic, analytical methods of optimization would not be applicable. Continuous effort toward improving the process, even incrementally, can result in a significant saving of resources.

Man-machine cooperative efforts will be useful in preparing partial and aggregate specifications to take care of relatively invariant conditions and operations and in providing necessary adjustments to changing conditions as they arise. Job shop scheduling, transshipment scheduling and air traffic control have this property.

• *Decisions that must adapt to changing conditions are often delayed.* If a particular prepared decision has served well for some time, use of habitual decisions may continue even after changes in the environment have rendered them inadequate. This moves the decision from the prepared to the unprepared category. However, people tend not (or refuse) to recognize such a decision as unprepared for cognitive economy as long as the consequences of doing this are not too serious. When they become serious, whatever adjustments made then are already too late and, to compensate for delayed reactions, overcorrection can result. In a rapidly changing environment, the adjusted course becomes inadequate before it is adjusted to the previous change. The resulting picture is an out-of-phase "hunting" syndrome.

Another difficulty with time delay is that the effects of man's actions often do not become visible or evaluable until several years have passed. Objectives and criteria acceptable at the time of the decision may have undergone changes.

There is no "cure-all" for these problems. More research is needed for the potential power of the man-machine partnership to be brought into realization. Man-machine techniques used in these types of problems could allow an evolutionary, multifaceted, but coordinated approach to problem analysis and decision making. In an evolutionary process, we need not look for an exact "solution" once and for all or for a single massive proposal that takes into account all possible events and consequences. It is more important to be able to indicate the relative merits of the various schemes and identify variable critical factors. Incompleteness and impreciseness of first analyses can be corrected and refined iteratively in an adaptive plan generation, which will continue to evolve with changes in the environment, in technology, in human value systems, and in our understanding of the problem.

2-6 GAKU: A STEP TOWARD MAN-MACHINE SYNERGISM*

Gaku embodies our current understanding of the workings of cognitive economy and of machine capabilities that are believed to be important in promoting "co-evolving" man-machine partnerships. As such, Gaku represents a systematic eclecticism of many borrowed ideas and techniques, mixed with our own.

2-6-1 Basic Structures

The basic framework of Gaku is derived from the two simpler structures, representing generalized planning processes. The first structure represents the iterative nature of planning; the second, the hierarchical nature of planning.

Iterative Nature of Planning. Earlier discussion included the four-step decision cycle commonly used in planning.

1. Define the objectives and set appropriate criteria.
2. Generate alternative courses of action.
3. Identify or estimate possible consequences of each alternative.
4. Evaluate the consequences in terms of the criteria and choose the alternative which best achieves the objectives.

Since the initial attempt at defining objectives and criteria is often inadequate and incomplete, these steps are usually repeated. The iterative nature of the process is shown schematically as a feedback

*Gaku, a Japanese word meaning adaptive, is the name given to a system of computer programs which has been evolving for several years. Gaku was first designed and implemented on the AN/FSQ-32 computer in the context of artificial intelligence research (Hormann, 1962, 1964, and 1965). It was later redesigned for man-machine cooperative problem solving in an artificial environment and was partially implemented on the same computer (Hormann, 1966 and 1969). The latest design features, which incorporate team planning and problem solving and are aimed at real-world problems, are currently being implemented on the IBM 360/67 computer under SDC's ADEPT time-sharing system.

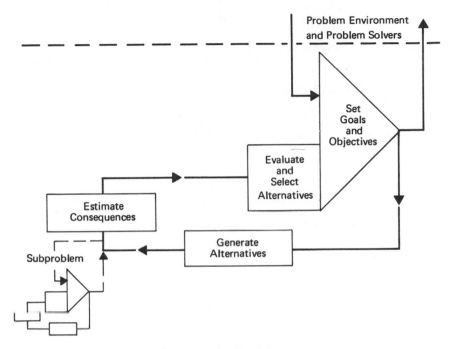

Figure 2-1.   Decision steps forming a feedback loop.

loop (Fig. 2-1). Much more flexibility is needed in real-world planning; a design structure derived from Fig. 2-1, as incorporated in Gaku, will be shown later.

Hierarchical Nature of Planning.   The hierarchical nature of planning comes into existence through the following two related aspects:

Evolvement of plans from general to concrete. Planning usually starts with the conceptualization of a given problem situation and, as such, is an aggregated, low-resolution consideration of various factors ranging over the full scope of a situation. As understanding of the problem increases, more details are added and vague or fuzzy concepts are clarified. Then, as more variables become identified and relations among variables become better understood, a reasonable separation may be made between decision variables (those variables the planner can, or chooses to, control) and other variables (over which he has little or no control) which also determine the outcomes. This process of progressive articulation and substantiation, including adjustment to

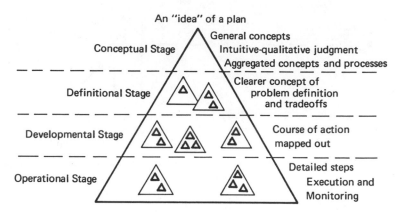

An "idea" of a plan

Conceptual Stage — General concepts
Intuitive-qualitative judgment
Aggregated concepts and processes

Definitional Stage — Clearer concept of
problem definition
and tradeoffs

Developmental Stage — Course of action
mapped out

Operational Stage — Detailed steps
Execution and
Monitoring

Figure 2-2. The hierarchical nature of planning.

changing environmental conditions, continues down to the very last step of implementation. It is a continuum of transitions although it is commonly divided into four stages for convenience. These are the conceptual, definitional, developmental, and operational stages (Fig. 2-2).

Subdivision of the task. For a large-scale, complex situation, it is important that the planner subdivide the problem into its subparts, each of which is presumably easier to manipulate and analyze. After the separate subparts are examined in appropriate detail, resulting plans of attack for these subparts are synthesized to furnish insights into the original problem (Eastman, 1969; Green, 1969). This process of subdivision is practiced in individual problem solving and in group planning.

Typically, in a hierarchical organization, the planning task is broken into a number of subtasks, which are assigned to particular division heads who, in turn, subdivide their assignments and delegate portions to department heads, and so on. Subplans generated are successively channeled back to be coordinated into an integrated plan. The importance of choosing appropriate subdivisions and the possibility of using more than one are treated later.

These processes of generating subproblems and attacking them separately are schematically depicted as small pyramids and sub-pyramids scattered within the outer pyramid shown in Fig. 2-2. The small feedback loop in Fig. 2-1 also depicts the generation of a sub-problem from the larger feedback loop.

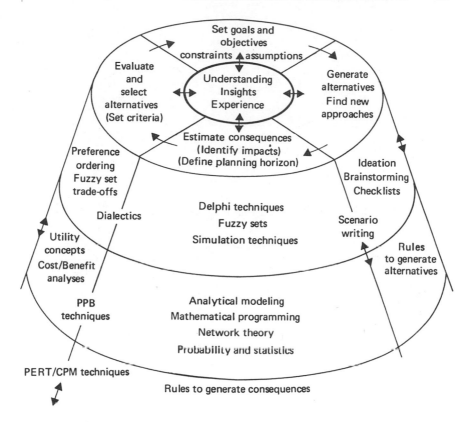

Figure 2-3. Gaku's framework.

2-6-2 Composite Structure: The Basic Framework of Gaku

Gaku's framework, which incorporates both of the structural characteristics shown in Figs. 2-1 and 2-2, is shown schematically in Fig. 2-3. It consists of a truncated cone structure with the top surface showing the four-step feedback loop similar to that in Fig. 2-1. The tower-like appearance of the structure suggests the hierarchical nature—the higher on the cone, the nearer to the conceptual stage of planning. The four sections at the top with clockwise arrows indicate the usual sequence of steps, but two-way arrows connecting the center circle with each of the four sections indicate that any section may be revisited at any time before completing the visits to all four sections in sequence. These four sections and the common center comprise a guiding mechanism for interaction, which is called a "user-modifiable feedback loop."

A variety of decision-aiding tools and techniques are shown along

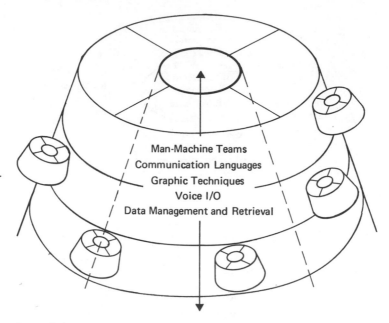

Man-Machine Teams
Communication Languages
Graphic Techniques
Voice I/O
Data Management and Retrieval

Figure 2-4. Substructures for team planning.

the outer "wall" of the cone, merely to indicate that decision aids should be made available to fit the needs of the decision maker(s). These decision aids must be geared to the needs occurring in the decision step and the stage of the planning hierarchy he is currently in. A rich assortment of tools, rather than a single powerful tool, appears to be needed. Some of the tools and techniques, such as statistical routines and the Critical Path Method (CPM), have been generalized and are available as "library" programs (Montalbano, 1965; Shure, et al., 1967). Other techniques, however, will have to be tailored to fit a particular situation or devised during the actual involvement of the man and the system.

Figure 2-4 depicts the various aspects of subtask handling which are represented by small cones within the main cone. The center "core" of the cone is shown here to indicate that some common resources and techniques are made available to man-machine teams at various levels of interaction. Man-machine teams themselves are included here since their actions and the information they generate are also used as resources and techniques.

If an individual has generated a number of subproblems and is attacking them one at a time, only one mechanism at a time within the outer cone is needed. Moving from the original problem to one of its subproblems is done by recursive use of the guiding mechanism.

Upon receiving a new subproblem, the mechanism reapplies itself, using a push-down list to keep track of the various levels of activities in which the planner is engaged. On the other hand, if a number of planners are using the system simultaneously, a copy of the guiding mechanism is created as needed (not prestored) for each individual, who can generate and handle his own subproblems by the recursive use of his own mechanism. All such guiding mechanisms, one for each individual, can operate simultaneously and independently of each other but can also contact and influence each other through the communication channels. Such channels or links among these mechanisms are usually specified in advance, but new links may be established during planning activities and old ones altered or deleted.

A hierarchical planning structure, which is typically influenced by the existing organizational structure, is shown in Fig. 2-5 as *organization-oriented planning*. The planning task is divided into a number of subtasks and assigned to division managers who, in turn, subdivide their assignments and delegate these subtasks to lower-level managers who may continue this process of subdivision and delegation. More details are added at each level and the assumptions and constraints that have been passed down are added to and clarified. In the man-machine context, Gaku can facilitate the timely information exchange among many planners at the same level and on different levels. It can solicit information from different planners, sort and distribute information to designated persons, and make up complex

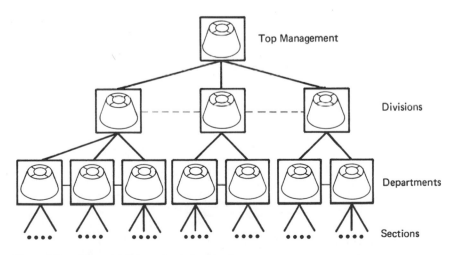

Figure 2-5.   Organization-oriented planning.

displays rapidly. "What if" questions generated by one planner may be answered by one or more planners at a lower level, or by making a "side" calculation, e.g., by exercising a simulation model relevant to the question. Some internal inconsistencies and/or conflicting subgoals may be revealed, and unstated or vague assumptions and different policy interpretations may be spelled out. The timeliness of the information exchange will permit the iterative process of plan generation and modification to be more efficient. This, in turn, facilitates timely identification of potential trouble spots and contingencies and further generation and examination of more alternatives, thus leading to a better plan.

So far, the hierarchical nature of team planning has been discussed in terms of the organizational structure. However, different ways of subdividing the total task may supply new insights into the problem situation, since information relevant to an important planning question may be scattered across departmental lines. For example, local government work on "personal and property safety" may be supported by a number of agencies, including the police and fire departments, the district attorney's office, the office of civil defense, and the medical examiner's office (Laska, 1970).

Such *function-oriented planning* is schematized in Fig. 2-6. A strategic plan may be generated by a group of planners who have been chosen from all the divisions contributing to the function in question. Contributing subtasks may appear in parallel or in sequence; thus, the resulting flow of activities will be very similar in appearance to a

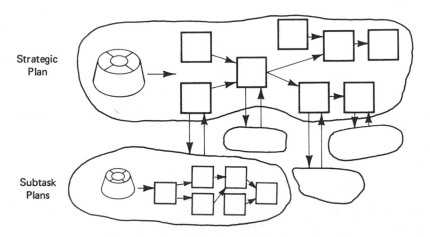

Figure 2-6. Function-oriented planning.

PERT network. Since each step in a strategic plan is usually a highly aggregated, broad-brush description of what is to be done, each node in the network is subsequently expanded to another network by another group of planners who represent a relatively narrower domain of functions and specialized skills. This successive expansion continues to the very concrete level of plan implementation. The hierarchical nature of planning is still visible, but it is often different from that of the organizational hierarchy.

For large-scale planning that uses complex combinations of diverse functions, it may be desirable for planners to test several ways of subdividing and structuring the problem. This activity often contributes toward insightful moments of creative problem solving. When constructing such tentative models becomes truly easy and inexpensive, man may be encouraged to try out "rough and ready" versions without commitment in order to see the same problem from different viewpoints, one of which may lead to methods or answers that could not have been attained in any other way.

2-6-3 An Example of Man-Machine Interaction

The framework of Gaku has been described in the previous section. Let us now see how the guiding mechanism of Gaku assists the man in defining and exploring the problem situation. This hypothetical interaction also includes capabilities of Gaku that are desirable to reduce man's cognitive load, i.e., to achieve cognitive economy.

Our discussion will concentrate on relatively high level planning characterized by imprecise, aggregated, intuition-guided activities. For simplicity, the focus will be on a single high-level planner interacting with Gaku and will occasionally shift to lower-level planners. In the following, steps are described in general terms first, and corresponding examples are given by using a food processing company interested in creating new products and marketing them. This hypothetical example is included here merely to illustrate the type of planning that evolves through multilevel interactions and iterative decision steps. The example itself should not be taken seriously because of its oversimplification in avoiding voluminous explication.

Goal Setting (Step 1). When the planner enters the guiding mechanism, he is in the "goal setting" step. He can start by stating (in English phrases*) some of the obvious goals and objectives, keeping in mind that he can modify or add to this initial list later. Gaku simply records this list under the "goals and objectives" section. If the planner wishes, he can bypass this and go to the next step.

In the food processing example, the objective may be stated as "new product creation and marketing" and corresponding criteria as "attractiveness to consumers" and "high rate of return on investment." Note that many assumptions are unstated and criteria are vague at this conceptual stage. Assumptions regarding the rest of the company's operation, such as continued production and marketing of other existing products of the company or phasing out of any of them, are not stated. Later in definitional and developmental stages, however, assumptions will have to be spelled out as completely and clearly as possible.

Alternative Generation (Step 2). In the "alternative generation" step, the planner lists possible alternatives, keeping in mind that these, too, are tentative. Gaku records this list under "alternatives." If the planner's inclination is to generate new ideas, he can request to be in an "ideation" mode with Gaku (and other planners). This may lead to the discovery or invention of new alternatives (see Hormann, 1965, for the description of "ideation"). This exercise may prompt him to restate goals and objectives, some of which may now be recognized as assumptions and constraints. If not, he goes to the "consequence estimation" step.

An example of alternatives for new products may be "freeze-dried dinners" and "existing product X with new packaging and a new promotion campaign."† Ideation with Gaku and other planners may

---

*The use of sophisticated English discourse analysis is not assumed here since simple recording and housekeeping of the record is sufficient for this phase of man-machine interaction. However, natural language (usually a subset of English) communication, including semantic-disambiguation and fact-retrieval techniques (Kellogg, 1970; Minsky, 1968), will be desirable for some classes of problems and users. Our own man-machine communication language (Hormann, et al., 1970) will be described later.

†Before new product alternatives can be suggested, preparatory work is needed that includes market exploration for potential growth areas related to the company's capabilities, required adjustments to the current operation, competitors' strengths (current and projected) in these areas, etc. Findings from these studies can be summarized as "opportunities and risks." Although these studies are assumed to have been done as preplanning procedures, simplified examples here do not reflect that assumption.

convince him that the current consumer interest places increased emphasis on nutritive values. So, he adds a new criterion, "high nutritive value" to the previously listed criteria and generates (or another planner suggests) a new alternative "fish cakes made from protein of the sea (small fishes, clean and wholesome scraps from processing large fishes, sea weed, etc.)."

Consequence Estimation (Step 3). Consequence estimation can be made in a number of ways, depending on the nature of the problem and the level of the planning hierarchy. The planner may use his own judgment to state the consequences; he may combine the Delphi technique and scenario writing to map out future conditions and possible events; he may subdivide the original problem and ask his staff members, with their specialized knowledge and experience, to estimate the consequences of subparts, while he himself synthesizes the total picture from those subparts; he may use Gaku's aids in computer simulation of the "relevant states of the world" to generate consequences. When future conditions and events must be projected and taken into account, this task is proportionately harder in relation to the length of the "planning horizon."

In our food processing example, consequence estimation will include examination of raw material requirements (what sources at what cost), production and packaging requirements (whether new equipment, new machine layouts, specially trained manpower, and other resources are needed), advertising media and retail outlets, distribution means and costs, and competition (current and projected) in each target area. A set of assumptions and constraints regarding federal and local regulations will also enter into the picture.

Assignment of subtasks. These are formulated as subtasks for making rough estimates of requirements and are channeled to responsible department heads who, in turn, break up the tasks and assign them to their subordinates or specialists. For example, the production and packaging department may have created two subproblems: production procedures with different assumptions and options, and package design alternatives and automatic packaging devices to be incorporated into the production procedures. Each of these can create its own decision cycle (see the small cone within the main cone in Fig. 2-4), stating its objectives and decision variables, generating alternatives, estimating consequences, etc., and can come up with one or more proposed plans for the subtask.

At the higher level, these subplans and estimates of costs from each department must be coordinated and sequenced properly in order to get a total picture. For example, as soon as target retail locations are identified, the distribution department can map out the network for distribution, but it cannot estimate transportation means and cost of distribution until given the characteristics of the products such as prespoil period (with and without refrigeration for perishables) and the size, shape, and weight of the packages. The marketing department would also need to know special selling points (e.g., "high nutritive value") since advertising campaigns and costs will reflect different strong points of the products.

Evaluation and Selection (Step 4). In the evaluation and selection step, the planner is asked to identify criteria or attributes that determine the desirability and undesirability of the various plans of action. Each alternative is then described in terms of the attributes as completely as possible and as quantitatively as possible. However, total quantification is either impossible, or when forced, would result in artificial values that are not reliable or meaningful.

The attributes selected for the food industry example may be "taste," "eye appeal," "convenience in preparation and serving," "nutritive values," "development cost,"* "selling price per unit," "projected rate of return in two years," etc. These are mixtures of qualitative and quantitative information, and determining their worth in relation to the objectives requires judgmental decisions. For this type of evaluation, traditional cost/benefit analysis is not adequate to summarize the value of a given plan since the analysis requires not only total quantification but also a single "quantitative measure of effectiveness" even when a variety of impacts are visible.

We have developed a set of methods and techniques to deal with this type of evaluation problem. It is incorporated into Gaku as one of its tools and is called "Machine-Aided Value Judgments." This interactive tool is an attempt to augment and sharpen the user's value-oriented judgments by guiding him in handling, systematically and consistently, both subjective value information and factual information. Immediate feedback and ease of adjusting criteria enable the user to explore complex trade-off possibilities that are usually very difficult or impossible to evaluate. In addition, group interaction

---

*Since the current stage of planning is still at the borderline of the conceptual-definitional stages, each of these figures can be given in the form of a three-valued set—i.e., lowest value, most likely value, and highest value.

through Gaku can facilitate the direct involvement of people (experts as well as other evaluators representing a variety of value systems). A brief description of the techniques is included in Appendix B, but a detailed description of the techniques in a step-by-step fashion with examples is found in Hormann (1971a).

Let us assume now that an evaluation of the current set of alternatives, including trade-off possibilities, has been made with Gaku's assistance. This type of exercise can help the planner become aware of complex value assumptions often hidden in trade-off considerations, and group interaction tends to bring them out more explicitly. As a result, he may be prompted to add or modify criteria, generate new alternatives, identify indirect consequences that become relevant in light of the new insights, and go through the evaluation process again. A better understanding gained in cause-and-effect relations (both direct and indirect) may help him to identify crucial decision variables among other variables over which he has little or no control.

In our food industry example, comparing the alternatives, "freeze-dried dinners," "existing product X with new packaging," and "fish cakes from protein of the sea" in terms of the attributes listed earlier, may reveal that fish cakes rate superior in "nutritive values" to the other products, nearly equal in "taste" and "convenience," but very low in profit potential. Upon examination of the breakdown of the profit projection for two years, special handling cost incurred by refrigeration for distribution was exceedingly high. Moreover, large volume production and nationwide distribution were not planned because of the product's perishability. Group ideation then produced suggestions such as adding preservatives, vacuum packing, freezing, and making into powder form. Powder was at first rejected, but was picked up again when a suggestion was made to experiment on different recipes for making fish cakes from the powder and other ingredients. Some of them, as it turned out, made not only tasty fish cakes, but dumplings, pies, and salads.

Tentative selection and delegation of details. So, the story goes—the fish powder becomes a tentative candidate for a new thrust by the company. It is to be packaged with suggested recipes on the wrapper and a proud display of its nutritional content. Large volume and wider distribution will now be possible with no extra handling costs.

The top management planner again delegates the development of more detailed plans to be worked out by the same lower management who made the initial report. This time, more detailed instructions can be given (e.g., "production plans for fish powder, not perishable for a long period, in large volume, and with nationwide sales targets"). This instruction, in turn, may be broken down into subtasks in the production, marketing, and distribution departments. While these subtasks are being worked on, the planner can continue examining other alternatives.

Let us now focus our attention on lower management in generating detailed alternative plans.

Developmental Stage of Planning (Steps 1 through 4).   Once a product has been selected as a tentative candidate and additional details have been requested, a more systematic means can be used for generating alternative implementation plans and their hypothetical consequences. For example, production of fish powder beginning with the raw material acquisition may be broken down into four operations, each having a number of choices:

A   different mixtures of fishes in different proportions;
B   different means of cleaning them;
C   different ways of making them into powdered form; and
D   different ways of packaging the powder.

Since these component operations are interdependent, choices within a single parameter cannot be made independent of other parameter choices. A certain combination may create a more efficient total operation than others even though some of the component operations are considered less efficient than other components. There will be many trade-off considerations. Impacts of this new operation on the other on-going operations in the company must also be examined. When the interface between components and interdependencies among their operations are very complex, a simulation approach may be taken to assess the total effects of a given combination in question and to try out many other possible combinations.*

Even without simulation, exhaustive enumeration of all combinations of all parameter choices will create $A \times B \times C \times D$ alternative production schemes. For example, if $A = 15$, $B = 7$, $C = 11$, and $D = 12$, all possible combinations created by these choices ($15 \times 7 \times 11 \times 12$) would total 13,860. Other combinatorial decision

---

*Simulation techniques deserve a topic of their own and are discussed in Section 2–7-2 of this chapter.

situations such as production of chemicals, for which possible combinations are too numerous, will also benefit from man-machine techniques.

Gaku can generate these combinations one by one, changing one parameter value at a time. Each combination generated may be displayed for the production department to examine for feasibility and desirability. Or, more important, Gaku's generation process can be guided by the planner as to what parameter values to change and in which direction rather than generating all combinations exhaustively. Man's pattern recognition capability with intuitive "warmer" or "cooler" feelings can guide Gaku in selective search toward a near-optimal combination.

When modeling is employed, a technique analogous to sensitivity analysis in operations research can be used to observe how minor changes in the value of a decision variable tend to affect the outcome in terms of desirability attributes. If the planner judges that the effect of these changes is significant, he may try ways of obtaining additional information about the collective behavior of outcome variables as influenced by the particular decision variable in question. This could contribute to a more refined model, and a "fine tuning" experimentation may then be possible which, in turn, will help the planner gain a "feel" for empirical relations among variables.

Varied Levels of Information Needs and Processing.   As planning proceeds from the conceptual stage to the developmental stage, more and more details are added in each decision step. A general plan passed down for more detailed planning is "fleshed out" by the lower-level processes. However, details that were necessary for the lower-level decisions are often not necessary for the higher-level ones and must be summarized when the results are communicated to the planners. The information can be structured in graded levels of detail so that at the top level, only important implications of the plan are shown and trouble spots that must be ironed out by the management are indicated. When more information is needed, each item can be expanded successively—finally reaching the factual data level.

Displays of graphs and charts are also important summarization techniques since visual information, when appropriately formatted, effectuates powerful and quick communication. Making an appropriate level of abstraction and generalization for summary construction and recognizing unique needs of information for each planning level and situation are a difficult but important part of the planning process. More research is needed to amalgamate hardware advances with the findings of information scientist and human factors specialists (Miller, 1965; Newell, 1970).

Ideal conditions toward which we strive are those in which information needs are met at all levels, and coordination and integration of subplans are easily achieved through effective communication channels throughout the hierarchy. The man-machine system can then allow higher-level planning to be broad and comprehensive while exploiting the detailed knowledge and specialized skills available at the lower levels. "What if" questions generated at a higher level may be answered at a lower level, and quick feedback and the ease of adjusting decision choices will enable the planners to examine a much larger number of alternatives, weighing many different factors, than they normally can before a final decision has to be made.

Decision-Aiding Tools at a Concrete Level. As the planning process evolves into a detailed and concrete level, more and more quantitative measurements and more precise relations among variables may become discernible. Many decision-aiding tools are available from mathematical programming, decision theory, network analysis, scheduling and resource allocation techniques, queuing theory, inventory analysis, PERT/CPM techniques, and similar support methods (Wagner, 1969), some of which can be used more economically in an off-line, batch mode. Most of these are aimed at optimizing well-defined operations and conditions; human creativity and judgment enter only in problem formulation and interpretation of results.

Man, however, can always find creative ways to use routine tools. For example, linear programming can be used in an iterative, experimental fashion to generate a plan. Computational results are *not* to be taken as the final "solution," but as indicators toward different formulation or different parameter settings. Retaining the same set of constraints, the planner may experiment with various objective functions, or various weightings of them to ascertain the sensitivity of solutions to criteria. The planner can determine how minor changes in data or coefficients affect a solution through parametric and post-optimality analyses.

Creative use of PERT/CPM methods is possible, especially in an interactive mode. Changing the precedence relations—thus changing the network configuration—can generate various alternative plans for which different "critical paths" can be generated. By manipulating the network structure, a new flexible means of arriving at an optimal schedule will be available to the planner. Superimposed on the above is the use of human judgment where the objectives to be reached are not completely defined in advance or where there is conflict among them. For example, meeting the project completion time while minimizing the total cost and maintaining a smooth rate of manpower utilization may be extremely difficult. Only after many "what if" questions can an acceptable compromise be reached.

An interactive use of visual input/output—charts, graphs, and network displays that can be changed easily online—will also help man formulate his questions more astutely than without such aids (Sutherland, 1970). The planner can quickly "zero in" on the troublesome areas to be corrected or the fruitful areas to be explored further.

2-7 BUILT-IN AND EXTENSIBLE CAPABILITIES OF GAKU

The foregoing section on man-machine interaction was presented to illustrate types of capabilities needed in Gaku in addition to the guiding mechanism within its framework. In the design of Gaku, an attempt has been made to incorporate our *current* understanding of cognitive economy and the techniques of partial and aggregate specifications. This includes an attempt to separate those features and capabilities that are relatively problem independent, and thus can be built-in for Gaku, from those that are problem specific and are generated or extended through man-machine interaction. To do this, built-in capabilities must include a means for user modification and extension through interaction.

The basic design philosophy followed is embedded in our definition of *adaptive planning*. Let us restate the definition by replacing the word "planning" with the word "designing," i.e., designing a man-machine system.

> Adaptive designing is an evolutionary process which starts with partial and aggregate specifications but which adapts, by progressive articulation, substantiation, and adjustment, to changing conditions in the environment and to new knowledge and techniques as they become available.

This definition recognizes the necessity of designing processes to anticipate uncertainties in the environment and also to allow for incompleteness in the designer's knowledge and understanding of the problem situation.

The "environment" here is the man-machine co-evolving situation, the nature of which cannot be predetermined or anticipated in any certain way. The partial and aggregate specifications we can make are limited to the basic framework and certain basic capabilities. Additional capabilities included are relatively *ad hoc* in nature, but they are modifiable and can be made to adapt to changing conditions and to new knowledge and experience. The many unspecified portions must be filled in by man during his interaction within the system. Certain degrees of freedom are maintained to achieve the generality of the system, but man, who brings with him his own specific problem, background knowledge and experience, can make the system more special purpose and powerful as the man-machine system coevolves.

It is difficult to make a clear distinction between the two ways of extending Gaku's capabilities, which are (a) by user-Gaku interactions that cause new terms and functions to be generated, some of which may be permanently incorporated into the Gaku system, and (b) by designer-Gaku interactions that change or add to Gaku's basic capabilities as well as create a new framework and new mechanisms.* The following summarization will focus primarily on ways to assist the user within a problem-solving context.

2-7-1 General Executive with Guiding Functions

The general executive portion of Gaku includes the guiding mechanism at various levels of planning and provides the "user-modifiable feedback loop" in the decision cycle (see Fig. 2-3). The major objective is to enable the user to start interacting even at the initial imprecise problem-definition stage, prompt him through the intuition guided problem-solving stage, and assist him to formulate detailed

---

*The design of Gaku and the language with which it is being implemented allow the designer to interact with Gaku's executive to make additions and changes to Gaku's internal mechanisms or rules of behavior. Changes in Gaku's behavior made in this way do not appear any different technically than changes caused by user-Gaku interaction. The only difference is that certain internal mechanisms of Gaku are guarded against indiscriminant changes that might be attempted by the user, but the designer and the systems specialists can use authorized codes to make system changes.

solution steps. In these stages, problem-definition and problem-solving processes are seen to be inextricably mixed.

The tree-generating questionnaire is a technique for narrowing the range of possibilities successively to a specific area of consideration by a conditional branch-generation of questions. Unlike the static questionnaire, which has many fixed questions with blanks to be filled in, this technique guides the user with a few questions at a time. Answers to only a few initial questions can circumscribe the total area considerably. The next set of questions generated is conditioned by these answers, and the process is continued until the man-machine team is able to "zero in" on the target area.

This technique can be used to assist the user in constructing new decision-aiding tools that are problem specific. It is also used to help the user circumscribe the problem context.

A context circumscriber is useful after Gaku acquires a large repertoire of capabilities and when a relative novice enters the man-machine system. This novice, instead of having to learn all of the possible combinations of Gaku capabilities and decision aids, will be guided to circumscribe the problem context. Only then will he need to learn the relevant parts of Gaku's capabilities and what the overall system can offer in his particular problem context. Gaku can take an initiative role of suggesting a certain set of tools and techniques or present the man a selected set of building blocks with which he can generate higher-level, special-purpose procedures and data structures. This will permit him to start at a relatively high level of planning/problem-solving activities.

When a natural-language input is desirable, the context circumscriber will have an important role in assisting in resolving ambiguities. A relatively simple semantic analysis can go a long way when the context of the discourse has been circumscribed. The interactive mode itself can be exploited to prompt the user to rephrase his statements and queries for successive disambiguation.

An online portraying technique is used to prompt the user to fill in previously unspecified portions. The "top down" approach is used. Gaku promotes *partial specification* by allowing the user to define rules and conditions, leaving some details to be filled in later. These unspecified portions may become knowable later and eventually be filled in. When a certain decision cannot be supplied due to the absence of specific conditions, Gaku can present a set of concrete decision situations to which man must react. By portraying, online, the portions of a decision-making model that cannot be defined at the outset and repeating the process under "similar" conditions, either the decision maker himself or the experimenter may be able to formulate the underlying decision rule as a hypothesis. This rule is a type of *aggregate specification.*

An example of this portrayal technique is a manager of a shop with job-shop scheduling responsibility. Most likely, he cannot formulate, in the abstract, the decision rules he himself is using. However, he can readily decide what is to be done when a set of specific conditions is explicitly given. Gaku can generate sets of similar conditions within a given framework of job-shop operations to repeat the decision portrayal. After a while, the manager (or an experimenter) may be able to formulate a tentative decision rule. This rule is given to Gaku, which then uses it under varying conditions to produce consequences. The manager then examines the consequences (generated and displayed by Gaku) of applying the rule; he can approve, disapprove or suggest a new or modified rule. After a certain "confidence level" is reached, the rule can be incorporated* into that part of the decision processes partially delegated to Gaku initially.

This portrayal technique can be a valuable research tool to gain insight into human judgment and intuitive decision processes. The interaction process and automatic recording of it makes internal, inaccessible phenomena to be externalized, at least partially. Such gain in understanding, in turn, can be used to carry the Gaku design closer to man-machine synergism. We can test influences of various decision aids on man's performance under varied conditions and problem situations.

2-7-2   Modeling Assistance

A simulation technique that includes a man in the model is useful for probing complex phenomena. A complex phenomenon, for which analytical modeling techniques are difficult or only partially suitable, is simulated by computer programs in which a man is included as a component. In such a simulation, the machine represents the environmental conditions and decision processes that can be clearly defined, and the man provides the behavioral-procedural information that was unknown to the modeler or that is idiosyncratic. Gaming situations,

---

*This type of rule may still be unsatisfactory in an actual operation. Human value judgments, such as giving a preferred customer high priority, are difficult to include in the rule since preferences are changeable and not clearly specifiable.

such as a corporate decision-making model and a community-development game, use this technique by having the man role-play or by using experts. This is another portrayal situation but one which is incorporated explicitly in modeling.

Many assumptions are usually built into the model. For example, assumptions on functional relations or cause-and-effect relations are made to depict the real-life situation. These assumptions are the product of management's (or modeler's) judgment and are difficult to test for validity. They may be wrong or they may become invalid. Therefore, it is important to make models and modeling techniques flexible and responsive to change (Jones, 1967). Asking "what if" questions can help the planner test his partial theory and identify areas of greatest uncertainty and explore these areas in greater depth.

Two types of "what if" questions can be asked. One type is for examining possible consequences of his decisions before commitment to a decision. This type causes a set of decision variables to assume certain values (e.g., decision to buy new equipment). These questions constitute an effective dialogue between man and machine during the planning session.

The other type of "what if" question causes a set of outcome variables to assume certain values. For example, new tax laws, price changes of the raw material, competitor's new products, etc., are not under the planner's control but nevertheless affect the outcome. The act of answering these questions leads to *contingency planning* and the answers may be called "as if" specifications. Uncertainties in the environment are treated *as if* they have occurred and a plan for the conditions is specified. Including these contingencies explicitly in the planning model can eliminate or minimize emergency, on-the-spot decisions.

Modularized simulation techniques can be used to exercise the model with a wide variety of inputs and conditions quickly and economically, especially for rough estimates of the consequences of a tentative plan. The total simulation model* can be partitioned into submodels, and sensitivity analysis can be performed with input-output variations for each submodel. Then exercising the total model for a large number of varied conditions can be done relatively quickly by activating only those submodels that are "sensitive" to that particular set of conditions, while using a "representative" set of outputs

---

*The "total" simulation model itself may still be a representation of a small portion of the problem environment under consideration.

from the "insensitive" submodels without executing the submodels themselves. This can be done by placing a checklist at the entry point for each submodel. If the input conditions, usually generated by other submodels, are within the sensitivity range allowed, then the output is given from the set of representative values without actually activating the submodel. The submodel is exercised fully if the input conditions are not met. The specification of sensitivity variations can be relaxed or tightened, depending on how rough an estimate can be tolerated.

These options are useful when meeting different information requirements generated in different stages of planning (conceptual, definitional, etc.) for certain levels of detail and accuracy. This technique, however, must be used with caution when the model is designed to create feedback which would cause changes to the model itself.

2-7-3 Delegation of Details to Gaku

Delegation of details to a machine, as these become identified as useful and delineable, is one of the most powerful ways of gaining a cognitive economy. Since human memory is limited in storing many pieces of information accurately, the delegation of details, especially in an aggregated form, enables man to concentrate more on higher conceptual problems and idea generation. In man-machine collaborative efforts, a set of decision steps, once prepared and stored, can be manipulated conceptually as a single action, while the machine retains all its details. Higher-level decisions are composites of many such prepared decisions, which serve as building blocks, of various sizes and complexity. Man can create a new higher-level function out of these building blocks, focusing attention on *what* they do and the *way* they fit together, rather than on *how* they are made up of constituent details.

In an interactive "co-evolving" planning situation, progressive articulation of rough plans and delegation of these decisions to Gaku provides a basis for a step toward man-machine synergism through cognitive economy. Then, partly because man continues to learn and partly because Gaku becomes increasingly more helpful and responsive to him, the style and degree of interactions between man and Gaku can change radically. This phenomenon is analogous to two people who have worked together on a project for some time. They begin to share a great deal of common knowledge and work load:

When they discuss their work, they need not go back to basic definitions, assumptions, and reasonings every time. An outsider to the
project will become quickly confused.

Building-block construction can be assisted by Gaku using the
"tree-generating questionnaire," described earlier, in addition to other
usual editing and diagnostic assistance. The questionnaire is first used
to narrow down the range of possibilities successively to a small area
of concern. Then the mechanism in the "user-modifiable feedback
loop" prompts him to specify goals (set of criteria in the form of
results to be obtained and/or of operations to be performed). This
time Gaku can take the initiative for generating alternatives (from
its repertoire of subroutines and basic functions) as suggestions. The
user, if experienced, may also generate his own or choose one or
more of the suggested alternatives to be tried. These alternatives may
already be relatively high-level building blocks or made up of many
low-level primitive operations, depending on the complexity of the
task and on Gaku's repertoire that had been built up in this area.

Next, consequences are generated by monitoring execution of the
chosen alternatives, and the results are fed back to the user. The user
checks the results against the stated criteria for goal achievement (and
also some unstated goals and assumptions that he overlooked or could
not state precisely at the outset). He may then wish to modify the
goals or add new criteria and repeat the process until he is satisfied
with the consequences (the performance and/or the results) of the
generated building block.

This building-block construction may be very tedious with many
small steps to be examined and monitored or may be a simple modification of an "off-the-shelf" building block. The resulting building
block is given a name (either a descriptive English word or a code)
and may be stored in tentative, personal, or public repositories:

Tentative repository: Building blocks in this repository are of a
tentative nature. Their workability or usefulness is not yet established.
Since this part of the storage is destroyed after each man-machine
session, those that are to be saved for later use should be transferred
to the personal repository.

Personal repository: Each user maintains his own building blocks
here. These are usually problem specific and reflect the user's current
interests and special skills. Other users of Gaku may use these only
with his permission. If some of these can be generally useful, the user
can suggest to the system that they be entered in the public repository.

Public repository: Those building blocks that have established their usefulness and general applicability are stored here by their names and descriptions and are available to all users. Some of these are built-in functions of Gaku and some are suggested by users. Those from the personal repository are checked for possible redundancy with the existing ones, recompiled for efficiency, and catalogued.

Use of check lists at strategic points will be helpful when a complex structure is being built from various building blocks. These can be numerical values to specify a range of acceptable (or unacceptable) values of operation; when the outcome of an operation falls outside the acceptable range, the user is notified and a decision response is prompted. This can be used as a "management-by-exception" technique. For example, in a PERT/CPM network, a delay in a project which is on the critical path can automatically be reported. Exception reporting could also be used in group planning to reveal conflict or inconsistent assumptions—e.g., in the use of the same limited resources by two or more divisions of the company. A check list can be used as a reminder or a memorandum to management.

A check list can contain commentary words and phrases that the user himself inserts at certain crucial junctures (as in model building from modules). When the model is exercised and a particular module of the model is reached that requires special handling, these comments, along with other outputs, are printed. The comments could be reminders to himself that a new set of parameter values is about to be requested or that a portion of the module has deliberately been unspecified.

2-7-4 Special Tools

Some special-purpose decision-aiding programs can be used independently as special tools. Some statistical routines are used in an off-line batch mode, but most decision-aids are used in an interactive mode. We are planning to incorporate existing programs whenever possible. Tools such as TRACE, online statistical routines (Shure, et al., 1967); network-related programs (Montalbano, 1965); and fuzzy-set techniques (Hormann, 1971a) are among those in the current list of candidates for the library.

Along with these tools, tutorials of graded levels of assistance will be developed for both the selection and use of appropriate tools.

2-7-5 Man-Machine Communication

All the features of Gaku that have been described must be facilitated through an effective communication means. There are many difficult problems yet to be solved but the future holds many exciting possibilities that are opening up through current research efforts. These include written and spoken natural-language communication and pictorial (2-D, 3-D, moving, and color) input/output.

We would like to apply and coordinate the results from all research in multiple modes of communication into an integrated medium in such a way that switching from one mode to another, or using more than one mode simultaneously, can be done smoothly. For example, while man is examining moving diagrams and pictures, he should be able to vocally direct the control program to change the contents or format of presentation, simultaneously pointing at parts of the display screen to indicate where and what to change—all without abrupt change to his physical position or to the direction and momentum of his thinking.

Of course, we are still far from the scene just described. Let us concentrate on what we can do now and in the near future. Successful implementation of Gaku's features and their extensions depends on effective communication languages, both from the points of view of the designer/implementer and of the users during cooperative problem solving. Traditionally, a system is implemented in one language, and another language is developed to allow for user-oriented and problem-specific expressions.

We have, instead, developed a language called *User Adaptive Language* (UAL) and associated techniques to serve both purposes. The basic UAL is used for initial Gaku implementation (as a programming language) and extended UAL is used for user-Gaku interaction and also for designer-Gaku interaction in system modification. This is possible through the extensible features of UAL and its techniques for building problem-oriented primitives from which higher-level, user-oriented functions and capabilities can be constructed for the users' convenience. Thus, the same language can be used for both purposes, affecting different characteristics in each case.

The extensibility of a language refers to the ability of the language to modify itself, that is, to create new primitive terms and functions and to define new language structures. This becomes important when the problem situation dictates a new notation that the original language does not accept or when new primitive terms and functions are required to reduce complexity. These new terms and functions may not be known at the outset but, through interaction, new ideas may be generated and the need for new terms and procedures realized. Thus, extensibility permits dynamic definition.

With these features, the user can start interacting with Gaku from the initial problem-conceptualization and definition stage and step through the decision cycle in problem solving iteratively. The conventional separation between the problem-definition and the problem-solving stages caused by specialists or programmers, or by extra languages, is not necessary. Gaku implemented in UAL can handle user-defined terms and procedures *directly* without internal translation since expressions in UAL are made up of the basic items that Gaku can understand, generate, and manipulate. For partially defined or ill-defined problems, the problem-definition phase cannot be separated from the problem-solving phase because of their iterative, evolving nature. Gaku can bring these phases together by allowing the undefined portions to be supplied by the user in the light of new information and insight as supported by his background knowledge and past experience.

UAL, in short, is designed to provide a convenient means for us to apply the techniques of partial and aggregate specifications at the design level—we do not know all the features that are needed or desirable, and we wish to reserve degrees of freedom for generality so that specific features and capabilities can be supplied by the users through interaction. The user, in turn, can use the techniques of partial and aggregate specifications by allowing the initial problem definition to be incomplete, nonspecific, and aggregate, but progressively adding more details and clarifying concepts, functions, and relations as new insight and understanding are gained. A detailed description of UAL is beyond the scope of this chapter, but it is available (Hormann, et al., 1970).

2-8 SUMMARY AND CONCLUSIONS

This chapter presented a pragmatic approach to man-machine synergism combined with a theoretical-analytical examination of cognitive elements and the relations among them. This combination forms the basis for the development of the Gaku concept and its design features.

Potentially fertile areas of application are recognized to be in the relatively early stages of planning and at the higher levels of problem-solving activities where new insights and innovative ideas are needed. Promoting a cognitive economy in man's intellectual pursuits by man-machine techniques can be seen to promote computational economy. Man can employ his intuitive judgments with pattern recognition and inductive reasoning in guiding the machine process selectively along fruitful paths of problem solving and away from unpromising ones, as the problem unfolds. The combinatorial complexity and ill-defined nature of many real-world problems make indiscriminate use of the computer futile. Faster and bigger computers alone cannot meet the challenge.

The powerful heuristics witnessed by researchers in human problem solving are characterized by astuteness in recognizing certain idiosyncracies of the problem structure and in devising methods to exploit these peculiarities in the search for short cuts or "pruning" the decision tree. The power of such heuristics seems to hinge on problem-specific pattern recognition. Therefore, such heuristics defy generalization and transferability. The author believes, however, that *conditions* in which man may be led to discover such idosyncracies can be provided by man-machine techniques. Better understanding of the workings of cognitive economy, with and without machine aids, and an optimal combination in the use of partial and aggregate specifications are needed for the full realization of such power.

Gaku can be thought of as an embodiment of our current understanding and, as such, represents a systematic eclecticism of many borrowed ideas and techniques, mixed with our own. The extended capabilities of Gaku achieved through man-Gaku interaction also would be eclectic in that the users' sense of utility eventually determines what is worth saving and extending and what should be discarded. The framework of Gaku is designed to coordinate separate capabilities and techniques for providing man with comprehensive cognitive aids.

Many problems of both a conceptual and a technical nature are yet to be solved in the realm of man-machine communication devices and techniques—large data-base manipulation and exploration, the intermeshing of man's inductive-deductive capabilities with the limited deductive capability of the machine, and many other areas. Many issues arising from the moral-philosophical and political concerns must also be dealt with.

When the pressure to "solve" is strong and methodological constraints and requirements dominate reasoning, too narrow specialization often results and science tends to trade-off wisdom for knowledge and even knowledge for information* (then, to some extent, information for data).

This sequence of trade-offs is depicted schematically:

$$\text{Data} \xrightarrow{\text{vs.}} \text{Information} \xrightarrow{\text{vs.}} \text{Knowledge} \xrightarrow{\text{vs.}} \text{Wisdom}$$

The men behind this, however, can strive collectively toward a broader, interdisciplinary grasp of the total ecosystem by supplying the "missing ingredients" (meanings, patterns, values, feelings, ethos, etc.) at each stage of synthesis during the reverse processes of going from the lower-level specialization into a more encompassing level of understanding.

A diagram summarizing the evolving roles of man-machine systems is presented in Fig. 2-7. Principles and techniques involved in developing such systems are shown in abstraction. Dots on the vertical lines suggest transitional points at which changes in the level of abstraction and the amount of specification may take place by the use of these techniques.

As stated earlier, Gaku cannot by itself be a planner or problem solver; but, in a given problem context, Gaku can be made to co-

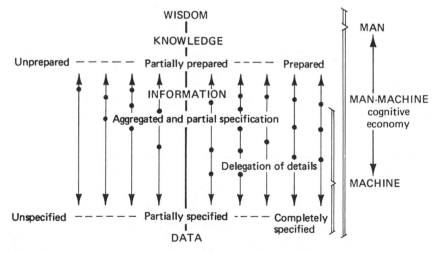

Figure 2-7. Evolving roles of man-machine partnerships.

*This tendency is discussed in a slightly different context by Seaborg (1970).

evolve into an increasingly helpful assistant. Starting with man-machine systems like Gaku as prototypes, we must continue to explore different ways of promoting man-machine synergistic capabilities and examine their implications. In view of the increasing complexity and seriousness of our real-world problems, more intensive research is required so that potential payoffs need not remain merely potential, idle thoughts entertained by man.

APPENDIX A

FUZZY CONCEPT AND COGNITIVE ECONOMY

Many concepts manipulated in the human mind are fuzzy. This fuzziness appears to be caused by:

Partial specifications, not only in plan generation, but also in specifying and classifying prepared conditions and processes and making associations between them. To achieve cognitive economy, some partially specified conditions and processes may be remembered as "prepared" if they are almost completely specified. Also for cognitive economy, parts of the specification may be in terms of aggregate specification, in which case additional processes are necessary to reach the concrete level. The total picture is even fuzzier if this aggregate specification is itself only partially specified.

Aggregate specifications, especially when aggregation is many levels removed from the concrete level. Some connecting links in defining the generating principles for reaching down to the specific level may get lost, or wrong connections may be made in time. Again, fuzziness increases when portions of the aggregate specification are partial specifications.

Changing criteria and attributes for grouping. Grouping objects, events, relations, and processes is done for cognitive economy by applying such concepts as "similarity" and "relevance," which are fuzzy concepts themselves. Such criteria tend to change when the context or point of view is changed. The increasing rate of change in the environment that we are witnessing seems also to be responsible for shifting categories and changing attitudes.

Having a range of values instead of clear-cut binary values of 0,1 or a yes, no situation for many of the judgmental attributes, e.g., good food, pretty girls.

There may be other causes for fuzziness, but this list is adequate for the moment. It should be clear by now that a certain degree and mixture of some of the above in a given situation can provide greater or lesser cognitive economy (including undue economy). The question of how to promote a better cognitive economy by machine assistance may be answered gradually, though not completely. Because of the changing nature of man's "cognitive map," which is conditioned by a changing environment and man's own growth, "prescriptive" cognitive economy (in the sense of "what *should* be done") may never be satisfactory in that it may take insufficient account of individual idiosyncracies.

APPENDIX B

FUZZY–SET CONCEPTS AND TECHNIQUES

Most papers written on the topic of fuzzy sets are abstract, and few deal with specific applications. In this Appendix, an intuitive meaning of a fuzzy set will be given, and the use of such a set in handling fuzzy attributes will be discussed. Fuzzy notions of trade-offs among these attributes will be presented, as well as techniques by which the decision maker can be assisted in refining his own preference logic successively in searching for an optimal alternative.

Let us suppose that a planner is attempting to assess a proposed set of design alternatives or to find new alternative designs for a new cargo vehicle. He may be currently considering attributes such as cost of construction, cost of maintenance, reliability, operating lifespan, business or military usefulness (now and a given number of years to come), and versatility of such a vehicle. For simplicity, let us list only three attributes to be considered:

> Cost
> Military usefulness
> Versatility

Assigning numerical values to the first attribute may be difficult because of the future consideration of currently nonexistent vehicles, although the concept of "cost" itself is not fuzzy. The last two attributes are intrinsically fuzzy. What does the phrase "alternative A_i is more useful militarily than alternative A_j" mean? The meaning will depend on the planner and the context in which he views the problem.

Numerical value assignment at this point would be difficult or arbitrary. Comparability rather than preciseness is the main consideration at this stage. Preference ordering of alternatives for each attribute is accomplished by comparing two items at a time or by an ordering of the list as a whole. After completing this preference ordering of alternatives, the planner must still deal with a fuzzy trade-off concept when he begins to evaluate the alternatives in terms of all relevant attributes simultaneously. Note that individual attributes themselves may be fuzzy and are often not commensurable.

The planner's subjective preference system can now be represented by a function. Suppose X is the set of alternatives. Let A be a subset of X possessing attribute α. The function $\mu_\alpha(x)$ for an alternative x in X associates with x, a number in the interval $[0, 1]$. The value $\mu_\alpha(x)$ represents the grade of membership of x in A (see Fig. 2-B1). If

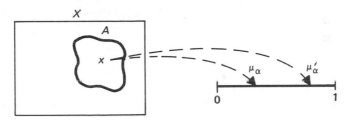

Figure 2-B1. An example of fuzzy-set mapping.

$\mu_\alpha(x)$ is close to 1, then x has a high grade of membership in A. Similarly, if $\mu_\alpha(x)$ is low and close to 0, it is not a high-valued member of A.

In our example, A represents the set of alternatives which are militarily useful. If x, a particular alternative, is viewed as very useful, then it is given a high value close to 1. This function allows the ingredient of the planner's experience to be taken into account. Each planner will presumably construct his own function; thus, for the same alternative x and the same attribute α, a different value, $\mu_\alpha'(x)$, is likely to be assigned.

A fuzzy set is a class of objects with a continuum of grades of membership or preference functions μ_α. This is convenient mathematically although it does run counter to intuition. The set of all functions for α can be viewed as the set of all possible orderings. One of the most important benefits we get from the use of this function is that trade-off concepts can now be dealt with because all the attributes have been made comparable. In our example, three attributes are cost, military usefulness, and versatility; say, α_1, α_2, and α_3, respectively. The planner's preference functions for these are μ_{α_1}, μ_{α_2}, μ_{α_3}, the values of which all lie in the interval [0, 1]. These values represent the grades of membership that are comparable rather than the attribute values themselves. Figure 2-B2 shows the three μ_α's for each alternative x_j. Displaying the useful information visually will enhance the planner's judgment and awareness of trade-off implications.

If the number of alternatives is large, he can specify an "acceptable" range of values for each μ_{α_i}, thus eliminating some alternatives before display. He can tighten or relax such restrictions to see what he "catches" and include weighting specifications for certain attributes to represent their relative importance. Then, the summation

$$S = \left\{ S_j \middle| S_j = \sum_{i=1}^{m} C_i \mu_{\alpha_i}(x_j) \right\}$$

of all the weighted preference values over m attributes can be made for all the "caught" alternatives, $x_1, x_2, \ldots, x_n$. Comparing the sums is a meaningful operation now and can be done by Gaku very rapid-

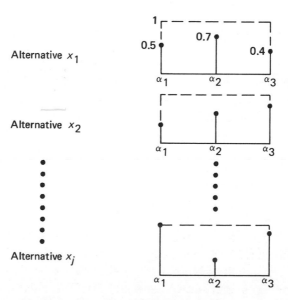

Figure 2–B2.   Trade-off comparisons of alternatives.

ly. Adding new attributes and changing his own preference functions can also be done easily and may lead to an interesting insight for a planner or experimenter.

Another important application of fuzzy sets is to help a group of planners, each with his own preference logic, to come to an agreement regarding "rational" choice of an alternative by making trade-off implications clear and by allowing each planner to adjust his preference functions while interacting with the other planners and with Gaku. To do this, we must first modify the notion of fuzzy sets to account for (a) probabilistic elements within the fuzzy sets and (b) the time element in the planning process.

Probabilistic elements enter into the lower levels of a planning hierarchy, so at least part of the planning activities should account for this.

The time element is important since the planner in most instances must re-evaluate and alter his set of priorities, after seeing some of the alternatives and consequences and their evaluations. Let us examine $X(t)$, a set of alternatives to a given problem situation at time t, and $B(t)$, a set of alternatives of current interest. (In our example, these are reasonable cost, military usefulness, and versatility. We will use β to represent a composite attribute of all three.) Presumably, as a planner studies the problem and considers consequences and evaluations, his conception of the problem grows and his fuzzy set changes and becomes more defined. That is, if $\mu_{\beta(t)}$ is his preference function operating on the fuzzy set at time t with respect to the criteria imposed by $\beta(t)$, then as t increases, $\mu_{\beta(t)}$ converges toward a more precise function; i.e., the planner is better able to sort out alternatives.

These preference functions will also be different for different planners. In general, however, there will be some acceptable preference functions and some which are not as desirable. In our example, the evaluation of a proposed design for a cargo vehicle on purely economic grounds would be considered undesirable to some degree. This could be indicated by imposing a "distance" measure d on the set of functions $\{\mu_{\beta(t)}\}$ so that $d(\mu_{\beta(t)}, \mu'_{\beta(t)})$ would represent the disparity in the two functions. This would not be a metric distance in the true mathematical sense but would indicate relative positions of preference functions to each other and to the desired set. A set of preference functions would be selected according to criteria generally agreed upon for a given context. This set would also be fuzzy.

In the cargo-vehicle example, suppose a planner is excessively cost oriented and his selection of alternatives reveals this tendency (the correlation can be easily established). Gaku can remind the planner of other important factors and trade-off implications. Fuzzy-set techniques can be employed in this situation in a very natural way. Recall that the planner's logic at a particular time t can be viewed as the function $\mu_{\beta(t)}$ where $\beta(t)$ is the composite attribute desired at time t. The purpose of Gaku relative to this setting is to guide the planner rapidly to the desired set with each step being made more precise.

If $\mathscr{F}\bar{\beta}_{(t)}$ is the set of planning logics which are precise and admissible in the sense of accounting for various factors, then Gaku can help the planner make the distance $d(\mu_{\beta(t)}, \mathscr{F}\bar{\beta}_{(t)})$ shrink rapidly as a function of time. The underlying phenomena in this shrinking is that as the planner's logic becomes more precise, his function $\mu_{\beta(t)}$ becomes more precise, and he comes closer to the goal of precision and efficient decision making. Besides Gaku's assistance, interacting with other planners through Gaku may influence the planner to take additional factors into account or to adjust his preference functions. In an ideal setting, of course, as time goes on, the distance between planners and the set of admissible fuzzy sets diminishes. The Delphi technique might be modified to include this approach.

A dynamic display of such changes over time may be dramatic (provided that a proper distance function is defined). Suppose we provide several distance functions for an experimenter to choose from in order to adjust to changing conditions until one appropriate for display is found. Time sequenced movements of $\mu_{\beta(t)}$'s and $\mu'_{\beta(t)}$'s for two planners may be seen in Fig. 2-B3.

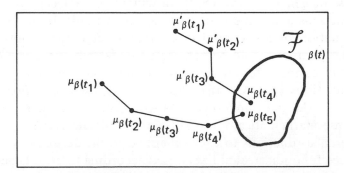

Figure 2-B3.   An example of two planners successively adjusting their preference functions.

In this diagram the encompassing rectangle represents a set of all fuzzy sets, and the points represent the preference functions for these sets. For convenience $\mathscr{F}_{\beta(t)}$ is assumed unchanged over time, but it may indeed change in real life. Since in real life there is seldom one exactly defined preference algorithm that is superior to all other $\mathscr{F}_{\beta(t)}$'s, the collection of admissible and precise preference functions is fuzzy. This further represents the real-world environment.

Other potential applications cover the areas of utility theory, Bayesian treatment of natural and psychological phenomena, correlation and manipulation of incentives by manipulating outcome variables and their probability measures, and other areas dealing with personal value orientations.

An important side issue may be worth noting. The planner's interactions with each other and with Gaku can be recorded and hard copies made, thus a very rich record of externalized accounts of how personal preferences are registered initially and how these may be changed through interaction, either as the result of better understanding of the environment or as the result of influence from others, or both, can be made available.

The same record can be used to protect the decision makers. The record can be summarized and its "hard" copy stored away for each important planning/decision-making situation. This will furnish protective evidence in the event the cost of a project is criticized by an outsider who does not have a good understanding of all of the factors that have been considered. Detailed accounts of how certain alternatives were rejected and others preferred in terms of complex trade-off implications would be valuable in such circumstances.

APPENDIX C

A SHORT DESCRIPTION OF THE USER ADAPTIVE LANGUAGE

The User Adaptive Language (UAL) is an extensible, functionally oriented language that has been designed to incorporate desirable features from many existing computer languages such as LISP* and TRAC† as well as some new ideas. User extensibility and readability are emphasized among other major features described below.

The "extensibility" of a language is its ability to modify itself. That is, its ability to create new primitive terms and functions and to define new infix operators. This becomes important when the problem situation dictates a new notation that the original language does not accept, or when new primitive terms are required to reduce complexity. These new terms and functions may not be known at the outset, but through interaction new ideas may be generated and the need for new terms and procedures realized. Thus, extensibility permits dynamic definition. The "readability" of a language is the rate at which information can be gathered from the language expressions themselves.

UAL is designed to provide a convenient and flexible means for man-machine communication in cooperative problem-solving/decision-making efforts. It enables the user to start interacting with the com-

*C. Weissman, *LISP,1.5 Primer,* Belmont, Calif., Dickenson Publishing Company, 1967.
†C. N. Mooers, "TRAC:A Procedure-Describing Language for the Reactive Type-writer," *Communications of the ACM*, Vol. 9, No. 3 (1966), 215–219.

puter even at the initial "rough-and-ready" stage of problem defini-tion and the "hunch-generation-and-testing" stage of problem solving (and perhaps back to the problem-definitional stage to repeat the process, if necessary). The user can easily define his own terms and concepts, procedures, relational assumptions, etc.; manipulate these terms and procedures in his own problem environment; view the results either statically or dynamically; and change or aggregate the previously defined terms and procedures. With these features, the user can communicate those actions and decision rules he wishes to delegate to the computer so that his own thinking can be focused on higher-level, strategic decision making. As a result, increasingly more complex situations can be analyzed thoroughly and quickly.

Some important features of the language are summarized here:

The basic data type is the set. Elements in a set can be sets, units of data, or even functional expressions, thus allowing functions and procedures to be stored and manipulated in the same manner as data elements and sets.

There are two types of assignments which can be done in the lan-guage: value changing and pointing. Each variable "points to" and is separate from its value. Thus, either the value itself may be changed, or the variable can point to a new value. The language makes use of a full list-structured technique. Lists, trees, and arrays may be manipu-lated as easily as single values. In addition, two or more lists may share members so that each is "aware" of a change in the other.

Arbitrary functions and infix operators may be defined or rede-fined, depending on the user's preference. New terms and procedures may be created to fit specific needs in the given problem situation, and to express complex ideas in a clear, readable fashion. The language is capable of redefining its own parts. The user may change the actions of any operator or change the way expressions are processed after entry.

The language is capable of supporting a semantic linkage for a given problem environment by defining a set of problem-oriented primitives; this allows other more specialized problem-oriented languages to be built upon it. The user may, if he wishes, work ex-clusively in the new language and divorce himself from the old one. Therefore, the new language can be made to assume characteristics close to the English language, or it can be made into a more stylized form.

Since the normal mode of operation is evaluation, expressions are evaluated immediately upon entry, and functional expressions themselves control the sequence of operations to be performed—a feature which makes it naturally suited for interaction. However, a means is provided to suppress evaluation when desired so that functional expressions can be stored and manipulated without evaluation.

The language is self-terminating. Each expression is built up from combinations of other expressions. Therefore, no special terminator for any statement is required. The entry of an incomplete expression simply results in the prompting of a continuation line.

A great deal of power and flexibility is provided in functional definition. The user has control over evaluation argument mapping, and the scope of variables.

REFERENCES
and Related Readings

Alexander, Christopher, *Notes on the Synthesis of Form*, Cambridge, Mass., Harvard University Press, 1962.

Amarel, S., "On the Mechanization of Creative Processes," *IEEE Spectrum*, Vol. 3, No. 3 (1966), 112–114.

_____, "An Approach to Heuristic Problem Solving and Theorem Proving in the Prepositional Calculus," in J. F. Hart and S. Takasu (eds.), *Systems and Computer Science*, Toronto, Canada, University of Toronto Press, 1967, 125–220.

_____, *On Representations and Modeling in Problem Solving and on Future Directions for Intelligent Systems*, Scientific Report No. 2, Princeton, N. J., Radio Corporation of America, June 1968.

Balzer, Robert M., "Search for a Solution: A Case Study," *Proceedings of the International Joint Conference on Artificial Intelligence*, Washington, D. C., 1969, 21–32.

Banerji, E. B., *The Theory of Problem Solving: An Approach to Artificial Intelligence*, New York, American Elsevier Publishing Company, 1969.

Becker, Joseph D., "The Modeling of Simple Analogic and Inductive Processes in a Semantic Memory System," *Proceedings of the International Joint Conference on Artificial Intelligence*, Washington, D. C., 1969, 655–668.

Bellman, R., and S. E. Dreyfus, *Applied Dynamic Programming*, RAND document R-352-PR, The RAND Corporation, Santa Monica, Calif., 1962.

Berlyne, D. E., *Structure and Direction in Thinking*, New York, John Wiley & Sons, Inc., 1965.

Bobrow, Daniel G., *Natural Communication with Computers*, Cambridge, Mass., Bolt, Beranek, and Newman, Inc., 1967.

_____, and Warren Teitelman, *Debugging in an On-Line Interactive LISP*, Cambridge, Mass., Bolt, Bernaek and Newman, Inc., 1967.

Bruner, J. S., Jacqueline J. Goodnow, and G. A. Austin, *A Study of Thinking,* New York, John Wiley & Sons, Inc., 1956.

_____ , "The Act of Discovery," *Harvard Educ. Rev.,* Vol. 31 (1961), 21–32.

Cady, George M., *Planning Activities and Applicable Techniques,* SDC document SP-3481, System Development Corporation, Santa Monica, Calif., 1970.

Citrenbaum, Ronald L., *The Planning Problem and a Survey of Applicable Techniques from the Field of Artificial Intelligence,* SDC document SP-3479, System Development Corporation, Santa Monica, Calif., 1970.

Colby, Kenneth M., and David C. Smith, "Dialogues Between Humans and an Artificial Belief System," *Proceedings of the International Joint Conference on Artificial Intelligence,* Washington, D. C., 1969, 319–324.

_____ , Lawrence Tesler, and Horace Enea, "Experiments with a Search Algorithm for the Data Base of a Human Belief System," *Proceedings of the International Joint Conference on Artificial Intelligence,* Washington, D. C., 1969, 649–654.

Coles, L. Stephen, "Talking with a Robot in English," *Proceedings of the International Joint Conference on Artificial Intelligence,* 1969, 587–596.

Culler, Glen J., "An Attack on the Problems of Speech Analysis and Synthesis with the Power of an On-Line System," *Proceedings of the International Joint Conference on Artificial Intelligence,* 1969, 41–48.

Curry, James E., "A Tablet Input Facility for an Interactive Graphics System," *Proceedings of the International Joint Conference on Artificial Intelligence,* 1969, 33–40.

Dalkey, Norman, "An Experimental Study of Group Opinion: The Delphi Method," *FUTURES*, Vol. 1, No. 5 (1969), 408–426.

Davis, M. R., and T. O. Ellis, "The RAND Tablet: A Man-Machine Graphical Communication Device," *AFIPS Conference Proceedings,* Vol. 26, Part 1, 1964 Fall Joint Computer Conference, Baltimore, Md., Spartan Books, 1964, 325–331.

Davis, Ruth M., "Man-Machine Communication," in Carlos A. Cuadra (ed.), *Annual Review of Information Science and Technology,* New York, Interscience, Vol. 1, 1966, 221–254.

Eastman, Charles M., "Cognitive Processes and Ill-Defined Problems: A Case Study from Design," *Proceedings of the International Joint Conference on Artificial Intelligence,* Washington, D. C., 1969, 669–690.

Emery, J. C., "The Planning Process and Its Formalization in Computer Models," *Proceedings of the Second Congress of Information Systems Science,* 1964, 369–389.

Engelbart, Douglas C., and William K. English, "A Research Center for Augmenting Human Intellect," *Proceedings of the Fall Joint Computer Conference,* 1968, San Francisco, 395–410.

Engelman, C., *MATHLAB: A Program for On-Line Machine Assistance in Symbolic Computations,* MITRE Report MPT-18, MITRE Corp., Bedford, Mass., 1965.

Evans, T. G., "Machine-Aided Design of Context-Free Grammars," *Association for Computing Machinery, Proceedings of the 20th National Conference, 1965,* New York, Lewis Winner, 1965, 344–353.

Feigenbaum, E. A., and J. Feldman (eds.), *Computers and Thought,* New York, John Wiley & Sons, Inc., 1963.

Findler, Nicholas V., and Wiley R. McKinzie, "On a Tool in Artificial Intelligence Research: An Associative Memory, Parallel Language, AMPPL-II," *Proceedings of the International Joint Conference on Artificial Intelligence,* Washington, D. C., 1969, 259–270.

Frye, C. H., F. D. Bennik, and S. L. Feingold, *Interim User's Guide to PLANIT: The Author-Language of the Instructor's Computer Utility,* SDC document TM-3055/000/03, System Development Corporation, Santa Monica, Calif., 1968.

Green, Cordell, "Application of Theorem Proving to Problem Solving," *Proceedings of the International Joint Conference on Artificial Intelligence,* Washington, D. C., 1969, 219–240.

Greenberger, M., et al., *On-Line Computation and Simulation; the OPS-3 System,* Cambridge, Mass., M.I.T. Press, 1965.

Helmer, O., "The Delphi Technique and Educational Innovation," in O. Helmer, et al., *Social Technology,* New York, Basic Books, Inc., Publishers, 1966.

Hormann, Aiko M., "Programs for Machine Learning, Part I," *Information and Control,* Vol. 5, No. 4 (1962), 347–367.

_____, "Programs for Machine Learning, Part II," *Information and Control,* Vol. 7, No. 1 (1964), 55–77

_____, "How a Computer System Can Learn," *IEEE Spectrum,* Vol. 1, No. 7 (1964), 110–119.

_____, Gaku: An Artificial Student," *Behavioral Science,* Vol. 10, No. 1, (1965), 88–107.

_____, *Designing a Machine Partner—Prospects and Problems,* SDC document SP-2169/000/01, System Development Corporation, Santa Monica, Calif., 1965.

_____, *A New Task Environment for Gaku Teamed with a Man,* SDC document TM-2311/003/00, System Development Corporation, Santa Monica, Calif., 1966.

_____, *Problem Solving and Learning by Man-Machine Teams (Summary of Current and Projected Work),* SDC document SP-3336/000/01, System Development Corporation, Santa Monica, Calif., 1969.

_____, *Application Problems of Man-Machine Techniques,* SDC document TM(L)-4452, System Development Corporation, Santa Monica, Calif., 1969.

——, *Planning by Man-Machine Synergism: Characterization of Processes and Environment,* SDC document SP-3484, System Development Corporation, Santa Monica, Calif., 1970.

_____, David Crandell, and Antonio Leal, *User Adaptive Language (UAL): A Step Toward Man-Machine Synergism.* SDC document TM-4539, System Development Corporation, Santa Monica, Calif., 1970.

_____, *Machine-Aided Value Judgments Using Fuzzy-Set Techniques,* SDC document SP-3590, System Development Corporation, Santa Monica, Calif., 1971a.

_____, "A Man-Machine Synergistic Approach to Planning and Creative Problem Solving: Part I," *International Journal of Man-Machine Studies,* Vol. 3, No. 2 (1971b).

_____, "A Man-Machine Synergistic Approach to Planning and Creative Problem Solving: Part II," *International Journal of Man-Machine Studies,* Vol. 3, No. 3 (1971c).

Hunt, E. G., *Concept Learning: An Information Processing Problem,* New York, John Wiley & Sons, Inc., 1962.

Jefferson, David K., "An Introduction to the Heuristic Programming System," *Proceedings of the International Joint Conference on Artificial Intelligence,* Washington, D. C., 1969, 253–258.

Jones, Malcolm M., *Incremental Simulation on a Time-Shared Computer,* Thesis, Massachusetts Institute of Technology, 1967.

Kahn, Herman, and Anthony J. Wiener, *The Year 2000,* New York, The Macmillan Co., 1967.

Kellogg, C. H., "Natural Language Compiler for On-Line Data Management," *Proceedings of Fall Joint Computer Conference,* Vol. 33 (1968), 473–494.

_____, and J. Burger, "Progress in Natural Language Data Management," *Proceedings of the Third Hawaii International Conference on System Sciences,* 1970, 846–849.

Kelly, J. L., Jr., and O. G. Selfridge, "Sophistication in Computers: A Disagreement," *IRE Transactions on Information Theory,* IT-8, (1962), 78–80.

Kleine, H., and R. L. Citrenbaum, *An On-Line Interactive Hierarchical Organization and Management System for Planning,* SDC document SP-3482, System Development Corporation, Santa Monica, Calif., 1970.

Kleinmuntz, Benjamin, (ed.), *Problem Solving,* New York, John Wiley & Sons, Inc., 1966.

_____, (ed.), *Formal Representation of Human Judgment,* New York, John Wiley & Sons, Inc., 1968.

Kochen, Manfred, "Adaptive Mechanisms in Digital 'Concept' Processing," in Manfred Kochen (ed.), *The Growth of Knowledge: Readings on Organization and Retrieval of Information,* New York, John Wiley & Sons, 1967, 185–202. Discussion by Merrill M. Flood, 202–203. (Reprinted from *Proceedings of the Joint Automatic Computer Conference,* American Institute of Electrical Engineers, 1962, 49–59.)

Laska, R. M., "MIS: Rx for Local Government Malaise," *Computer Decisions,* Vol. 2, No. 2 (1970), 28–36.

Lederberg, Joshua, and Edward A. Feigenbaum, *Mechanization of Inductive Inference in Organic Chemistry,* Stanford Artificial Intelligence Project Memo No. 54, Stanford University, Stanford, Calif., 1967, 29.

Licklider, J.C.R., "Interactive Dynamic Modeling," in George Shapiro and Milton Rogers (eds.), *Prospects for Simulation and Simulators of Dynamic Systems,* Washington, D.C., Spartan Books, 1967, 281–289.

_____, "Man-Computer Communication," in Carlos A. Cuadra (ed.), *Annual Review of Information Science and Technology,* Vol. 3, Chicago, Encyclopaedia Britannica, Inc., 201–240.

_____, "Man-Computer Partnership," *International Science Technology,* No. 4 (1965), 18–26.

_____, and Robert W. Taylor, "The Computer as a Communication Device," *International Science Technology,* No. 76 (1968), 21–31.

Lientz, B. P., *On Time-Dependent Fuzzy Sets,* SDC document SP-3485, System Development Corporation, Santa Monica, Calif., 1970.

McCarthy, J., "Programs with Common Sense," in *Mechanization of Thought Processes,* Vol. 1 (National Physical Laboratory Symposium No. 10), London, Her Majesty's Stationery Office, 1959, 75–84.

Manheim, Marvin L., *Hierarchical Structure: A Model of Planning and Design Processes,* Cambridge, Mass., M.I.T. Press, 1966.

____, *Problem-Solving Processes in Planning and Design,* Professional Paper P67-3, Massachusetts Institute of Technology, Department of Civil Engineering, Cambridge, Mass., M.I.T. Press, 1967.

Miller, G. A., "The Magical Number Seven, Plus or Minus Two," *Psychology Review,* Vol. 63 (1965), 81–97.

____, E. Galanter, and K. H. Pribram, *Plans and the Structure of Behavior,* New York, Henry Holt and Co., 1960.

Milne, Murray, *The Design Process,* Master's Thesis, University of California at Berkeley, 1965.

Minsky, M., "Steps Toward Artificial Intelligence," *Proceedings of the Institute of Radio Engineers,* Vol. 49 (1961), 8–30.

____, "Matter, Mind, and Models in Information Processing," in *Proceedings of IFIP Congress 65,* W. A. Kalenich (ed.), Washington, D. C., Spartan Books, Vol 1 (1965), 45–59.

____, (ed.), *Semantic Information Processing,* Cambridge, Mass., M.I.T. Press, 1968.

Montalbano, M. S., *High-Speed Calculations of the Critical Paths of Large Networks,* Technical Report 320–3204, IBM Scientific Center, Palo Alto, Calif., 1965.

Newell, Allen, *Learning, Generality, and Problem Solving,* RAND document RM-3285-1-PR, The RAND Corporation, Santa Monica, Calif., 1963.

____, "On the Representations of Problems," in *Computer Science Research Review, 1966,* Annual Report, Carnegie Institute of Technology, Pittsburgh, Pa., 1966, 19–23.

____, and George W. Ernst, "Some Issues of Representation in a General Problem Solver," *Proceedings of the Spring Joint Computer Conference,* 1967, 583–599.

____, and George W. Ernst. *GPS: A Case Study in Generality and Problem Solving,* New York, Academic Press, Inc., 1969.

____, and H. Simon. "Problem-Solving Machines," *International Science and Technology,* No. 36 (1964), 46–62.

——, "Remarks on the Relationship Between Artificial Intelligence and Cognitive Psychology," in Banerji and Mesarovic (eds.) *Theoretical Approaches to Non-Numerical Problem Solving,* Berlin. Springer-Verlag, 1970, 363–400.

Nilsson, N. J., "Searching Problem Solving and Game Playing Trees for Minimal Cost Solutions," *Proceedings of the IFIP Congress,* 1968, H-125–H-130.

____, "A Mobile Automation: An Application of Artificial Intelligence Techniques," *Proceedings of the International Joint Conference on Artificial Intelligence,* Washington, D. C., 1969, 509–520.

Oettinger, Anthony G., *Technological Aids to Creative Thought (Project TACT),*

Progress Report, Cambridge, Mass., Harvard University Computation Laboratory, 1966.

Press, Lawrence I., Miles S. Rogers, Gerald H. Shure, "An Interactive Technique For the Analysis of Multivariate Data," *Behavioral Science,* Vol. 14, No. 5 (1969), 364–370.

Quillian, M. R., and D. G. Bobrow, "Growing a Semantic Memory from English Text," Presented at *Fifth Annual Meeting of the Association for Machine Translation and Computational Linguistics,* Atlantic City, N.J., 1967.

Quinlan, J. R., "A Task-Independent Experience-Gathering Scheme for a Problem Solver," *Proceedings of the International Joint Conference on Artificial Intelligence,* Washington, D.C., 1969, 193–198.

Raphael, B., *SIR: A Computer Program for Semantic Information Retrieval,* Ph.D. Dissertation, Cambridge, Mass., M.I.T. Press, 1964.

Reitman, W. R., *Cognition and Thought,* New York, John Wiley & Sons, Inc., 1965.

Restle, F., *Psychology of Judgment and Choice,* New York, John Wiley & Sons, Inc., 1961.

Roberts, L. G., "Graphical Communication and Control Languages," in J. Spiegel and D. E. Walker (eds.), *Information System Sciences; Proceedings of the Second Congress, Hot Springs, Va., 1964,* Washington, D. C., Spartan Books, 1965, 211–217.

Rosove, P. E., *A Provisional Survey and Evaluation of the Current Forecasting State of the Art for Possible Contributions to Long-Range Educational Policy Making,* SDC document TM-3640, System Development Corporation, Santa Monica, Calif., 1967.

Rovner, Paul D., and Dugald A. Henderson, Jr., "On the Implementation of AMBIT/G: A Graphical Programming Language," *Proceedings of the International Joint Conference on Artificial Intelligence,* Washington, D. C., 1969, 9–20.

Sackman, H., *Advanced Research in On-Line Planning: Critique and Recommendations,* SDC document SP-3480, System Development Corporation, Santa Monica, Calif., 1970.

Sandewall, Erik J., "Concepts and Methods for Heuristic Search," *Procedures of the International Joint Conference on Artificial Intelligence,* Washington, D.C., 1969, 199–218.

Seaborg, Glenn T., "Birth Pangs of a New World." *The FUTURIST,* Vol. 4, No. 6, (1970) 205–208.

Shaw, J. C., *JOSS: Conversations with the Johnniac Open-Shop System,* RAND document P-3146, the RAND Corporation, Santa Monica, Calif., 1965.

Shelly, M. W., and G. L. Bryan (eds.), *Human Judgments and Optimality,* New York, John Wiley & Sons, Inc., 1964.

Shure, Gerald H., Robert J. Meeker, and William H. Moore, Jr., "TRACE—Time-Shared Routines for Analysis, Classification and Evaluation," *Proceedings of the Spring Joint Computer Conference,* 1967, 525–529.

Simmons, R. F., *On-Line Interactive Displays in Application to Linguistic Analysis and Information Processing and Retrieval,* SDC document SP-2432/001/00, System Development Corporation, Santa Monica, Calif., 1966.

Simon, Herbert A., *The Sciences of the Artificial,* Cambridge, Mass., M.I.T. Press, 1959.

Slagle, J. R., and J. K. Dixon, "Experiments with Some Programs that Search Game Trees," *ACM Journal,* Vol. 16, No. 2 (1969), 189–207.

Sutherland, Ivan E., *Sketchpad: A Man-Machine Graphical Communication System,* Lincoln Lab Technical Report 296, Massachusetts Institute of Technology, Lexington, Mass., 1963.

____, "Computer Displays," *Scientific American,* Vol. 222, No. 6, June 1970, 56–81.

Sutherland, William R., "Language Structure and Graphical Man-Machine Communication," in Donald E. Walker (ed)., *Information System Science and Technology,* Washington, D. C., Thompson, 1967, 29–31.

Teitelman, Warren, "Toward a Programming Laboratory," *Proceedings of the International Joint Conference on Artificial Intelligence,* Washington, D. C., 1969, 1–8.

Tolman, E. C., "Cognitive Maps in Rats and Men," in E. C. Tolman (ed.), *Behavior and Psychological Man, Essays in Motivation and Learning,* Berkeley and Los Angeles, University of California Press, 1958, 241–264.

Uhr, Leonard, and Manfred Kochen, "MIKROKOSMS and Robots," *Proceedings of the International Joint Conference on Artificial Intelligence,* Washington, D.C., 1969, 541–556.

Wagner, Harvey M., *Principles of Operations Research, with Applications to Managerial Decisions,* Englewood Cliffs, N. J., Prentice-Hall, Inc., 1969.

Waldinger, Richard J., and Richard C. T. Lee, "PROW: A Step Toward Automatic Program Writing," *Proceedings of the International Joint Conference on Artificial Intelligence,* Washington, D. C., 1969, 241–252.

Wigington, R. L., "Graphics and Speech, Computer Input and Output for Communication with Humans," in. F. Gruenberger (ed.), *Computer Graphics,* Washington, D. C., Thompson, 1967, 81–98.

Willmorth, N. E., *Human Factors Experimentation in An Interactive Planning System,* SDC document SP-3483, System Development Corporation, Santa Monica, Calif., 1970.

Zadeh, L. A., "Fuzzy Sets," *Information and Control,* Vol. 8 (1965), 338–353.

3

PLANNING AND
ARTIFICIAL INTELLIGENCE

R. L. Citrenbaum

Abstract

Among the initial problems in developing online computer systems for planning is the identification of desired capabilities for such systems, and the specification of techniques and methods useful for implementation. To provide background on the overall problem of planning, the paper opens with an overview of generalized planning. A subjective definition of generalized planning is included along with the role and scope of planning. The hierarchical structure of planning is discussed, and introductory thoughts on computer-aided planning are presented. Newly emerging disciplines are reviewed, and several general-purpose, problem-solving techniques are considered briefly.

The remainder of the chapter is devoted to artificial intelligence as a basis for techniques in computer planning. The field of artificial intelligence is surveyed in its primary areas of study. After criticism of approaches taken and general assumptions made by workers in the field, the basic techniques utilized in artificial intelligence are extracted and briefly analyzed.

The primary conclusion is that planning problems fall

into the realm of nonformal, ill-defined problems, precisely the area in which the payoff in artificial intelligence research has been minimal. It is suggested that interactive man-machine systems may provide an answer to this difficulty, and man-machine systems are discussed relative to the independent capabilities of both man and machine.

3-1 THE GENERALIZED PLANNING PROBLEM

3-1-1 Definition and Role of Plans

"Planning" is a process in which an individual or group of people endeavor to handle a given problem by a well-thought-out procedure. "Generalized planning" is the formal process of explicitly generating the alternative courses of action for a given abstract problem and selecting one of these alternatives by means of some evaluating criteria. Such planning may encompass a variety of tasks. Among them are the design of an appropriate model (abstract or real) of the problem under study, the selection and implementation of tools to manipulate the model, the choice of techniques to evaluate data generated by the model, and the development of resources and details to handle the actual planning process chosen.

The output of any planning process is the choice of a "plan" or set of plans constituting a technique to elicit behavior leading to desired outcomes. Thus, for a given problem a plan must specify the necessary inputs, required actions, and predicted outcomes. The complete specification of a plan consists of determining the problem variables and either placing values on the variables or establishing their functional form by use of an appropriate model.

Often a plan is used as a structural model itself. This is evident in the use of a plan to display the hierarchical structure of a corporation. Here the plan provides a means of coordinating activities of various levels, indicating both command and communication structure.

3-1-2 The Scope of Planning Problems

The scope of planning may be classified into two distinct categories—types of planning and general areas of application. Branch (1966) distinguishes three types of planning. In order of increasing complexity they are "functional planning," "project planning," and "comprehensive planning." Functional planning is detailed planning, usually within the realm of a single discipline, of a subsystem or small portion of a larger operation. Project planning normally includes a wider range of disciplines than functional planning. A diverse variety of scientific fields may be involved—some on the basis of quantitative precision, others utilizing aspects of reasoning, testing, and even accumulated experience. In essence, project planning embodies the application of progressive knowledge and successive experience to attain desired goals. Comprehensive planning is the highest-level planning process, encompassing the whole of human awareness, knowledge, and capacity to consider and act as applied to achieving a major endeavor. While it includes functional and project planning, it transcends them in both magnitude and complexity. The fantastic accomplishments by the space program that placed man on the moon are a prime example of comprehensive planning. Note that the scope of this project includes far more than the marvelous engineering feats involved; an enormous expenditure of money attaches profound social and philosophical sidelights which deeply affect the overall planning decisions.

The general areas of planning application include "city planning," "corporate planning," and "military planning."

City planning involves two distinct categories: planning a new city, and the evolutionary shaping of an existing blossoming community. The history of city planning dates back to ancient Egypt and much of the existing literature on planning is devoted solely to the layout of cities.

Organized comprehensive planning, on the other hand, is a relatively new vehicle for top corporate management. The sophisticated discipline of operations research, management science, general systems theory, and systems engineering are newly emerging from pure research techniques and accumulated corporate management experience. (These disciplines are individually described and discussed in Section 3–1-5.) Comprehensive corporate planning attempts to apply scientific method and quantitative analysis to the corporation, utilizing the aforementioned techniques when applicable. It is concerned not only with elements presently enveloped in the system but projects into the future, coping with intangible as well as quantifiable aspects. It is often constrained by time to produce a best or alternative set of plans within some formal limits—changing perhaps by on-going events. Resultant plans must be formulated clearly so as to be understandable to middle and lower management, and in addition must be amenable to be placed into operation immediately, while being flexible enough to be periodically reviewed and revised. Most important, a corporate plan must be responsive to the needs, potentials, and realities of the overall enterprise such that it produces demonstrable results and confidence in its execution.

Military planning is similar to corporate planning in that the basic logistics are comparable. Most of the fields fundamental in nonmilitary planning are likewise important in military planning. The differences in military planning lie in the nature of the military's objectives: preparation for conflict, victory in war, and national survival regardless of cost. The flow of information and use of information and solution techniques may be severely restricted because of security classification. This has the effect of strengthening the chain of control by concentrating knowledge as well as authority.

The dividing line between the various areas of planning described above appears to be becoming less distinct. Matters of overall national objective and productive activities are of prime importance during both war and peace. Developmental strategy during peacetime illustrates that war is more or less continuous—its immediate state being either "hot" or "cold."

3-1-3 The Hierarchical Structure of Planning

The development of a complex plan often cannot be handled as a single independent problem. The objectives must be decomposed and partitioned into more manageable subobjectives, each of which may be further decomposed into still smaller subobjectives. This process continues until the resulting subobjectives generated are manageable with no further decomposition necessary. The overall structure of objectives and subobjectives forms a hierarchy.

The hierarchical structure of planning can be represented both geometrically and by means of tree-like structures. A detailed description of these representations is presented in Sections 7–2-3 and 7–2-4 of Chapter 7. The planning of any particular subobjective in the hierarchical structure of a given planning problem constitutes a "single-level" planning process. This process is characterized by five steps (Emery, 1964):

1. Determine the planning data.
2. Generate alternate plans and predict their capabilities.
3. Choose the best alternative.
4. Convert the plan into an executable form.
5. Revise the plan periodically using iterative feedback.

The determination of the planning data is highly dependent on the relative level of the subobjective being planned within the planning hierarchy. In general, the higher the level in the hierarchy, the less detailed the data. Thus, high-level planning can basically constrain lower-level planning by restricting the data to be considered. In addition, it can constrain lower-level planning by restricting goals, specifying structure, resources, and policy, and by defining procedural techniques to be utilized.

A strong hierarchical planning process maintains the capability of revising plans by means of an iterative cycle. Such a cycle begins with the formulation of a high-level preliminary plan. Lower-level planners using this plan as a guide, and supplemented with more detailed information obtained from planners at still lower levels, may propose plans which they consider realistic. Then the higher-level planner may utilize these proposals to modify the original plan in a constructive manner. This cyclic procedure continues until the planning process has converged to the satisfaction of all involved. The transference of planning information across hierarchical levels aided by the iterative cycle may reveal a low-resolution, high-level planning model to be unrealistic due to poor basic assumptions. Thus, it is the responsibility of low-level planners to point out unrealistic aspects of high-level plans and to generate more realistic plans through an explicit iterative cycle. It is important that no strong bias against "upward" flow of information (low-level to high-level) is present in a planning hierarchy, or unrealistic high-level plans can result.

3-1-4 Computer-aided Planning

Basic Facets of a Man-Machine System. The use of computers as an aid to man in the formulation of plans and for improved decision processes offers exciting potentialities. The overall planning process can be vastly improved by a man-machine symbiosis utilizing the best features of both man and machine. As men are superior to machines in the vague areas of pattern recognition and generalization to determine meaning and representation, a man could assume the higher-level planning tasks: proposing interesting basic assumptions in conjunction with a variety of constraints. The computer, utilizing its prowess as an incomparable data processor in both speed and accuracy, could generate the appropriate alternatives and test them for some desired criteria, yielding a set of utility values.

To date, computers have been used in just this way. Comparatively little use has been made of computers for high-level "strategic planning," while their use for low-level operational control has been widespread.

There are several inherent advantages to a man-machine system. First, and perhaps foremost, is that the decision processes need not be completely formalized. The computer model of the planning process can incorporate those decision processes which are formalized, while the human can handle the vague concepts. By means of iterative feedback the vague concepts can become better understood, resulting in a completely formalized model. Another advantage of the man-machine system is the vast amount of power gained by the planner. Whereas planning may remain a hierarchical structure, a single planner can have access to several levels in the hierarchy. Not only can he formulate a high-level plan, but, by use of the computer to sequentially search through a low-resolution lower-level planning space described by an aggregate model, he can immediatley iterate and explore the plan in greater depth by means of higher-resolution models. In addition, the global planning objective need not be subpartitioned to the extent necessitated by the lack of a computer, since the computer can handle far greater complexity than the unaided planner. While computer models will not change the basic iterative aspects of hierarchical planning, the identification of unrealistic high-level plans during the search through low level derivatives of these plans will be greatly enhanced in a man-machine system. Finally, by speeding up the planning process by means of a man-machine team, a greater number of alternative plans can be considered in a present time period. With more alternatives considered, the probability rises that a superior plan will be found. Furthermore, the increased time allotted the planner to consider alternatives rather than perform detailed calculations, combined with the quick turnaround time of his queries, is conducive to creative thought. Hopefully, this "bonus" time will be utilized in creating new alternatives, or trying interesting combinations of those previously considered.

A residual advantage of the man-machine system is the possibility of a change in the balance between cost and value of additional planning. If the use of the information processing equipment is low compared with the use of a team of planners, this could provide a strong argument for consideration of additional alternatives to strengthen the resulting plans.

Interactive Aids—Graphic Displays and Voice I/O.   Graphic displays have become quite prominent in the last few years as a means of increasing man's capabilities and his overall flexibility in dealing with the computer. A variety of support media for graphic I/O has been and continues to be developed. Prominent among these are light detecting "light pens," electron beam detecting "beam pens," capacitive and inductively coupled tablets or writing surfaces, mechanically coupled wheels, two-dimensional sheet potentiometers, and shaft encoded knobs. Although graphics displays have provided unique applications in open loop systems (such as producing animated cartoons, processing nuclear event bubble-chamber photographs, data reduction and plotting, etc., their prime interest in man-machine systems is in the closed loop mode. Some of the more interesting applications (Wigington, 1967) in the area include (a) computed and displayed effects of drawing models of objects as design alterations are made, (b) real-time plotting of online parameter insertion, (c) online recognition of handwriting using time sequence information, (d) graphical presentation of alternate process decisions for choice by human user, (e) development of problem solutions as directed by user.

The use of speech for computer I/O is strongly motivated by the desire to exploit the computer as a utility for the masses. As telephones are readily available in almost every home and office, this could have far-reaching consequences. However, while a few commercial speech output devices for computers or computer-controlled systems have been announced, automatic recognition of speech by machine is proving to be a highly complex task. One of the best experimental systems, investigated at Stanford, is limited to a vocabulary of only 560 words with a recognition time of approximately 15 seconds per word and an accuracy of 95 to 98 percent. This system uses recognition techniques based on "easily extracted acoustic distinctive features (which may or may not be related to phonological distinctive features) and depends strongly on structural relationships of work-level and sentence-level syntax," (Stanford Artificial Intelligence Project Memo, 1969).

3-1-5   Disciplines and Techniques Useful in Planning

A variety of disciplines, tools, and techniques pertinent to the planning process has developed in recent years. A brief examination of four general disciplines, each of which has given rise to its own types of methods and techniques, is followed by a discussion of those particular techniques which may be useful in an online planning system.

Operations Research: An area which utilizes the scientific method to employ mathematics and techniques from the physical and social sciences for the quantitative-numerical solution of problems. The major phases of an OR project include formulating a problem, constructing a mathematical model to represent the system under study, testing the model and the solution desired from it, establishing control over the solution, and, finally, implementing the solution. In the last several years OR has brought about significant advances in the methods of analyzing business operations and functional planning, particularly in the areas of inventory studies, allocation problems (linear programming), waiting-time models (queuing theory), replacement criteria, and competitive considerations (game theory).

Systems Engineering: A new approach to engineering problems focusing on the mathematical interrelationships between components in a complex system. It is particularly concerned with the organization and integration of the components or subsystems to achieve a desired end result in an optimal fashion. Modern advances in feedback-control systems and optimization theory, leading to such wonders as space vehicles, large interconnected computer complexes, and complex communication hardware, are direct beneficiaries of this newly developing science.

General Systems Theory: An attempt to abstract the fundamental basis of systems theory in one quantitative formulation. Because of its general and loose structure, it has not yet led to any meaningful new applicable techniques for solving real problems. Most likely, it will remain theoretical for some time yet because of its almost unlimited depth and complexity.

Management Science: An outgrowth of operations research that places great emphasis on econometrics. As such it may be considered broader in scope and intent than OR. Management science has become a prominent topic in graduate courses in business administration, and its emphasis on mathematics and the scientific method is bringing great changes to the area of business administration.

In 1967 an interesting survey of forecasting methods, useful for estimating value in stimulating public dialogue, was made by Rosove. Although he applied his results to long-range educational policy making, many of the methods he outlined (some of which are derived from the above disciplines) are equally applicable to the planning problem. The twenty-one methods he distinguished are listed below in their rank order of capability to provide seven major functions, including generating possible alternatives, exploring the alternative pathways, exploring the decision consequences, achieving public dialogue, training policy makers, conducting selected research, and identifying information needs. The methods are:

1.	Gaming	12.	Benefit-Cost Analysis
2.	Operational Simulation	13.	Input/Output Tables
3.	Delphi Technique	14.	Time-Sense Extrapolation
4.	Deterministic Models	15.	Morphological Analysis
5.	Probabilistic Models	16.	Contextual Analysis
6.	Scenarios	17.	Content Analysis
7.	Social Accounting	18.	Primary Determinant
8.	Expert Opinion	19.	Historical Analogy
9.	Decision Matrices	20.	Historical Sequences
10.	Relevance trees	21.	Literary Fiction
11.	Brainstorming		

In addition to these techniques, other useful methods include linear and nonlinear programming (Hadley, 1964), dynamic programming (Bellman, 1956; Bellman and Dreyfus, 1962), graph theoretic analyses (Berge, 1962; Busacher, et al., 1965), PERT and CPM (Moder and Phillips, 1964), PPB (Chapter 4 of this book), dialectical planning (Mason, 1969), allocation and transportation problem methods including shortest path algorithm, etc. (Chapter 6 of this book), mathematical optimization techniques, and various extensions of these techniques amenable to online operation. Although a wealth of methods have been named above, it should not be inferred that each should be considered as an independent approach to a planning problem. For many objectives, whole strings of methods may be needed. This was stressed by Rosove in his work. Thus, for any given problem type a planner may either apply a preset string of methods which were useful in solving similar problems in the past, or may attempt to synthesize a suitable string from the available "library" of methods.

3-2 ARTIFICIAL INTELLIGENCE

Perhaps computer-aided planning can be enhanced by using some of the techniques that have been developed and investigated in recent years in the area of artificial intelligence. Artificial intelligence is a budding field, growing out of the realm of heuristic data processing and encompassing the theoretical and experimental study of perceptual and intellectual processes by using computers. Its ultimate goal is to formulate and thereby understand these processes sufficiently to enable a computer to perceive, comprehend, and behave in a manner now possible only for humans.

In this section the techniques utilized in artificial intelligence are scrutinized and applicability to the generalized planning problem is considered. First, however, an orderly examination of the field provides a suitable framework for this study.

To achieve a consistency with established literature, the ordering of much of the information included in this survey of artificial intelligence follows that found in a critique of the field by Dreyfus (1965).

3-2-1 Basic Areas of Artificial Intelligence

The most important work in artificial intelligence to date can be classified into four main areas:

1. Game playing.
2. Problem solving.
3. Semantic information processes and language translation.
4. Pattern recognition.

Game Playing. Of the four areas mentioned above, perhaps the most fascinating to the researcher is game playing. Game environments are useful in studying the nature and structure of complex problem-solving processes, and, in addition, provide man the amusing opportunity to challenge his wits against a machine. The relatively highly regular and well-defined problem environments characteristic of games in general provide an excellent foundation for the use of intelligence and symbolic reasoning skills. Hopefully, a thorough understanding of the theory of game playing will enable man to formulate problems closer to realistic applications. It should be stressed that games are not studied because they are clear and simple. To quote Minsky (1968): "It is that they give us for the smallest initial structures, the greatest complexity, so that one can engage in some really formidable situations after a relatively minimal diversion into programming." Thus, many game-playing situations (such as in chess) exhibit a complexity of structure beyond those of the problem-solving situations one normally encounters in everyday life (provided the intangibles of the real-life situation can somehow be removed). A primary difference between game playing and planning situations lies in the origin of the uncertainties. In a game, the uncertainties result from the large number of alternatives available, while the objectives as well as the rules are rather simply stated. However, in many actual planning situations, the uncertainties are essential attributes resulting from an imperfect knowledge of the environment. Furthermore, the problem itself is usually stated in a fairly complex manner, involving a large number of variables. Hence, the study of game playing might be relevant to only those real-life planning problems in which the structure remains complex even after removal of the intangibles.

The game which has received the most attention thus far in artificial intelligence is chess. Obviously, any game which is sufficiently complex and subtle in its implications to have allowed a deepening analysis through centuries of intensive study and play without becoming exhausted is an excellent target for machine studies. Work to date is based mainly on a pioneering paper by Shannon (1950) which pointed out that although chess is a finite game (there are approximately 10^{120} move possibilities—as contrasted with 10^{16} microseconds in a century), application of a minimaxing technique would be impossible on even the fastest digital computer because of the large number of possibilities to be explored. Shannon proposed that minimax continuations be explored to a certain practical depth and static evaluations then be made to determine the move with the highest effective value. To do this he suggested a numerical measure, based on various features that chess experts consider important, be formed by summing a number of factors that can be computed for any position. While Shannon did not present a particular computer program, his specifications helped pave the way for many prototypes, the latest of which has achieved success in novice chess tournaments (Newell, et al., 1958; Greenblatt, 1967).

However, the classic research in game playing is a checker-playing program which has progressed to a championship level by means of clever learning heuristics (Samuel, 1958 and 1967). It is an example of pure artificial intelligence in that it does not attempt to simulate human information processing. Positions are evaluated by using a weighted sum of a selected set of "property" functions (features) of the positions (i.e., center control, advancement, mobility, etc.), and a move is made on the basis of the difference between what the evaluation function yields directly of a position and what it predicts on the basis of extensive continuation exploration (i.e., looking ahead). The difference calculated is used for reinforcement and the system effectively learns at each move.

It should be emphasized that the major importance of game playing is not so much to solve any particular game, but to utilize the game as a vehicle to derive new heuristic techniques for computer application. Because of this goal, the emphasis has shifted in the past few years from obtaining optimal solutions to problems of great complexity (such as chess) to developing techniques capable of handling whole classes of problems. Generality rather than complexity has become the vogue (Newell, 1963; Ernst and Newell, 1967). In this movement a major trend is the stress placed on effective problem representation. Many seemingly difficult problems can be easily solved when placed in a proper frame of reference and represented accordingly (Newell, 1969; Citrenbaum, 1969; Amarel, 1968).

Problem Solving.   Research in this area is concerned with understanding the complex heuristics effective in problem solving. Methods which guarantee solutions, but which require vast amounts of computation, are not of interest. Instead, emphasis is placed on understanding how a sicentist arrives at a conjecture or proof, even though he does not know how or if he is going to succeed when he starts.

Often during the course of solving a problem, one becomes involved with a set of interrelated subproblems. Should the subproblems prove to be a large set, only a few of the best alternatives may be explored; the selection being made by heuristic techniques based on estimates of relative difficulty and desirability. For really difficult problems, step by step heuristics to reduce search may fail, and an overall technique for analysis of the global problem structure may become necessary. In short, "planning" is necessary. Thus, planning itself may be considered as a technique to aid in problem solving.

The value of decomposing a complex problem by subdividing it into a number of parts, each of which can be attacked by a smaller search (or divided still further), should not be underestimated. The following discussion from Minsky (1961) elaborates on this point:

"Generally speaking, a successful division will reduce the search time not by a mere fraction, but by a *fractional exponent.* In a graph with 10 branches descending from each node, a 20-step search might involve 10^{20} trials, which is out of the question, while the insertion of just four *lemmas* or *sequential subgoals* might reduce the search to only 5×10^4 trials, which is within reason for machine exploration. Thus, it will be worth a relatively enormous effort to find such islands in the solution of complex problems. Note that even if one encountered, say, 10^6 failures of such procedures before success, one would still have gained a factor of perhaps 10^{10} in overall trial reduction. *Thus, practically any ability at all to 'plan' or 'analyze' a problem will be profitable* if the problem is difficult."

The initial significant achievement in problem solving within the realm of artificial intelligence was the Logic Theory Machine developed in the late 1950's (Newell, Shaw, and Simon, 1957). Using heuristically guided planning techniques, this program was successful in proving 38 out of 52 theorems from Russell's *Principia Mathematica.* The Logic Theory project was criticized by Wang (1963) on the grounds that there are mechanized proof methods (which he demonstrated) capable of ultimately finding proofs for any provable proposition by using far less machine effort. However, the goal of the Logic Theory project was primarily to develop heuristic techniques for solving complex problems by nonexhaustive methods, and to this end it succeeded marvelously.

An outgrowth of the Logic Theory project was a more general problem-solving system known appropriately as the GPS or General Problem Solver (Newell and Simon, 1963). The GPS uses the technique of means-end analysis to guide a heuristic tree search in attempting to solve problems. Essentially means-end analysis is a general technique which involves subdividing a problem into easier subproblems. It is applied in the GPS by taking differences between given and desired information. It then utilizes the differences to select a desirable operator, one relevant to reducing the differences. This yields a new "given" object and the original problem is rephrased by replacing the initial situation with the new object. Recycling follows. If no operator is applicable to an object, the reason it is not applicable is generated as a difference, and the GPS attempts to reduce this difference in the same way it reduces a difference between two objects.

Tasks which the GPS has successfully tackled include proving theorems in the first-order propositional calculus (similar to the logic theorist), the missionaries and cannibal problem, solving integral calculus problems, the tower of Hanoi puzzle, the monkey task, parsing sentences, three coins puzzle, father and sons task, and various other puzzles.

Banerji (1969) has written a book describing a formal theory of problem solving as an approach to artificial intelligence. It attempts to generalize the essential ingredients of several game playing techniques, the problem-solving methods of the GPS, and various pattern recognition schemes. We expect that other works along the same line with emphasis in general systems theory will follow.

Semantic Information Processing and Language Translation. The earliest successes in the field of artificial intelligence were accomplished in the mechanical translation of languages. In the middle 1950's translation research efforts were among the few well-financed nonnumerical projects. After solving many of the comparatively simple mechanical dictionary-type applications, however, linguistic workers in the area ran into a major stumbling block—linguistic ambiguities. The ambiguity problem that arose from word-by-word and sentence-by-sentence substitutions were found to be far more formidable than had previously been expected. So great have been the resulting problems that pessimism has clouded the entire field. It has generally been concluded that a high-quality automatic translation mechanism should be capable of representing situations as complex as those handled by a human translator. To assume this capability, the machine must assume an intelligence akin to that of a human subject learning material by reading a book.

Much of the work in recent years aims at this goal. Some of the interesting papers produced in the last several years are classified in the area of "semantic information processing," as opposed to language translation, and include reports on the following:

- An attempt has been made to build a memory structure that converts its input into an efficient systematic model (Raphael, 1964). The model provides a means of answering various kinds of questions by understanding statements as they are made, and using this understanding to add to or modify the existing model. The system is capable of utilizing context and past relationship usage to resolve statement ambiguities.

- A program has been written to solve algebra word problems by assuming that a collection of sentences must contain some algebraic relations between its objects and by making good guesses as to the relevant objects and relations to determine meaning. It is capable of setting up algebraic equations directly from verbal statements: precisely the problem that stymies many algebra students (Bobrow, 1964).

- A technique has been developed to resolve word ambiguity by building a network of objects and relations, and then comparing plausibilities of different interpretations by the strength of links between the various meanings (Quillian, 1966). This approach is a direct projection of earlier work on the logic theorist attempting to discover heuristics by modeling human behavior.

- A program has been developed which is capable of recognizing analogies between complex objects (Evans, 1963). On its highest level it can determine the similarities and differences between comparisons of objects in terms of relations between their descriptions, and thus is a realization of a concept of analogical reasoning. It has solved several problems taken directly from college-level intelligence tests.

- Work is progressing toward the development of a system for online conversation using ordinary English grammatical patterns. In such a system data bases of diverse content and structure may be described, interrogated, and modified. Data management in ordinary English will be accomplished by composing a user-extendable subset of English, a natural-language compiler to translate the English sentences into storage and search procedures, and a data-management machine to execute these procedures. Hopefully, this will provide the user with a natural, easy-to-use and powerful means of man-machine communication (Kellogg, 1968).

Pattern Recognition. Progress in the area of pattern recognition has been painstakingly slow. A prime reason lies in the enormous difficulty in the nature of the task. A man when abstracting a pattern from complex stimuli essentially has classified the possible inputs. But often the basis of the classification is unknown even to him; moreover, it is too complex to specify explicitly. Often patterns are defined ostensibly—only by example. (Consider, for example: these speech sounds are a request to throw the ball; that object is a history book; Most important patterns are defined by experience and the process of learning.

Initial areas of concern in the area of pattern recognition included optical character recognition and voice recognition. Additional areas which have come under study include hypothesis formation by machine, discrimination learning in random nets, perceptual learning in human beings, and recognition of meterological phenomena.

The typical pattern recognition program is either elaborately preprogrammed to handle specific types of input patterns, or is designed with ability to adjust its values and "learn." The former type cannot identify large classes of patterns that appear only trivially different to the human eye, and the latter type of self-adjusting program does not yet possess methods for accumulating experience sufficiently powerful to succeed in interesting cases. Much of the work in self-organizing systems is characterized by the latter approach.

The most important learning process in pattern recognition is the generation and evaluation of the crucial features of an input pattern. An early program which met limited success in this regard was one by Uhr and Vossler (1963), designed to recognize hand-printed letters using a 20×20 digitized input matrix. Today the trend is away from the general, and toward solving specific pattern recognition problems with hard, sure-fire methods.

3-2-2 Underlying Difficulties Facing Artificial Intelligence and Criticism of Basic Assumptions

The review of artificial intelligence in Section 3–2-1 pointed out some of the difficulties encountered by workers in the various fields. A basic assumption commonly shared by artificial intelligence researchers is that human subjects face the same difficulties as machines, and therefore by applying human-like techniques machines will be able to overcome all obstacles. Dreyfus elaborates on this argument and considers four important human forms of information processing as contrasted with their machine surrogates. His four arguments are summarized in the following four sections.

Subconscious Selection. A prime procedure in devising game playing programs is to utilize heuristics to cut down the exponential growth of the game tree, thereby running the risk of excluding some possibly good moves. Essentially, these heuristics eliminate many supposedly unfruitful possibilities and then "count out" or "explore" all remaining possibilities by brute force enumeration. Supposedly for a game such as chess, this is how the masters proceed. However, Dreyfus points out that in reality a human utilizes two distinct information processes. First, he uses a "global" process to "zero-in" on an area formerly on the fringe of consciousness which other areas still on the fringes of consciousness make interesting, and then he counts out specific alternatives. As an example, a human chess player considers only a few distinct move alternatives at a given position; the particular alternatives being those chosen by a seemingly undefinable subconscious global pattern recognition of that position.

Early success in game-playing programs was obtained by working with games or portions of games in which the counting out was of importance and was feasible. Failure began occurring when global awareness became necessary to avoid exponential growth. The game of chess is certainly a case in point. In 1957, after the game had been set up on a computer and initial successes were achieved, one of the originators of the field of artificial intelligence, H. A. Simon, predicted that within ten years a digital computer would be the world's chess champion. Now, with the best program able to beat only rank amateurs, and with major breakthroughs required for significant advancement, the folly of this prediction is evident.

Essential and Unessential Discrimination. The work in problem solving and pattern recognition is highly dependent on the researchers' instructing their programs as to the essential features of the problem under study. It seems that the ability to distinguish between the essential and the unessential is a unique human form of information processing and is not readily amenable to mechanical search techniques.

In general, work in problem solving requires two types of thought: associationistic, elementary reasoning, and a more complex type requiring creative insight. The former type has been used to solve problems, once the programmer has used the latter type (involving his own insight) to set up a proper program schema. In complex problem solvers such as the GPS, in which more than simple association is required, the resulting program performance is little more than that of a "blind muddler" groping in the dark. The means-ends analysis of the GPS is not strong enough to provide truly creative heuristics for planning. Unfortunately, problem solving research seems to have assumed that there is a distinction between the essential and the accidental.

Ambiguity Tolerance.   The hang-up in language translation as discussed earlier lies primarily in the complexities introduced by ambiguities. To illustrate the difficulty of direct language comprehension, consider the simple sentence: "The box was in the pen" (Bar-Hillel, 1960). The pen referred to is almost certainly a playpen. But the computer, knowing only that pen had two meanings, and unaware of the relative size of pens in terms of boxes and other objects, would be effectively stymied. Thus, the human ability to use a global context to sufficiently reduce ambiguity without having to formalize it is a major information processing advantage over a machine. Hopefully, by proper heuristics and formalization this gap will be narrowed by some of the recent work described in the earlier discussion of semantic information processing and language translation.

Perspicuous Grouping.   Pattern recognition requires each of the forms of human information processing discussed thus far. To summarize these briefly: subconscious selection makes humans aware of contextual features too numerous to state explicitly; a sense of contextual essentiality allows humans to "zero-in" on important features and ignore the irrelevant; and ambiguity tolerance allows humans to use information about goals and context to narrow down the number of possible parsings without requiring the resulting interpretation to be absolutely unambiguous.

The combination of subconscious selection, insight, and context determination, which allows humans to understand and perceive connections, has been labeled "perspicuous grouping." This integrated form of human information processing is as important as the three fundamental forms from which it is derived since many problems, particularly those in pattern recognition, require all three forms in varying degrees.

Dreyfus feels that further progress in game playing, problem solving, and language processing requires a breakthrough in pattern recognition.

Assumptions and Misconceptions in Artificial Intelligence. According to Dreyfus a primary conviction of workers in artificial intelligence is that human information processing must proceed in discrete steps like a digital computer and, with proper programming, a computer should be capable of performing human-like functions. This assumption is naive for it does not consider the possibility that the brain might process information in an entirely different manner. Perhaps some processing is done globally, as an analog computer solves a differential equation.

The philosophy that thinking is analyzable into simple, determinate operations has been expressed in the stimulus-response school of psychology, and earlier in the associationist philosophy. In opposition, the gestaltists claim that thinking is a global process which cannot be modeled by either sequential or parallel processes. However, early success in artificial intelligence has strengthened the associationist position to the point that most workers are no longer aware of this basic assumption and the limited outlook it bears.

3-2-3 Basic Techniques of Artificial Intelligence

Heuristic Techniques. As stated previously, the objective in artificial intelligence is to produce techniques enabling a computer to exhibit intelligent behavior. Because algorithmic techniques are often inadequate in solving complex problems because of time and space considerations, such problems must often be approached by techniques more sophisticated than mere brute-force. In such cases problem solving is conducted by means of a highly selective search resulting in a drastic pruning of the tree of alternatives. In dealing with real-life situations, humans have evolved two general-purpose heuristic problem-solving methods: "means-ends analysis" and "planning." In the former, an initial state is transformed into a desired state by selecting and applying operations which reduce the difference between these states at each step of a multistep procedure. In the latter, the original problem is simplified, and means-ends analysis is applied to the newly stated simpler problem. Hopefully, the result is a set of plans capable of solving the original problem. As previously mentioned, the technique of means-ends analysis is the basis of the GPS. Several complex combinatory problems have been approached with varying degrees of success by the planning approach.

Other less general heuristic problem-solving methods are also available. Many problems can be quickly solved by working backwards from the solution to get the initial hypothesis, and then reversing the process: beginning with the hypothesis and obtaining the solution. Such a tactic is often used in proving mathematical theorems and in manipulating trigonometric identities. Another useful heuristic is that of approaching new problems with methods that have solved similar problems in the past. However, while this technique is often quite helpful, it tends to hinder innovative problem solving and the development of new techniques.

Search Techniques.   Many problems in artificial intelligence, particularly in the areas of game playing and theorem proving, involve the searching of large trees of alternative possibilities. A variety of procedures, ranging from the brute-force minimax technique to a new method called "dynamic ordering," is found in the literature. Here are brief descriptions of each of these techniques along with appropriate references:

Minimax Technique (Shannon, 1950).   This is the classical approach for determining a path through a game tree leading to a desired final state in a two-person game. In the minimax technique, the following question is asked recursively until the terminal branches of the tree have been reached and the end of the game has been determined: "Where can I move, such that my position after my opponent's move will be the best I can hope for, should he make the best countermove?" Each node in the game tree is examined for the above criteria, and the resulting solution is one of brute-force in that an algorithm rather than heuristic is utilized.

Alpha-Beta Technique (Edwards, et al., 1963).   This is a tree search procedure that is several orders of magnitude faster than minimax but nonetheless equivalent in the sense that it still finds the best solution by algorithmic means. It saves time by not searching certain nodes of the tree when their values do not affect the value of nodes at higher levels.

Fixed Ordering Alpha-Beta Cutoffs (Slagle, et al., 1969).   This technique is an improvement on the alpha-beta technique, accomplished by an ordering procedure of nodes based on their computed values.

Dynamic Ordering (Slagle, et al., 1969).   A further improvement on alpha-beta beyond fixed ordering which becomes worthwhile in searches within trees of "depth" six or more. It is shown that almost "perfect ordering" is obtained by this procedure.

Other Procedures. There are several problem-specific search procedures. Five such procedures have been proposed by Amarel (1967), Doran and Michie (1966), Nilsson (1968), Slagle and Bursky (1968), and Samuel (1967).

Evaluation Techniques. When search techniques are not sufficiently effective to render a problem deterministic, some sort of evaluation must be made. In this regard, Shannon's proposal for an intermediate evaluation from a minimax approach in the game of chess has been discussed earlier in the section on game playing.

Static evaluation functions, mostly of the linear threshold variety, have been used extensively in the area of pattern recognition, particularly involving adaptive and self-organizing systems (see, for example, Klopf, 1965). The basic element of an adaptive system is an adaptive threshold element as illustrated in Fig. 3-1. Each of the inputs

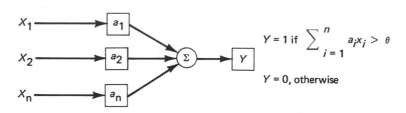

Figure 3-1.   Adaptive threshold element.

$X_1, X_2, \ldots X_n$ have a corresponding value of 0 or 1. The output Y is 1 if the sum of the inputs times their corresponding weights $a_1, a_2, \ldots, a_n$ is greater than some threshold value θ. Otherwise the value of the output is 0. Several interconnected adaptive threshold elements form the basis for a loose pseudo-net. Each of the inputs, such as a summing element of a net, is the output of a lower-order adaptive threshold device. Hopefully, weight assignments allow a net to discriminate between different sets of input patterns. The problem solving technique employed by a net is the reinforcement of weights. After a large number of reinforcements, it is hoped that the weights will converge to an optimal value and will be capable of causing the net to perform the correct discrimination.

Work in the area of adaptive and self-organizing systems has not been very fruitful. To date no adaptive systems have demonstrated capabilities of recognizable higher cognitive activity.

Learning.   Learning can be divided into four basic areas:

Rote Learning.   The most elementary type of learning is simple rote learning in which past experiences are stored for future playback. This can be quite useful in experimental techniques such as regenerative recording (see Chapter 9), and finds ready application in storing board positions encountered in game playing, together with their computed scores.

Generalization.   Continuous storage of all learned information via rote learning can result in severe problems in both data storage and retrieval. One way to decrease the amount of storage needed is to generalize on the basis of experience and save only the generalization. This, of course, is the basic problem of pattern recognition: choosing the general features which should be retained. In Samuel's checker playing program in the game-playing section, a set of features has evolved through both human choice and machine generation to yield an effective game player. Thus, in specific cases, success can be and has been obtained. In general, however, learning by generalization remains an unsolved problem.

Deductive Learning.   This is an area in which artificial intelligence is particularly strong. In the problem area, work in mechanical theorem proving has provided realistic evidence of deductive learning by computer. Interesting exploratory work in this regard includes the Logic Theory Machine of Newell, Shaw, and Simon, and the Geometry-Theorem Proving Machine of Gelernter (1963).

Inductive Learning.   Whereas artificial intelligence is quite strong in attacking problems by using deductive inference, little has been done in the area of inductive inference. The latter is certainly the more significant problem, as it encompasses the interesting possibility of hypothesis formation by machine. In reality *this is the really difficult problem in generalized planning—* deciding just what the problem is and what a good plan should accomplish. It can be equated with the general pattern recognition problem discussed earlier.

In an attempt to explore the processes of problem solving, hypothesis formulation and theory formation in scientific work, as well as to solve a realistic problem, researchers at Stanford embarked on the DENDRAL Project, an ambitious task aimed at determining the mollecular structure of organic molecules directly from mass spectral data. The overall structure of the program was a scientific method cycle, consisting of phases of preliminary inference making, systematic hypothesis generation, predicting from hypothesis, and testing against empirical data with evaluation using goodness-of-fit techniques. Significantly, the problem-solving behavior of the program is remarkably good for the limited set of organic molecules considered; in fact, the program's ability is at least equal to, and usually better than, that of professional mass spectral analysts (Lederberg, et al., 1969; Duffield, et al., 1969). Using DENDRAL as a springboard and the field of chemical inference as a context, Stanford researchers are currently addressing themselves to some of the key problems of artificial intelligence, including representation, knowledge assimilation, man-machine communications for the transfer of knowledge, and efficient systems design (Stanford Artificial Intelligence Memo AI-87, 1969).

3-2-4 Classification of Artificial Intelligence Techniques and Application Considerations

If the techniques used in artificial intelligence are classified according to types of intelligent activities into which they fall, four main classifications are evident:

Associationistic: Simple repetitive problems amenable to rote techniques or alternatively, a list search or decision tree.

Simple Formal: Simple games, decidable mathematical theorems, etc., which can be handled by search algorithms limiting the growth of the search tree.

Complex Formal: Complex games, well-defined complex patterns in noise, proofs of undecidable theorems, etc., all of which can be tackled by means of efficient search pruning heuristics and various learning techniques.

Nonformal: Ill-defined problems often requiring insight and inductive inference. No strictly artificial techniques have succeeded in handling difficult problems of this sort. A prime difficulty lies in the basic assumptions inherent in most artificial intelligence work, as previously discussed.

The formulation of a plan and the generation of the possible alternative courses of action (see the definition of planning in Section 1-1) fall into the realm of nonformal problems. By its very nature, plan formulation is ill-defined. Consequently, pure artificial intelligence provides no readily applicable techniques or heuristics to handle this problem. However, once a set of alternatives is formulated, and the problem structures revert to the simple or even complex formal types, efficient heuristic search algorithms can be applied to reduce the number of possibilities to be considered.

The picture changes drastically when a man-machine system is constructed. By adding a human to the process, solutions to ill-defined problems requiring insight and inductive inference are no longer unobtainable. Many interesting problems of this sort, involving interactive graphics in particular, have been solved.

Of prime importance is the fact that most of the problem-solving techniques used in artificial intelligence are designed to replace the intelligence of man, or at least to provide a usable substitute for his deductive abilities. Having a human partner alleviates the computer of much of this responsibility. In essence, the computer can fall back onto its inherent data-processing strengths.

Thus, to obtain a better handle on the relative merits of man-machine planning systems, the useful data-processing capabilities of each should be considered. This is done below. (For a more detailed analysis of human and machine capabilities, see Chapter 8.)

Human Data-Processing Capabilities:

- Has superior inductive abilities and can act on relevant ill-formulated data to fill in gaps, recognize emerging patterns, and decipher trends.
- Excellent at generating new hypotheses and in utilizing inductive powers for insight and creativity.
- Naturally adaptive and able to adjust quickly to new and changing situations.

Computer Data Processing Capabilities:

- Can handle large amounts of complex data, and is capable of sifting through such data and signaling for human intervention when an interesting situation arises.
- With proper filtering techniques, is capable of detecting signal in situations in which unaided human observer detects only noise.

- Adept at comparing data at high speeds to identify well-defined patterns.
- Excellent at carrying out detailed complex processes with few, if any, errors.
- Useful in quick and accurate data sorting and information distribution. Particularly good at rapidly forming complex graphical displays.
- Excellent bookkeeper, capable of maintaining and updating large files of detailed records.

Any man-machine planning system should attempt to combine the useful capabilities above to utilize the inherent advantages of both man and machine along these lines. Willmorth (in Chapter 8) has suggested converting large amounts of data to a graphical or pictorial representation via graphic I/O and allowing a human planner to utilize his inductive abilities to determine essential relationships. From these relationships the planner might reformulate his hypotheses concerning the data, thereby effectively lessening the necessary overall data processing.

A number of useful ideas have been proposed by Hormann (1965) under the context of developing a machine partner for man. Among the more promising is the design of a cognitive map providing the computer with an internal model of the external world and allowing it to answer appropriate "what if" questions asked by its human partner. Another possibility is a man-machine ideation session in which the machine could present the user with possible relationships within a body of queried information, hopefully opening up new possibilities of stimulating and capturing man's creative activities. Hormann also considers the possibility of using an associative memory in a unique fashion to provide the computer with an effective "parallel processing of background information at the 'subconscious' level," thereby minimizing human rumination.

An interesting learning machine, aptly named Gaku and containing coordinated mechanisms of induction, planning, problem orientation, and programming, has been considered as a major implementation device to tie together these objectives (see Chapter 2). An extensible man-machine communication language, UAL (User Adaptive Language) has been designed as a vehicle for the Gaku Project (Hormann, 1969).

Perhaps with an advanced learning machine, one that works hand in hand with a human partner to provide true man-machine synergism, the computer will aid man in the creative problem of problem finding as well as in its more traditional role of problem solving. Originality of this sort would mark a new era of scientific inflation (Mackworth, 1965), with a multitude of innovative possibilities materializing.

3-3 SUMMARY AND CONCLUSIONS

Planning is loosely defined as a process in which an individual or group of people endeavor to handle a given problem by a well-thought-out procedure. Following an elaboration of this definition, the scope of planning is bounded by two classifications: types of planning and general applications of planning. Included in the types of planning discussed are functional planning, project planning, and comprehensive planning, while the primary applications discussed are city planning, corporate planning, and military planning. The planning process itself is characterized as a hierarchical structure with a single-level planning process within the hierarchy described by five distinct steps: determining the data, generating alternatives, choosing the best alternatives, executing the plan, and periodically revising the plan by iterative techniques.

Some considerations of the advantages of a man-machine system are presented. This is followed by a discussion of the use of graphic displays as a means of increasing man's capabilities, and the potential advantages of the use of voice input/output.

Various techniques useful in planning along with newly emerging disciplines such as operations research, systems engineering, general systems theory, and management science are presented and discussed. Included in the techniques for planning are 21 interesting methods documented by Rosove (1967), and a few additional pertinent techniques which he failed to consider.

The field of artificial intelligence is closely surveyed in an attempt to distinguish further fruitful techniques and methods useful in on-line interactive computer planning. To this end the basic research areas of artificial intelligence (including game playing, problem solving, semantic information processing, and pattern recognition) are reviewed, and relevant highlights are acknowledged. Following the format of a major critique of the field (Dreyfus, 1965), some of the underlying difficulties facing artificial intelligence are considered along with a criticism of some of the field's basic assumptions. With these preliminary observations concluded, the basic techniques utilized in artificial intelligence research are extracted. Those considered include heuristic techniques, search techniques (minimax, alpha-beta, fixed ordering alpha-beta, dynamic ordering, etc.), evaluation techniques, and learning techniques (rote, generalization, deductive, and inductive). These techniques are classified into four categories of intelligent activity: associationistic, simple formal, complex formal, and nonformal. It is observed that the formulation of a plan and the generation of possible alternative courses of action can be categorized as involving inductive inference, falling into the realm of nonformal problems, precisely the category in which achievement in artificial intelligence has been minimal. Barring a significant development in artificial intelligence research, it is concluded that such problems in planning are not immediately suited for application of pure artificial intelligence techniques, but may instead be handled efficiently by a man-machine team, each using its particular strengths. As an indication of a possible delegation of responsibilities between man and machine, the data-processing capabilities of a human are contrasted with those of a computer, and references for future study along these lines are made.

REFERENCES

Amarel, S., "An Approach to Heuristic Problem Solving and Theorem Proving in the Propositional Calculus," in J. F. Hart and S. Takasu (eds.), *Systems and Computer Science,* Toronto, Canada, University of Toronto Press, 1967, 125–220.

____, "On Representations and Modelling in Problem Solving and on Future Direction for Intelligent Systems," Princeton, N.J., RCA Labs., 1968.

Banerji, E. B., *The Theory of Problem Solving: An Approach to Artificial Intelligence,* New York, American Elsevier Publishing Company, 1969.

Bar-Hillel, Y., "The Present Status of Automatic Translation of Languages," in *Advances in Computers,* Vol. 1, F. L. Alt (ed.), New York, Academic Press, 1960, 91–163.

Bellman, R., "Dynamic Programming," The RAND Corporation, R-295, Santa Monica, Calif., 1956.

____, and S. E. Dreyfus, "Applied Dynamic Programming," The RAND Corporation, R-352-PR, Santa Monica, Calif., 1962.

Berge, C., *Theory of Graphs and Its Applications,* New York, John Wiley and Sons, 1962.

Bobrow, P. G., "Natural Language Input for a Computer Problem Solving System," Ph.D. Dissertation, M.I.T., 1964.

Branch, M. C., *Planning: Aspects and Applications,* New York, John Wiley & Sons, 1966.

Busacher, R. G., and T. L. Saaty, *Finite Graphs and Networks,* New York, McGraw-Hill Book Co., 1965.

Citrenbaum, R. L., "Efficient Representations of Optimal Solutions for a Class of Games," Systems Research Center, Report SRC 69-5, Case Western Reserve University, 1969.

Doran, J. E., and D. Michie, "Experiments with the Graph Traverser Program," *Proceedings Royal Society,* **294,** 1437 (1966), 235–259.

Dreyfus, H. L., "Alchemy and Artificial Intelligence," The RAND Corporation, P-3244, Santa Monica, Calif., 1965.

Duffield, A. M., et al., "Applications of Artificial Intelligence for Chemical Inference II. Interpretation of Low Resolution Mass Spectra of Ketones," *Journal of the American Chemical Society,* May 1968.

Edwards, D. J., and T. P. Hart, "The $\alpha-\beta$ Heuristic," in Artificial Intelligence Memo No. 30, MIT Research Laboratory, Cambridge, Mass., October 1963.

Emery, J. C., "The Planning Process and Its Formalization in Computer Models," *Proceedings of the Second Congress of Information Systems Science,* 1964, 369–389.

Ernst, G. W., and A. Newell, "Generality and the GPS," AD 807-354, Carnegie Institute of Technology, 1967.

Evans, T. G., "A Heuristic Program to Solve Geometric Analogy Problems," Ph.D. Dissertation, M.I.T., 1963.

Gelernter, H., et al., "Empirical Explorations of the Geometry-Theorem Proving Machine," in *Computers and Thought,* E. A. Feigenbaum and J. Feldman (eds.), New York, McGraw-Hill Book Co., Inc., 1963, pp. 153–163.

Greenblatt, R. D., et al., "The Greenblatt Chess Program," *Proceedings Fall Joint Computer Conference,* 1967, pp. 801–810.

Hadley, G., *Nonlinear and Dynamic Programming,* Reading, Mass., Addison-Wesley Publishing Co., 1964.

Hormann, A. M., "Gaku: An Artificial Student," *Behavioral Science,* Vol. 10, No. 1, (1965), 88–107.

  , *Problem Solving and Learning by Man-Machine Teams,* SP-(L)-3336/ 000/01, System Development Corporation, Santa Monica, Calif., May 1969.

Kellogg, C. H., "Data Management in Ordinary English: Examples," in *Computer Studies in the Humanities and Verbal Behavior,* Vol. 1, No. 4, December 1968, 159–182.

Klopf, A. H., "Multi-Element Pattern Recognition Systems," Case Western Reserve University, 1965 (unpublished).

Lederberg, J., et al., "Applications of Artificial Intelligence for Chemical Inference I. The Number of Possible Organic Compounds: Acyclic Structures Containing C, H, O, and N," *Journ. of American Chemical Society,* May, 1969.

Mackworth, N. H., "Originality," *American Psychologist,* Vol. 20, January 1965, 51–66.

Mason, R. O., "A Dialectical Approach to Strategic Planning," *Management Science,* Vol. 15, No. 8, April 1969.

Minsky, M., "Steps Toward Artificial Intelligence," *Proceedings of the Institute of Radio Engineers,* 49, 1961, 8–30.

_____, (ed.),. *Semantic Information Processing,* Cambridge, Mass., M.I.T. Press, 1968.

Moder, J. J., and C. R. Philips, *Project Management with CPM and PERT,* New York, Reinhold, 1964.

Newell, A., *"Learning, Generality, and Problem Solving,"* RM-3285-1-PR, The RAND Corporation, Santa Monica, Calif., 1963.

_____, "On the Representation of Problems," Carnegie-Mellon University, 1969.

_____, J. C. Shaw, and H. A. Simon, "Empirical Explorations of the Logic Theory Machine: A Case Study in Heuristics," *Proceedings of the Western Joint Computer Conference,* 1957.

_____, J. D. Shaw, and H. A. Simon, "Chess Playing Programs and the Problem of Complexity," *IBM Journal of R&D,* 2, 320, October 1958.

_____, and H. A. Simon, "GPS, A Program that Simulates Human Thought," in *Computers and Thought,* E. A. Feigenbaum and J. Feldman (eds.), New York, McGraw-Hill Book Co., 1963, 279–293.

Nilsson, N. J., "Searching Problem Solving and Game Playing Trees for Minimal Cost Solutions," *IFIP Congress,* 1968, H-125–H-130.

Quillian, M. R., "Semantic Memory," Ph.D. Dissertation, Carnegie Institute of Technology, 1966.

Raphael, B., SIR: A Computer Program for Semantic Information Retrieval. Ph.D. Dissertation, M.I.T., 1964.

Rosove, P. E., *A Provisional Survey and Evaluation of the Current Forecasting State of the Art for Possible Contributions to Long-Range Educational. Policy Making,* TM-3640, System Development Corporation, Santa Monica, Calif., 1967.

Samuel, A. L., "Some Studies in Machine Learning Using the Game of Checkers," *IBM Journal of R&D,* 3, 210, July 1968.

_____, "Some Studies in Machine Learning Using the Game of Checkers, II– Recent Progress," *IBM Journal of R&D,* November 1967.

Shannon, C. E., "Programming a Computer for Playing Chess," *Philosophy Magazine,* 41, 256, March 1950.

Slagle, J. R., and P. Bursky, "Experiments with a Multipurpose, Theorem Proving Heuristic Program," *ACM Journal,* 16, 2, April 1969, 189–207.

Stanford Artificial Intelligence Project, Memo. AI-87, Computer Science Department, Stanford University, June 1969.

Uhr, L., and C. Vossler, "A Pattern Recognition Program That Generates, Evaluates, and Adjusts Its Own Operators," in E. A. Feigenbaum and J. Feldman (eds.), *Computers and Thought,* New York, McGraw-Hill Book Co., 1963, 251–268.

Wang, H., "Toward Mechanical Mathematics" in K. M. Sayre and F. J. Crosson (eds.), *The Modeling of the Mind,* South Bend, Ind., Notre Dame University Press, 1963, 91–210.

Wigington, R. L., "Graphics and Speech, Computer Input and Output for Communication with Humans," in F. Gruenberger (ed.), *Computer Graphics,* Washington, D.C., Thompson Book Company, 1967, 81–98.

II

Management and
Project Planning

In Part II, planning is examined from the vantage point of project
management in a system development context. Cady's chapter sets
the pace with a functional description of comprehensive planning in
the system development cycle with special emphasis on the Planning,
Programming, Budgeting process. Citrenbaum reviews planning procedures using various forms of network analysis, including critical
path methodology and PERT. He indicates the promise of interactive
graphic techniques to expedite the representation of planning networks. Loubal describes an online resource allocation model with
experimental examples for a community problem. In Chapter 7,
Kleine and Citrenbaum tackle the problem of modeling hierarchical
management planning; they indicate a possible framework into which
a variety of planning tools can be effectively utilized.

165

These four chapters expand the notion of comprehensive planning developed earlier in Part I. Various planning roles emerge from the project planning context: management, professional planners, information systems specialists, and technical users. These roles are integrated in terms of the rational division of labor throughout the evolutionary planning process. The potential of selected interactive planning techniques is highlighted for key points in the planning cycle.

4

PROJECT PLANNING PROCEDURES

G. M. Cady

Abstract

This chapter analyzes the entire planning process into twenty specific identifiable activities. Logical precedences are established among the activities and a three-level hierarchical representation of planning activities is presented. This view of planning is developed as an aid in the discussion of various techniques which are, or might be, used to assist planners in the performance of their tasks. Opinions on the most beneficial role of the computer at all activity levels are drawn. One large-scale planning system, PPB, is examined in the light of the previous analysis of the planning process. PPB functions which might potentially derive the greatest benefits from the use of computers are pointed out, and the advantages and disadvantages of implementing an online computer-assisted PPB-like system are discussed.

In recent years there has been a remarkable growth in the number and variety of computer-adaptable techniques which are applicable to problems in military and corporate planning. As a result, computer assistance in planning exists today and formalized computer-assisted planning systems, dealing with virtually all aspects of planning, are near at hand. We may expect that the computer will assume an ever more important role as new insight into the nature of planning leads the way to more sophisticated computerized planning techniques.

In this chapter we will analyze the planning process in some detail, breaking it down into a structured collection of subactivities by identifying what it is that planners do.

Such an approach, it is hoped, will be useful in coming to terms with exactly what a man-computer planning system must accomplish, where the man and where the machine may best be used in the scheme, and what techniques are applicable to each of the given functions. Obviously, no claim is made either that this is the only way to cover the subject or that the techniques described represent a complete list. The intent is, however, to stimulate some thought on how the ill-defined task of planning may be improved by formalization and extensive and variegated use of computer techniques.

4-1 THE PLANNING PROCESS AS A TRI-LEVEL HIERARCHY

Figures 4-1 to 4-4 constitute a schematic representation of the generalized planning process in terms of smaller, readily identifiable activities. Figure 4-1 represents a breakdown of the whole process into three gross levels of function; Figures 4-2 to 4-4 show expansions of these three levels into specific activities. Outputs of the activities of the first level (policy) act as constraints on those of the second level (strategy); a similar relationship exists between strategy and logistics.

The prime danger of this representation of planning is that it may convey the idea of a one-shot, almost linear process which takes a set of very general inputs and proceeds inexorably in a forward direction,

Figure 4-1.   Three levels of planning activities.

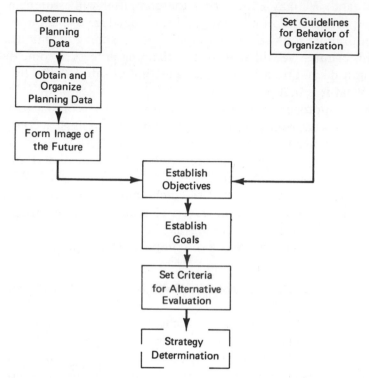

Figure 4-2. Policy determination.

producing a single plan with sufficient detail to act as an adequate mechanism of control. It should be made quite clear, however, that this interpretation is not intended, for two very important reasons.

First of all, the planning environment is continuously changing, as is the planners' interpretation of that environment. This forces changes in the organization's view of the future, its view of itself, and its goals and objectives. These changes, in turn, dictate revision of any plans which had previously been formalized. In a direct manner, for example, changes in the availability of resources may affect plans.

Planning must also be viewed as an interactive process. New information generated by any activity may be used as a revised input to any other activity, and thus the planning process must recycle from that activity. The importance of iteration in planning can hardly be overemphasized.

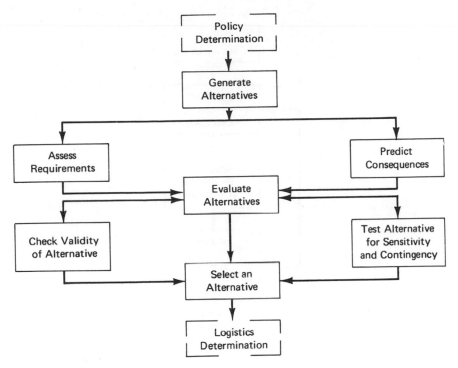

Figure 4-3.   Strategy determination.

A planning system must, then, allow for periodic repetition of its various activities, with resultant updating and revision of the components of the plan. The diagrams given here give no indication of this aspect of the planning process. Their intent is merely to identify fundamental activities of planning, categorize them into related groups, and establish some sort of logical (not necessarily temporal) precedence relationships among them.

4-2 LAYING THE FOUNDATION FOR THE PLAN: DETERMINATION OF POLICY

Policy determination (Fig. 4-2) addresses itself to those problems of planning which are the most poorly defined and ill-structured. At this level, problems are formulated rather than solved and, in general,

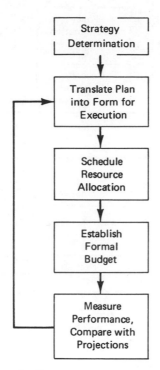

Figure 4-4. Logistics determination.

formulation of problems is a much more nebulous task than their solution. In this realm, man's judgment is presently the most valid decision-making mechanism; the mathematical and analytical techniques provide only supplemental help. It should be pointed out, however, that since this area has been by far the least formalized and receives, at present, the least sophisticated assistance from computers, it also seems to offer the most wide-open field for new research in computer application. While technology development at the other planning levels would primarily take the form of synthesizing, optimizing, polishing, and integrating known techniques, and adding to them features which become available through interactive implementation, the potentially greatest payoffs (and risks) seem to lie in the area of assistance in policy determination. Since policies must be determined before plans can proceed, the importance of this field is obvious; gaining credibility and acceptance for new systems, however, may present a very severe problem at this level, partly because of the poorly defined structure of policy problems, partly because of the inertia associated with the high organizational rank of the potential users, and partly because it would take years to evaluate any real-world plans which were generated using such systems.

The best established computer applications at this level are the data base management systems which can make vast amounts of planning data into a manageable and useful entity, and the myriad techniques of statistical analysis and projection which aid the planner in forming his image of the future.

Certain new techniques give promise of aiding in other activities at this level, particularly in the establishment of goals and objectives, the formation of criteria for the evaluation of alternatives, and in forecasting (McCarthy, 1970; Helmer, 1966; Mason, 1969). These techniques aim to forge the divergent views of two or more well-qualified groups or individuals into a consensus through a strictly formalized debating process. The formal structure of the debate is intended to eliminate many of the well-recognized faults of round-table, or committee, planning while at the same time forcing due consideration of all relevant aspects of, or approaches to, the problem at hand. Mason's dialectical approach has been applied to the generation and selection of alternatives (this activity is described at the next lower level in our hierarchy of planning activities), but, as demonstrated in the example in his paper, it also produces powerful new inputs to the policy formulation process. So far the Delphi technique of consensus formulation seems to have been used only for questions which demand a single-valued, quantitative, answer; but the establishment of criteria for plan evaluation, if viewed as a process of ranking or weighting of previously selected objectives and performance measures, could possibly lend itself to a Delphi-like approach. The application of the computer to both the Delphi and dialectical techniques may be a fertile area for investigation, although there is serious question as to whether or not manual and mechanical techniques would serve just as well and be considerably more cost-effective.

The two activities at the top of Fig. 4-2, setting general guidelines for the behavior of the organization and determining the variables which will form the basis for the whole planning process, are functions of the highest management level of the organization. Only indirectly do they lend themselves to any known techniques where computers could play a significant role as when the outputs of other planning activities dictate the acquisition of more information, or even a new look at the general purposes of the whole organization.

The exercise of scenario formulation appears to be the closest thing to a formalized procedure for setting general guidelines for an organization's behavior. In scenario formulation, future conditions are postulated and the implications of the various futures upon current planning decisions are analyzed. One way to examine alternative futures is to construct an "event graph"; an example of the use of this technique to create a possible scenario of computer/communication technology is given in Fig. 4-5. Each box represents an achievement with the branches flowing out representing the alternative developments which might logically follow that achievement. Developments which are logical consequences of other developments are linked together on the graph. With visual aids such as these, the planner is able to see clearly the consequences of various possible alternatives and trace those paths which may be taken to achieve a given condition in the future. By assuming that the most probable path will be taken at some points and exerting strong control to influence the decision at other points, the gross outlines of a plan to achieve the most desirable future may be discerned.

The logical role of the computer in this exercise, although its effectiveness has yet to be demonstrated here, would be to maintain and display alternative graphs, accept and process changes input interactively through a graphical device, and preserve the scenarios for future use. The computer might also handle probabilistic calculations so that the analyst could quickly see the effect on the final scenario of altering the probability of any given development.

4-3   SELECTING A PLAN: DETERMINATION OF STRATEGY

In strategy determination a plan actually arises for attaining the goals and objectives formulated as policy. The problem has been formulated in terms of goals, objectives, and criteria; its solution begins with the selection of a strategy. Policy determination tries to establish where the organization is going; strategy determination tries to establish how the organization may best get there. It is at this level, when the problem is somewhat better structured than at the preceding level, that the techniques of modeling and simulation are likely to make their greatest contribution.

Several notions concerning the roles of men and machines in the generation, evaluation, and selection of alternatives, should be made

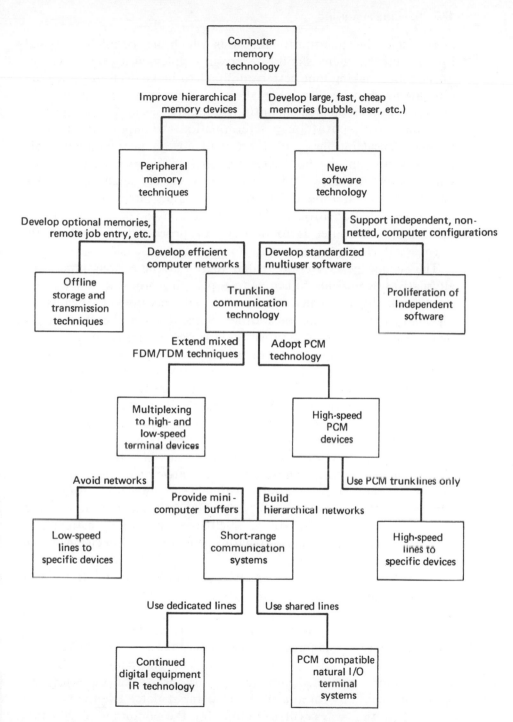

Figure 4-5. Graph representation of computer/communication scenario.

clear. First, the quantitative methods which are, or might be, used for the activities here, should be aids in supplementing the judgment of man and making him better qualified to make decisions; they are not intended to be decision makers in their own right. Qualitative analysis must supplement quantitative analysis as an integral part of the total function of strategy determination. All important nonquantifiable considerations (and there will always be nonquantifiable considerations in any nontrivial planning problem) must be treated with qualitative analysis, and only in this way can quantitative work be intelligently interpreted. The role of man in strategy determination is to generate alternatives and to evaluate consequences. The proper role of the computer is to translate proposed actions into consequences which the planner may evaluate.

The second general point is that there may be a large number of alternatives as possible solutions to a planning problem. A man can, in general, discard many of them on sight because of obvious infeasibility for one reason or another. Since it would therefore be expensive and wasteful to perform detailed computer analyses on the discarded alternatives, the conclusion is that any man-machine system for alternative selection ought to relegate to man the prime responsibility for weeding out "bad" solutions at an early stage. A genuinely interactive environment would facilitate this process.

Considerable attention has been given recently to the determination of strategies by using probabilistic decision trees (Brown, 1970). Decision forks, representing alternatives from which the planner may choose, and event forks, representing alternative events over which the planner has no control, are related in logical sequences to form a decision tree. The probable utility (profit) associated with the end point of each path in the tree is calculated based on an estimate of the probable utility associated with each event and decision in the tree, along with the probabilities of traversing the different paths leading out of event forks. The series of decisions leading to the end point with the highest expected utility is then presumably selected as the plan strategy.

Decision-tree analysis presents a fascinating area for research in computer-assisted planning. We can envision, as a first step, computerized systems with graphical input, automatic housekeeping of tree structures and associated data, path utility calculations, and simplified methods for the planner to input data. Eventually, it is anticipated that ways will be found for the computer to generate alternatives. This would allow more alternatives to be considered (thus improving plan quality), and the planner could concentrate on consequence evaluation and tree-pruning functions where it is likely that man will always be more efficient and capable than the computer.

Mason's dialectical approach to planning and strategy, mentioned in the previous section, addresses itself directly to the problem of plan selection, although the results which the structured debate produces can, and apparently do, have constructive repercussions at all levels of the planning hierarchy (Mason, 1969). Two conflicting alternatives are selected, based on two different interpretations of the same planning data. The proponents of each plan are forced to look at the assumptions on which their plan is based, and expose those assumptions very clearly. Quite often the result is that a new alternative is generated, based on those assumptions from the previous two plans which prove to be the strongest. The technique, which could be iterated to further refine the selected plan, is evidently highly regarded by those who have used it.

The next five activities in Fig. 4-3, all parts of the process of evaluating alternative plans, leading to the actual selection of an alternative, are analytical in nature and appear to be excellent candidates for the techniques of modeling and simulation. The Department of Defense and other organizations perform this analysis in terms of cost and utility functions (Novick, 1965; Bureau of Budget, 1965). One model of a cost-utility analysis process has been worked out in detail by Jones (1969). More often than not, either cost or utility is assigned a fixed value and the value of the other function is estimated for each alternative, but occasionally the difference between cost and utility or the cost/utility ratio is the basis of optimization. Care must be exercised when the cost/utility ratio is used because the optimum solution may occur at an extreme point, resulting in either an inordinate cost or an unsatisfactory benefit. When neither cost nor utility is fixed, therefore, an obvious requirement is to constrain the problem by carefully assigning a maximum tolerable cost and a minimum tolerable performance benefit.

Techniques of simulation will not be discussed here, but some important considerations which relate directly to the use of simulation and modelling in the evaluation of alternative plans will be listed. Most of them are points which were emphasized by Fisher (1965). They apply equally well to analytical models and process simulation.

1.   No matter how good a model is, the user must ask the right questions to get meaningful results.

2.   The design of the user's approach may have to be frequently modified and restructured; this implies the need for an interactive and highly flexible modeling package.

3.   All assumptions which underlie a model should be explicit and visible. Many of these assumptions will come, of course, from actions taken at the policy determination level of the planning process.

4.   Uncertainty should be treated explicitly. Uncertainty about the state of the world in the future must be handled by such techniques as sensitivity analysis (variation of key, but uncertain, parameters away from expected values to see how sensitive the rankings of alternatives are to such changes) and contingency analysis (testing how well an alternative's ranking holds up under major changes in the evaluation criteria or in the general environment). Statistical uncertainty must be handled either with a Monte Carlo-type simulation technique, or one of the many curve-fitting techniques currently available. In Monte Carlo simulation, also known as synthetic sampling, a statistically valid sample of experiments on the test system is performed by selecting numerous values of input parameters at random, according to what is believed to be the statistical distribution of those parameters. This results, in turn, in a set of values for output parameters, rather than a single value, and much better information about the behavior of the system under the range of likely conditions is obtained. These results may then be statistically fitted to curves which describe a system performance distribution. From these, the probability of obtaining various performance levels may be calculated. The analyst may select from alternatives with considerably more confidence when the performance distribution is known than when only single-valued performance figures are available. The value of computerized techniques here is obvious.

5.   It will probably be important for the model to handle time considerations, as when the flow of costs, information, or objects through time represents a significant constraint.

6.   The validity of any model and the information it yields need to be tested by answering such questions as: Can the model describe known facts and situations? Are the results consistent and plausible when the principal parameters are

varied? Can it handle special cases where the outcome is known? Can it assign causes to known effects? Validity checking is represented in Fig. 4-3 as a separate activity in the plan evaluation and selection process.

7.   Analysis at this stage of the planning process may require inputs from, or simulation of, the activities at the third level which are concerned with actual plan implementation, thus belying, again, any linear interpretation of the planning process.

4-4 IMPLEMENTING THE PLAN: DETERMINATION OF LOGISTICS

Logistics determination might also be called the operational or management control level. A plan has been established which spells out what the organization should do; it remains to be decided how to do it.

The problem by now is quite clearly specified; generally it is to meet the specifications of the strategic plan at minimal cost, or maximize output at a fixed cost, or some such problem. It is an optimization problem with budgeting and control considerations, and the solution of optimization problems has been a prime area of research by applied mathematicians, systems analysts, industrial engineers, operations researchers, etc., for a number of years, resulting in a great array of solution techniques.

All of the activities at the logistics level of planning have successfully been accomplished or strongly assisted by computers, usually in a batch-processing system. Some organizations have attempted to automate more than one activity in a single system which is, possibly, a fruitful direction in which to proceed and one in which progress has been made only at the lowest levels of the planning process. One anticipated obstacle along the way, however, is generality. Most combinations of techniques have been strongly oriented to one specific application; whether or not any kind of generality could be achieved in an integrated package is a moot point. It is difficult to conceive at this point of a single system which could do justice to such problems as inventories, scheduling, resource allocation, sequencing, queuing, and budgeting for more than one narrow type of user.

The types of analyses which might assist a planner in translating a plan into a form for execution involve a host of optimization techniques included under the generic term "mathematical programming." Among the most fundamental techniques are:

Linear programming and its derivatives.
Graph theory and network analysis.
Search techniques.

Linear programming itself will solve only problems with linear objective functions and constraints, and it has been said that no real world situation is linear. Yet the ideas and approaches of linear programming have spawned many similar approaches to other problems of more complexity, many of which can be transformed into a form which linear programming techniques will solve directly. Integer, quadratic, and geometric programming fall into this category, as do many of the methods for the solution of more general nonlinear programming problems.

Network analysis and graph theory have solved a number of problems dealing with such matters as activity scheduling, resource allocation and scheduling, budgeting, and problem control. The most widely known techniques are CPM (Critical Path Method) and PERT (Program Evaluation and Review Technique). With PERT, a network representation of a project in terms of its milestones and activities is established. The strength of the idea lies in two advantages over more intuitive approaches:

- Visual representation of project achievements and the steps which must be taken to attain them provides powerful assistance to the planner who must grasp the interrelationships among activities, spot the critical areas of the project, and comprehend the consequences of proposed changes in schedules and manpower and equipment allocation.
- A PERT network superimposes on the activities a logical and formal structure which is well suited to the types of quantitative analysis which would be difficult or impossible with a less structured approach.

An IBM document (IBM, 1967) lists the following functions which may be performed by PERT programs:

1. Compute the expected time required for completion of a project.

2. Find the critical path through the activity network, revealing which activities are limiting the projected completion date.
3. List an optimal sequence of events.
4. Provide descriptive statistics for performance time probability curves.
5. Relate network and time data to program deadlines.
6. Indicate slack areas.
7. Compute the probability of meeting scheduled completion dates.
8. Compare current forecasts against scheduled completion dates.
9. Provide summaries of progress and outlooks for future progress.
10. Compute the effects of alternative courses of action.
11. Schedule resource acquisition.
12. Assist in budget preparation.
13. Update all of the previous outputs on the basis of more current inputs.

PERT systems are widely used because of the obvious values of these functions to managers concerned with actually carrying out a plan.

Widespread research is being conducted into refinements, extensions, and new applications of PERT-like concepts. Hormann (1969) has suggested areas of research for some improvements which might be made to man-machine PERT systems. These suggestions all would seem to enhance the versatility of the system and its creative use by the planner:

- Move away from fixed network structures, and allow users to alter precedence relations (and therefore network structure), thus quickly generating alternative plans and hopefully optimizing project scheduling better than fixed structural considerations would allow.
- Allow incomplete specification of objectives, or conflicting objectives, making it possible for the user to reach a compromise solution through the use of "what if" questions.
- Dynamically display charts and numerical values for various alternatives, so that users may more easily formulate incisive questions.

Other potential areas of research are in the inclusion of quality as well as time, costs, and quantity as PERT variables, and facilitating the interactive incorporation of fundamental changes in the activities and end products of the PERT network. All of the items which have been suggested here point in the direction of a truly interactive, flexible, and more powerful use of the PERT idea for faster and more creative planning by quickly allowing the planner to consider more alternatives in his trade-off analyses. Automatic optimization of PERT networks according to combinations of various criteria should also be made available. A final area which seems fertile is to try to better relate PERT inputs and outputs to other phases of the planning process.

Other important network optimization techniques have been developed for other types of problems and are likely to find important applications in planning. One of the most promising is the Out-of-Kilter Algorithm (Durbin, 1967) which finds the optimal solution to a problem where the process under consideration can be modeled as a steady-state network flow process. A wide variety of flow constraints, costs, etc., may be incorporated. Among its many applications are transportation problems, personnel assignment, system reliability optimization, and equipment allocation.

Finally, a few words should be said about the capabilities and drawbacks of search techniques. A search technique involves making a local observation of the value of a function to be optimized and then, using information gleaned from such direct observations, moving in a direction that appears promising for the next observation. This procedure is repeated until the optimal solution is found (or approximated). A large number of such techniques have been formulated for optimization of various functions. Many of them depend on some specialized assumptions which can be made about a function and therefore applicability in generalized situations may be severely restricted. But the beauty of search techniques is that they are readily understandable, easily implementable, and often more efficient than any other known method. In fact, for optimization of certain complex functions, they appear to be the only way to go.

A technique currently enjoying widespread use is SUMT (Sequential Unconstrained Minimization Technique) (Fiacco, 1968), but newer ones are coming out as considerable effort is going into this area.

Optimization of very large systems may present a considerable barrier, in terms of computer time and storage, using most of the techniques mentioned so far. Analysts have generally preferred to use simulation techniques for the representation of complex systems, and to find a "good" solution essentially by trial and error. Others prefer to beat the cost problem by using less detailed representations of their systems and precise optimization methods.

On the philosophy that a good solution to a complete system problem is more valuable than the best solution to an incomplete version of the problem, techniques are being developed which attempt to combine features of simulation and optimization (Karr, 1965; Luther, 1966). These techniques, integrated under the generic term "Simoptimization," operate on detailed models of large systems and efficiently produce solutions which are invariably better than those produced by trial-and-error or "good guess" methods, although they may not be optimal. There is a gradation of techniques producing increasingly refined solutions, at correspondingly increasing costs. The analyst must decide whether the expected improvement in the solution from a more refined technique will pay for itself during the life of the system.

The computer-assisted techniques mentioned in this section exist primarily in batch mode applications. Referring to the activities listed under logistics determination, however, a natural division may be seen between those activities which are best left in the batch mode and those which could be allowed to do these things in an interactive environment. During the actual operation of the system, however, the repetitive and mechanical nature of budgeting and control imply that offline processing would be more economical and effective.

Almost needless to say, only the barest outline of techniques applicable to plan implementation are given here; further investigations and decisions await better definition of the objectives and applications to be fulfilled by a particular planning system.

Specifically, the translation of a general plan (strategy) into an executable form (tactics), scheduling, and, to some extent, resource allocation, involves exploration of alternatives and requires some imagination on the part of the planner; these functions, then, are well-suited to interactive implementation. When considering the budgetary and management control processes, however, a distinction should be made between their set-up and their operation. It may be desirable to allow the planner to specify operations to be performed on the data and report formats interactively. The actual processing, however, is suitable only for offline implementation.

Directions for Planning Research. We have depicted the planning process in a form which would lend itself to the necessary analysis which must be performed prior to the design of a man-machine planning system. The whole process has been broken down into three levels of activities. Various techniques which have been, or might be, used to assist planners in the performance of the activities at each level have been mentioned, and some opinions on the most likely role of computers at each level have been given.

Some of the prime contributions to planning which a new planning system might make include:

1. Generality. Previous computer-oriented planning systems usually cover an incomplete subset of planning activities, and are set up solely for special-purpose applications.
2. Integration of a given level's activities with each other, as an aid to the simplification of the analysis required at each level. This may be achieved through such techniques as a common data base and well-defined interactivity communication protocol.
3. Integration of the three major levels of activities with each other.
4. True interactivity between man and machine to make the best use of the capabilities of each, and of new graphical and natural I/O techniques, to break down the barriers which inhibit man-computer communication.
5. Availability of the system for direct use by nontechnical personnel. The ideal is to have very sophisticated techniques embedded in the system, without requiring the user to learn a great deal of technical detail before using them, thus enabling the planners who make the decisions to use the system directly.
6. Comprehensiveness, in the sense that a single, well-integrated system may be used for assistance in all activities of the planning cycle. In such a comprehensive system, plan quality and timeliness would be improved by formalization of the interfaces among all planning functions. "Holes" where planning information is needed but no formalized methodology exists would be minimized.

What are the prospects of such a comprehensive planning system being realized? It appears to be arriving by a process of evolution. We can see the process already as planning techniques are combined in twos, threes, and fours to form specialized planning systems in industry, government, and the military. Gaps between computer-assisted planning functions are narrowed and filled as progress in hardware and software technology, as well as developments in planning-related analytical and interactive techniques, makes it feasible to do so. It is likely that new ways for computers to assist planners will be found as long as man feels the need to plan his future.

4-5 THE PLANNING–PROGRAMMING–BUDGETING SYSTEM

PPB is a large-scale planning, budgeting, and control system developed at RAND under the aegis of the Department of Defense, and now adopted by all major departments of the Federal government and by other institutions in the public and private sectors. Various parts of the system take care of all activities listed in this chapter except the highest policy-making functions. The main purpose of PPB is to make it possible to base budget decisions on the results of formalized planning and systems analysis. The basic principles which make the system work are not particularly new, but they *are* organized into a fairly well-integrated and defined system which specifies what activities shall be performed and how they interrelate with each other, but not how to perform them. PPB essentially guides the planning process by asking questions and requiring certain information at various stages of that process; planners must devise their own means of supplying the data.

At the beginning of the Kennedy Administration, the planning function within the Department of Defense was found to be in disarray. The basic problem was that substantive, or military, planning was completely separated from fiscal, or budgetary, planning (Hitch, 1967). Military planning was performed by the Joint Chiefs of Staff and other military personnel. It was carried out in terms of such departmental outputs as military units and weapons systems. Although long- and intermediate-range military plans were drawn up, their budgetary requirements were never adequately assessed. The resulting financial infeasibility of the long-range plans meant that they were generally ignored by the department's civilian managers, who made the vital financial decisions.

All fiscal planning was done by the civilian comptroller agency, under the direction of the Secretary of Defense. The categories of fiscal planning were departmental inputs rather than outputs, such as personnel, maintenance, research, construction, etc. No attempt was made to correlate these inputs and the output categories of the military plans. Fiscal planning was done on a one-year basis, which encouraged a lot of new projects for which the long-range costs were not at all apparent. This unrealistic mode of planning therefore, fostered numerous project cancellations, stretchouts, and postponements. The largest organization in the world had no approved plans for more than a year in advance.

The old system did not force the substantive planners to be responsible to financial constraints in their choices, so all fiscal responsibility and, ultimately, the important decisions were borne by the comptroller's office. Another fault was the system's decentralization, which deemphasized joint missions between the services and encouraged each service to think only in terms of its own priorities and its own favored missions.

The prime contribution of PPB, then, is the full integration of substantive and fiscal planning. But, as we shall see as we examine the characteristics of the system, other inherent faults of the old system are also overcome. Program review becomes essentially a year-round operation, rather than something to be performed annually in a concentrated period of several weeks; planners are forced to specify both their objectives and their accomplishments in precise terms for meaningful analysis; more alternatives are given adequate consideration by high-level officials (although the system, by itself, still does not force out all good alternatives); and the future costs of programs which result from present decisions are projected and considered. These benefits are essentially independent of the many that accrue simply from uniting fiscal and substantive planning.

We turn now to an examination of the design and basic concepts of PPB, drawing primarily from the Bureau of the Budget specifications (1965). The system will be analyzed in terms of its basic features, processes, outputs, and specific identifiable activities.

Basic System Features.   Essential to the system is an objectives-oriented (or output-oriented) program structure. In the nomenclature of this chapter, program corresponds to the alternatives which are selected as the seemingly optimal means toward accomplishment of the organization's objectives. The program structure, which represents the objectives, serves as the basic framework for all processes of the

PPB system. A three-level tree structure is used, headed by broad *program categories,* corresponding to the broad objectives of the organization, such as improvement of higher education would be for the Department of Health, Education, and Welfare. The next level is that of *program subcategories,* which break down program categories to a level that defines more specific goals encompassed within a broad objective. Carrying out our example, a program subcategory would be improvement of engineering and science training. The lowest sub-division is the *program element,* a specific activity, expressed in quantitative terms, which contributes to achievement of the subcategory. An example would be to train a certain number of teachers in using "new math." No single element may appear under more than one subprogram. The important thing is that plans are organized around programs, not objects of expenditure. This scheme affords the analyst a much clearer picture of the organization's activities in relation to its goals. Furthermore, since programs may or may not correspond to the organizational structure, duplication is easier to spot and inter-agency cooperation in pursuit of common goals is facilitated. It is interesting, incidentally, that people who have implemented a PPB system say that establishment of a meaningful program structure is the longest and most difficult task.

Also essential to PPB is the process of cost-benefit analysis, which is performed on alternative programs for meeting goals and on specific goals themselves in terms of meeting the agency's mission or basic objectives. Thus, the evaluation and comparison of alternatives is put on a systematic basis, although the planners must develop their own evaluation criteria and their own methods of estimating cost and benefits. Under this system the objective function to be maximized may be the difference between benefits and cost, or the benefit/cost ratio. A formal model of the cost-benefit analysis process has been developed by Jones (1969). In his model, a cost matrix is developed from consideration of the costs of basic resources, system elements, and system characteristics, with a constraint imposed on each of these costs by an equation. Benefit measures are also input, and the benefit/cost ratio is maximized. Sensitivity analysis is applied to the results. Similar models might also be developed from different assumptions. For example, we might assume the constraints to be inequalities, or we might seek to maximize the benefit-cost difference. Other good opportunities for research in this field are given in Jones' paper.

Adherence to a time cycle is also a fundamental part of PPB. In many applications, programs are laid out in five-year plans, although it is sometimes necessary to plan considerably farther into the future. Program costs are estimated right up to the planning horizon, but immediate budgets are drawn only from the first year of the plan. As an annual event, the past year is removed from the plan and a new year's plan is added at the other end.

Basic System Processes.   Three fundamental processes are involved in the operations of PPB:

An *analytic process* carries out continuing in-depth analyses of the organization's goals, the programs which have been selected to meet those goals, and possible alternative programs. Information generated by this process serves as the main input to the other two processes.

A *planning and programming* process organizes data into meaningful categories, and selects and schedules programs for implementation.

A *budgeting process* translates program decisions into a budget context for formal presentation to top-level management.

Basic System Outputs.   The principal output of PPB, the item which might be called the actual plan, is the *Multi-year Program and Financial Plan* (PFP): The important characteristics of the PFP are:

- It is set forth on the basis of the previously described program structure.
- It covers a long-range period of time.
- It shows program levels considered appropriate over the entire period covered by the plan.
- Goals and planned accomplishments are expressed, wherever possible, in quantitative, but nonfinancial, terms.
- The entire cost for the achievement of each program element is indicated. Since the sum of these costs will be reflected in the total budgeting allotment for an agency, the planners are forced to arrive at these costs through *total systems* considerations.
- Costs (and receipts) of each program are translated into a prescribed budgetary format. Among other things, this facilitates comparison of different programs with similar objectives by standardizing the format and units of measurement for all programs.

- The PFP is in continuous existence and should be the perpetual guide for agency activities and operational decisions.
- Except for the annual reappraisal and updating of the PFP, only minor adjustments may be made to it without approval from very-high-level management.

Another fundamental output of the PPB system is the *Program Memorandum,* a document which is prepared annually for each program category in the PFP. The program memorandum represents the culmination of a great deal of analytic effort to assess the adequacy and efficiency of the PFP to meet the needs expressed in the program category. Modifications to previously approved plans, when deemed advisable, are recommended. Specific information in the Program Memorandum should include:

1. A listing of specific programs being recommended, including costs and anticipated benefits.
2. Objectives of the program, described in quantitative, non-financial terms, wherever possible.
3. Comparison, on the basis of cost-benefit analysis, of alternative programs which would also meet the described objectives.
4. Explicit identification of all assumptions which support the recommended programs. (In a dialectical approach, assumptions which support each alternative would have to be identified.)
5. Explicit identification of the criteria used in evaluation of alternatives.
6. Identification of uncertainties in the assumptions which support the recommended alternatives, along with analysis of the sensitivity of alternatives to variations in these uncertain variables, in terms of cost and benefit.
7. Although not required in Bureau of the Budget specifications, the Program Memorandum would also be the proper vehicle for the results of contingency, validity and *a fortiori* analyses, mentioned earlier in this chapter.

The third output of the system consists of *Special Studies,* drawn up by the analytic staff, on topics of interest to high-level planners where the information cannot be found in the PFP or Program

Memoranda. The emphasis may be on either broad reviews of a wide area of information, or intensive examination of narrow topics.

Identifiable Activities in PPB. PPB might well provide a good starting framework for an integrated large-scale online planning system. Such a system might incorporate modules based on well-known techniques, while at the same time exposing many areas for the development of new techniques.

In Table 4-1 are listed identifiable functions which must be performed in order to fulfill the requirements of a PPB system. The four columns after the PPB activities serve to classify them in four different ways. All classifications are, of course, highly subjective opinions of the author, giving little or no recognition to the fact that we are dealing with "fuzzy" areas with considerable overlap between them.

Under "Hierarchical Level" each activity is classified according to its appropriate level in the planning process, as depicted in Figure 4–1.

The "Process" column associates each activity with one or more of the basic PPB processes (planning-programming, analytic, and budgeting).

Under "Output" the file which serves as the primary vehicle for information generated by each activity is listed.

The most conjectural column of all is headed "Computer Role." Here will be found the author's estimate of the importance of the computer to each function, in the past and in the near future, according to a code given at the bottom of the table. Those functions which, because of creative or exploratory aspects, coupled with some foreseeable form of computer assistance, would appear to be most beneficially affected by man-machine interactive implementation are indicated in the fourth column by asterisks.

Some further considerations should be borne in mind while studying Table 4-1. First, the represented activities do not, in themselves, constitute a closed system. All of the activities are undertaken within the framework of policies and constraints from above. These arise outside the system due to the many constraints imposed by such factors as economics, politics, ethics, and the organization's mission. Furthermore, no claims are made as to the completeness of the list or the separability of the activities from each other. Finally, no inferences should be drawn from the order in which activities are presented, except that they are roughly grouped according to their level in the planning process hierarchy.

Computer-Assisted PPB: Pro and Con. We have examined the characteristics of the PPB system and seen some of its advantages; what, then, are its major pitfalls?

In a large organization, which is the only kind which would be interested in this system, installment of PPB procedures tends to foster centralization of the planning process. It is quite conceivable that this could have some creativity-stifling side effects, such as premature elimination of planning alternatives, or the creation of a built-in bias in favor of "safe" but not necessarily creative proposals. Managers should seek ways to overcome these effects as the planning mechanism is made more visible through PPB.

Overly tight linkage of policy analysis with the budget cycle can also have bad effects, as discussed at length by Wildavsky (1969). Emphasis on the PPB program structure and schedules can easily lead to a ritualistic *pro forma* performance of planning duties at the expense of sound and imaginative policy analysis which, by nature, is a much less structured activity.

Implementation problems associated with the installation of PPB procedures can also be tremendous. Inertia on the part of personnel who have, or think they have, vested interests in policies and procedures of the past, must somehow be overcome. Also, well trained personnel must be secured to manage the system. Perfunctory filling in of blanks by analysts not properly trained to perform the necessary functions of PPB can be a particularly insidious fault of a new system, since the formal PPB structure can tend to give the faulty data far more credibility than it merits.

Certain other defects might arise in a strongly computerized version of PPB. All of the faults mentioned so far would tend to be magnified by computerization and certain special problems would be introduced specifically by extensive computerization.

First of all, computer systems which attempt to be too general in purpose are generally not successful. The breadth inherent in PPB and the depth required for meaningful solutions to significant problems may be an incompatible combination on the computer.

Also, users of all phases of such a system would undoubtedly require considerable training and technical expertise. As has usually happened in the past, the managers who should be using the system would then probably assign others to perform the technical interface activities. This development would virtually negate any provisions the system had for creative and explorative work by isolating the system from the real planners.

Table 4-1. Summary of PPB Activities

	Activity	Hierarchical Level	Process	Output File	Computer Role[1]
1	Explore future needs in relation to planned programs.	Policy	Analytic	Special Study	1
2	Determine program categories.	Policy	Planning-Programming	PFP	0
3	Determine program subcategories.	Policy	Planning-Programming	PFP	0
4	Translate subcategories into quantitative goals (program elements).	Policy	Planning-Programming	PFP	1*
5	Determine program levels through timespan of PFP.	Policy	Planning-Programming	PFP	1*
6	Set criteria for evaluation of accomplishments.	Policy	Planning-Programming	Pgm. Memo	0
7	Relate programs to total universe to be served.	Policy	Analytic	Pgm. Memo & Sp. Study	1
8	Generate feasible alternatives.	Strategy	Planning- and Analytic	Pgm. Memo	1*
9	Associate financial data with physical data.	Strategy	Analytic and Budgeting	Pgm. Memo and PFP	3
10	Perform cost-benefit analysis of alternatives.	Strategy	Analytic	Pgm. Memo	2*
11	Perform validity checks on alternatives.	Strategy	Analytic	Pgm. Memo	2*

Table 4–1. Summary of PPB Activities. (Cont'd.)

Activity	Hierarchical Level	Process	Output File	Computer Role[1]
12 Recommend alternatives.	Strategy	Analytic	Pgm. Memo	2*
13 Expose all assumptions which support recommended programs.	Strategy	Analytic	Pgm. Memo	0
14 Identify uncertainties in assumptions.	Strategy	Analytic	Pgm. Memo	1
15 Perform sensitivity analysis on recommended programs.	Strategy	Analytic	Pgm. Memo	2*
16 Select alternatives.	Strategy	Planning-Programming	PFP	0
17 Schedule programs.	Logistics	Planning-Programming and Budgeting	PFP	2*
18 Translate first-year financial data into budgetary format.	Logistics	Budgeting	PFP	3
19 Evaluate actual costs.	Logistics	Budgeting and Analytic	Pgm. Memo	3
20 Evaluate measures of performance.	Logistics	Analytic	Pgm. Memo	2
21 Perform micro-economic studies.	All	Analytic	Sp. Study	2
22 Perform special project studies.	All	Analytic	Sp. Study	1

[1]Code: 0 = minimal computer assistance likely.
1 = substantial computer assistance possible.
2 = substantial computer assistance demonstrable.
3 = computer can essentially perform task.
*especially benefited by online implementation.

Finally, there is a potential danger in collapsing the time span during which plans are made. This results from elimination of the "incubation" period after exposure to a problem, during which a person is likely to produce his best solution. If the minimum amount of time during which the imagination of the planner may be permitted to operate is greatly shortened, it seems quite possible that the creative function of the planning process will suffer unless it is enhanced by other features of the system.

On the other hand, it is likely that many system improvements could be made as a direct result of introducing computers into an active role in the process. For example, benefits would accrue from

1. Removal of mundane work which essentially interferes with the planner's more important tasks.
2. Greater uniformity at the interfaces between planning activities.
3. Shortening the time span required to produce and maintain plans.
4. Availability of more planning data at a lower cost for data base maintenance.
5. Support provided by the availability of an integrated library of automated planning techniques.
6. Advantages of online techniques for problems which are open-ended and require considerable insight.
7. Potential for thorough and systematic testing and comparison of much larger numbers of alternative plans.

All of these positive and negative considerations should be thoroughly weighed by anyone contemplating a computer-assisted, PPB-based, integrated planning system. Final evaluation of the idea, however, must necessarily await its actual implementation and application.

REFERENCES

Brown, R. V., "Do Managers Find Decision Theory Useful?," *Harvard Business Review,* May-June 1970.

Bureau of the Budget, *Planning-Programming-Budgeting,* Bulletin No. 66-3, 1965.

Durbin, E. P., and D. M. Kroenke, "The Out-of-Kilter Algorithm: A Primer," RM-5472-PR, Santa Monica, Calif., The RAND Corporation, 1967.

Fiacco, A. V., and G. P. McCormick, "The Sequential Unconstrained Minimization Technique for Nonlinear Programming, A Primal-Dual Method," *Management Science,* October 1964.

Fisher, G. H., "The Role of Cost-Utility Analysis in Program Budgeting," in D. Novick (ed.), *Program Budgeting-Program Analysis and the Federal Budget,* Santa Monica, Calif., The RAND Corporation, 1965.

Helmer, O., "The Delphi Technique and Educational Innovation," *Social Technology,* New York, Basic Books, 1966.

Hitch, C. J., "Program Budgeting," *Datamation,* September 1967.

Hormann, A. M., *Application Problems of Man-Machine Techniques,* TM-L-4452, System Development Corporation, Santa Monica, Calif., 1969.

IBM Corporation, *PERT-Dynamic Project Planning and Control Method,* Manual No. E20-8067-1, 1967.

Jones, C. R., "On Modeling a Planning, Programming, and Budgeting System," Naval Postgraduate School, NPS55Js 9072A, 1969.

Karr, H. E., Luther, H. Markowitz, and E. Russell, "Simoptimization Research—Phase I," No. 65-P2.0-1. C.A.C.I., Santa Monica, Calif., 1965.

Luther, E., and H. Markowitz, "Simoptimization Research—Phase II," No. 66-P2.0-1, C.A.C.I., Santa Monica, Calif., 1966.

Mason, R. O., "A Dialectical Approach to Strategic Planning," *Management Science,* Vol. 15, No. 8, April 1969.

McCarthy, J. F., and A. Ginn, "A Systematic Approach to Setting and Implementing Product Objectives," *Management Review,* January 1970.

Novick, D. (ed.), *Program Budgeting-Program Analysis and the Federal Budget,* Santa Monica, Calif., The RAND Corporation, 1965.

Wildavsky, A., "Rescuing Policy Analysis from PPBS," *The Analysis and Evaluation of Public Expenditures: The PPB System,* Washington, D.C., Joint Economic Committee, Congress of the United States, 1969.

5

GRAPHIC NETWORK ANALYSIS IN PROJECT PLANNING

R. L. Citrenbaum

Abstract

The objective of Graphical Network Analysis (GNA) is to identify the most desirable features of CPM and PERT critical path methodology, and to place them in a single package suitable for use with interactive graphic displays. The resulting system would provide project management with an effective, easy-to-use planning tool which emphasizes operational optimization as opposed to solely mathematical optimization.

5-1 INTRODUCTION

5-1-1 General Background of Graphic Network Analysis in Planning

Before the late 1950's there was no generally accepted formal procedure useful in aiding planners with project scheduling and management. The development of CPM (critical path method) and PERT (Program Evaluation and Review Technique) in 1958–59 fulfilled this need. Both of these techniques involve a graphical portrayal of interrelationships among elements of a given project. They utilize simple arithmetic procedures for identifying those activities which are most important or most "critical." The overall goal of these

199

methods is to produce better plans by properly balancing the cost and time to complete the project while avoiding excess demands on key resources.

PERT was developed as a management control scheme to provide a guide for the planning of the Polaris missile system. Because several phases of the Polaris program were dependent on technological advances and "breakthroughs," there was a considerable degree of uncertainty in the performance time of various activities. Such problems were the basis for the statistical treatment of uncertainty in activity performance time found in PERT.

In general, PERT is used for planning projects composed primarily of variable activities: those containing a considerable number of chance elements which may never have been previously performed. PERT treats the uncertainty in performance times of activities and is based on three time estimates: a minimum time for completion, a maximum time for completion, and a most likely time for completion of activities.

On the other hand, CPM was developed to determine how best to reduce the time required for routine tasks such as plant overhaul, maintenance, and construction work. Such activities generally show small variations from job to job, and costs for each activity can be readily estimated. Therefore, CPM is useful in planning and scheduling a project with emphasis on performance time and total costs. Projects composed primarily of deterministic activities may best utilize CPM techniques. CPM is based on a single time estimate and, therefore, is simpler to use than PERT.

The objective of Graphical Network Analysis (GNA) is to abstract the most desirable features of CPM and PERT critical path technology and to place them in a single package suitable for use with online interactive graphics, thus providing an effective planning tool for project management. In this chapter the components of CPM and PERT are reviewed and discussed in detail. Much of the material in Sections 5-4 to 5-6, including the basic nomenclature, has been taken from the unpublished notes of Brousil (1965). A philosophy for online GNA and a discussion of relevant work to date is discussed in Section 5-7.

5-1-2 The Role and Objectives of Project Management

The basic functions of project management can be subdivided into several important phases:

Policy Formulation: Determining the basic policies to be followed in the fulfillment of any tasks or projects.

Strategic Planning: Selecting the objectives of the project, generating and evaluating various alternatives, and finally selecting a suitable strategy for carrying out the objectives.

Operational Planning: Determining the specific requirements necessary to complete the project.

Resource Allocation and Scheduling: Allocating the available resources to complete each activity in the project according to a master plan and schedule.

Project Control: Overlooking the entire process all the way from the initial point of decision to the project completion.

Critical path techniques such as PERT and CPM are particularly useful in the strategic and operational phases. The former is illustrated by the use of GNA in generating and choosing among a variety of alternatives in Section 5–3; the latter by the resource leveling techniques in Section 5–4.

5-1-3   The Elements of a Project

The project is the basic operational unit of management. In general, projects fall into two categories: continuous and static. The continuous type is evident in certain operations in which there is a continuous production cycle such as a chemical process or a manufacturing assembly line. Static projects, on the other hand, are characterized by one-shot jobs such as the construction of a shopping center or the goal to place a man on the moon. Thus, a static project is basically one with a definable beginning and a desired end, containing a number of interrelated and interdependent activities, all of which utilize resources, and which may depend on certain imposed internal and external constraints. Because they can be subdivided into recognizable activities, static projects are suitable for analysis by critical path methodology; thus, it is this type of project that is the subject of this chapter.

From the definition of a static project just given, its three basic elements are evident: activities, resources, and constraints. The activities are the jobs which must be performed to meet the project's objectives. In any project there are certain jobs which must be performed before others, and there are jobs which can be done concurrently. In addition to determining the sequence, the method, time, and cost of performing each activity must be specified by the project planner. The second project element, the resources, consists of five components: manpower, money, machinery, materials, and time. Although time is often overlooked as a project resource, it is usually the one that must be spent most judiciously, and is often a function of various constraints imposed on the project. The third project element, imposing conditions or constraints, may include effects of deliveries of machines, materials, etc., from outside agencies. Activities must be carefully planned around the delivery of a key piece of machinery such as a large computer. Needless to say, an ill-timed delivery can be quite costly.

5-1-4 Potential Benefits in the Use of Critical Path Methodology in GNA

The use of critical path methodology and GNA extensions gives rise to a variety of planner benefits. Some are presented below as a motivational force; others are indicated toward the end of this paper.

The construction of an activity network for a project and the associated arithmetic computations provide management with the following benefits:

- They require a logical discipline in planning, scheduling, and control of projects.
- They encourage long-range and detailed planning.
- They assist status reporting in providing a standard method of documentation and communication of project plans.
- They identify the critical activities in a project, making it possible for management to focus attention on the most constrained portion of the project.
- They illustrate the effect of technical and procedural modifications on the overall schedule.
- They assist the planner in determining how to best allocate limited resources across the duration of the project. Often the start of certain activities must be rescheduled—sometimes increasing the total project duration—to keep within the constraint that the demand for a limited resource (e.g., men or materials) does not exceed the supply.
- They assist in determining better plan alternatives by indi-

cating those critical activities for which time-cost tradeoffs are most effective. In addition, CPM methods may be used to balance direct costs (e.g., regular labor, materials, overhead, bonuses, penalties) and thereby minimize the total project expense.

While it is true that CPM and PERT methods require greater planning effort and may double planning costs, the resultant savings in managing a carefully planned project more than compensate for this expenditure.

5-2 PROJECT NETWORK

5-2-1 Preliminary Requirements

Central to all critical path methodology is the development of a project network in which all activities in a project are depicted, and their interrelationships specified. Before indicating the technique of drawing networks, let us consider the requirements of both the project planner (the observer) and the project engineer (the manager). The primary needs of the planner are:

1. A rapid method of determining the "correct" project status at any point in time.
2. A means of handling expected lapsed times to determine the expected completion times for each milestone.
3. A means of determining the key milestones and relating them in the overall project.
4. A means of assessing the scope of the project.
5. An evaluative technique for determining the effects of various alternatives or modifications before committing a decision.

The primary needs of the engineer are:

1. A rapid means of determining his current work status in relation to the overall project.
2. An assessment of resource needs and their order of commitment; hopefully, a schedule for resource allocation.
3. A means of overlooking the scope of the project.

4.   A means of alternative generation and evaluation to find the best course of action before proceeding.

The needs of the planner and engineer do not widely differ, as is evident from the above. In following the action of the project, the planner is interested in "where" it is, the engineer in "what" it is. The best solution for their combined needs is an activity-oriented arrow diagram depicting the project under consideration. The development of such a diagram is the topic of the remainder of this section.

5-2-2   Network Terminology

A *network* is a graphical representation of a project plan, depicting the interrelationships of the various activities making up the project. When the results of time estimates and computations are added to a network, it may be used as a project schedule. The basic components of project networks are activities and events. An *activity* (or synonymously, "task" or "job") is any portion of a project which has a definable beginning and end. It may involve any time- or resource-consuming element of the project. Activities are represented by arrows, with activity description and time estimate written along the arrow as shown in Fig. 5-1. The dependency of one activity on another may be indicated by means of a *dummy activity*. Dummy activities are represented by dashed-line arrows, and carry a zero time-duration and cost as shown in Fig. 5-2. They are introduced to keep the logic correct and to provide unique numeric activity designation (as will soon be evident).

Figure 5-1. Activity representation.   Figure 5-2. Dummy activity representation.

The beginning and ending points of activities are called *events.* Although theoretically an event is a node representing an instantaneous point in time, it is often represented by a numbered circle, the number specifying the event. If an event represents the beginning or completion of an important accomplishment in the project, it is often termed a *milestone.* An event which signifies the joint completion of

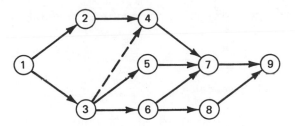

Figure 5-3. An example network.

several activities is called a *merge event*. One that represents the joint initiation of several activities is called a *burst event*. In the project network shown in Fig. 5-3, events 3 and 6 are burst events and events 4, 7, and 9 are merge events. By not allowing two or more activities to have the same predecessor and successor node as portrayed in Fig. 5–4(a), activities may be uniquely specified by the numbers of its predecessor and successor events. A revised version of Fig. 5-4(a), using dummy activities, is shown in 5-4(b). Notice that it is good practice to number events such that the number at the tail of any arrow is always smaller than the number at the head. This provides the user with an easy means of interpreting a sequential network.

5-2 3 Rules and Common Errors in Network Diagramming

Activity arrows imply logical precedence only; neither the length of the arrow nor its "compass" direction in the network has any significance. (An exception occurs, however, in time-scaled networks.)

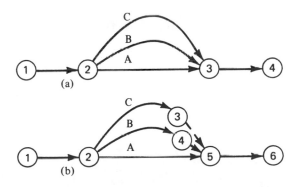

Figure 5-4. Use of dummy activities for unique activity numbering.

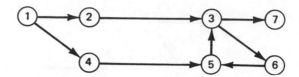

Figure 5-5. Illegal loop condition.

Before an activity may begin, all activities preceding it must be completed. Thus, in Fig. 5-3, activities 4–7, 5–7, and 6–7 must be complete before activity 7–9 can begin. This *does not imply* that activities 4–7, 5–7, and 6–7 must be completed simultaneously.

Because all preceding activities must be completed before an activity can begin, the loop condition exemplified by activities 3–6, 6–5, 5–3 in Fig. 5-5 is not permitted.

Often events are partially but not wholly dependent on the completion of an activity. Thus, if activity 5–6 in Fig. 5-6(a) depends on activities 2–5, 3–5 and only the first part of activity 1–5, activity 1–5 can be broken into parts 1–4 and 4–7 with the dependency of 5–6 indicated by dummy activity 4–5, as in Fig. 5-6(b).

Redundant dummy activities should be eliminated to simplify the network. Thus, in Fig. 5-7 dummy activity 2-4 can be eliminated since it is evident that activity 4–5 depends on event 2.

Ambiguities arising at merge events may be removed by the use of dummies. For example, in Fig. 5-8(a) it is not clear whether the completion date (8-20-70) above event 5 refers to activity 1–5 or 2–5. The ambiguity is resolved in Fig. 5-8(b).

Ambiguities may also be removed by time-scaling the network. *Time-scaled networks* have their activities and events spaced by a horizontal time scale. The projection of each arrow on the horizontal scale represents the activity's duration. Dashed portions of an arrow

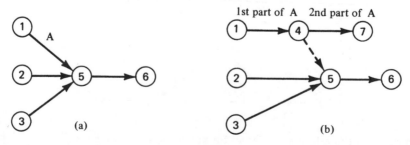

Figure 5-6. Illustration of partial dependency.

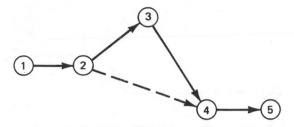

Figure 5-7.   Use of redundant dummy activity.

indicate "slack" time. Thus, Fig. 5-8(a) may be corrected by a time-scaled network as indicated in Fig. 5-9. The advantage of time-scaled networks is that the temporal relationships of all activities and events are clearly represented. In addition, such a representation provides the planner with an aid in the task of resource allocation. The disadvantage of time scaling occurs when the network must be modified and a large number of events and activities repositioned along the time scale.

One of the most difficult problems facing the user of critical path methodology is the diagramming of a realistic network. Often a network which is acceptable to the novice may be totally unrealistic to the experienced planner. For example, consider Fig. 5-10(a), a project network for digging and pouring concrete for the foundations of the building in 5-10(b). Under the condition that one digging crew and one pouring crew are available, 5-10(a) indicates that six days are required for the job. If, however, one divided the digging and pouring tasks into three parts as in 5-10(d), a more efficient project network may be obtained as shown in 5-10(c). The task may now be completed in four days, utilizing the crew far more efficiently. Thus, it is evi-

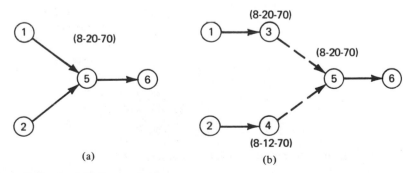

Figure 5-8.   Ambiguity resolution.

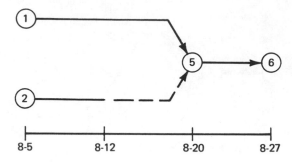

Figure 5-9. Time-scaled network.

dent that the efficient drawing of a project network requires a degree of experience in addition to knowing the network rules and the details of the project.

5-2-4 Level of Network Detail and Time Estimates

The level of activity detail in the project network depends on several factors such as

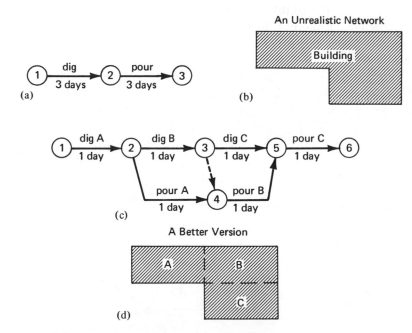

Figure 5-10. Laying the foundation for a building.

- What level of management will use the network?
- Is it feasible to make activities more detailed?
- Does someone require a more detailed network?
- Will the accuracy of the time estimates be affected by more or less detail?

There is a set of general conventions for handling activity duration (time estimate). Typical units for activity duration are hours, days, or weeks (a measure of time) rather than man-hours (a measure of effort). Delays caused by uncontrollable conditions such as fires, floods, strikes, etc., are not included in the time estimates nor is any safety factor employed to take care of them. However, anticipated effects of weather may be incorporated into the time estimates. In addition, certain activities such as the curing of concrete may extend into weekends, whereas the use of the labor force on that task might not. Appropriate modification in time estimates can account for this.

5-3 BASIC SCHEDULING COMPUTATIONS

The ultimate objective of applying network analysis to a project is to produce a schedule giving the calendar dates on which each activity should start and end. After a project network has been constructed as prescribed in the previous section, a series of computations is performed to schedule activities and determine the critical paths through the network.

The computations to be performed are the *forward pass* and *backward pass*. These will determine the values for "total activity slack" and "free slack," and will provide for specification of all "critical" and "subcritical" paths in the network.

5-3-1 Computation Nomenclature and Definitions

The important parameters associated with events and activities are:

a) $E_1(i)$ = earliest expected occurrence time for event i.

b) $E_2(i)$ = latest expected occurrence time for event i.

c) $A_1(i\text{-}j)$ = latest allowable start time for activity whose predecessor event is i and whose successor event is j

d) $A_2(i\text{-}j)$ = earliest expected finish time for activity $(i\text{-}j)$
e) $T_M(i\text{-}j)$ = single estimate of mean duration time for activity $(i\text{-}j)$
f) $S_T(i\text{-}j)$ = total activity slack for activity $(i\text{-}j)$
g) $S_F(i\text{-}j)$ = free activity slack for activity $(i\text{-}j)$

The total activity slack S_T is equal to the latest allowable time of the activity's successor event minus the earliest expected finish time of the particular activity [i.e., $S_T(i\text{-}j) = E_2(j) = A_2(i\text{-}j)$]. It is equal to the amount of time that the activity completion time can be delayed without affecting the earliest start or occurrence time of any activity or event on the network critical path. Activity free slack is equal to the earliest expected time of the activity's successor event minus the earliest finish time of the activity in question [i.e., $S_F(i\text{-}j) = E_1(j) - A_2(i\text{-}j)$]. It is equal to the amount of time that the activity completion time can be delayed without affecting the earliest start or occurrence time of any other activity or event in the network. Notice that $S_T(i\text{-}j) \geqslant S_F(i\text{-}j)$.

The critical path through a network is that path whose activities contain the least total slack. If the convention of letting $E_2 = E_1$ for the final network event is followed, then the critical path has zero slack; otherwise, the slack on the critical path may be positive or negative.

5-3-2 Modified Network Representation

To incorporate the computational nomenclature presented above, let us replace the activity symbol, the arrow, with the more sophisticated arrow in Fig. 5-11(a), and the event symbol, the numbered circle, with the subdivided circle in 5-11(b). Scheduling information is now located in the various blocks and spaces of these symbols. Pertinent scheduling information associated with an activity and with its predecessor and successor events is shown in Fig. 5-12.

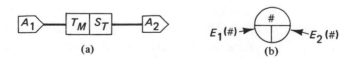

(a)   (b)

Figure 5-11. Modified symbols.

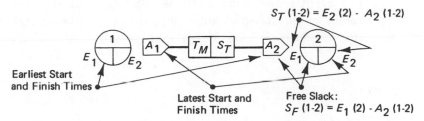

Figure 5-12.   An activity with its predecessor and successor events.

5-3-3   Network Computations

Forward Pass Computation:

1. Start with a network of modified symbols with events numbered and activity duration times T_M given.
2. Let $E_1(i) = 0$ for the initial network event i.
3. For each activity following an event j with earliest start time $E_1(j)$, compute the earliest finish activity time $A_2(j\text{-}p) = E_1(j) + T_M(j\text{-}p)$ and place the result in the head of the activity's arrow.

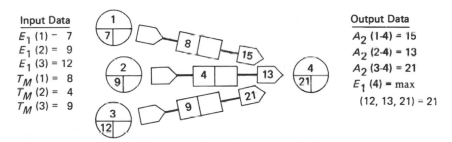

Figure 5-13.   Illustration of forward pass calculations.

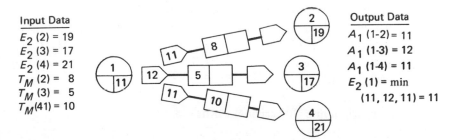

Figure 5-14.   Illustration of backward pass calculations.

4.   For event j determine $E_1(j)$ as the largest of the $A_2(i\text{-}j)$ values of the activities merging to the event; place $E_1(j)$ on the left bottom side of the event symbol, i.e., $E_1(j) =$ max $[A_2(i_1\text{-}j), A_2(i_2\text{-}j), \ldots, A_2(i_n\text{-}j)]$. See Fig. 5-13.

Backward Pass Computation:

1.   The forward pass must be completed for the network, then set $E_2(p) = E_1(p)$ for the final network event p.
2.   For each activity merging to an event p with latest allowable time $E_2(p)$, compute the latest allowable activity start time $A_1(j\text{-}p) = E_2(p) - T_M(j\text{-}p)$ and place the result in the tail of the activity's arrow.
3.   For each event determine $E_2(j)$ as the smallest of the $A_1(j\text{-}p)$ values of activities bursting from the event; place $E_2(j)$ on the right bottom side of the event symbol, i.e., $E_2(j) = $ min $[A_1(j\text{-}p_1), A_1(j\text{-}p_2), \ldots, A_1(j\text{-}p_m)]$. See Fig. 5-14.

Slack Computation:

1.   The backward pass should be completed for the network. Compute the total activity slack for activity $(i\text{-}j)$ as $S_T(i\text{-}j) = E_2(j) - A_2(i\text{-}j)$. Notice that an alternate equivalent computation is $S_T(i\text{-}j) = A_1(i\text{-}j) - E_1(i)$.
2.   Compute the free activity slack for activity $(i\text{-}j)$ as $S_F(i\text{-}j) = E_1(j) - A_2(i\text{-}j)$.

An Example Network Computation.   For the project network in Fig. 5-15(a) with activity duration times shown along the arrows, the modified network symbols complete with forward pass, backward pass, and slack computations are shown in 5-15(b).

The critical path for the network in Fig. 5-15(b) is the path with the least total slack; clearly it is made up of activities (1–3), (3–6), (6–8) as this path has a total slack of 0. The path can be designated by its successive events: 1–3–6–8.

5-3-4   Critical and Subcritical Paths

In addition to determining the critical path through a network, we can identify various subcritical paths which have varying degrees of

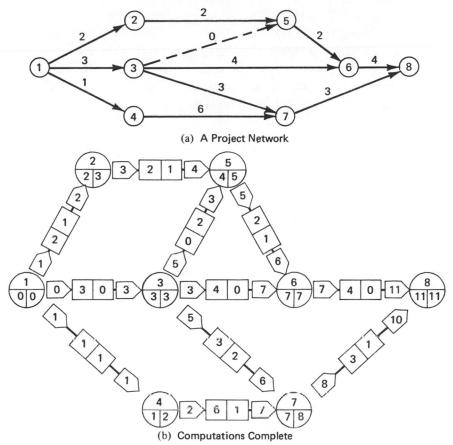

(a) A Project Network

(b) Computations Complete

Figure 5-15. An example network.

total activity slack and, thus, depart from criticality by varying amounts. The subcritical paths can be found as follows:

1. Sort the activities in the network by total activity slack, placing those activities with a common total slack in the same group.
2. Order the groups according to the magnitude of their total slack, small values first.
3. The first group comprises the critical path(s) and the subsequent groups comprise subcritical paths of decreasing criticality. Their "distance" from the critical path, in units of time, is given by their associated value of total slack.
4. If an activity with a given criticality begins at an event, and no activity with the same total slack terminates at that

event, then this event is the beginning of a particular path of the given criticality.

5. Paths of a given criticality are composed of successive activities which have the same total (activity) slack.

6. An event upon which a member of a path of given criticality terminates, but from which no activity with the same total slack emanates, is the end of the particular path of given criticality.

To illustrate the application of these rules let us reconsider the network in Fig. 5-15(b). The total slack for each activity and the resulting paths (as defined above) are shown in Table 5-1. Note that to find the total slack along a path of given criticality, one *does not* sum the total slack of each activity of the path! The total slack along a given path is a measure of "distance" of the path from the critical one(s). This is automatically obtained from forward-backward-slack computations, and may be seen more clearly if we draw a time-scaled network diagram.

5-3-5 Variations in Network Computations

Determination of Critical Path From Forward Pass Only. When only the critical path is desired and subcritical paths are unnecessary, then the critical path may be obtained by applying the following rules immediately after the forward pass:

Table 5-1.   Critical and Subcritical Paths in the Network of Fig. 5-15(b)

Total Slack	Activities	Paths
0	1-3	1-3-6-8
	3-6	(this is the critical path)
	6-8	
1	1-2	1-2-5-6
	2-5	
	5-6	
	1-4	1-4-7-8
	4-7	
	7-8	
2	3-7	3-7
	3-5	3-5

1. Start with the project final event (which is critical by definition) and proceed backward through the network.
2. Whenever a merge event is encountered, the critical path follows the activity(ies) for which $A_2(i-j) = E_1(j)$.

Applying these rules to the network in Fig. 5-15(b), it is observed that the critical path 1–3–6–8 easily emerges.

Event Constraints.   Sometimes events are constrained to occur at some particular time. The conventional method of handling such constraints depends on whether the event constrained is an initial event in the project, a final event to the project, or an intermediate event.

1. The constraint of an initial project event i to a given time T_S is interpreted to mean that the earliest event occurrence time $E_1(i)$ is not zero but that $E_1(i) = T_S$.
2. In the case of constraint of a final event i in a project to a given time T_S, the latest event occurrence time $E_2(i)$ is set equal to T_S rather than equal to the value obtained by the forward pass.
3. A specification of time of occurrence of an intermediate event i is usually interpreted as placing a maximum value on its latest occurrence time $E_2(i)$. For such events, the earliest event occurrence time $E_1(i)$ is determined by standard forward pass computations. The latest event occurrence time is taken as the smaller of the scheduled time T_S or the backward pass calculated time $E_2(i)$, i.e., $E_2(i) = $ min $[T_S, E_2(i)_{\text{back. pass}}]$. See Fig. 5-16.

Constraint: $T_S(2) = 2 = E_2(2)_{\text{max}}$

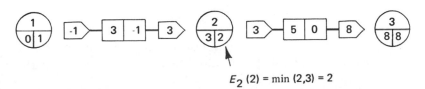

$E_2(2) = $ min $(2,3) = 2$

Figure 5-16.   Illustration of scheduled network with specified time for intermediate event.

5-4   RESOURCE ALLOCATION CONSTRAINTS

There are several possible approaches to allocating resources to fulfill the schedule computed by the network calculations. One possibility is to start all activities as soon as possible and to provide resources accordingly. Obviously, this practice could be quite wasteful. Another approach is to establish an arbitrary resource limit and attempt to revise the schedule to suit this limit. If the limit is too low, of course, the project duration may be longer than necessary. On the other hand, if the limit is too high, waste may result. Both of these approaches are inadequate (although the latter may be realistic) because each ignores resource "leveling." In this section we will consider techniques for leveling resource requirements, and in addition, will observe the case in which there is only a limited resource availability.

5-4-1   Leveling Resource Requirements

Consider a project for which sufficient resources are available; however, it is desired to minimize the daily variation in the amount of resource used. A useful arithmetic tool in the minimization procedure is the sum of the squares of daily resource requirements. This sum of the squares will have a minimum value when a minimum variation in the daily resource requirements is achieved.

In the procedure to be discussed it is convenient to list the activities in the network in tabular form. If the convention is followed of having the successor event number larger than the predecessor event number for each activity, then the project activities should be listed in the table by:

- Order of precedence, i.e., by ascending successor event numbers.
- Ascending predecessor event numbers when two or more activities have the same successor event.

The procedure for resource leveling is:

1. Construct the activity table (see Table 5-2 as an example) with a time-scaled bar chart. Schedule activities as early as possible and indicate any slack available.
2. Starting with the activity at the bottom of the chart,

schedule it so as to give the lowest total sum of squares (i.e., by rescheduling it later). If more than one scheduling time gives the same sum of squares, then select the latest scheduling of the activity (to provide as much slack as possible for varying predecessor activities).

3. Repeat step 2 for every activity listed in the table, proceeding from the bottom of the list to the top.

4. Repeat this cycle (steps 2 and 3) until no further reduction in the sum of squares can be achieved. The resultant schedule

Table 5-2. Allocating a Resource to Project Activities

Activity	Resources Per Day	PROJECT DURATION (days)										
		1	2	3	4	5	6	7	8	9	10	11
1–2	4											
1–3	6											
1–4	1											
2–5	2											
3–5	0											
3–6	5											
5–6	2											
3–7	3											
4–7	3											
6–8	4											
7–8	6											

	1	2	3	4	5	6	7	8	9	10	11	
Initial Total Daily Resource Requirements	11	13	11	13	13	13	8	10	10	10	4	
Modification 1: Moving Activity 7-8	11	13	11	13	13	13	8	(4)	10	10	(10)4	$\Sigma(\ )^2 = 1298$
Modification 2: Moving Activity 4-7	11	(10)	11	13	13	13	8	(7)	10	10	10	$= 1298$
Modification 3: Moving Activity 3-7	11	10	11	(10)	(10)	13	(11)	(10)	10	10	10	$= 1262$
Modification 4: Moving Activity 1-4	(10)	(11)	11	10	10	13	11	10	10	10	10	$= 1232$
Final Total Daily Resource Requirements	10	11	11	10	10	13	11	10	10	10	10	$= 1232$

of activities provides a "best" resource leveling. (Note that some other ordering of activities in the table might give a better leveling—or it may not.)

As an example of resource leveling, consider once again the project of Fig. 5-15(b). The activities of this project are listed in tabular form along with the resources per day necessary for each activity in Table 5-2. All critical activities (those with no slack) are cross-hatched for convenient reference. The initial total daily resource requirements are derived from Step 1 of the procedure, scheduling activities as early as possible. The sum of the squares of this initial allocation (as shown at the bottom) is 1298. Following Step 2 of the procedure, the activities are rescheduled one at a time (starting from bottom of the chart) to lower the sum of the squares. Rescheduled activities are redrawn on top of and slightly below their former location. For the reader's convenience the effect of each modification to the chart is indicated at the bottom of the table. Circled daily resource requirements indicate those affected by a given modification. Although modifying the chart to reschedule activity 7–8 does not lower the sum of the squares (but does not raise it either), this rescheduling is done to provide as much slack as possible for varying predecessor activities. The final total daily resource requirements as shown at the bottom of the table are seen to be far more level than the initial requirements. Notice that the sum of the squares is not changed by allocating activity 1–4 to either day one or day two. The final decision could rest in the hands of the project planner. If the resource being allocated is manpower, it is possible that the planner would prefer to keep activity 1–4 at day two so as to allow for a smoother transition in daily manpower requirements.

5-4-2 Limited Resource Availability

In many "real-world" projects there is a preset fixed amount of a given resource available (i.e., the maximum number of work crews available per day), and activities must be scheduled such that this amount of resource is not exceeded. This may be done by rescheduling activities within their slack time, and extending the duration of the activity.

The activity table is also useful for this scheduling. Activities are listed by:

- Order of precedence (ascending successor event, numbers).
- Order of increasing total slack when two or more activities have the same successor event.

Scheduling activities for limited resources is still very much an "art"; however, the following procedure may be helpful:

1. List the activities in tabular form as specified above.
2. Check all activities to see that no individual activity requirement exceeds the total availability. If this should occur, either adjust activity requirements or increase resource availability.
3. Starting with the first activity, schedule activities as early as possible. If lack of resources makes earliest scheduling of an activity impossible, go to Step 4.
4. If one or more activities competing for the resource have slack available, reschedule one or more of them within the limits of their total slack if this will permit scheduling the activity in question. If not, go to Step 5.
5. If the duration of the activity in question can be increased or decreased, or if it can be split, do so if this will permit scheduling. If not, go to Step 6.
6. If one or more activities competing for resource in question can be split, or its duration increased or decreased, do so if this permits scheduling. If not, go to Step 7.
7. A different ordering of activities in Step 1 may make it possible to schedule activities with resource availability. If not, there is no solution for the constraints imposed.

As an example of this limited-resource allocation technique, let us reconsider the network of Fig. 5-15(b) and the same specification of required daily resources in Table 5-2. In addition, let us specify the following constraints:

1. Only 10 units of resource are available per day.
2. An integer number of units of resource must be used by each activity per day, and an integer number of days must be utilized by each activity. (Assume that $2n$ men working for m days can do the same work as n men working $2m$ days.)
3. Activity 6–8 may take only four days.

The solution is shown in Table 5-3. Modifications to the initial daily resource requirements are shown step-by-step below the chart. The changes in daily resource requirements are indicated for each modification, and the final total daily resource requirements fulfill the constraints at the cost of increasing the project duration by two days. Notice that rescheduling a task to meet the constraints requires rescheduling all subsequent activities depending on the successor event. Thus, rescheduling activity 1–4 requires that activities 4–7

Table 5-3.   Allocating a Limited Resource to Project Activities

Activity	Resources Per Day	PROJECT DURATION (days)												
		1	2	3	4	5	6	7	8	9	10	11	12	13
1–2	4													
1–3	6													
1–4	1													
2–5	2													
3–5	0													
3–6	5													
5–6	2													
4–7	3													
3–7	3													
6–8	4													
7–8	6													
Initial Total Daily Resource Requirements		11	13	11	13	13	13	8	10	10	10	4	0	0
Mod. 1: Move 1-4,4-7 and 7-8, one day		(10)	(11)						(7)		(10)			
Med. 2: Move 1-4,4-7 and 7-8, one day			(10)	(9)						(7)		(6)		
Mod. 3-5: Move 3-7 one day, (3 times)				(10)	(10)	(10)	(11)	(10)	(10)					
Mod. 6: Move 3-7 and 7-8, one day								(8)			(7)			(6)
Final Total Daily Resource Requirements		10	10	9	10	10	10	8	10	10	7	10	6	6

and then 7–8 also be rescheduled. In this example, the only network changes were those caused by rescheduling activities. However, if constraint 1 had stated that only 9 units of resource were available per day, then it would have been necessary to stretch activity 1–2 from two days to four days and make a variety of similar changes in other activity durations.

Since the final solution shows a project duration of 13 days, this new figure can be replugged into the network as $E_2(8) = 13$. This will yield new values of $A_1(i\text{-}j)$ for each activity $(i\text{-}j)$ and new total slack times for each activity. If this exercise is carried out, it is seen that every activity has increased its total slack time by two days, and the initial path, while remaining 1–3–6–8, now has a total slack of two, rather than zero. It is important to realize, however, that to accomplish the project under the constraints imposed in the manner specified in the solution of Table 5-3, every activity must be considered critical. Moving any activity within its supposed slack will upset the calculated resource allocation.

5-5 TIME–COST TRADEOFF PROCEDURE

5-5-1 Introduction

The cost of the project is the sum of two basic costs, the direct expenditure made in carrying out the work and the indirect cost related to the control or direction of the project. The direct cost increases as project duration is shortened from a given "normal" duration time [see Fig. 5-17(a)]. Such a shortening or "crashing" might be vitally necessary because of a change in job priority, or the necessity to meet a given deadline. The indirect cost (i.e., financial overhead, lost production, etc.), on the other hand, increases with project duration. If supervisory overhead is the only indirect cost element, then the total indirect cost is a straight line with a slope equal to the daily overhead as indicated in Fig. 5-17(b). However, outage loss (due to an inability to meet demands) is also an indirect cost element and tends to make indirect costs rise more steeply with increased project duration time [Fig. 5-17(b)]. The combined effect of direct and indirect costs on a project is to determine an optimum duration time, shorter than the normal time along the critical path(s) where it can be obtained at least cost.

For every activity on the critical path and on near critical paths,

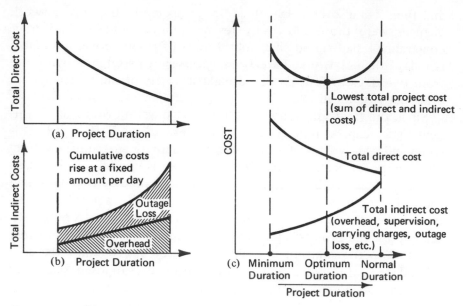

Figure 5-17.   Direct and indirect project costs.

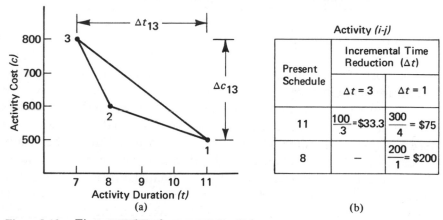

Figure 5-18.   Time-cost data for an activity $(i\text{-}j)$.

"feasible" time-cost points are determined. Each feasible point specifies the activity direct costs for a specified duration of the activity. As can be observed from Fig. 5-17(a), which can be considered a continuous plot of time-cost points, time-cost points should have cost decreasing with increasing duration. The cost of buying a decrease in activity duration time is obtained from the slopes of a line segment between two time-cost points. For example, in Fig. 5-18(a) the additional cost incurred in decreasing an 11-day activity to 7 days is Δc_{13} = \$800 - \$500 = \$300. The cost per day is $\Delta c_{13}/\Delta t_{13}$ = 300/4 = \$75. For every set of time-cost points for an activity, a table which indicates the various costs of reducing activity time can be constructed. Such a table for the above example is shown in Fig. 5-18(b).

5-5-2 Time-Cost Trade-off Rules

The direct cost duration curve can be found through a process of compression and relocation applied first to initial critical activities and proceeding until all activities have been compressed for at least one critical path. An approximation to the total direct cost curve can be obtained by using these rules:

1. If the network has one critical path, consider all activities with time-cost data tables and select that activity which has the lowest cost slope $\Delta c/\Delta t$; select that with the smallest Δt. If this modification causes the path to become subcritical, do not make the modification, but go to Rule 2. If more than one critical path exists initially, go to Rule 3.

2. This rule should be applied when modification causes a formerly critical path to become subcritical. Consider all activities on the critical path for which $\Delta t \geqslant \Delta t_c$ (where Δt_c is the minimum decrease in time required to make other paths critical). Select from among these activities that activity which has the lowest cost Δc, and denote its cost slope by $\Delta c_m/\Delta t_m$. If $\Delta t_m = \Delta t_c$, then modify and the step is complete. If $\Delta t_m > \Delta t_c$, then the path becomes subcritical ($\Delta t_m - \Delta t_c = \Delta t_s$). In this case choose the activity (ies) whose Δt's $\leqslant \Delta t_s$ with the largest cost Δ_c which has previously been modified. "Sell back" these costs to increase the activity duration and make the path critical again. The total cost of modification will be $\Delta c_m - \Delta c$ (sold back)/Δt_m.

3. This rule should be applied when there is more than one critical path.
    (a) Divide critical paths into Part A containing all activities common to all critical paths, and Part B containing activities not common to all critical paths.
    (b) Apply Rule 1 or Rule 2 to activities in Part A.
    (c) Modify two or more (depending on the number of

critical paths) activities simultaneously. There is no definite rule on how to choose these modifications. We must pick likely combinations which keep $\Delta c / \Delta t$ small.

(d)   Select the modification determined in (b) or (c) as the modification to be applied so that $\Delta c / \Delta t$ is minimum.

As an illustration of the time-cost trade-off rules, consider the network in Fig. 5-19(a). Forward and backward pass computations yield the network of 5-19(b), and the critical path 1–4–5. The time-cost data table for each of the five activities is given in 5-19(c). From 5-19(b) it is evident that the duration of the project with any time-cost tradeoff is 18 days. Let us investigate how costs increase as this duration time is lowered.

First, on critical path 1–4–5, activity 1–4 has the smallest $\Delta c / \Delta t = \$50$. Therefore, modifying according to Rule 1, the project duration can be decreased to 17 days at a cost (Δc) of \$50. Doing this results in both paths now becoming critical. Thus, to continue decreasing duration time, Rule 3(c) must be applied. The minimum cost slope is 50 with $\Delta t = 1$ for activity 3–5. Corresponding to this on the other critical path, the lowest cost for $\Delta t \geqslant 1$ is activity 4–5. Such a selection causes 1–4–5 to go subcritical, so by Rule 3(b) we can "sell back" the cost of Δt obtained in the first step above (the reduction of 1–4 by one day). Thus,

$$\Delta c_{net} = 50 + 150 - 50 = 150, \quad \Delta t = 1, \quad \Delta c / \Delta t = 150/1 = 150.$$

Project duration has now been decreased to 16 days and the total accumulated cost is \$200. If a still further reduction in duration is desired, apply Rule 3(c) again. This time, the best selections are $\Delta c / \Delta t = 50$ for activity 1–4 and $\Delta c / \Delta t = 100$ for activity 2–3. Thus, project duration becomes 15 days, incremental change in cost is \$150, and accumulated cost is \$350. One can continue in this manner until a satisfactory project duration is achieved, or until the time-cost points for some activities are exhausted.

Applying time-cost analysis as outlined above will generally result in significant reductions in total project investment and will contribute to the understanding and overall comprehension of the project planners.

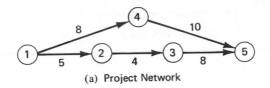

(a) Project Network

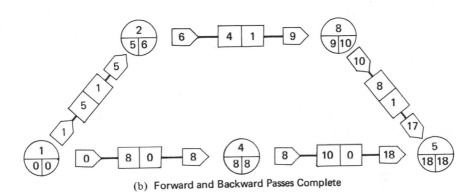

(b) Forward and Backward Passes Complete

Activity 1–2
No tradeoff possible

Activity 2–3		
	$\Delta t = 1$	$\Delta t = 1$
4	$\dfrac{100}{1} = 100$	$\dfrac{300}{2} = 150$
3	—	$\dfrac{200}{1} = 200$

Activity 3–5		
	$\Delta t = 1$	$\Delta t = 2$
8	$\dfrac{50}{1} = 50$	$\dfrac{250}{3} = 83$
7	—	$\dfrac{200}{2} = 100$

Activity 1–4		
	$\Delta t = 1$	$\Delta t = 2$
8	$\dfrac{50}{1} = 50$	$\dfrac{250}{3} = 83$
7	—	$\dfrac{200}{2} = 100$

Activity 4–5		
	$\Delta t = 2$	$\Delta t = 1$
10	$\dfrac{150}{2} = 75$	$\dfrac{300}{3} = 100$
8	—	$\dfrac{150}{1} = 150$

(c) Time-Cost Data Tables

Figure 5-19.   Time-cost tradeoff example.

5-6 THE PERT STATISTICAL APPROACH TO PROJECT SCHEDULING

5-6-1 Introduction

Calculations are made in the same manner for PERT as for general critical path methods for all the preceding applications illustrated. The introduction in this section of a probability distribution for activities makes it possible to calculate the probability of meeting a scheduled date.

It is virtually impossible to exactly determine the distribution function and variance of project activities. Moreover, even if the data were available during the planning stages, their validity would be questionable and the cost of attempting to use them impractical. As an alternative to assuming a fictitious deterministic case with a single time estimate, the PERT technique was developed to assume some form of probability distribution function (see Fig. 5-20) and proceed from there to establish a range of confidence. The initial goal was to estimate the time required to achieve an event (i.e., to complete all activities terminating at that event) together with a measure of uncertainty.

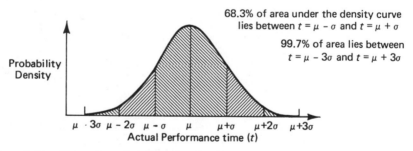

Figure 5-20. Normal probability distribution.

The mean of the distribution (with discrete case) in Fig. 5-20 is $\mu = (t_1 + t_2 + \ldots + t_n)/n$ where $t_1, t_2, \ldots, t_n$ are n observations of actual activity durations. The standard deviation of the distribution is

$$\sigma = \sqrt{\frac{\sum_{i=1}^{n} (t_1 - \mu)^2}{n}}$$

The variance of t is the square of the standard deviation.

5-6-2 PERT Time Estimates

For m independent tasks $t_1, t_2, \ldots, t_m$ with means $\mu_1, \mu_2, \ldots, \mu_m$ and variances $\mu_1{}^2, \mu_2{}^2, \ldots, \mu_m{}^2$, if we form the sum $T = t_1 + t_2 + \ldots + t_m$, then $\mu = \mu_1 + \mu_2 + \ldots + \mu_m$ and $\sigma^2 = \sigma_1{}^2 + \sigma_2{}^2 + \ldots + \sigma_m{}^2$; where μ is the mean of T, and σ^2 is its variance. For large m (say, $m > 4$), T tends toward a normal distribution. This is known as the Central Limit Theorem.

An activity time distribution, as typically illustrated in Fig. 5-21, is estimated for every activity with an uncertain duration. PERT expected time estimates are based on the premise that the duration distribution is unimodal (only one most likely activity completion time exists), and that its standard deviation can be roughly estimated as one-sixth of the range, where the range is defined as the distance between the pessimistic and optimistic estimates (see Fig. 5-21). Thus, the mean and the standard deviation are approximated as in Fig. 5-21.

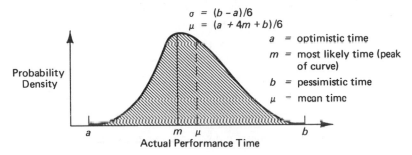

$$\sigma = (b - a)/6$$
$$\mu = (a + 4m + b)/6$$

Probability Density

a = optimistic time
m = most likely time (peak of curve)
b = pessimistic time
μ = mean time

Actual Performance Time

Figure 5-21. PERT time estimates.

5-6-3 Network Calculations of Mean and Variance

Rules for calculating event variance are

1. σ_T^2 for the initial network event is assumed equal to zero.
2. σ_T^2 for the event succeeding the activity in question is obtained by adding the activity's variance σ^2 to the variance of the predecessor event, except at merge events.
3. At merge events, σ_T^2 is computed along the longest path. In cases of ties, we choose the path which gives the larger variance.

As an example, consider the network in Fig. 5-22(a) in which three time estimates (optimistic, most likely, and pessimistic) are given for each activity. The values of σ_{ij}^2 and μ_{ij} for each activity (i-j) can be

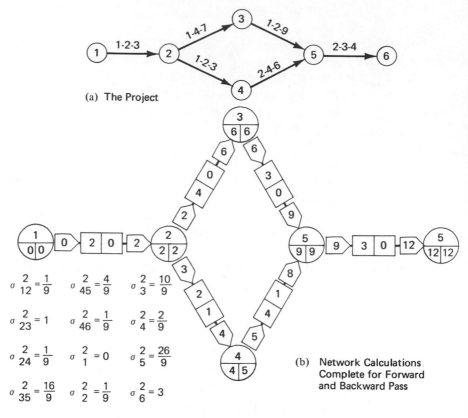

$$\sigma_{12}^2 = \frac{1}{9} \qquad \sigma_{45}^2 = \frac{4}{9} \qquad \sigma_{3}^2 = \frac{10}{9}$$

$$\sigma_{23}^2 = 1 \qquad \sigma_{46}^2 = \frac{1}{9} \qquad \sigma_{4}^2 = \frac{2}{9}$$

$$\sigma_{24}^2 = \frac{1}{9} \qquad \sigma_{1}^2 = 0 \qquad \sigma_{5}^2 = \frac{26}{9}$$

$$\sigma_{35}^2 = \frac{16}{9} \qquad \sigma_{2}^2 = \frac{1}{9} \qquad \sigma_{6}^2 = 3$$

(b) Network Calculations
Complete for Forward
and Backward Pass

Figure 5-22.   Calculations of mean and variance in a network.

calculated by the formulas in Section 5-6-2. Then the mean times (μ_{ij}) calculated for each activity are used in the same way the duration time T_M was previously used in Section 3-3. If $E_2 = E_1$ for event 6 (as no constraints have been placed on the finish time), then the complete network calculations for forward and backward passes are as shown in Fig. 5-22(b). (Note that the values for $T_{M_{ij}}$ have been replaced by μ_{ij}.)

In calculating the forward and backward passes, the basic assumption was that activity times were independent (not the activities themselves), and the Central Limit Theorem was used to obtain the project mean and variance. Thus, along the critical path 1–2–3–5–6.

Total Project Duration = $T = T_{12} + T_{23} + T_{35} + T_{56}$
Mean of $T = \mu = \mu_{12} + \mu_{23} + \mu_{35} + \mu_{56} = 2 + 4 + 3 + 3 = 12$
Variance of $T = \sigma^2 = \sigma_{12}^2 + \sigma_{23}^2 + \sigma_{35}^2 + \sigma_{56}^2 = 1/9 + 1 + 16/9 +$
$\qquad 1/9 = 27/9 = 3$

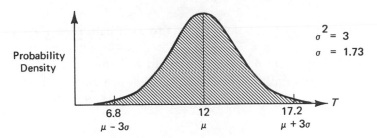

$\sigma^2 = 3$

$\sigma = 1.73$

Figure 5-23.   Probability density distribution for example.

The Central Limit Theorem assumes a normal distribution for T and is illustrated in Fig. 5-23 with appropriate values of μ, $\mu - 3\sigma$, and $\sigma + 3\sigma$.

5-6-4   The Probability of Meeting a Scheduled Date

The cumulative normal distribution function is utilized in calculating the probability of meeting a scheduled date. This distribution is depicted in Fig. 5-24. Table look-up of the cumulative normal distribution function provides a convenient method of determining the probability $\phi(Z)$ (the probability of completing a project in at most T_S days) for a given value Z, where Z is computed as

$$Z = (T_S - \mu)/\sigma$$

Thus, if we are interested in the probability of completing a project in T_S days, we compute Z by the above formula and find $\phi(Z) \times 100\%$ confidence that the project will be completed in T_S days.

If it is desired to find the probability that the project of Fig. 5-22 will be completed in 14 days or less, then

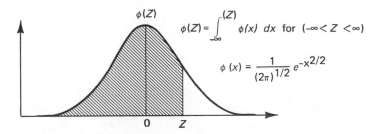

$$\phi(Z) = \int_{-\infty}^{(Z)} \phi(x)\ dx \quad \text{for } (-\infty < Z < \infty)$$

$$\phi(x) = \frac{1}{(2\pi)^{1/2}} e^{-x^2/2}$$

Figure 5-24.   Cumulative normal distribution function.

$$Z = (T_S - \mu)/\sigma = 14\text{-}12/1.73 = 1.16$$

By table look-up, $Z = 1.16$ corresponds to a probability $\phi(Z) = 0.8770$. Thus, we can say with 88% confidence that the project will be complete in 14 days. Alternatively, we might be interested in finding the number of days required for a 95% confidence statement. For this, the procedure is worked in reverse. $\phi(Z) = 0.95$ corresponds to $Z = 1.65$. Thus,

$$
\begin{aligned}
T_S &= Z\sigma + \mu \\
&= (1.65)(1.73) + 12 \\
&= 2.8 + 12 = 14.8 \text{ days}
\end{aligned}
$$

5-7 INTERACTIVE GRAPHIC NETWORK ANALYSIS

5-7-1 Overview

Online planning has been exemplified in recent years by the interactive scheduling of dynamic systems on a digital computer. An interactive approach becomes necessary when automated scheduling algorithms cannot be mathematically defined, and the scheduling process must depend on human judgment. The persons performing the task must be able to interact directly with their data, allocating resources and appropriately modifying the schedule. The interactive process lends itself to the use of a time-sharing computer system in which one or more terminals of a multiterminal system are devoted to the scheduling process.

In practice, there are two levels of user interaction; conversational interaction and interactive computer graphics. In conversational interaction, the planner specifies his scheduling inputs and/or queries to the computer via a teletypewriter and receives output information over the same teletypewriter. He can then call on his own experience and insight to modify the scheduling inputs and obtain alternative plans. Iterating in this fashion he will eventually converge to what he deems an acceptable solution to the problem.

The second-level approach, interactive computer graphics, is more costly to initialize but far more convenient to use. Here the layout and modification of the schedule are done on a cathode-ray tube display, with a light-pen providing direct input to the data base and schedule information. There is usually a function or display selector for calling up any display from a "display repertoire." After requesting a schedule display, the planner can adjust the schedule by using the light-pen until he finds the most suitable set of conditions.

5-7-2   Desirable System Features

There are several features a planner should consider including in an online system for graphic network analysis and scheduling. Foremost, perhaps, is the nature of the interaction. As pointed out in the preceding section, the most convenient vehicle for user interaction is a graphic display system in which the user has immediate cathode-ray tube display responses to his queries and can input information via the light-pen or typewriter keyboard. A well-designed system allows the planner instantly to call up additional structured or hierarchical data about items in the display. In particular, it allows the planner to determine the effect of any action on the overall schedule before executing that action.

It is essential that the system be user-oriented in that the displays are presented in terms of users' needs and the language is in the users' terminology. Both inputs and outputs should be simple and designed to reflect the operating environment of the user.

As scheduling tasks often have basic constraints and priorities associated with them, the accommodation of these should be intrinsic to the overall system. Furthermore, the system should have the capability to predict and resolve (perhaps by alerting the planner) any conflicts as they arise.

The foundation of the system must contain a data base that includes all static as well as dynamic aspects of the system being scheduled.

5-7-3   State of the Art

There is no question that an interactive graphics system providing the capability of online PERT would make a big hit with the management community. Surprisingly, there is little in the literature to indicate that extensive research is proceeding in this direction. The high initial development cost, coupled with cool economic conditions, has apparently forced business management to wait for "someone else" to develop such a package. An interesting initial attempt at interactive graphic CPM was made by Anderson (1969) in his MS Thesis at Dartmouth. The most interesting work to date is the development at Stanford of a graph manipulator for online network picture processing (DiGiulio and Tuan, 1969). In this research a system was developed to provide a "drawing board" through the use of interactive graphics to compose, transform, decompose, partition, simplify, merge, and regenerate network pictures for the purpose of facilitating rapid convergence in new computer experiments. The study is based on a theoretical graphics framework and should provide a foundation for further work in interactive GNA. It seems inevitable that interactive GNA is destined to become a key management tool of the near future.

5-8   CONCLUSION

5-8-1   Objective of GNA

Basically, GNA endeavors to coordinate all elements of a project into a master plan by creating a working model to complete the project in a desirable time period at least cost. The phases in a GNA undertaking include network diagramming, forward and backward pass calculations, resource allocation, and activity time-cost tradeoff procedures.

5-8-2   Project Management and Control with GNA

There are four primary interdependent functions in controlling the management of interrelated project activities. These include:

Strategic Planning: Establishing the overall objectives; making the decision to proceed, selecting completion dates, etc.
Operational Planning: Establishing the necessary activities required to implement the strategic plan and determining resources for each activity.
Operational Schedule: Determining start and finish times for each activity based on the availability of resources.
Plan Control: Revising operational plan and schedule to correct deviations between predicted and actual progress.

Critical path methodology combined with resource allocation and activity time-cost tradeoff considerations fulfills these management control functions. Essentially, given a preliminary network diagram and estimates of normal activity durations, critical path techniques aid the planner in (1) developing better network alternatives (as is done in the example in Fig. 5-10); (2) refining the network logic (eliminating redundant dummies, observing the true flow of work, etc.); (3) refining estimates of critical activities (by focusing attention on these activities); and (4) resolving conflicting requirements. Resource allocation techniques, applied to the network diagram after forward and backward pass calculations have been completed, aid management in determining how best to level the specific resources to satisfy budgetary requirements. Time-cost tradeoff charts for project activities help determine optimal or near optimal procedures to crash the project duration time at minimum additional cost. Finally, time-scaled network diagrams aid in determining a predicted calendar use of resources as well as the start and completion of each operation.

5-8-3 Computer Usage

Virtually every phase of the GNA process can make effective use of speedy, accurate computer computation. However, the most effective utilization of computers is as an online interactive graphic aid to the planner. Oddly, while a great deal of information on batch applications of critical path methodology can be found in the literature (see, for example, Sippl, 1966, or Goodman, 1969), a void exists in the interactive applications. The only reference the author has encountered on interactive CPM is the preliminary work by Anderson (1969), and two excellent papers describing a graph manipulator by DiGiulio and Tuan (1969). By placing GNA in an online interactive graphic system, the planner would be able to get instantaneous responses to desired modifications, providing him with a means of quickly generating and testing alternative plans. In addition to aiding his intuitive (and hence creative) insights to the project and its control, such techniques would enable the planner to make far more effective use of the heuristic methods for resource allocation and activity time-cost trade-offs. It appears that interactive computer graphics should be the next big step to be taken by researchers in the area of management planning and control.

REFERENCES

Anderson, J. L. "A New Management Tool: Critical Path Charting Applied to Graphical Display," MS Thesis, Dartmouth College, Hanover, N.H., June 1969.

Brousil, J. "Systems Optimization Course Notes" (unpublished), Case Institute of Technology, 1965.

DiGiulio, H. A., and P. L. Tuan, "A Graph Manipulator for On-Line Network Picture Processing," *Proceeding of the Fall Joint Computer Conference,* AFIPS Press, 1969.

____, and P. L. Tuan, "A System for Network Picture Processing and Interactive Computer Graphics," *Proceedings ACM 1969 National Conference and Exposition,* 1969.

Goodman, I. F., "Planning and Scheduling Jobs on a Computer Using CPM," U.S. Army Tank Automative Command, Warren, Mich., 1969.

Martino, R. L., *Project Management and Control: Vol. I, Finding the Critical Path,* New York, American Management Assoc., 1964.

____, *Project Management and Control: Vol. II, Applied Operational Planning,* New York, American Management Assoc., 1964.

Moder, J. J., and C. R. Philips, *Project Management With CPM and PERT,* New York, Reinhold, 1964.

Sippl, C. J., *Computer Dictionary and Handbook,* Indianapolis, Ind., Howard W. Sams and Co., 1966.

6

ALLOCATING RESOURCES OVER A NETWORK

P. S. Loubal

Abstract

This chapter describes a model and an online computer procedure developed for resource allocation over a network. In its full generality, the procedure is applicable to a variety of commercial and public facility locational problems involving a transportaiton network with given link costs (distance, traversal time) and supplies or demands associated with nodes or links.

The objective of the model is to allocate demands to supplies so as to achieve not only a close-to-optimal solution with regard to overall costs (such as total travel time) of the solution, but also to keep the maximal cost in the solution (such as the longest distance to be walked) within reasonable bounds, and to develop contiguous service areas around each supply facility (i.e., links allocated to that source). The values of supply and demand can be given either directly or as functions of transportation costs determined during the computations.

The procedure will provide, at substantial savings in computer time and with smaller core-size demands, re-

sults very close to those obtained by means of optimizing procedures, such as a least-cost flow (out-of-kilter) program, or a series of minimum-path tree runs (one for each source) followed by a least-cost transportation (Hitchcock, 1941) program. Because of swift computer solutions yielded by the model, it is an ideal tool in assisting an online planner in obtaining a feel for his problem and in reaching an operationally feasible solution.

6-1 INTRODUCTION*

The resource allocation procedure described in this chapter forms the basis of an interactive planning tool applicable to a variety of problems in logistics, locational planning and transportation. The main variables that are considered are the costs associated with a network of movement possibilities, the locations (either on nodes or on links) of points of supply and demand of a given commodity, and the capacities of a limited number of the links. The procedure determines the routes and amounts of flow between the points of supply and demand.

6-1-1 Available Approaches

The large number of models and a substantial body of literature dealing with the above type of problem tend to belong to one of three categories, depending upon which variables are treated as an input, and which variables are provided as an output. These three categories are summarized in Table 6-1.

Table 6-1. Summary of model categories; I-input, O-output.

Type of model	Complete Network	Supply (locations, amounts)	Demand	Allocated Flows
Transportation models	I	I	I	O
Locational models	I	O(I)	I(O)	O
Network Selection models	O	I	I	O

*This was originally a paper presented at the ORSA/ORSIS Conference, Tel Aviv, Israel, 1969, and published in their proceedings.

The resource allocation model attempts to fill the need for a single model for all three categories, each of which has so far been treated by separate models, briefly reviewed below.

Transportation Models are used to allocate flows, via a given network, from specific supply to specific demand locations. In the well-known Hitchcock (1941) Problem, the costs on links that directly connect the points of supply and demand for a single commodity are given. The objective is to minimize the total cost of shipment, while sending the maximum flow through the network that the amounts of supply and demand will permit. The above problem can be solved efficiently by means of the Out-of-Kilter Algorithm (Fulkerson, 1961), which can also be applied to situations where the source-to-link flows are routed via networks capable of representing the complex movement possibilities, with regard to both costs and capacities. A basic related problem is that of finding the shortest path between two points of a network. Other models in this category deal with the problem of determining the maximal flow that can be achieved through a network, given the link capacities (the maximal flow problem) or both link capacities and traversal times (the maximal dynamic flow problem). Another problem is that of minimizing the maximal cost that will affect any unit of flow needed to satisfy given levels of demand (the bottleneck allocation problem). Various solutions to the above problems can be found in Ford, et al., (1962); and Berge (1962).

Lately, research in this area has concentrated on problems where link costs are flow dependent, without, so far, providing any efficient cost minimizing algorithms for the multicommodity case, the single-commodity case with nonconvex link costs, or the fixed-charge problem in which an additional cost is incurred for any link that has flow assigned to it.

Locational Models are used to determine, for a given network, the optimal location for sources of supply, if the locations and amount of demand are known, or vice-versa. The usual objective is to determine the number of such sources, their location and the necessary capacities, in order to minimize the sum of investment and transportation costs on the basis of some common denominator. The literature in this area dates back to the beginning of the century (Weber, 1909), with the newer contributions generally utilizing either heuristic methods or optimization methods of the branch-and-bound type. In the more mathematically oriented literature in this field, a substantial amount of work on industrial, residential, and re-tail location has been published lately by researchers in regional science.

Network Selection Models are used to determine new or improved networks to carry flows between given locations of supply and de-mand, the usual objective being to minimize the sum of investment and transportation costs. The methods employed range from simu-lation, heuristics, and graph-theoretical approaches to the use of calculus of variations, branch-and-bound, and a discrete version of Pontryagin's Maximum Principle. Any practical network selection problem will, of course, require some information on the connection possibilities, such as the topography and geology of the terrain, or the street system to be used by a network representing the lines and schedules of a public transit system.

Whenever it was necessary to treat problems encompassing all three areas, the usual approach was to use a combination of methods. In regional planning, for instance, the standard approach is to use several traffic estimation models for solving problems of flow alloca-tion and network selection, and to use a variety of land-use models for locational planning. This creates complex interfacing problems, which have never been successfully solved.

In the simpler area of single-commodity problems, it would be possible to use the out-of-kilter procedure (Fulkerson, 1961) to provide optimal solutions to the flow problem on alternative net-works that represent various location and network selection possi-bilities. Questions relating to land and transportation network investments would then be treated by a heuristic approach, in which various possibilities are compared and alternatives formulated.

6-1-2 The Proposed Procedure

The present procedure was developed for a similar type of com-bined application. It will allocate the locations of demand for a commodity to a close source of supply, making sure that the sum of demands does not surpass the amount available at any location, and taking into account the transportation costs and identifying the route to be taken. Although the present model has some deficiencies with respect to the exact out-of-kilter procedure, it bears some im-portant advantages for many applications.

Among the disadvantages are:

- The model will not, in general, determine the optimal least-cost flow allocation. It does, however, tend to achieve close-to-optimal results in a combined objective of achieving low overall costs and a low maximal cost (e.g., the longest distance to be walked or driven by anyone). It furthermore eliminates cross-traffic on any link and tends to form contiguous service areas around any source. The latter is a very practical planning objective for most applications.
- The model can efficiently take into account the capacity constraints on only a limited number of links.
- The model will, under certain circumstances, lead to less-than-satisfactory allocation patterns, the correction of which will require an intervention by the user.

Among the advantages are the following:

- The procedure is very simple and easy to program, and can be adjusted for specific applications.
- It is substantially faster and has smaller demands on computer core space. It can, therefore, be used to treat much larger networks or operate at a greater level of detail.
- Different variables, such as supply, demand, or link costs, need not be specified directly, but can be functions of results obtained during the computational process.

These advantages can be translated into some very practical properties. The simplicity of the procedure makes it possible for an adequately trained user to easily adjust the basic program and incorporate any additional routines to deal with specific problems, account for different constraints, provide additional output, or use nonstandard input or output formats.

The speed of the procedure makes it an ideal planning and design tool. The user can evaluate a large number of alternatives and utilize the outputs to formulate new alternatives to be evaluated. He can, furthermore, easily compensate for any deficiencies in the output the procedure provides. Since in the current-generation interactive computing environment the results are available practically instantaneously, the full utilization of the procedure will require the development of fast display and input methods, such as cathode-ray tube displays with light-pen input. The man-machine interaction problems that have to be dealt with in this connection are beyond the scope of this chapter.

The procedure is applicable to most single-commodity allocation and planning problems, and to those multicommodity problems where each commodity can be dealt with separately, with the common variables adjusted after each allocation. It is particularly suited for evaluating possible new locations for schools, warehouses, industries, parking lots, retail centers, etc., and for deciding which existing locations should be expanded. Other problems that can be solved by means of the procedure include the evaluation of the effect that changes in the network will have on such locations or on flows. A very fruitful area for applying the model is advance emergency planning and operational control in emergency situations. Such applications include the allocation of scarce resources to surviving populations, the allocation of people to hospitals or to fallout shelters, and the development of contingency evacuation plans.

The procedure should, therefore, be characterized as quite general and applicable to a variety of practical problems. Any particular situation will, in general, require that a separate program be written, based on the basic routine described in the next section, and incorporating additional routines of the type described in the last section to account for specific constraints and considerations.

A really efficient operational computer program of this type can, of course, be written only by experienced programmers, both familiar with the procedure and its possible extensions, and capable of correctly interleaving the routines within a common index addressing framework.

6-2   DESCRIPTION OF BASIC PROCEDURE

6-2-1   General Description

The basic procedure is an extension of the well-known Moore (1963) or Dijkstra (1959) Minimal Path Algorithm, based on an essentially dynamic programming approach. Two major changes make this algorithm applicable to the allocation problem:

1. All sources must act as simultaneous origins in a tree-building process. The final *single* minimal path tree will be

composed of branches stemming from the individual source nodes.

2. Whenever a node is reached in the computational process, it will be allocated to the source node from which it was reached only if its demand can be met by the remaining supply.

Whenever additional factors and constraints have to be considered in any practical application, other routines will have to be included in the process.

6-2-2 Notation and Algorithm

The network N is composed of nodes i, which belong to either a set X of "reached" nodes or a complementary set X of "unreached" nodes. The nodes are connected by links (i,j) with costs $c(i,j) \geq 0$. Associated with each node i are the labels $x(i)$, cost from origin; $s(i)$, source number; $v(i)$, the supply value $(v(i) \leq 0)$, or the demand value $(v(i) \geq 0)$; and $a(i)$, the allocated demand value.

Step 1—Initialization: for all nodes i set $x(i)=\Lambda$ (large number); $s(i)=0$.

Step 2—Source identification: for all nodes i such that $v(i) < 0$ set $x(i)=0$; $a(i)=0$; $s(i)=i$, and assign these nodes i to the set of reached nodes X.

Step 3—From all links (i,j), $i \in X$, $j \in X$: find the one that has the minimal value $x(i) + c(i,j)$ and satisfies the condition $a(s(i))+v(j)+v(s(i)) \leq 0$, which guarantees that the supply at the source can meet the allocated demand. If such a link cannot be found, STOP.

Step 4—For the link (i,j) determined in step 3: set $x(j)=x(i)+c(i,j)$; $s(j)=s(i)$; $a(s(j))=a(s(j))+v(j)$; assign node j to the set X. Go to step 3.

This algorithm will assign, if possible, each node to a source node with an adequate remaining capacity. Some nodes may remain unallocated.

The speed of this basic routine can be greatly increased by using a sequence table, so that each link will be considered only once in the computational process. In order to utilize the computer core to treat as large networks as possible, such a sequence table should be of the rotating form. Additional savings can be attained by using a somewhat different labeling method, various counters, etc.

Existing standard least-cost path programs are capable of performing all the computations necessary to determine a single tree in less than 1 second of computer time on IBM 360 or CDC 3800 computers, on networks of up to 8000 nodes. Since the above algorithm includes only one additional test to check the adequacy of the source supply, it is possible to achieve a comparable speed with the present process. Novel network coding schemes can be used to treat networks of up to 10,000 nodes, with up to 4 outbound links per node on, say, a CDC 3800 computer of 64K capacity.

6-3 EXAMPLE

A prototype program, utilizing a somewhat adjusted version of the basic routine, was applied to a specific allocation problem—the development of a community fallout shelter plan. Given census-derived data on the number of people on each link (street segment) of a street network of some 2300 links, the objective was to allocate the population on each link to a nearby shelter. Various alternative shelter plans with different locations and capacities were tested. Since the demand for shelter space was associated with links, the supply of shelter space was similarly treated as a link-associated variable and the algorithm was adapted to allocate links rather than nodes. The movement to shelter was by walking, and the link length or distance (equal in both directions) was used as the link cost. The following small 61-link example will explain this particular application of the procedure. Shelters are treated as sources of supply, and the number of people on any link as a demand.

The 61 links are identified by number as shown in Fig. 6-1. The four circled links represent shelter location (sources) for a particular alternative to be tested. The supply values (in circles), and the demand values, associated with any link are shown in Fig. 6-2. The program automatically determines the available net supply at each source link.

The input to the program is of the form:

LINK	COST	DEMAND	SUPPLY	NEIGHBOR LINKS							
1	4	5	0	2	5	6	0	0	0	0	0
2	3	20	0	1	3	6	7	0	0	0	0
.	.	.	.	.	.	.	.	.	.	.	.
.	.	.	.	.	.	.	.	.	.	.	.
29	0	10	800	25	26	28	30	36	61	24	0
.	.	.	.	.	.	.	.	.	.	.	.
.	.	.	.	.	.	.	.	.	.	.	.
.	.	.	.	.	.	.	.	.	.	.	.
61	0	0	0	32	35	36	29	24	0	0	0

Note that the cost on the source links (e.g., 29) was assumed to be zero. It could, of course, be any other value.

The output of the program lists, for each source, each link that was allocated to it, the distance (computed on the basis of the "pessimistic" assumption that all demands are located at the far end of the

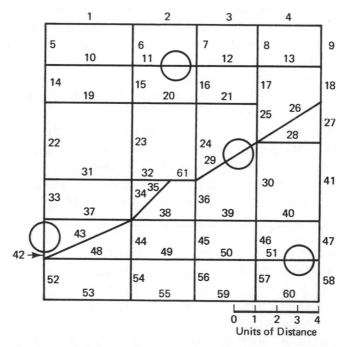

Figure 6-1. Link identification.

link) and the predecessor link on the optimal route from the source.
The output is of the form:

LINK	SOURCE	COST	PREDECESSOR
1	11	6	6
2	11	5	6
3	11	5	7
.	.	.	.
23	11	7	15
4	29	9	8
8	29	6	17
9	29	8	18
.	.	.	.
.	.	.	.
.	.	.	.
60	51	5	58

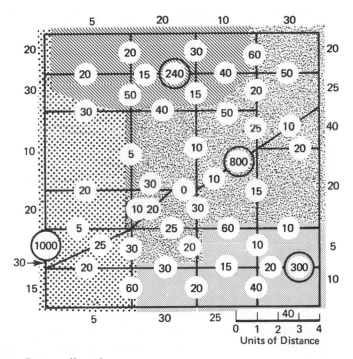

Figure 6–2. Source allocation.

The four shaded areas around each source in Fig. 6-2 indicate for each link the source to which it was allocated. Although in this example all links were allocated, other input data could lead to results where some links remain unallocated because they cannot be reached from a source with adequate capacity, or because such a source is beyond a maximal permitted distance.

In the present example note that link 5 with a demand of 20 units was allocated to the source on link 42 rather than the closer source on link 11. This is due to the limited capacity of the closer source. Similarly, link 20 was not allocated to the source on link 11 since the demand (40 units) would have surpassed the remaining available capacity, but the 5 units of demand on the more remote link 23 were accepted. The procedure did not permit any partial allocation of the demand on a link since it was considered more practical to allocate all people on the same segment to a single source link.

The following additional output was obtained in order to simplify the evaluation of different plan alternatives. This output indicates, for each source link, the amount of demand allocated, the percentage of available capacity that was allocated, and the mean cost (distance) to each source. A similar result is obtained for the sum of all sources.

SOURCE	LINK	SUPPLY	DEMAND	%DEM/SUPP	MEAN DISTANCE
1	11	240	225	93.8	2.7
2	29	800	525	65.6	5.1
3	42	1000	890	89.0	6.1
4	51	300	255	85.0	3.8
	TOTAL	2340	1895	81.0	5.1

Note that the procedure does not permit the links allocated to one source to be used by some other source. This will lead to possible unsatisfactory results:

(a)   Unallocated links may not be reached from a source with adequate capacity because the intervening links have been allocated to one or more closer sources of insufficient capacity.

(b)   The intervening allocated links will not completely block off an appropriate source, but just prevent the more remote links from being reached via the shortest path.

Though the algorithm could be adapted to automatically correct such situations, this would greatly reduce its efficiency. It is, therefore, recommended that such unsatisfactory allocations be corrected by the user, for instance, by a multistage application of the procedure. Only sources with "adequate" capacities would be used in the first round. Results of the first round would be used to adjust the input data by means of an auxiliary program. The remaining sources would then be allocated in a second round.

In an interactive environment the experienced user can quickly determine the areas where the computer results seem to be unsatisfactory and take the necessary corrective action. In many planning situations deficiencies of this type will indicate that the plan itself is deficient, e.g., the capacities at some sources are inadequate. The user is thus provided with information he can use in formulating alternative plans. Any other approach, such as the out-of-kilter method, would also require a possible correction of results in a practical application. In most situations it is more important to have a process in which necessary adjustments can be made quickly and easily, rather than a slow, cumbersome, theoretically exact procedure.

The need to account for additional factors that cannot all be considered in the computational process will, of course, compromise the optimality of any result. It is, therefore, felt that the other advantages of the present process will in many practical applications outweigh the mentioned deficiencies. It is also possible to use the present procedure in evaluating alternatives; an exact procedure can then be used to determine the cost minimizing flows on any alternative selected.

6-4 EXTENSIONS OF BASIC PROCEDURE

One major advantage of the model is its simplicity and speed. These make it possible to add additional routines without any great difficulty and still have a reasonably fast efficient process, suitable for specific application. Only some major possible extensions will be mentioned here.

It might be desirable to associate with each source a variable cost which depends on the total amount of demand allocated to the source.

The demand being allocated to a source could, for instance, be vehicles, with those arriving first finding close parking spaces, and those arriving later being parked further away. The variable source cost would then represent the terminal time associated with the parking problem at each source, and would influence the allocation process.

Since information is available, at any time during the computational process, on the total amount of demand allocated to each source up to that time period, this information can be used to constantly adjust the cost (terminal time) associated with each source. This source cost can then be taken into account whenever new nodes (or links) related to that particular source are added or removed from the sequence table in the basic routine of the procedure. Thus, it can influence the allocation process.

The capacity of a source can be interpreted as a constraint on flow rather than as a limit on the total demand that can be allocated to a source. A source terminal cost can then be determined as zero if this capacity exceeds the flow arriving at the source from the furthest points of demand so far reached, or as a value representing the time lost in the queue if the entering flow surpasses this capacity.

In developing an evacuation plan, where the main bottlenecks occur on the escape routes from a region, it might be desirable to take into consideration the capacities of these bottlenecks. When allocating the demand on the network of the region to the various escape routes, the critical capacities on these links should be correctly accounted for as additional time losses. A similar approach would be needed if, instead of taking into account the capacity of a parking facility, there is a limit to the number of vehicles that can enter per unit of time, and queues build up if this limit is exceeded.

Again all the necessary values, including the time separation between points of supply and demand, are known. Such time losses can, therefore, be correctly taken into account during the computational process and thus affect the resulting allocation.

Instead of associating flow-dependent time costs with a source, such variable values can be associated with links so as to take into account link capacities. In allocating vehicular traffic flow it will certainly be desirable to consider at least the limiting capacities of the most critical links. The procedure suggested for taking into account flow constraints on sources can be applied to links. It is not a very efficient procedure for situations where the capacities of all links have to be checked, but is suitable where only some of the links need be considered, their flows monitored, and costs adjusted accordingly.

The demand (or supply) values in many practical applications will depend on transportation costs. For instance, a person living close to a shopping center will make more trips than a person living far away. The basic routine provides the transportation cost from the location of demand to a source that is being considered, and the actual amount of demand can be generated at that point in the computational process by means of some suitable formula. Similarly, the supply can be adjusted on the basis of calculations up to that point in time.

The output of the basic routine can be used to directly provide additional information required by the user. In an application related to the allocation of vehicular traffic, it might be desirable to predict the total amount of flow on each link or the mean distance driven by all vehicles.

The routine used will, of course, depend on the information required. For instance, the total flow on each link can be obtained by means of a loading procedure which assigns flow to paths determined on the basis of predecessor information. An efficient loading procedure will consider each link only once and will hardly affect the computational speed of the allocation program. It will require, as input, a list of links ordered by distance (cost) from each origin, which can be easily obtained from the basic routine. If different distances are associated with each direction of a link and the sources of supply are really the destinations of flow, the basic routine in which sources act as origins of flow can still be used. It will only be necessary to reverse the link directions on input, i.e., associate the cost c(i,j) with the link direction (j,i).

REFERENCES

Berge, C., *The Theory of Graphs,* New York, John Wiley & Sons, Inc., 1962.

Dijkstra, E. W., "A Note on Two Problems in Connection with Graphs," *Numerische Mathematik,* **1**, 1959, 269–271.

Ford, L. R., and D. R. Fulkerson, *Flows in Networks,* Princeton, N. J., Princeton University Press, 1962.

Fulkerson, D. R., "An Out-Of-Kilter Method for Minimal Cost Flow Problems," *J. Soc. Indust. Appl. Math.,* **9**, 1961, 18–27.

Hitchcock, F. L., "The Distribution of a Product from Several Sources to Numerous Localities," *J. Math. Phys.*, **20**, 1941, 224–230.

Moore, E. F., "The Shortest Path Through a Maze," *Procs. Int. Symp. on the Theory of Switching*, Cambridge, Mass., Harvard University, 1963, 1–3.

Weber, A., *Uber den Standort der Industrien*, Tubingen, Germany, J.C.B. Mohr Publishers, 1909.

7

INTERACTIVE MANAGEMENT PLANNING

H. Kleine and R. L. Citrenbaum

Abstract

An overview of strategic management planning is presented by indicating the role of management along with a conceptual framework for planning. The strategic development of a plan via tree representation and the geometric interpretation of the resulting "window effect" are indicated. This is followed by brief remarks on the man-machine interface in interactive planning.

On the basis of the hierarchical structure of planning, an approach toward an interactive coordination system for management planning is outlined. Initial considerations and elements of such a system, as well as examples of management organization utilizing the system, are presented. The feasibility of handling structural assignments, retrieving information, and producing status reports is indicated. In addition, the generality of the system is stressed, and inclusion of problem-specific planning techniques such as Delphi, PERT–CPM, gaming, and simulation is discussed.

7-1 INTRODUCTION*

The generalized planning process can be characterized as consisting of four identifiable activities. In chronological order of execution, these include (1) considerations of policy to determine what is to be planned, (2) choice of strategy, (3) determination of tactics, and (4) establishment of suitable logistics.

In this chapter an interactive system for management organization and planning is developed through considerations of strategic planning within a comprehensive hierarchical structure. The topics of policy making, tactics determination, and logistics determination are not considered.

After examining hierarchical strategic planning by observing the nature of the planning tree, and the window effect and its geometric interpretation, some facets of man-machine interaction on tree generation and creation are briefly considered. Then, a specific management-oriented online interactive hierarchical planning system is outlined, and application examples are presented. Several useful planning tools are discussed with respect to their incorporation into the planning system.

The goals of the system described in this chapter are to:

- Provide a model for management coordination.
- Promote faster organizational planning by
  - (a) placing a super-structure over planning data;
  - (b) providing superior communication facilities;
  - (c) allowing clear subdivisions of planning tasks into subtasks.
- Ensure higher quality planning by having the computer handle bookkeeping and repetitive tasks, freeing the planner to devote more time and creative insight into the generation alternatives.
- Provide planning flexibility by incorporating various essential forecasting and planning techniques such as Delphi, PERT-CPM, gaming, and simulation.
- Aid layman user development by providing an extensible evolutionary system.

*This chapter is a revised version of a paper which appeared in the *Proceedings of the 7th Annual National Information Retrieval Colloquium* sponsored by the ACM Special Interest Group in Information Retrieval (SIGIR).

7-2 AN OVERVIEW OF STRATEGIC MANAGEMENT PLANNING

7-2-1 The Role of Management Planning

Planning and project coordination is a universal component of management. In the broader sense, the management planning process refers to the advance specification of action for a given undertaking. Effective management often distinguishes itself through astute analysis and subdivision of a complex project into tractable components, and through formal communication of the resulting decision to interested parties throughout the organization. The planning network by which the organization governs itself consists of various activities, including the design of the organizational structures and goals, the selection of manpower and other resources, the specification of policies and procedures, budgeting, and detailed scheduling. The output of the planning process is a "plan," the purpose of which is to elicit behavior leading to desired outcomes. Thus, a plan must serve both as a formal vehicle of management, guiding lower level activities and communicating throughout the organization, and as a means for describing actions and outcomes, representing continuing "performance programs" which allow higher organization levels to govern lower levels.

7-2-2 The Framework of Planning

In general, a plan progresses through four stages of transition. After the idea of the plan is hatched, the plan begins its "conceptual stage" in which the plan consists of vague, often intuitive, concepts. As further consideration is given to the problem, understanding increases and vague conceptions are clarified, giving rise to a clearer problem definition. This is the "definitional stage" of the plan. When a still clearer concept of problem solution is available, the plan is said to be in the "developmental stage." Finally, when detailed steps toward plan implementation can be specified, the plan is said to be in the "implementation and monitoring stage."

The four transitional stages of planning may apply to individual components of a problem as well as to the overall problem itself. Actually, we can define a "single-level planning process" which encompasses the philosophy of the transitional stages. The primary constituents of the single-level planning process are:

1. Set goals and objectives; make initial assumptions.
2. Propose alternate plans and generate their predicted outcomes.
3. Estimate consequences by defining a planning "horizon" and identifying planning impacts.
4. Set criteria and evaluate alternatives.
5. Reset constraints and objectives based on experience gained thus far; iterate on the planning process by returning to step 1.

Hormann, 1970, depicts the single-level planning process via the interesting framework shown in Fig. 2-3. The understanding, insight, and experience of the planner (at the core of the truncated cone) are seen to contribute to each stage of the cyclic planning process (at the crust of the cone). The usual sequence of cyclic steps is indicated by clockwise arrows, with the two-way arrows indicating that any section might be revisited at any time before completing the four-section tour. The overall guiding mechanism is thus a "user-modifiable feedback loop." A variety of decision-making and forecasting tools are shown along the outer surface of the cone. Their positions on the cone are related to the single-level planning process via clockwise arrangement, and to the four transitional stages of planning via vertical position—the higher on the cone, the nearer to the "conceptual stage" of planning.

7-2-3 The Strategic Development of a Plan

A structure useful in indicating the division of a task into subtasks, or, alternatively, the formation of an organizational hierarchy, is the tree representation as shown in Fig. 7-1. In this figure, the "chain of command" or subdivision is indicated by subscript. Thus, b_{211} indicates that this node is subservient to b_{21} and that, in turn, to b_2.

Another interpretation of the tree structure is obtained by considering the "ancestors" of any node in the hierarchy to be the set of feasible alternatives available at that node. This interpretation is quite useful in the theory of game playing and in problem-solving systems in general (Citrenbaum, 1965).

The tree representation clearly shows a prime difficulty in dealing with hierarchical situations: the number of possibilities grows ex-

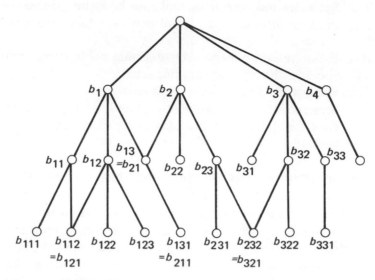

Figure 7-1. Development of a tree.

ponentially with choice number as viewed from the initial node. In addition, because several routes may lead to the same task or subproblem, the tree may be nonunique; thus, in Fig. 7-1, $b_{131} = b_{211}$.

It is important to realize that the standard notion of analysis as a tree search is misleading to the extent that it implies that each step consists solely of selecting a choice from many available alternatives. In reality, a planner generates choices as he goes along, effectively building his own tree. This is an important distinction between decision making and planning: decision making implies a given number of alternatives, whereas in planning the alternatives must be created. Thus, planning involves both choice behavior and the finding or creating of alternatives.

Of primary importance is the consideration of how to effectively build a tree. To visualize this process, consider a planner climbing a tree as he builds it. Crawling along a branch in one direction corresponds to making a choice in the current state, while traversing it in the other direction corresponds to unmaking a choice and restoring the previous state. This ability to back up a tree is the crucial ingredient in enabling a planner to abandon unpromising lines of investigation and start anew. In addition, in starting anew, the planner may have gained fresh insight into the problem and may either investigate branches he has previously built or create new ones. Furthermore, as the planner builds and creates, he also accrues and retains information, effectively "developing" the problem. Often this type of development lays the foundation for the actual "problem formulation." Thus, the planner's conception of the problem at any time consists of the information he has about the problem, how he has evaluated this information, and how it has shaped his definition of the problem. An interesting discussion of the organization of the thought process is presented in De Groot (1965).

7-2-4   The Window Effect and a Geometric Interpretation

Due to the nature of planning, a tree for planning is of necessity quite different from a tree structuring a game such as chess. In chess, each node in the game tree represents a board position and each choice an alternative move connecting possible positions. Thus, each node is well defined and can be measured precisely for numerous characterisitcs by various criteria. However, a node in a planning tree, particularly one near the apex, may consist of a set of aggregate low-resolution variables—by definition, poorly structured. The resolution

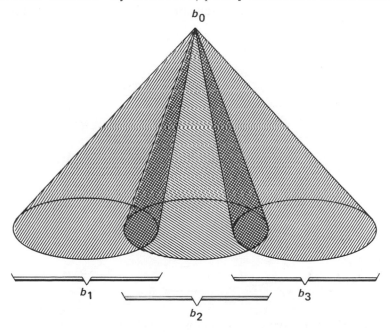

Figure 7-2.   Window effect.

of the variables in the plan becomes finer as we progress down the planning tree. Hopefully at the terminal branches the nodes represent well-formulated plans, each having a well-defined utility in terms of a calculable function of its variables. Therefore, terminal plans can be ordered in terms of preference by the utility function.

Because of this dependence of resolution of aggregate variables in a given node in a planning problem on the relative position of the node in the tree, a more concise tree representation is necessary. To properly portray the planning tree, consider the "window effect" shown in Fig. 7-2. Branches are no longer discrete, but instead appear as "fuzzy rays" emanating from an originating node. In fact, due to their fuzzy, poorly defined nature it is possible for branches to overlap each other as shown. Of course, branches originating from any branch b_i are constrained to be within the boundaries of the "ray" or "window" which defines b_i. Because of this fact, the further one travels down the tree, the finer the resolution of b_i becomes. This follows since b_{ij} is a "partition" on b_i; b_{ijk} is a partition on b_{ij}; etc.

A geometric structure providing an alternate picture of the hierarchical structure of planning is shown in Fig. 7-3. The window effect is more evident in this diagram. Essentially, the geometric description considers an n-dimension abstract space containing all

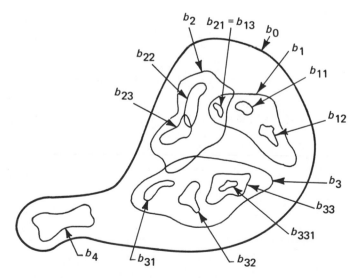

Figure 7-3. Geometric representation of window effect.

planning alternatives, with each dimension representing a variable to be used in describing a plan. Then every point has an associated desirability value or "utility value" based on a function of the n variables defining that point. A high-level plan is represented by a large set of points consistent with its specified aggregate low-resolution variables. It may consist of whole ranges of variables and, thus, have a distribution of utility values. The particularl utility chosen depends on the resolution of high-level into detailed lower-level plans. Because pertinent detailed information is often not available to the high-level planner due to the number of low-level alternatives, his choice of plan may be based on a subjective estimate of the probability distribution of utility values. At each planning level, the planning space is further constrained, narrowing the number of remaining alternatives under consideration. Unfortunately, a poor constraint choice at a relatively high level of planning may inadvertently constrain the possible alternatives in a manner which eliminates from the low-level planners' considerations either the best plan or a set of excellent possible final alternatives. Due to the low resolution of high-level plans, this "inconsistency" in hierarchical planning is often known to occur. For example, a computer systems group designing an advanced software package may severely constrain the flexibility of their package and greatly reduce its potential value by their initial choice of either hardware or computer language.

Consistency of hierarchical planning can be portrayed by the constraint of a low-level plan within the "bounds" (range of variables) set by its higher-level predecessors. This is evident in Fig. 7-3.

7-2-5 Interactive Planning

When considering a specific planning problem, the resolution of planning variables determines the methods and relative difficulties facing the planner as he generates choices in the planning tree. Humans often make decisions based on "what if" extrapolations, simulating abstractly some real-world conditions. However, well-defined accurate answers to "what if" questions provide calculable answers only if asked at low levels of the planning tree. High-level choices corresponding to more ill-defined situations yield consequences which can only be estimated or approximated by some probability distribution.

Since computers are excellent at fast and accurate data processing and calculating, they could provide excellent vehicles for the rapid examination of "what if" questions for low-level choices. On the other hand, since man is superior at present to machines in the vague areas of pattern recognition and generalization, "what if" questions could best be utilized by man to break down high-level planning into parts which can be applied to a computer. By using both man and machine in their respective specialties, the problem can be handled through effective interaction in a manner superior to the exclusive capabilities of either. Speedy, accurate computer analysis of detailed low-level planning facilitates this process even further, and more alternatives and combinations of interesting possibilities may be considered in the time saved through quick analysis.

In addition, freeing man from detailed analysis and calculation at low-level planning enables him to concentrate his energies on the creation of more interesting high-level alternatives. Thus, the availability of analyzed information, combined with concentration on the abstract features of the planning and deep interest resulting from the fascination of having an online computer servant, may provide the necessary catalysts for creative insights and intuition (Mackworth, 1965).

7-3 TOWARD A MANAGEMENT COORDINATION SYSTEM

7-3-1 Initial Considerations

The process of organizing and managing plan development is known to be cyclic, interactive, incremental, involuted, and maybe irrational. A large planning operation involving many people and many activities encounters complexities because of such factors as:

- Changes in constraints, estimates etc., occurring at unpredictable parts of the planning structure (assuming there is a structure) and having unpredictable effects.
- The downward movement of information within a hierarchical structure becoming a burdensome task, and the upward movement an overwhelming implosion.
- Coordination problems.
- Events (i.e., status changes) occurring at random times, producing interactions ranging from violent to subtle.

A computerized management system based on a hierarchical foundation could provide a framework on which a user could "hang" the operational modules of his plan. The system could then assist with the intercommunications, and provide other services to help the user manage his plan.

A key feature of such a system would be the data structure used to represent the planning operation. Preliminary exploration has shown that many available and some new interactive computer services (i.e., application programs) could be effectively integrated into such a proposed system, e.g., Delphi, information retrieval, data management, natural language processing, gaming, and simulation. In the following discussion the system is proposed, and applications of these techniques are exemplified by a planning operation for a fictitious convention.

7-3-2 Elements of the System

A planning project initiator must view his task as a collection of subtasks (area-of-responsibility nodes) which are interrelated by information flow, work subordination, or other connectives. The initial assessment may be as simple or complex as the user wishes, with development of the plan proceeding incrementally. The system is designed so that at any stage of the process the user may expand or contract the plan structure—adding or deleting nodes. He may also expand or contract the content of individual nodes adding or deleting data specific to a node. In addition to maintaining the data base, the system will be able to explore the ramifications of changes and perform other bookkeeping chores.

Experience with this system will uncover node attributes which are common to all planning projects. These attributes may then be standardized within the structure of a node, leaving the remainder of the node data free-form and open-ended. The description or definition of a node may contain functional subprograms to be executed by the system in carrying out the node's assignment.

The format of basic attributes appropriate to most management coordination and planning structures, GROUPS and ACTIVITIES, are shown in Fig. 7-4.

As shown, the information associated with a GROUP is its NAME; its hierarchical LINKS with other groups, Superior ones, Subordinate ones, and Lateral (associate) ones; and its MEMBERS, the first member being designated the Head. Associated with an ACTIVITY is

```
GROUP

    NAME

    LINKS:  SUPERIOR, SUBORDINATES, LATERAL

    MEMBERS:  HEAD, OTHER MEMBERS

ACTIVITY

    NAME

    DESCRIPTION

    STATUS

    LINKS:

        SUPERIOR:

            PARENT:  LINK, NAME, FORWARD, DATA—TEXT

        OTHERS

        SUBORDINATE

        LATERAL

    MEMBERS:  HEAD, OTHER MEMBERS

    DURATION

    TASK REQUIREMENTS

    TASK RESULTS

    DATA
```

Figure 7-4.   Data structure for GROUP and ACTIVITY.

a variety of information including the NAME of the activity, its DESCRIPTION, its STATUS (indicating whether the activity is finished, in operation, waiting, or unstarted), its LINKS with other activities (including Superior, Subordinate, and Lateral ones), its MEMBERS, its expected DURATION time, a specification of the TASK REQUIREMENTS along with the output TASK RESULTS, and the DATA or information accumulated for use in fulfilling the activities tasks.

7-3-3 An Example of a Management Coordination Problem

The exercise of planning a fictitious convention is used in following sections to exemplify a simple application of the proposed system. Presuppose that the initiation of the convention plan is the responsibility of a single individual.

Structural Assignment. The planner, addressing the computer, can describe the superstructure of his project in terms of action of area-of-responsibility nodes. A rough syntax to indicate possible planner interaction is:

CREATE GROUP:	CONVENTION CHAIRMAN
Let MEMBERS be:	Mr. A, Mr. B, Mr. C.
Create GROUP:	TREASURER
Let MEMBERS be:	Mr. C.
Create GROUP:	PUBLICITY
Let MEMBERS be:	Mr. D.
Create GROUP:	ACTIVITIES
Let MEMBERS be:	Mr. E.

The development of actual primitive functions and building blocks for this particular convention example in an extensible natural language can be found in "User Adaptive Language: A Step Toward Man-Machine Synergism," (Hormann, et al., 1970).

The relationship between nodes can be established by task assignment, as shown here:

To TREASURER from CONVENTION CHAIRMAN: (1) prepare a plan for collection and disbursement of funds; (2) provide an itemized estimate of the total cost of the convention and the cost per person; (3) note your own independent assumptions; (4) estimate completion time of assigned tasks; (5) establish constraints: (a) 1000-1500 attendees, (b) 20 hours of meetings, (c) publicity budget of $20,000.

To PUBLICITY from CHAIRMAN: (1) prepare a plan for publicizing the convention; (2) estimate the delivery date of the

plan; (3) assume tentatively a publicity budget of $2,000.
To ACCOMMODATIONS from CHAIRMAN: Reminder—don't
forget accommodations.
To ACTIVITIES from CHAIRMAN: (1) prepare a schedule of
meetings; (2) prepare a selection list for lecturers and/or meeting
chairmen; (e) estimate completion time of assignment.

The input of this example generates in the computer a representation of the items as shown in Fig. 7-5.

With this information the computer can automatically produce "attention" memos addressed to the participants to inform them that they have been drafted for the project. In general, any change in status of any node can trigger the computer production of attention memos notifying heads of nodes affected by the change. This feature can play a very important role in very complex structures where interconnections might be subtle but effects drastic, as dramatized by the quotation: "For want of a nail the horse was lost. For want of the horse the man was lost, ..."

The notifications need only be in the form of a terse memo calling attention to the fact that a status change took place that *might* affect the node. The specific details of the change could be obtained by directly querying the computer. Typically, a change in the status of a lower-level node would propagate status changes upward toward the top of the node. It can easily be seen that such actions might constitute an information implosion that could inundate top-level nodes with (for that level) trivia. This effect could be avoided by implement-

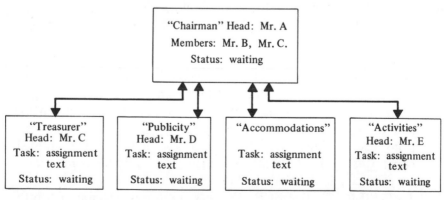

Figure 7-5. Computer representation of management example.

ing a blocking option for each node that would allow the node head to bar upward propagation of lower-level status changes.

Notice that no head has been named for the "Accommodations" node. In this circumstance, the head of the node above would be recognized as responsible for the "Accommodations" node. The planning activity could proceed without ever naming a head for this node, in which case Mr. A, the head of the "Chairman" node, would be responsible. Alternatively, a head of the "Accommodations" node could be named at any time, in which case the individual named would be notified as before. He could then interrogate the computer to learn the status of the project. By describing nodes and leaving heads unnamed, a planner could conveniently subdivide his own assignments.

Continuing with the example, suppose that Mr. C, the head of the "Treasurer" node, begins by retrieving a check list of convention expenditures and selects the following items as appropriate:

1. Meeting rooms   4. Luncheon
2. Clerical personnel   5. Printing
3. Parking

Mr. C may now subdivide his duties as follows:

GROUP: "Meeting rooms"   HEAD: Mr. Γ.
From "Treasurer to Meeting rooms"—TASK:
1.   Locate and ascertain the approximate cost of meeting rooms for the following schedule: Five rooms 200–300 people for three days (9:00 AM to 5:00 PM), and one room 700–900 people for one day (8:30 PM to 10:00 PM).
2.   Estimate completion time of assignment.
GROUP: "Clerical personnel"
From "Treasurer" to "Clerical personnel"—TASK: Estimate the cost and the number of people required to handle clerical duties (e.g., collect registration, mail brochures, etc.) for a convention of 1000–1500 people.

Information Retrieval.   Suppose now that the "Treasurer" wishes to select a head for the "Clerical personnel" node. He may address the personnel file, applying descriptive statements to screen a selection of possible candidates. He may then make his final selection and designate him as the head of the "Clerical personnel" node. This designation, as all others, will be in the form of cross reference between the node and the personnel file. This means that all of the information on an individual becomes accessible within the organizational structure. Of course, some data from personnel, and other data sets as well, would have access restricted. Furthermore, each person involved in the structure also becomes a node in the hierarchy, and the effect of changes in his status can be investigated automatically by the system. For example, if an employee terminates association with the organization, the removal of his record from the active personnel file also removes the employee's record from any and all activity structures of which he is a member. His removal causes the heads of affected higher-level nodes to be alerted by computer-generated attention memos. A graphical representation of this data structure is shown in Fig. 7-6:

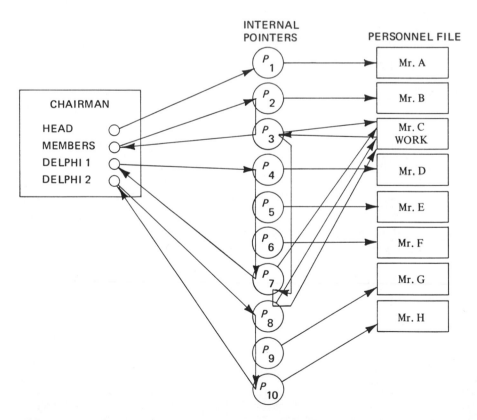

Figure 7-6. Graphical representation of data structure.

1.   The CHAIRMAN and "other activity" nodes are connected by their relationship.
2.   HEAD is connected to Mr. A via pointer P_1.
3.   The MEMBERS list is threaded through P_2 and P_3, which point to Mr. B and Mr. C, respectively.
4.   The Delphi 1 set is threaded or chained through P_4, P_5, P_6 and P_7, which point to Mr. C, D, E, and F.
5.   The Delphi 2 set of another ACTIVITY is chained through P_8, P_9, and P_{10}: Mr. C, H, and G, respectively.
6.   The *WORK* list of Mr. C is chained through P_3, P_7, and P_8, which point, respectively, to MEMBERS of CHAIRMAN node, Delphi 1 set of CHAIRMAN node, and Delphi 2 set of another ACTIVITY node. These are the tasks with which Mr. C is involved.
7.   In the event that the MEMBERS set of the CHAIRMAN node were to be eliminated, the P_2 and P_3 links would automatically be removed from the work chains of Mr. B and Mr. C.
8.   If Mr. C were to retire, the links of his work chain, P_3, P_7, and P_8, would automatically be removed from MEMBER of CHAIRMAN node, Delphi 1 set of CHAIRMAN node, and Delphi 2 set of another ACTIVITY node. Since this action represents a change in the status of the coordination system, the node HEAD—in this example Mr. A—would be automatically alerted.

Continuing with the example, Mr. C., the TREASURER, loads the computer with:

GROUP: "Parking"	HEAD: Mr. G.
GROUP: "Luncheon"	
GROUP: "Printing"	HEAD: Mr. H.
From TREASURER to "Parking"	Task: get parking cost–300 cars/day
From TREASURER to "Luncheon"	Task: get lunch cost
From TREASURER to "Printing"	Task: get printing cost

Mr. C. has now assigned all of the duties. He may now estimate his DURATION TIME as a function of the completion-time estimates of the assigned tasks:

> Duration time = max of duration time ("meeting rooms"; "cleri-
> cal personnel"; "parking"; "luncheon"; "printing")

Figure 7-7 depicts the structure of the planning project as it might appear after a few more steps. Note that nodes TREASURER and "PAID ADS" both require printing services, which are easily coordinated by naming Mr. H as head of both subnodes. An alternative would be to link the PRINTING subnode to both of the upper nodes.

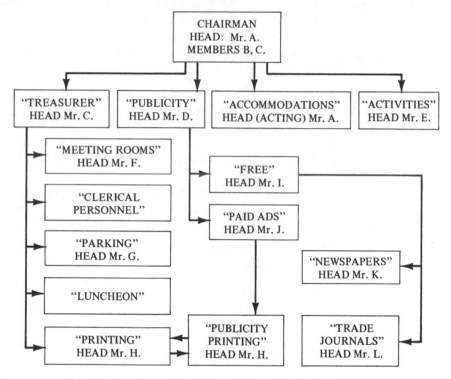

Figure 7–7. Organizational structure of convention project.

Compilation of Status Reports. From the moment that the project was initiated by Mr. A., the planning activities have been proceeding independently at each node with the system monitoring the interactions. All of the individuals involved are executing their functions at times of their own convenience as they wait for lower-level input or supply output (answers). Thus, the system can be viewed as a real-time data processor with interdependent data. As the lower-level nodes perform their functions, the "ready" signal filters up to the top of the structure under control of the people responsible for the nodes. If the head of a node can formulate his output as a function of his input, he may describe this function for the system to execute, eliminating the need for his personal attention. Any time he wishes to do so, the head of any node may query the computer to learn the status of the lower-level nodes; e.g.:

REPORT STATUS ON CHAIRMAN

The system would respond by reporting the status of all lower-level nodes. The following example is based on the plan represented in Fig. 7-7.

ASSIGNMENT STATUS REPORT

Level			Node	Finished	Working	Waiting
(1)	(2)	(3)	"TREASURER"			*
	(2)		"MEETING ROOMS"	*		
	(2)		"CLERICAL PERSONNEL"		*	
	(2)		"PARKING"	*		
	(2)		"LUNCHEON"	*		
	(2)		"PRINTING"		*	
(1)			"PUBLICITY'			*
	(2)		"FREE"	*		
		(3)	"NEWSPAPERS"	*		
		(3)	"TRADE JOURNALS"		*	
	(2)		"PAID ADS"			*
		(3)	"PUBLICITY PRINTING"		*	
(1)			"ACCOMMODATIONS"		*	
(1)			"ACTIVITIES"	*		

The system can also ascertain the nodes which are blocking the completion of the project:

Level	Nodes Blocking Project Completion
(2)	"CLERICAL PERSONNEL"
(2)	"PRINTING"
(3)	"PUBLICITY PRINTING"
(1)	"ACCOMMODATIONS"

Notice that TREASURER and "PUBLICITY" are not listed since they are both waiting for lower-level input to complete their tasks. The "TRADE JOURNALS" node is not included in the list because its next-level node, "FREE," has finished its job independent of "TRADE JOURNALS" response.

7-3-4 Problem-specific Planning Techniques

Delphi. Recently researchers at The RAND Corporation (Helmer, 1966; Brown, et al., 1969) have devised a new approach for obtaining a consensus of opinion among a group of experts in a particular area. This technique, known as Delphi, is an interactive procedure cycling through the steps of opinion polling, ranking opinions, and reporting the outcome of the polling. It has been shown that a consensus can be obtained with a few iterations of this process.

Returning to the preceding example; while Mr. C has been interacting with the system, the other members of the team have also been busy. Mr. A, the CHAIRMAN, has been concerned about his estimate of the number of attendees. Suppose he elects to try for a better estimate by utilizing the Delphi technique. He first applies information retrieval techniques to the computerized personnel file to screen it for people who might have the kind of information he needs. The entire selection is easily joined to his node and designated as consultants for Delphi iteration. He next submits a message describing his problem and requesting the designees to respond by disqualifying themselves or agreeing to participate. In addition, they are asked to suggest others who may be knowledgeable on the subject. Upon receiving the alert, the individual goes to the computer to retrieve the message. He then indicates his willingness to participate by answering yes or no. If he knows of another person who has some expertise in this area, he can suggest this person by adding his name to the list of Delphi consultants in natural language similar to the following:

Add Mr. I to Delphi consultants of "CHAIRMAN"

If Mr. I is already on the list, no action will be taken. If not, he will be added to the list and notified with the original message, which is still on file. At any time, Mr. A, the CHAIRMAN, can modify his message (e.g., deleting the request for additional names and thereby closing the list). Furthermore, at the conclusion of the Delphi iterations Mr. A can delete the list of consultants or retain it for future reference. Suppose that as a result of this operation Mr. A now believes that attendance might number 3000–4000 if a certain conflicting convention is cancelled. To investigate this possibility, he can simply propagate the additional information downward and wait for the outcome. If, however, the planning operation is near completion, he may elect to preserve the initial plan before initiating the development of the new plan. Both completed plans can be held for recall in case of either eventuality.

While Mr. A has been conducting his Delphi iteration, Mr. D, the head of "PUBLICITY," may also be using this technique. This presents one individual handling the bookkeeping for both studies, even in the case where one individual may be concurrently on both Delphi studies, the head of one node, and a member of another.

PERT/CPM. The structure outlined thus far can be seen to be amenable to critical path method analysis. If the estimated task completion time (DURATION) is a standard requirement of all nodes, the system can easily examine the planning structure and produce a PERT or CPM diagram (or a display of nodes which are delinquent with their estimated task completion time, as in the example above); e.g.:

> User Input: TASK COMPLETION ESTIMATE Feb. 5, 1970
> or ESTIMATED COMPLETION TIME 2 weeks
> DISPLAY PERT DIAGRAM FOR NODE "TREASURER"

Since the PERT analysis routine references a data structure that is dynamic, it too is dynamic. Thus, a change in a completion-time estimate of a node would be reflected immediately in the PERT diagram.

The system should be capable of providing hard copy of any displays with little effort from the user, so that progressive PERT diagrams can be obtained as desired.

Note that techniques such as PERT and assignment status reporting are examples of functional requirements of the system which are suggested for inclusion without the user's specific request. In addition, the user should be provided with a capability for explicitly specifying functional requirements, global to all subnodes, to which the subnodes must respond. To illustrate, consider a large operation in its early stages of planning. Suppose that the top-level planner must have current estimates of the dollar requirements of his operation. As the operational plan evolves, more costs are added with every node. Obtaining cost data with current methods would require a flood of cost reports. If the cost reports were submitted directly to the top-level node, they would have to be collected, summarized, delinquent reports expedited, etc. If cost reports filter up through the planning hierarchy, delay would be compounded by the necessity for handling the cost data at each node. In this case it is doubtful that a system could respond quickly except in an occasional all-out emergency crash effort. Crash efforts for any purpose often have a high price.

In the proposed system, the top-level planner could specify that a cost estimate be supplied by each subnode. This cost estimate would be stated as a global functional requirement, with each subnode planner specifying the descriptive details of the function for his particular case and in his own terms. The commonality between these functions would be in the function name as prescribed by the top-level planner. Figure 7-8 depicts an example project. The cost functions associated with each node have been accepted and recorded by the system. In this example, all information necessary to evaluate total cost is available, and the top-level planner can query the system and expect a current estimate in seconds. The system calculates the cost estimate

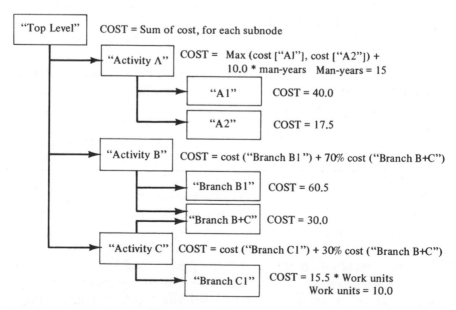

Figure 7-8. PERT example project.

by tracing down through the tree. The function name "COST," appearing on the left of the replacement operator(=), is interpreted as the calculated value to be returned to the upper-level node. The appearance of COST on the right is interpreted as a reference to the cost estimate to be returned by a lower-level node. Thus in the example shown, the calculation takes place as follows:

COST ("A1") = 40.0
COST ("A2") = 17.5
    COST ("Activity A") = MAX (40.0, 17.5) + 10.0 * 15 = 190.0
COST ("Branch B1") = 60.5
COST ("Branch B+C") = 30.0
    COST ("Activity B") = 60.5 + 0.70 * 30.0 = 81.5
COST ("Branch C1") = 15.5 * 10.0 = 155.0
    COST ("Activity C") = 155.0 + 0.30 * 30.0 = 164.0
        COST ("Top Level") = 435.5

The units of measurement of the cost function could be established by the top-level planner, with the responsibility of unit conversion left to the system.

A planner could obtain a breakdown of cost estimates by simply requesting estimates from lower level nodes. In addition, changes in cost estimates at lower-level nodes could be made more freely, since the new information would be incorporated in subsequent calculations without delay. With such a system, the top-level planner could program a combination of budget constraints and cost estimates resulting in the production of attention memos; e.g.:

IF COST IS GREATER THAN BUDGET, ALERT "TOP LEVEL"

Simulation.   Simulation is destined to play a vital role in organization and planning, just as it has in the investigation of systems in general. An existing simulation language such as SIMSCRIPT or GPSS could be developed into an online interactive simulation system and integrated with the management coordination system. This would permit the planner to generate and test a variety of alternatives in an inexpensive manner. More will be said about simulation as an independent entity in a management coordination system in Section 7–4.

Gaming.   As the plan evolves, the user (at any level) may direct the system to record the current state of development. Later he may decide to return to a previous step and continue from there. With this capability it is easy to visualize a gaming situation. The user need only take a snapshot of the system at some point in time and then experiment (with or without other participants) with the further development of the plan. It might also be possible to incorporate into the system a method for organizing the branches of the plan development "tree," and perform an evaluation and comparison of the outcomes of each branch.

Miscellaneous Techniques. A variety of additional techniques may be incorporated into the hierarchical planning system. It is not difficult to imagine managers at particular nodes applying techniques such as decision matrices, deterministic and probabilistic modeling, input/output tables, cost-benefit analysis, contextual analysis, scenarios, etc. (A listing of 26 such planning techniques, complete with accompanying explanation, is given by Sackman in Chapter 1.)

Additional Computer Services:

Text Editing. A significant part of the input to the system will be in the form of memos or messages composed in natural language. This makes it mandatory that the system provide the user with text-editing capability. This facility should be broadened to encompass editing of data and user programs.

Graphics. The potential role of graphic I/O in this system is so broad and far-reaching that it seems premature to list examples or suggest specific applications at this time. It is sufficient for now to point out that graphic I/O will be useful almost everywhere, and vital in many parts of the system.

File Management. The file management characteristics of the system are assessed as:

1. The size of the data structure generated by the user for a single application can be expected to range from very small to medium.
2. The user-generated data structure can be easily managed.
3. The user-generated data will be required to interface with existing files, which may be quite large.
4. User-generated data and programs will need to interface with existing programs.

5. It can be expected that user-generated data and programs will need to be retrieved, changed, and restored very often. This activity may occur at diverse times and locations; however, the problem of conflict in access and storage of files should not be difficult to handle.

7-4 SIMULATION

The role of simulation as an experimental test bed in the study of systems is well established, with countless examples in the literature. Certainly, in the study of management planning, simulation is assured a continuing role as an efficacious vehicle for testing and comparing alternative plans and planning techniques.

Simulation applications occur on two levels: the study of specific problems and the generalized modeling of problem areas. The precedence of the dual levels is established in studies of the problem areas such as computer configuration and time-sharing. It is evident from the state of the art of planning that much work with specific applications needs to be done. Many simulation references which allude to coordination and planning actually apply to resource allocation (Raju, Bendazzi, 1969), while in other cases simulation is discussed in broad general terms tied only loosely to planning. Only deep experience with many specific applications can provide the insights for uncovering and abstracting the underlying principles of management planning. At this early stage, it is even difficult to estimate the degree of success that can be expected.

Thus, it seems clear that the planners who use the management coordination and planning system will require a simulation capability. This capability may take the form of (a) external simulation languages already in existence, e.g., SIMSCRIPT, GPSS, GASP, SIMULA; or (b) an online interactive simulation language/system as an integral part of the system. Using existing languages has the overpowering advantage of low cost. However, there are compelling reasons for electing the other alternative. First, online interactive simulation is the next eagerly awaited evolutionary step in the development of simulation languages, and an online management coordination would provide an excellent vehicle for development, test, and promotion. Second, a powerful argument for an integrated system results from the integration of the simulation program with the hierarchical planning structure described in Section 7–3. The striking advantage of this merger is that it allows the actual data of the plan to be accessed directly and entirely by the simulation program. Thus, the necessity of developing and initializing a separate data structure for the simulation program is completely eliminated. Such data structures are a basic part of simulation programming and, hence, this simplification is a very significant gain.

As examples of the value of an integrated simulation capability:

Consider a plan whose formulation has been completed by using the hierarchical system. This plan could be tested by executing it against a simulation of a real-world environment. Of course, a plan formulated by any means could be tested against a simulated environment. The advantage gained by using the proposed system lies in the structure of the completed plan and its accessibility by the system. The planner could execute his tasks in simulated time by using the system to communicate, to replan subtasks, and in general to utilize the capabilities of the online system to access all associated information. The simulation program would generate environmental input, monitor the operation, record the activities, and summarize the results.

Again consider a completed plan, but in this case suppose that the results, answers, estimates, etc., reported from the planning structure nodes are probabilistic. The output of the system, assuming dependency on the probabilistic input, is, in turn, probabilistic. While in theory it is possible to compute these probabilities, it is often realistically impossible for a complex problem. In such a case the execution of the plan could be simulated, supplying input by sampling appropriate distributions and obtaining the expectation of the output.

During the formulation of a plan, the head of a particular node could write a simulation program to study the problems of his area. If the simulation language/system available to him were online interactive and could interface easily with the planning data, he could investigate his problem and return his conclusions to the main planning structure. The simulation program, which he developed to analyze his problem, could be retained for future use.

These arguments and examples support the inclusion of a simulation language/system for an interactive management coordination system. In addition, the similarity of the general data-structuring capability of simulation languages and the specific requirements of the proposed management coordination system lead to the conclusion that the development of the two parts can proceed independently.

7-5 SUMMARY AND CONCLUSIONS

The development of a complex plan often cannot be handled as a single independent task, and a task subdivision may be necessary. Subtasks must be further subdivided until the resulting subobjectives generated are manageable. In this manner, a complex plan yields a hierarchy of subtasks. It has been suggested that an online interactive hierarchical management coordination system may be an ideal method of handling such problems, and initial considerations for such a system have been presented.

An example of a management planning problem, organizing a convention, has been presented with specific considerations given to structural assignment, information retrieval, and the compilation of status reports. The incorporations into the hierarchical system of various planning techniques, including the Delphi technique, PERT-CPM, gaming, simulation, and others, have been discussed in detail. Indications have been made as to the possibility of utilizing additional computer services such as text editing, graphics, and file management. Finally, the field of computer simulation has been discussed with respect to planning, and the usefulness of an online interactive simulation language has been presented. Such a language would have far-reaching possibilities, beyond the scope of management planning, and would provide a much-needed and extremely useful tool.

REFERENCES

Brown, B., et al., "The Delphi Method II," RM-5958-PR, The RAND Corporation, Santa Monica, Calif., 1969.

Citrenbaum, R. L., "The Concept of Strategy and Its Application to Three Dimensional Tic-Tac-Toe," SRC 72-A-65-26, Systems Research Center, Case Western Reserve University, 1965.

DeGroot, A. D., *Thought and Theories in Chess,* The Hague, Mouton and Company, 1965.

Emery, J. C., "The Planning Process and Its Formalization in Computer Models," *Proceedings of the Second Congress of Information Systems Science,* 1964, 369–389.

Helmer, O., *Social Technology,* New York, Basic Books, Inc., Publishers, 1966.

Hormann, A. M., et al., "User Adaptive Language (UAL): A Step Toward Man-Machine Synergism," TM-4539, System Development Corporation, Santa Monica, Calif., 1970.

Mackworth, N. M., "Originality," *American Psychologist,* Vol. 20, January 1965, 51–66.

Raju, G. V., and A. Bendazzi, "A Generalized Manufacturing Line Simulator System for Production, Equipment, and Manpower Planning," *Third Conference on Applications of Simulation,* December 1969, 64–75.

III

Experimental Analysis

of Interactive Planning

Since planning is still in a predisciplinary stage, it is imperative to develop the experimental techniques that will elevate planning to a more advanced scientific level. Part III is addressed to methodological considerations for improved analysis of planning. These three chapters are aimed at the functional components of experimental method in online planning: experimental design, the collection of planning data, and the reduction and analysis of data.

Willmorth's chapter points up the design of planning experiments as essentially a challenge in the analysis of human problem solving with machine assistance. He reviews the problems and pitfalls of experimentation with human subjects in the online-planning context. The next

279

chapter, an abridgment of a Master's Thesis by Karush, treats a major advance in real-time data collection for interactive planning—regenerative recording. This technique completely captures the real-time transactions between man and computer so that the complete behavioral sequence can be rerun and reanalyzed as often as desired by the investigator. The last chapter by Swerdlow, reviews available techniques for online data reduction, and recommends promising leads for the planning context. All three chapters stress the significant advances in analytical power made possible by interactive experimentation with online planning.

8

HUMAN FACTORS EXPERIMENTATION IN INTERACTIVE PLANNING

N. E. Willmorth

Abstract

Although there are human engineering design criteria for equipment, these are poorly defined for information-processing systems. For ease and efficiency of use and maintenance, information and its controls and displays should be readily accessible, functionally grouped, easily discriminable, protected from destruction or disclosure, reliable, and compatible with the tasks to be performed. A planning language should be simple and easy to use, yet powerful enough to formulate, analyze and evaluate plans.

The computer is best at processing of voluminous and variegated data via extensive, but well-formulated algorithms. The human is relatively slow, inaccurate, and unreliable in such tasks, but relatively superior at detecting relationships, recognizing patterns, and performing ill-defined tasks with partial, inaccurate data. Although research into associative processes, heuristics, and semantic analysis is progressing, at present the information processing system should only aid, not replace, humans in interpretive problem-solving tasks.

To perform credible experiments in planning, experienced experts are desirable. Despite industry claims to the contrary, extensive training is required to use information-processing systems efficiently and effectively. The unavailability of expert planners will present some severe restrictions on experimental designs and problems, partially offset by experiments in using the system in training new planners.

Planning experiments will be concerned both with comparative system performance and comparisons of individual planning techniques. Covering the range of planning, measuring performance, and developing data recording and reduction tools are of key concern in experimenting with online planning systems.

8-1   HUMAN FACTORS IN ONLINE PLANNING

Any information-processing system designed to aid the human planner in solving the problem and making the decisions attendant upon formulating plans must be strongly oriented toward the needs of the human. Much of the task of planning involves seeing relationships and patterns in the presence of missing and erroneous data, and of creating innovative solutions to unstructured situations. Much of the rest of planning involves evaluating hypotheses about causes, possible courses of action, and contingency ("what if") questions advanced by the planner. Thus, the planner and his human weaknesses and foibles are central to the planning problem; the information system must be designed around helping him do his task, not about doing it for him.

The ways in which the data system can help are legion, of course, since it is largely information and little else that is being manipulated. The information-processing system can help the planner detect the need to plan by, for instance, comparing actual to desired (planned) performance. It can help investigate causes of problems and probable solutions by data analysis and runs of forecasting and predictive models. It can help to arrive at decisions regarding courses of action by simulation techniques, statistical decision functions, and resource allocation and network analysis models. It can use these and other techniques in evaluating the possible consequences of plans and helping to formulate contingency actions and safeguards against risks that cannot be safely ignored. In planning exercises of any size where the work must be divided among many planners and areas of responsibility, and where those responsible for contributing information and making decisions are widely separated, the information processing system can act as an information gathering, distributing, and coordinating device, for keeping books on the planning process, and for performing many other clerical, coordinative tasks. In all these activities, it is the human who stands at the heart of the system and whose capabilities and limitations must be primary constraints on the design of the system.

In establishing a planning system the central questions are:

What information does the planner need?
How will the information be used?

Formally, these are known as:

The specification of information requirements.
The design of planning procedures.

The task here is to determine how established human-factors knowledge may be used in deciding these two main goals.

Human factors impinge on system design in several aspects:

- Designing the system for ease and efficiency of use, operation, and maintenance.
- Allocating of functions to hardware, software, and personnel subsystems.
- Designing, developing and maintaining an efficient and effective personnel subsystem.

Providing an effective scheme for project management might be considered also, but we may defer that until a later date.

8-1-1 Human Engineering

Applying the principles of good human-engineering design to the design of equipment is fairly well understood (McCormick, 1964), although new data is added to the file of human engineering information at a fairly steady rate. Human-engineering design criteria for military systems is not quite so well determined (MIL-STD-1472, [1967]), partially because of the specificity of the requirements and partially because of system complexities and interaction. Although some attention has been given to ease and efficiency of using and maintaining software, and working with data bases, the actual amount of verified human engineering data for software is almost unknown. Some indication of this situation is given in the studies of Sackman (1967) through initial considerations of the pacing of man-machine interactions and time-sharing techniques. Designing an information system for human use implies task analyses to determine the human actions to be performed, the decisions to be made, and the information required to be displayed to the human and expected from him, followed by the optimal design of the man/system interface. To avoid continuing to contribute to this deplorable situation, time and effort must be devoted to designing a well-human-engineered planning system.

*Display and Control Subsystem.** The human will interface with the planning system through the medium of a display and control subsystem. Information will be presented on such displays as CRTs, hard copy, console lights and registers, instruments, graphs, and, perhaps on occasion, by voice, pressure, vibration, and other media. He will return commands and information to the system through punched cards, switches, keyboards, light-pens, and, if recent efforts are successful, by voice, graphic, and handwritten inputs.

Although far from determining the precise set of display and control equipment that might be desirable for planning, some criteria are available for specifying appropriate console layouts. These criteria will help in ensuring that easy and efficient methods are used in specifying displays to be generated, that displayed information is easy to work with, and that human-engineering criteria are observed in composing displays and laying out controls.

The major criteria for display and control design are:

Accessibility. Information must be delivered to man so that he can perceive it and react to it readily. Displays must be simple enough to

*Much of the information presented here is the result of an extensive but un-published survey of human engineering design criteria for information systems conducted by Marvin Detambel, James Baker, Richard Knight, and the author.

grasp the essential information readily, information must be pertinent to the task in hand, and sufficient time msut be granted for the human to assimilate the information, consider its implications and formulate a response. Controls, of course, must be readily reachable and easily manipulated. Required input information should be available to man, not too difficult to compose, nor too extensive (normative or default values should be supplied whenever possible). When working with a large amount of verbal material as we may be in generating problem statements, plan objectives and rationales, special care to compensate for and recover from human error must be included.

Functional Arrangement. Displays and controls should be grouped by logical, easily comprehensible categories. They should be grouped by system or subsystem goals and use, rather than by type of information or control action required. Priority in location should be given to frequency of use, required deftness or difficulty in understanding and using, and by criticality (e.g., life-or-death) or emergency action nature. Considering the diffuseness and arbitrariness of much planning data, considerable capability should be given the user to structure and organize the data to suit his needs.

Differentiability. To increase ease of comprehension and reduce errors, functional sets of controls and displays should be differentiated from one another by such characteristics as location, physical characteristics, color, and mode of use. The coding should be consistent across the system to facilitate transfer of training.

Safety and Security. Displays and controls should be designed to prevent accidental activation, especially of emergency controls and alarms. Classified or otherwise sensitive information should be protected from accidental disclosure via keys or other mechanisms. Potentially injurious (to the system, to data stores, or to the system environment) commands should also be verified by appropriate keys before execution, if at all feasible. "Working" (semiformulated) plans and unapproved plans should not be disseminated generally for the results of some planning hypotheses might be quite damaging to organizational morale.

Reliability. Measures to ensure reliability of interpretation of displayed information and input commands and data should be taken. Feedback should be provided on inputs, and controls and displays should be clearly labeled. On graphs, meters, and movable controls, the direction of movement (value change) should be clearly indicated or labeled. If labels and settings cannot be made obvious, "last state" information should be given the user, if possible.

Compatibility. Controls and displays should be compatible with one another and with the task to be performed. Controls should be mounted in close proximity to the display reacted to. For instance, selecting one of a series of illuminated buttons labeled with the choices offered or using a light-pen on displayed items represent optimal proximity. Display formats and contents should be dimensionally similar to control locations, direction of activation, and other physical characteristics. Coding of displays and controls such as color coding, numerics, mnemonics, etc., should be consistent for functional groupings. Differences in language, word, and symbol meanings between the two should be avoided, and advantage taken of the "natural" associations of words and symbols.

Language Standardization. Any information system today is faced with the possibility of using many different input languages for programming, simulation, information retrieval, and data analysis. If there are many cognates among the languages and many subtle syntactic and semantic differences, the user will be faced with considerable potential for making language errors. Further, if a multinode network is used for experimentation, it is likely each node will also have language anomalies. The seriousness of language difficulties cannot be overemphasized. The formulation of plans is already so fraught with special terminology that adding confusion at the system interaction level could be disastrous. It is also likely that a planning language or at least a subset of commands for planning will be developed for the system. Therefore, language standardization, insofar as it can be achieved and as desirable as it is from the human factors point of view, should be sponsored across the system, and courses of action, such as compiling a thesaurus of languages used, training courses, and performance aids, should be taken to compensate for the high probability of language input errors. Input editors in the software that may in part compensate for human errors by detecting syntactic input errors (if not semantic) should be encouraged.

Data Management System. Data files should be constructed to fit the planner's use and to be easy and efficient to maintain, insofar as technology exists to do so. While doing actual experimental investigations of data structures versus user requirements is beyond the strict scope of our investigation of planning, opportunities to establish human-engineering criteria in this area should be grasped.

Management of the Processing Flow. Modularity and flexibility of function and efficient operating sequences for the human should be sought. In view of the tentative nature of planning data, the iterativeness of the planning process, and the likelihood of input errors, the system should probably contain as many recovery, restart, and error-correcting features as is feasible. Provisions should be made for temporary or working stores for most work without affecting master files until a final decision is cast. To keep user-input requirements online to a minimum, considerable attention should be given to defining default values, selectable default sets, and similar techniques.

8-1-2 Function Allocation

One major activity of system design is the division of functions among the hardware, software, and personnel in the system. Conceptually, in terms of man-machine symbiosis, machines act to extend man's physical capabilities; whereas software extends his information-processing capabilities. Man must continue to perform those functions for which he needs no assistance, for which the costs of mechanization or automation are too great, or for which we have no mechanical or program solution.

For a data-processing system, the capabilities of man that are of concern are the data-processing ones of sensing inputs, identifying them, interpreting them, making a decision or an appropriate reaction to them, and communicating the decision. For a planning system, the cases of stimuli and responses that need to be considered are rather restricted.

Sensing. Although machines and programs can be devised whose sensing range, sensitivity, speed, and discrimination limen are all superior to man's, planning information is not normally of a nature for man to require sensing assistance. However, if there is a huge flow of data, as we might have in trying to detect anomalous situations for operational planning need-detection, or in evaluating the state of the economy, a data-processing system could be of considerable assistance in filtering the data. Of course, if the appropriate filtering conditions (mental set, what to look for) cannot readily be given to the system, much of the final evaluation (filtering) of the data might be left to man. That is, the system with its ability to handle complex streams of data very quickly, and with its untiring vigilance, might detect anomalous situations at a relatively low threshold and ring an alarm (output the data for evaluation by the human). The human, with superior pattern recognition abilities, easily reprogrammed attention sets, and better ability to fill in missing values, extrapolate trends, and read through noise, could perform the final filter—the input is one that should be detected. For most purposes, however, we should probably permit the planner to do his own sensing.

Identifying.   Since identifying requires comparing an input signal against possible classes of data to determine its exact category, it is here that the data system might reasonably come into its own. Of course, what was described above was not solely "sensing," but contained a certain amount of identification and interpretation in filtering a proper input out of a "noisy" environment. Here, having detected an input worthy of consideration, but which may or may not represent a critical situation (we had a low threshold, remember, and may get many false positives), the analytic power of the computer may be brought into play.

A data system has, of course, a near perfect memory, and will, once programmed, perform complex analytic procedures very quickly, or indeed a multitude of them, in evaluating the input conditions. Although the system is fast and has a large capacity for complex phenomena, it is also true that it operates best in fixed, predefined patterns. While probability models can be constructed and associative schemes incorporated into the procedures, decisions requiring remote associations, interpretation of context, and category inventions are difficult.

Man does have a large associative memory that is, depending to a certain extent on the unit selected, capable of very precise remote associations. Unfortunately, the memory is quite faulty (though its exact capacity has never been tested) and information often decays rapidly with time and other parameters and many faulty associations are formed. Channel capacity is also extremely limited and quite slow for specific detailed, precise data, creating some difficulty when placing complex situations into storage, but large for aggregated configurations and depictions. A scheme is needed that will take advantage of man's ability to extract complex relationships from equally complex contexts and compensate for his low channel capacity and faulty memory. Perhaps one symbiotic operation would be to take high-rate numeric and alphabetic inputs and transform them to pictorial (graphic) displays from which the human very readily extracts essential relationships and trends that the computer might find difficult. Further, the human might form new hypotheses concerning the data that the computer could then apply to the data. Also, in complex procedures, the human might perform tree-pruning operations that would help the computer limit its area of search.

Interpreting and Deciding.   The function here is placing phenomena into categories on the basis of their implications or meaning rather than by physical attributes or appearances. The human is perhaps best at forming hypotheses concerning the effects or implicaitons of complex phenomena, but the data-processing system may be best at testing these hypotheses via simulation models and other analytic devices. The system is best, of course, at testing with well-formed, algorithmic processes while the human may still have advantages, cost-wise, at testing with ill-formed, heuristic methods. The human is relatively more innovative or inventive in generating new hypotheses and problem solutions, and the system best at following long, complex processes with very few mistakes. The human is very good at changing his mental sets (and, in fact, may have difficulty in maintaining one for lengthy periods), but slow to learn long, complex procedures. The system normally finds it difficult to change its processing rules, but, once set up, follows long procedures easily. That is, a human seems naturally adaptive; it takes considerable work to make a data processing system so. Further, making a data system relatively adaptive destroys many of the speed and capacity capabilities that make it so attractive

Perhaps one of the most important functions that the human can perform is that of resolving uncertainty in the face of ambiguous, missing, and unreliable data. Equally important may be his ability to inject uncertainty; that is, to see alternative interpretations and re-structurings in what might be thought well-structured situations, and to be otherwise innovative.

If problem-solving is assumed to be the iterative evaluation of hypotheses, the proper symbiotic relationship would seem to be to assign to the human the hypothesis formation function (although some aid from the computer might be provided in terms of checklist, scratch pad memory, etc.), and to assign to the computer the task of running through iterations of the model involved to determine the detailed implications of the hypothesis.

Communicating.   Although face-to-face interchange of information is a highly desirable mode of communication, especially, say, in the hypothesis formation stage of planning, the data system really shines at performing communications so long as it can deal with the physical characteristics of data and not with the underlying meaning and implications of the informational contents of data. It converts, sorts, and distributes information at high speed. It has great "mailbox," store-and-forward capabilities and can make up quite complex displays rather readily. As a communication device, the computer can facilitate the interpersonal communications of many planners. It can solicit, store and display for further definition and interaction the semi-formulated ideas of planners. By performing essentially clerical recording and reporting tasks, by tabulating evaluative opinions, by digging up requested data and performing requested analyses on the data, and by serving as a general information coalescing and distribution device, the system may facilitate problem definition and solution formulation on the general, personal, face-to-face level as well as on the more detailed computational level of large data-base manipulations, complex simulation runs, and elaborate data analyses. Speeding up data processing, and, hence, the timeliness of the information collected, analyzed, and distributed, is also a most important advantage of computerized information systems.

It is on the level of the communication function that new modes of interaction between man and computer would seem to profit most. The general idea would be to generate a more natural manner of interacting, using voice and handwritten inputs and natural conversational entries. If the data system is awkward to use, such as using a special keyboard device located in an out-of-the-way place with limited display capability, with only a limited number of special purpose tasks performable, we cannot expect the system to operate very well as a partner in the planning process.

Allocation Analysis.   The basic task that the allocation function performs is to gather together the information-processing requirements for the system and determine what combination of men, machines, and programs would be best suited to answer the requirements. The allocation decision depends not only on the characteristics of the data processed, the processing performed, and the control exercised, but on the concept of operation for the system and the conditions of operation.

Information. Determining information requirements includes establishing the amount, variety, and kinds of information, along with such data characteristics as completeness, reliability, accuracy, and precision for each datum. Data with precision and volume requirements beyond human capabilities should be the purview of hardware and software, but some contribution with regard to incomplete and unreliable data may be made by the human. Depending on the nature and objectives of the planning done, planning data requirements involve a large variety of data types, much of it tentative and incomplete. Forecasting and trend detection may require seeing relationships (information) in the data not readily detectable by software. Hence, data requirements for planning will involve considerable human involvement.

Processing—The Transfer Function. Determining requirements for the collection, conversion, transmission, storage, and transformation of data is directly dependent on the types and amount of data to be processed, but also of course on the logistics of collecting variegated data from a multitude of sources, converting it and integrating it into coherent sets, and distributing it for display. For planning, the human may be best at detecting appropriate inputs from a complex and ambiguous environment and transforming them into machine-processible form. He may also be best at data interpretation tasks involving seeing patterns and relationships and in determining the meaning of information, such as, for instance semantic analyses of verbal messages. Hardware and software are best, of course, for complex searches and transformations of large data files, for rapid transmission of data, and for complex computations.

Control. Determining how decisions concerning the operating of the system will be made involves some analysis of how well-structured —cut-and-dried—the decision will be. Since planning involves many investigative, hypothesis formation, and testing operations, a large proportion of human control operations may be expected.

Concept of Operations. In designing a system there are many choices available concerning how processing to achieve the same result may be done (time-sharing versus batch processing, for instance).

One overriding determiner in making such choices should be the intended manner of employment of the system. Since the planning system is to be used directly to support the human planner at what is essentially a rather private, individualistic task, the concept of operation or use of the system must receive considerable thought. Just how does a planner want to do his job? How should the system operate to facilitate that mode of operation? The basic experimental question is whether or not an interactive system will aid teams of planners, but many operations might reasonably be run in a batch or background mode rather than under direct control of the human or operating system.

Environment. Certainly the environment within which planning will be done will influence the concept of operation and the formulation of transfer functions. For instance, does it take the same sort of system to support a committee (a group of relatively equal and unstructured participants) as it does to support a staff (a team of experts with specific skills and responsibilities)? Would the system that supports a team in a centralized planning center support a team of managers operating from their offices? Educational planning may present a different environment than does manufacturing or commerce, field operations different from headquarters, and so on.

8-1-3 Personnel Subsystem

Determining personnel subsystem design requirements for an interactive planning system will present many problems that may not be entirely foreseen. At present, on the basis of the preceding analysis, many crucial operations in the system will be allocated to humans. In fact, the whole system must be geared to supporting the human planner. However, specifying planning procedures when these may vary considerably from one area of planning to another may be difficult. Doing station or position analyses and designing jobs at these positions may be impossible for a general experimental model. That is, a job at a position cannot be defined until the nature of the planning experiment and the planning area has been selected. Similarly, specifying skills requirements, experience levels, and training needs is tricky until task and job analyses and designs have been done. Simply, the task is to determine the personnel requirements for the system in terms of skills and numbers of persons, and to determine plans for the procurement, selection, classification, training, promotion, and organization of these. To do this in an uncertain and ambiguous situation is not simple at all.

Task and Position Analyses. Determining requirements for the personnel subsystem requires task and job analysis, and job and procedure design. These analyses and syntheses are not carried on independently of hardware and software design activities, but are an integral part of the whole process. Designing the operator and user interface with the system employs the results of task and position analyses in the human engineering of the interface. Since, for planning, the human functions in the system are heavily loaded with improvisation, innovation, and problem-solving behavior, tasks whose performance can only be seen imperfectly, the tools of scientific task analysis (time and motion studies, comparative studies of methods, etc.) are not often directly applicable. Consequently, heuristic rather than scientifically determined job descriptions will probably have to be developed. Although the details of interacting with the data processing system may be fairly readily identified (displays read and interpreted, control devices manipulated), the complex nature of the operation in between may not be readily apparent. At a minimum, general statements of job and task functions must be given, major environmental conditions (especially stress and other contributing factors) and their impacts considered, and the possible contingencies that could arise during the performance of the task evaluated. Careful analysis should be made of each decision man must make and of the flow of decisions in the system especially as these are shared and supported by the data system.

Although some long-term problems of personnel subsystems, such as turnover and limited availability, may not be quite such problems for short term experimentation, others, such as individual differences and difficulty in procuring proficient planners, will be.

The planning task will have to be examined in great detail before a system is built, especially those functions allocated to man. With our present primitive state of understanding of the planning process and in the absence of guiding theories about planning behavior, the conduct of definitive research and the consequent generalization of results may be extremely difficult, perhaps impossible. However, even though there are certainly major differences from area to area and level to level in the planning process, and despite job differences in technique application, any experimentation will lead to useful knowledge about planning. Whether or not basic theorems about planning will appear is not at all obvious at this time. Hopefully, planning generalities will appear so that our results will apply to more than planning for a particular area, at a particular level, under particular conditions at a specific instance in time.

Skills Requirements. Besides procedures and job descriptions, one of the major results of task analyses is a specification of the skills areas and levels that are required in the persons who perform the job. Not only the individual skills required, but some conception of the organizational composition, numbers of persons, and conditions of performance should be given. Personality factors, if these are likely to be important in the performance of the tasks, may also be specified.

Although difficult to foresee entirely, there may be some difficulty in obtaining highly skilled, well-trained and experienced planning personnel to serve as subjects in experiments. Even if cooperating organizations are found, planners may not be readily available for lengthy experiments and may be subject to pressures from other tasks. If planning experiments could be integrated with ongoing operations as they might, say, with developmental planning and decision making for the proposed ARPA network, subjects might then be fairly readily available for a number of experiments.

The alternative to using already experienced planners and experts would be to train people in planning to be used as subjects. This alternative opens up several possibilities since, for instance, planning could be concentrated on those specific skills required for the particular planning task rather than being the more diffuse, uncontrolled process of learning by experience. Further, interesting experiments in the training of planning and problem-solving processes could be undertaken at the same time.

Training Requirement. One of the claims frequently made for complex data systems and for programming and data retrieval languages is that they are so easily understood that little or no training is required to use or operate them. Such statements are not true, neither in the general nor the particular. Although it may be true that the system instruction set and the possible action list is short and easy to describe, invariably the skill and task involved are complex ones and do require much more detailed instruction. Further, as is the case with many military and commercial systems, if the system is subject to a steady stream of changes, even well-trained users may require recurrent refreshing on language and operating detail.

The case for data processing in general has been made by Fred Gruenberger (1970). He states that whereas perhaps 50,000 persons a year are being introduced to data processing by formal classes, the overwhelming bulk of this instruction is aimed at elementary programming (coding) and very little at all is aimed at data processing itself. Although the student may learn the rudiments of a computer language, he does not learn to solve problems nor to apply the programming language to any problem other than the simple, well-defined tasks from the language text. In the practical situation, data processing problems are usually ill-defined, and ill-defined by someone who is not a data processor and whose definitions are filled with erroneous and superfluous information. Further, the problems are usually large, fraught with exceptional procedures, and difficult to standardize and/or parameterize. To state that familiarizing a person with a programming or data-processing language is tantamount to training him in the data processing art is indeed a gross exaggeration. Similar simple approaches have been taken, however, to time-sharing systems, to information storage and retrieval systems, and to many other application systems. That is, a simple user's manual is issued for the system that explains the rudiments of the operating instructions and available commands with the expectation that the "man off the street" will be able to read the manual and immediately use the system in a profitable manner. As with programming languages, such an assumption is valid only if the potential user is already well-trained in the application involved and only needs to pick up the details of doing in a slightly different way something that he already knows how to do well.

For military online systems, thorough training programs have been found desirable to bring new users and operators on board. With a planning system, the results of an error may not be so immediately catastrophic as with a command and control system, but potential impact may indeed be greater in the end.

Builders of time-sharing and online information retrieval systems have, on occasion, included user aids within their systems to lead the beginning user through the system by the hand. Again, however, such instruction usually ends with elementary operations and initial langauge instruction. Users of an information retrieval system may be shown the rudiments of working with their data bases, but are not taught how to ask a good or complex retrieval query, nor how to interpret the results they get. Conversations with system users indicate that they are frequently frustrated by their inability to perform more than the simplest sort of interactions with the system and by the lack of advanced instruction in making queries, building data bases, and interpreting (and oftentimes diagnosing) results.

Hence, whatever sort of planning system is designed, the plans should include within the system a thorough indoctrination in the command language and in the use of the system. This should include textual materials and practical exercises. It certainly should include some "diagnostic" aids or information that would help the user determine what he did wrong. If teams are used, some of the practical exercising should be in an interactive mode.

Computer-aided instruction beyond running practical exercises probably should not be included. While it might be of great value if the planning system were implemented for an actual application, the expense and effort do not seem justified for experimental purposes.

The question also arises as to whether or not to try to evaluate the training in a formal fashion. While it is not necessarily strongly advocated as a necessity, a demonstration of the effectiveness of training versus no or rudimentary training would indeed be of benefit to the industry. It should be noted that training is not universally procured as a new data processing system is procured. A demonstration of the cost-effectiveness of doing so would support the requirements, training, and other personnel subsystem people within DOD and might encourage commercial providers of data processing systems to provide the training that is necessary to use their systems.

8-2 EXPERIMENTAL DESIGN IN ONLINE PLANNING

To conduct any meaningful experimental test of interactive planning will require the performance of a complex task by skilled, experienced personnel. Any lesser task neither provides the abrasive onerousness nor the subtle complexities required to show the superiority of the data processing machine. Undoubtedly most small planning tasks can be done just as well, just as cheaply (if not cheaper), and just as fast (if not faster), as trying to use an interactive system that may introduce some inconveniences of its own. (That the interactive system may provide some slight conveniences in terms of clerical ease and excellence and easy communication to dispersed locations is hardly a convincing argument.) Such tasks will take time to prepare, accomplish and analyze, severely limiting possibilities of replications. Experienced planners as subjects will be severely limited in availability, both in number and time, reducing the possibilities of a large population.

With such restrictions on the number of subjects, trials, and experimental tasks, yet faced with complex methodological, task, and experimental materials variables, it behooves us to use experimental designs that will obtain optimal utilization of experimental material (subjects and stimuli) within the constraints of permissible run times and experimental costs. Usually this tradeoff results in the presentation of some subset of the experimental conditions to a given subject and the elimination of certain comparisons (usually the higher-order interactions) from the experiment. This would seem to place our experiments within the classes of orthogonalized squares, lattices, and partially replicated (incomplete block) factorial designs. The analysis of results would involve complex analyses of variance, some of which might offer a few difficulties. However, analytic problems may be relatively easily overcome; setting up meaningful experiments for online experimentation presents problems more difficult to resolve.

The many problems associated with online system experimentation complicate simplistic statements concerning factorial arrangements. In a system there are many complexities associated with the hierarchical, systems-within-systems structure or, as a tree, nodes-within-nodes, each node containing variables of interest that we might desire to inspect, but which would not be reflected in global measures. Hence, in an experiment involving more than one node, there is the problem of laying out experimental designs and planning statistical analyses for many subsystems. Such designs might be somewhat complicated by the possibility of replication differences between experimental units involved in the larger planning experiment. Thus, in a hierarchy with five subnodes, each producing some subpart of a larger plan, all different, the techniques employed in planning at each subnode might all be different. That is, the techniques applied at one node might not be applicable to any other node.

Further, however, in a hierarchy it cannot be assumed that higher and lower nodes in the tree structure are entirely independent, i.e., the actions at least at connected nodes do influence one another, and, indeed, perhaps differential action at subnodes will have differential effects on the success of employing subnode results at higher points in the tree. Devising means of testing such results could present some challenging design problems.

There may also be various time-trend and other sequential comparisons to be made, especially if experiments involving maintenance of plans are run simultaneously with plan generation. If the global experiment were to involve comparisons of the effects of differences in hierarchical structure, there might not be comparable nodes from one experimental block (team) to another. Even here, however, perhaps some descriptive statistics might be of value, even though no comparative statistics could be used.

The conduct of an experiment takes several major steps, including:

Planning the experiment
Preparing for the experiment
Running the experiment
Analysis of the results
Interpreting and reporting results

Although some of the factors involved in conducting experiments in online planning have been inspected, a more organized scrutiny might be helpful.

8-2-1 Planning the Experiments

In planning an experiment the questions to be answered and hypotheses to be tested must be explicitly stated followed by the determination of what experimental results will be taken as evidence that a hypothesis is accepted or rejected. The measures of experimental behavior that are to be taken must be selected and defined. An experimental design that will answer the questions and control extraneous conditions may then be selected. The final step is to establish the run requirement for the experiment in terms of time, materials, subjects, equipment, numbers of runs, and costs. The costs must be examined, of course, to determine whether the experiment can be afforded or not. If not, another iteration or so of the plan may be necessary before going ahead.

Experimental Hypotheses. Any planning experiment that is conducted is not likely to have a single, simple hypothesis, but instead a complex of hypotheses and questions. Considering the complexity of the phenomena that are to be studied and the initial state of experimentally verified information, some very rich experiments may result, but it also requires carefully stated hypotheses in a form in which they are testable. So should be the "questions" that are asked, "questions" being probes for information without specifically advancing a hypothesis to be tested, but for which descriptive statistics could be computed and that might form the basis for future experiments.

Some basic hypotheses to be tested are:

- An interactive planning system is superior with regard to characteristics x, y, and z to a manual and/or batch-process supported planning process.
- Planning (and/or decision-making) technique A is superior to technique B under conditions i, j, k.
- An interactive planning system provides better support for planning in content area x than for areas y or z (e.g., operational versus strategic and tactical; planning against nature versus planning for operations or for ill-structured problems; product planning versus production planning, etc.).
- A team with a hierarchical structure A is superior to a team with structure B (i.e., Organization A is superior to Organization B).

These hypotheses may be global as the first and last, or specific to a node as might be the second, or mixed as might be the third hypotheses.

Evidence. Quite often experiments are planned without an explicit statement of the conditions that should exist to elicit the differential behavior that will demonstrate that a hypothesis is borne out or not. Not only must the characteristics to be measured be selected, but some analytic evaluation should be made of how these characterisitcs should vary as a function of changing experimental conditions. Questions should also be asked if any other conditions might exist to elicit the response. Quite often such an evaluation will uncover further conditions that should be controlled to obtain meaningful and conclusive evidence and sometimes will indicate that the hypothesis as stated is not testable. The more tenuous and abstract the area of investigation, as planning behavior surely is, the more attention should be given to establishing crucial tests of the hypotheses and selecting appropriate statistical analyses.

Experimental Measures and Conditions.   Careful attention should be given to the precise definition of the measures to be taken, including their quantization and categorization. Too fine or too coarse measures may defeat a test or be inappropriate. Careless construction of categories without considering precisely what an entry in the category means can destroy a comparison and perhaps an experiment. I personally have been caught in this trap even when I thought I had a thorough definition of my variables, and I have quite often caught others at it. For instance, a few years ago I ran an experiment with photointerpreters (Willmorth, 1966) involving search priorities. I asked the interpreters to look for tanks alone, tanks and trucks, with tanks as the first priority of search, and for all classes of military targets; the hypothesis being that the simpler the search priority (tanks alone) the faster and more accurately imagery could be screened. Well, there was a decline in detection accuracy and completeness with more complex search priorities all right, but the number of tanks detected under each condition did not seem to vary (decline) in line with the hypothesis. Target difficulty and numerosity (which I had not considered or controlled) had messed up my test. Further, there was no difference in the times taken, either, but while this seemed to negate the hypothesis there was some indication that the interpreters might be consciously or unconsciously pacing themselves, another uncontrolled factor. I reran the experiment about a year later with better control and essentially confirmed the tentative results, but I could certainly not make that decision on the basis of the first run.

Some of the experimental conditions requiring control are training or learning, subject differences, plan differences, team differences, and technique differences. Some measures that might be taken are plan quality (if this can be defined), planning time, planning effort expended (man-hours, computer time), costs, trends, and, say, number and length (amounts) of personal interaction.

Experimental Design.   Having a complete grasp of the experimental questions, the measures to be taken, and the conditions to be controlled, a design complex may now be selected that will incorporate the crucial tests that are to be conducted. The basic concerns here were covered in the introduction to this section and will not be reconsidered. This is not, however, a trivial step, but one involving a lot of work and some expertise.

Run Requirements. The experimental plan is not complete until requirements have been established for conducting the experiment, including obtaining or setting up the system, generating test materials, planning test procedures and data collection procedures, procuring and training subjects and observers, and estimating costs for the lot. The latter may be important, for online experimentation is likely to be expensive and, if it proves too much so at this point, it may be necessary to replan the experiment with reduced goals, a more efficient design, or otherwise more economical procedure.

8-2-2 Preparations

Even if it is assumed that a planning support system is in place— a computer network with the appropriate display and control consoles, software to drive them and to support appropriate planning techniques and tools, data files all prepared—there are still a lot of preparations to be made. There are test vehicles to construct (i.e., sets of planning problems to be solved with supporting materials); recording procedures, forms, and means to be set up; instructional materials to prepare for subjects (planners) and observers; and subjects and observers to procure and train and assign to experimental conditions. Selection of subjects that meet planning experimental design requirements may present some difficulties, but, hopefully, this can be done without undue expenditures to train "experts."

Physical Arrangements. The extensiveness of the physical arrangements that must be made should not be underestimated. Any experiment involving data-processing equipment and a complex control and display interface with humans is likely to require facilities construction, hardware reconfiguration if not construction, and some software. None of these arrangements need to be as sophisticated and efficient as would a finished application system, but considerable time and expense will be involved in any case.

Building an experimental facility or laboratory can be very expensive and time-consuming. There have been numerous computer-based laboratories built over the past several years, including several at SDC (Sackman, 1967). For instance, at RAND (1952-1954), early system experimentation was done in a specially constructed simulation laboratory. Later, at SDC (1955-1956) experiments in air defense procedures and training were conducted in a simulated air defense direction center. An even more complex laboratory based on an AN/FSQ-32 computer was built at SDC to study problems of command and control systems. These laboratories included many features to facilitate human observers of experiments (galleries, one-way mirrors, and walkways) and for recording results (cameras, microphones, tape-recorded phone conversations as well as computer-recorded results). Such facilities are often expensive indeed and while dramatic results were sometimes obtained, if experimentation is the sole use of the laboratory, the limited use of the laboratories often casts doubt on the cost-effectiveness of such facilities.* It is quite possible that a planning laboratory could be constructed to permit ready observation of the planning team by both human observers and automatic recording equipment. Before going to any great expense, however, a great deal of thought should be given to the sort of experiments to be run and to providing for a considerable variety of planning configurations. Only if less expensive "field environment" experiments fail should the expense of a special laboratory be considered.

The interface between humans and the computer, as emphasized in the first section here, is a most important aspect of online systems. There remain a great many questions to be answered concerning the efficiency and effectiveness of various combinations of control and display devices and of various input modes singly, let alone considering them in the complex environment of a planning system. Although not proven, there seems little doubt that more natural graphic and conversational input modes would be easier and more effective methods for humans to use. Any extensive planning laboratory should consider the design and construction of "planning consoles" that would permit the incorporation of such features into a configuration really used by humans. However, initial experimentation should undoubtedly be done with relatively crude lash-ups and breadboard-type

---

*Consider, however, the even greater costs and limited use of some aerospace laboratories such as the acceleration lab at Ames Research Center. Many millions are spent in studying phenomena that are of less potential impact than interactive information systems promise to have.

gear. The human operator is capable of accommodating considerable awkwardness in equipment design, especially if he understands that it is for experimental purposes. In a planning environment, some degradation of physical arrangement can probably be tolerated if it does not interfere materially with mental performance.

Similarly, in the area of software design and construction, the experiments should be run by using lash-ups of existing software insofar as is possible. Some special software for planning and for conducting the experiments probably cannot be avoided, but again some operating inefficiency can undoubtedly be tolerated if the great expense of producing a complex software system can be avoided. Many of the functions required by an online planning system already exist in current time-sharing systems including operating executives, recording programs, data management systems, and some communications capabilities. While programming special planning tools cannot be avoided, full advantage should be taken of existing capabilities through relatively minor changes

Test Vehicle. Preparing the test vehicle for the experiments will also require considerable work. If comparative studies are to be done and if repeated measures of the same subjects are to be used (so that they act as their own controls), then several "planning problems" will be required. To be a real contestant for online applications, such planning problems will have to be relatively elaborate. This does mean, despite the labor involved, some extensive data bases and simulation vehicles. Under some circumstances (shakedown, for instance) the data bases may be largely simulated, and in some instances (scheduling, for instance) the data base may be built up during the planning process. Under others, such as simulating a competitive environment, and using optimizing tools, data must be collected elsewhere. For some experiments, it might be possible to obtain some precanned economic data from Census Bureau sources, or if a DOD problem is dealt with, perhaps real system data will be available. Those who do studies on planning and decision-making techniques might also be sources for data banks. It is also possible to build some data generators, but unless these are very simple a considerable amount of work would have to be spent on data specifications that might better be expended elsewhere.

Although the sort of planning problems to be solved must be determined by each experiment, it seems reasonable to hope to cover the planning-problem spectrum from natural environmental competitions to deductive-inductive strategic planning as Hormann (1970) proposes. If a partnership is entered into with a military or commercial agency, the planning problems will be dictated by the practical considerations of solving a problem that exists. Nevertheless, selecting an appropriate problem and building up supporting data files and, if a responsive environment is desired, constructing gaming and simulation vehicles to give the subjects feedback on the success of plans will take some serious thought and planning.

Recording Procedures and Devices. Means of collecting the measures desired must be devised, some of which may have to be manual. While most interactions with the system may be recorded dynamically, other measures may be the result of observation or of subject comment. For instance, if one of the experiments compares online planning with manual planning, measures of performance in the manual mode will undoubtedly have to be gathered manually. Recording forms, directions to observers, scoring formulas and data-gathering procedures will need to be laid out and arrangements made for keypunching and entry into the computer. Instructions to recording programs will have to be composed for the automated system.

Performing experiments with an online data processing system offers some special opportunities in recording dynamic, rapidly changing events that are normally denied to the experimenter. In fact, if all inputs, outputs, and environmental conditions are recorded, and the system is not changed, the whole experiment may be "played back" to re-observe experimental events at leisure, except, of course, unrecorded human reactions The advantages of "regenerative recording," as it is called by Sackman (1967), include replaying the experiment with system changes to observe their effects, leading to further hypotheses that can be verified by further experimentation.

Online experimentation further permits controlled interaction between the subjects and the experimenter in the form of simulated interactions with various agencies. It permits dynamic decisions to record special information, to make dynamic adjustment to experimental conditions, and similar realtime modifications to the experimental plan. To obtain definitive results, of course, such changes must be foregone, but during the exploratory, idea-generation, pilot study phases of the experimentation, such a capability would be extremely valuable.

Instructional Material. Depending on how complex the planning problems, experimental designs, and experimental procedures are, there could be more or less instructional materials required. At a minimum, there must be instructions covering, for the subjects, the planning system and any planning techniques that might be used and a careful presentation of the planning problem to be solved.

For experimenters, instructions covering the observations to be taken, the experimental procedures to be followed, and, if any functions are to be simulated that cannot be handled by the computer, the simulation procedures and simulation data to be used must be specified.

Note that the procedural and instructional materials areas are ones often slighted in experiments with humans. Mental sets are not only very easily engendered in humans, but are very sensitive to nuances in the way instructions are given and to subtle differences in the way runs are conducted. (Computers on the other hand are quite insensitive to such nuances, a factor to consider when comparing manual to automated observations.) It is always best to have instructions written down precisely for all procedures. Instructors should be rehearsed and debriefed to ensure skillful, consistent presentations, and the recipients checked to be sure they understand the instructions and will be able to do what they have been asked to do. Some experimenters record instructions to be sure that all information is given in precisely the same way each time. However, this procedure may suffer from some loss of the social facilitation of face-to-face interactions and may prohibit questions. On the other hand, if a large share of instructions to subjects is presented via computer interactions, subtleties and nuances in the instructional situation may be largely suppressed.

Subjects. It is highly desirable to obtain experienced planners, area experts, or persons with organizational responsibility to serve as subjects and to present these subjects with planning problems pertinent to their own interests. Using naive subjects casts considerable doubt on the credibility of results, and opportunities for profitable advice for the improvement and debugging of the system would be lost.

If experts are used, these will be assigned, in most experiments, into team positions reflecting their expertise. If a broad spectrum of planning problems is used, of course, some areas of expertise will not be applicable in all problems, casting some doubt on the use of a single team for all problems. If separate teams are used for different problems, however, team differences are confounded with problem differences, creating other difficulties. Further, different problem types may require different team organizations to handle them.

Two possible alternatives exist to the problem of not being able to acquire experienced subjects. The first of these (discussed in Section 1-3-3), is to use a developed planning system to conduct experiments in training planners. As a follow-on, the newly trained persons could be used in further experiments comparing techniques, team organization, and similar problems. However, under these conditions the taint of faint contact with "real-world experience" is never quite removed, however much face validity could be injected into the training and the experimentation.

Another alternative is to abandon, at least initially, the idea of comparative experiments and concentrate on building a system that would satisfy some set of real-world planners. That is, some group or agency could be enlisted for whom the planning system would be built. The planning experts in the agency would serve as system designers and together with the experimenters would work out, by trial-and-error or by successive iterations, sets of practical planning aids. Such an approach sacrifices classical experimentation that generates unequivocal tests of hypotheses, but might generate some planning tools with built-in acceptance by the recognized experts. This is, of course, the normal "demonstration" method of system design rather than the experimental design approach. On the other hand, once developed, differences in techniques and organization may be introduced to determine the effects created by varying basic parameters (if these can be distinguished) of the system.

The matter of instructing subjects in the use of the system, in the use of planning techniques, and in the problem area was discussed at some length in Section 8-1. There are some additional problems, such as subject preference for particular planning techniques, that need to be considered, but which should be alleviated somewhat by proper training and indoctrination. The training program will be important, no matter how trivial the planning problem, and must be given proper attention.

8-2-3   Conducting the Experiment

If proper plans have been laid, running the experiment and collecting data are the easiest operations of all. Considerable care must be taken to control all of the important variables in the experiment (or if they cannot be controlled, measured so that their effects may be accounted for in the analysis). Working with a new system presents some problems in maintaining consistency of conditions because of system reliability. New systems are notably unreliable, and (from personal observation) working with an unreliable system is most frustrating. Making it consistently so across several experimental runs and conditions is probably asking too much, and differential reliability may contaminate experimental results. Measures of satisfaction with a technique or the system, for instance, could be seriously affected by unreliability, and measures of time and costs may be adversely affected by run failures and down time.

The power of conducting experiments online has not yet been tapped. Many of the possibilities underlined by Sackman (1967) have hardly been grasped, let alone implemented. Online experimentation offers almost instantaneous data reduction so that sequential analysis and sequential decision functions are almost instantaneous events. Regenerative recording techniques provide the capability of capturing elusive operations as they occur and replaying them later for better understanding, or with minor changes to investigate the impact of modifications upon system performance.

Also possibilities are the techniques associated with system exercising programs like those used in air defense systems. Data reductions and presentations to support immediate debriefings are possible. Time-sharing systems offer many possibilities in this regard that have not been tried or exploited.

The possibility of simulating a responsive environment, or of speeding up "environmental" events simulating its responses, should not be ignored. Management games use this technique with apparent success. Certainly the use of online simulation to answer "what if" questions for the planner may be investigated both as a planning and a training technique for planners.

Hence, part of the planning for the experiments must be some detailed investigation of what could go wrong, and the laying of contingency plans for counteracting the effects of failures and goofups. Although we cannot hope to be completely successful, any action may help save considerable waste and negative effects.

8-2-4 Analyzing the Results

There are three sources of variance to be accounted for in an experiment: treatments variations, variations among experimental materials, and variations among replications of the experiment. A critical difference among treatments is usually established by comparing treatment variances to an appropriate variance among the experimental materials, or, as in the case of a complete factorial without replication, against some residual variance assumed to be "error" after all "true" variance has been accounted for. Most complications in design and analysis of experiment arise from arranging the experimental materials into aggregates or blocks that often represent (and control thereby) trends in the experimental materials and from confounding some portion of the treatment variance with these blocks. Groupings can be complex ("rows," "columns," "squares," "cubes") and subject to restrictions on the assignment of treatment conditions within the groupings. Some information on confounded effects may be recovered by repeating the experiment (replicating) and varying the effects confounded with arrangement groupings. Further complications may be expected if "sub-system" measures are obtained in addition to total "system" performance.

Some of the sources of variance whose effects should be controlled or isolated are learning or training effects, "subject" differences (including both individual subjects and teams), and order of presentation effects. Some important behaviors that seem especially allied to planning, but that may be difficult to control or measure, are planning and programming of responses (anticipating or forecasting events and taking preventive actions—such as pacing of work to fill or fit into a specified time period), inventing and problem solving by innovation (unanticipated responses and results), and communicating (uncontrolled or unmeasurable).

Insofar as possible, all measures and controls actions to be taken should be established in advance and analyses restricted to these variables. Manipulation of the data to derive new measures may be a rich source of hypotheses, but conclusions drawn on the basis of chance variations in data collection are scientifically tenuous and should be subjected to experimental verification before placing much credence in their substance.

8-3 PLANNING BY EXPERT CONSENSUS
(A PLANNING EXAMPLE)

As an example of planning as it might be done in a widespread computer network, let us choose the ARPA network as an outstanding possibility. The ARPA network (Roberts, 1969) is a resource-sharing network of computers located at universities and other research centers supported by the Advanced Research Projects Agency of the Department of Defense. Eventually, the network will have more than 20 nodes (locations), some of which will serve two or more computers. The computers connected by the network are of all sizes and varieties, with many differing hardware (word length, instruction repertoire) and software (languages, etc.) features. If capabilities at one node are to be utilized by projects at other nodes, a great deal of planning must be done. Therefore, over the next several years as the network is installed, checked out, and modified, many details will have to be coordinated and many decisions will need to be made.

It would be most convenient if the network had some vehicle to support and speed up the coordination and decision-making process that would take advantage of the net capabilities and avoid endless conferences and travel. It is quite possible that such a vehicle exists in an online, interactive Delphi (Helmer, 1966). Delphi would permit arrival at a consensus of opinion regarding an issue (a design detail, for example) permitting an authority to make a decision and to forward that decision to all concerned.

Many of the software requirements for a Delphi are similar to those for the basic network. These include the ability to:

- Forward a message from one computer to one or more others.
- Address specific processors in the receiving computer.
- Store and save messages that cannot be forwarded due to outages until queried (a store-and-forward "mailbox" capability).
- Receive and store a message until the recipient is ready (online, etc.) to have it displayed.
- Interpret input from several computers with different word sizes and representations.

Delphi does have some other requirements that may be specific to the polling and evaluation process (accumulating responses and performing statistical analysis, preparing displays, keeping book on responses and the reasons associated with them). If several inquiries are underway at one time, each involving slightly different sets of participants and somewhat different treatment of responses, clear identification of data files, mailing lists, and processes is required.

8-3-1 Delphi Operations

A Delphi experimenter at the console must be able to enter a series of messages (queries, multiple-choice responses, statements, etc.) into the computer and forward these messages to a list of recipients. The statements and response categories must be properly identified and saved for later reference. Provision for including additional information and reorganizing the reference file should be made. Text editing as the messages are constructed and later, as basic statements are revised, is required. In forwarding messages, if the receiving computer or console cannot be contacted (i.e., the device might be down or inactive), the messages should be saved in a "mailbox" for delivery when an inquiry for messages for the recipient is made.

At the receiving computer it would be convenient for messages received to be stored and, if the named recipient is not available (i.e., is not signed on), saved until he inquires after messages. After receiving his messages, the Delphi respondent may then or later respond to the queries and statement. He should identify the items he is responding to, and in the case of multiple choice, name the response category he selects. In the case of open-end or fill-in responses, especially if a long series of input information is to be supplied, fixed-order responses, response names, key words, or field identifiers should be supplied by the respondent. Arrangements to recognize these responses could be provided in the Delphi programs. The respondent must also be able to compose and send text or tabular messages, such as rationales for responses, positions on an issue, or additions of data. Again these messages should be identified and associated with the queries or statements.

At the host computer, replies to a query from many respondents should be stored, each reply identified by the respondent making the answer. In the case of fixed category or quantitative responses the experimenter should be able to specify tabulation of responses, statistical analyses or other transformations of the data. It is quite possible that with an interactive Delphi system a great deal of sophistication, branching, and response interpretation might be possible. However, with either fixed or free response, the experimenter should be able to display the responses at his console (and on hard copy) either immediately or on querying the mail box. If many planners are active at once, conflict resolution on displays and some clever merging and sorting of responses may be required. If a large number of free responses are received, the experimenter will have to perform various manipulative and editorial operations upon them, such as composing categories and assigning responses to them, compiling lists of reasons, and merging data. This information must be stored and new messages made up to transmit the reduced information to the Delphi participants along with, if desired, a new set of queries and statements, or perhaps a decision, plan, or directive as the result of the survey.

8-3-2 Possible Experiments

Besides an immediate practical payoff of obtaining rapid consensus and decisions in ARPA network problems, there are many experimental questions that may be answered concerning interactive planning. These answers would not all be restricted to online polling and consensus situations, but would have broad implications for all sorts of interactive information system operations. Some of the experimental questions that might be asked are:

1. Is immediate interaction (all planners in the net at one time) more effective than delayed interactions (via the store-and-forward "mailbox")? Immediate interactions implies, of course, that all computers are up and all lines working. Delayed interactions implies that either the Delphi system is cycling or on call in the host computer at all times, or that the "mailbox" message buffering system is operating in all computers.

2. Is spaced practice in interactive planning more effective than massed? If so, what is the optimum spacing, what is the optimum period of practice, and what is the optimum amount of work to do? Preliminary indications from Sackman (1969) are that the typical time-sharing user (largely programmers) spends between a half and a full hour at the console at a sitting with some indications of a regression toward 20 minutes as an accustomed practice period for experienced users. There is also some indication that this time represents a clerical input and hypothesis-testing period with planning and problem solving being done away from the console. Control over console activity (problem solving versus message composition, etc.) needs to be established if conclusions concerning this point are to be reached.

3. Are discrete iterations (ensuring relatively independent judgments from the participants) better or worse than continuous accumu-

lation of judgments and positions as the polling takes place? That is, does a continuous box score create a bandwagon effect?

4. Can sophisticated analytic and query devices be profitably employed in an interactive fashion?

Some possibilities are:

- Sequential analysis.
- Paired comparisons, ranking and other psycho-physical techniques and nonparametric statistics.
- Hierarchical branching in pursuing querying sequences.
- Rapid simulation, allocation, and analytic devices for response formulation and evaluation.
- Dialectic problem investigations.

REFERENCES

Gruenberger, F., "Formal Production of Trained and Educated People," *Data Processing Digest,* Vol. 16, No. 1, January 1970, 1–7.

Helmer, Olaf, "The Delphi Technique and Educational Innovation" in Helmer, et al., *Social Technology,* New York, Basic Books, Inc., Publishers, 1966.

Hormann, Aiko, "Planning by Man-Machine Synergism: Characterization of Processes and Environment," SP-3484, System Development Corporation, Santa Monica, Calif., 1970.

Kleine, Henry, and Ronald L. Citrenbaum, "An Online Interactive Hierarchical Organization and Management System for Planning, SP-3482, System Development Corporation, Santa Monica, Calif., March 1970.

McCormick, E. J., *Human Factors Engineering,* New York, McGraw-Hill Book Company, 1964.

MIL-STD-1472, "Human Engineering Design Criteria for Military Systems, Equipment and Facilities," October 1967.

Roberts, L. G., "Resource Sharing Computer Networks," IEEE International Conference, March 1969.

Sackman, H., *Computers, System Science, and Evolving Society,* New York, John Wiley & Sons, Inc., 1967.

———, "Experimental Analysis of User Behavior in Computer Utilities," TM-L-4293, System Development Corporation, Santa Monica, Calif., June 1969.

Willmorth, N. E., "The Influence of Target Priorities and Interpretation Methods on the Speed and Accuracy of Photo Interpretation," Unpublished Research Report, 1966.

9

THE CAPTURE AND REPLAY OF LIVE
COMPUTER SYSTEM OPERATION

A. D. Karush

       315

Abstract

Regenerative recording is a technique to allow complete digital computer system playback. A recording component records an initial system state and then time tags and records all subsequent input to the system. The regenerative component plays back the recorded input in its original sequence, starting from the same initial conditions and forcing the system to repeat its original behavior. This technique provides for the controlled reproduction of computer events as they occurred in a live computer run. The term "regenerative recording" was coined by Sackman in 1961 in connection with experimental studies of SAGE air defense.

Regenerative recording is one of the tools that should be available to the system investigator. It lies between system operation and measurement. Conventional measurement and recording tools are essentially partial or selective recording mechanisms. They contain no capability for reconstructing and rerunning the original system test. Regenerative recording permits capture of the system test and then iterative playback and analysis using the selective recording and measurement tools.

317

Regenerative recording has a number of additional diverse and powerful applications. The application of regenerative recording to time-sharing systems is a recent and still experimental development. Because online planning systems will be built within a time-sharing framework, and because there is a requirement to study these planning systems experimentally and scientifically, the existence of a regenerative recording utility becomes of paramount importance.

9-1 INTRODUCTION

Two underlying themes in this book are the central importance of a computer to the planning process, and the empirical validation of planning processes through advanced scientific techniques. To satisfy the latter requirement in light of the former context, we must develop a planning laboratory in which to conduct controlled planning experiments.

Construction of controlled experiments centering about complex man-computer systems has not been very successful. The major difficulties, the inability to conduct controlled experiments and to collect adequate data, arise because of the complexity of these systems. Conventional data collection schemes require the *a priori* specification of the data of interest—there is no way to retrieve additional information once the computer system has been exercised and the specified data collected. Furthermore, voluminous data collection can degrade the subject system's performance to the point that it is no longer representative. Controlled experiments, required by the experimental method, are difficult to attain because of the impossibility of controlling all variables in subsequent experiments. The human interaction, in particular, is extremely variable, having not only the obvious primary effect on the experiment's reliability, but also secondary effects by changing the sequence of events for all other components—man and machine—of the system.

The regenerative recording technique that has evolved over the past decade appears to be the only feasible solution to this problem. It is unusual among experimental techniques in that it utilizes the computer as a data-collection tool in addition to the computer's regular role as an experimental variable. It is unique among data-collection techniques in that it collects sufficient information to allow the computer system's behavior to be duplicated by rerunning the original system as often as desired. With each rerun, not requiring real users but duplicating original system behavior, data collection may proceed as a cyclic "specify-collect-evaluate-respecify" process, and the system may be modified to produce controlled experimental mutations for precise experimentation. Furthermore, negligible artifact is introduced as very little data need be collected in the original system operation; and time during the reruns is artificial, allowing temporal discontinuities in the system's operation.

This technique supports and facilitates both exploratory and experimental scientific investigation of online, complex, man-computer systems. It benefits the human-factors scientist by capturing all the man-computer interaction, both content and context. It aids the computer scientist by providing a temporal microscope to see into the complex innards of a computer system, and by facilitating experiments on computing strategies and algorithms. It especially supports the efforts of a system analyst by providing a mechanism for viewing system interactions in all their complexity, then allowing a narrowed focus into a specific area of interest. In summary, regenerative recording is a technique that makes visible the myriad relationships within a man-computer system, and allows application of the scientific method to elucidating the problems of these systems.

This chapter is concerned with an exposition of the regenerative recording technique. First, the concept is defined and background is described. Then we present a report of an experimental investigation into the regenerative recording of time-sharing systems. The significance of this report is due to the fact that online planning systems will evolve as interactive, time-sharing systems. An understanding of the application of regenerative recording to time-sharing systems is vital to the development of a computer-based planning laboratory.

9-2 DEFINITION

Regenerative recording is a technique to allow complete digital computer system playback. The recording component records an initial system state, and then time tags and records all subsequent input to the system. The regenerative component plays back the recorded input in its original sequence, starting from the same initial conditions and forcing the system to repeat its original behavior. This technique provides for the controlled reproduction of computer events as they occurred in a live computer run.

Regenerative recording is one of the tools that should be available to the system analyst. Its place in the analytic process is between system operation and measurement. Conventional measurement and recording tools are essentially partial or selective recording mechanisms. They contain no capability for reconstructing and rerunning the original system test. Regenerative recording allows the capture of the system test and then iterative playback and analysis, using selective recording and measurement tools.

The significance of regenerative recording to the system analyst derives from the complexity of contemporary digital computer systems. The analyst is faced with two problems. The first is attempting exploratory studies in a poorly understood, dynamically changing environment. He needs a method for rapidly and inexpensively exploring and probing the system to develop hypotheses. The second problem is the establishment of a laboratory in which to set up well-controlled experiments for testing his hypotheses.

Acquiring exploratory data about a complex system is not inexpensive with conventional tools. These tools require separate runs of a live system for each differing set of data to be examined. Each live run is accompanied by the concomitant costs of prime computer time and real users or, where the recording can be accomplished during normal operation, degradation of the computer service. There is also the attendant risk of system failure during a live run due to the additional recording mechanisms that must be activated for new recording requirements. Regenerative recording minimizes these problems by requiring only one live run with real users and slight system degradation. All exploratory recording and measurement is carried out in nonprime computer time as often as required. The failure of additional recording mechanisms is no longer critical. There is also more control over the quality of the observed system operation as the analyst can afford to wait until the system is being used in a manner consistent with his interests. For example, many investigations are concerned only with the behavior of the system under heavy load.

The second problem, performing well-controlled experiments to test hypotheses about the system's operation, is also aggravated by the complex characteristics of real-time digital computer systems. In a classical sense, well-controlled experiments imply that only the variables of interest will be subjected to systematic variation. With present experimental techniques, there are two basic ways to approximate this control. One is to apply statistical methods to the analysis of a large number of runs under standardized conditions. This technique is limited in the accuracy of the conclusions that can be drawn, and is also expensive because it requires many live computer runs. The other method for assuring a well-controlled experiment is to build abstractions, or models, of the system. The problem with this approach is credibility—laboratory surrogates often only crudely approximate the real world. Simulation models that may closely approximate the system are very costly and time consuming to build.

Regenerative recording is the technique which could, in theory, provide true experimental control for experiments on digital computer systems without sacrificing real-world credibility. This aspect of regenerative recording has been stressed by Sackman (1964). Control is achieved by creating well-defined mutations of the original system or its inputs after having recorded its original operation. The operation of each mutation corresponds to a well-controlled experiment. The mutations constitute the independent variables, the unchanged portions of the input and system constitute the experimental controls, and the changed outputs are the dependent variables.

The concept of regenerative recording and associated controlled experimental mutations are schematically described in Fig. 9-1. Regenerative recording has a number of additional diverse and powerful applications. Some of these have been realized in existing digital computer implementations while others are still hypothetical.

Program Applications. Regenerative recording allows the regeneration of complete program behavior. This facilitates the debugging process of new computer programs and systems by playing back the actual conditions surrounding an erroneous operation. It would be even more useful, if not essential, in debugging errors in an operational environment. In this situation errors occur at random and at infrequent times, and it is often impossible to duplicate the error. The only way to solve the problem is to regenerate the exact system behavior. In addition, the regenerative recording provides a test environment for checkout that is far more complete than manually generated test situations.

Training Applications. Many computer systems and subsystems require substantial training of the human users to assure effective

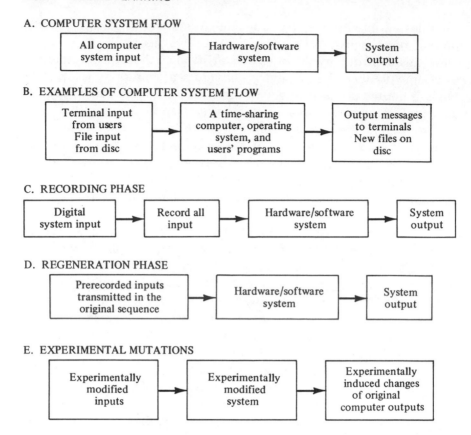

Figure 9-1. Schematic description of regenerative recording.

use of the system. Regenerative recording provides a vehicle for recording the users' behavior and its subsequent effect on the system and then playing it back for the users. This allows the users to observe their own behavior for corrective action and general debriefing. This also facilitates observation of the dynamic characteristics of users and their effect on the software, perhaps resulting in new software or user protocol design.

Operational Application. Regenerative recording provides a vehicle for studying the behavior of the system under real-world conditions and it allows this study to proceed iteratively in a nonreal-time environment. Unusual stresses, such as overloads and system degradation, may be captured for study when these conditions can neither be predicted nor simulated.

The study of specific system behavior, such as the security aspects of the system, is facilitated by regenerative recording. There are three facets to the security problem. First, to prevent security infractions; next, to detect security infractions; and last, to determine why the fault occurred and how to correct it. By being able to play back the system at the time the infraction occurred we could determine exactly where the fault lay. This function is similar to the flight recorder in commercial aircraft.

9-3 BACKGROUND

The idea of regenerative recording of digital computer systems is not recent. The earliest implementation goes back to 1960. Since then, the concept has occurred independently to many people; however, there have been few implementations. This section discusses the significant ideas and developments in regenerative recording that have appeared in the open literature.

9-3-1 Concepts

Van Horn (1968) has proposed three design criteria for specifying the structure of a system. These criteria assure that a user can control all the influences affecting the content and extent of his computer's output. The criteria are:

1. *Input Recordability (IR):* Any input stream of a computation (program) may be recorded.
2. *Input Specifiability (IS):* The content of any input stream to a computation may be prespecified.
3. *Asynchronous Reproducibility of Output (ARO):* The content and potential extent of the output streams of a computation depend only on the input streams and the computation's initial state. The asynchronous quality means that the relative timing of the production of several output streams is not necessarily reproduced.

These criteria are very similar to the system design features that are required to support regenerative recording. The IR criterion is equivalent to the recording requirement. The IS criterion says that the recorded input stream may replace the original input stream; this is equivalent to the playback portion of regeneration. The ARO criterion claims that the operation of the system with prerecorded data will produce the same output as the original operation. This criterion is weak, however, as it does not guarantee the reproduction of the original timing of the output. Van Horn has concentrated on the problem of regeneration for a single user, and thus he felt free to allow asynchronous reproduction. However, if we are attempting to regenerate the behavior of a complex operating system, exact timing reproduction of the output may be crucial. Apparently Van Horn did not envision the extent to which his ideas could support system investigation. He was primarily concerned with program checkout. There is no indication that any of his ideas were ever implemented, either in terms of specifying a system's design or of building a regenerative device.

Sackman (1964, 1967) was a major contributor to the earliest and most extensive implementation of regenerative recording. He has been the only individual to speculate upon its potential power and philosophize upon its ultimate significance. Sackman believes that the basic advantages of regenerative recording include total recording, efficient retrieval of digital system information, real-event libraries, support for system analysis, and experimental versatility and precision. It provides the foundation for making each digital system an applied science in the sense that each system will be capable of learning from and experimenting with its own real-time events in accordance with evolving hypotheses relating system performance to system design. Sackman has suggested that regenerative recordings be considered as automata, and that they be subject to experimental modifications through controlled regenerative mutations. This idea is plausible when we define a regenerative recording, or automaton, as a fixed and unambiguous set of inputs, an initial state and an associated set of states, and state transitions composed of the hardware/software system. With this interpretation, a real-world environment of men, machines, and natural system events can be transformed into a model. This is a significant concept, for it provides hope that segments of the real world—systems of such complexity that their details are beyond the grasp of a single human mind—can be converted to computerized counterparts that are amenable to formal study.

Sackman has made some worthwhile practical observations concerning the feasibility of regenerative recording. He points out that perfect reproduction is only an idealized goal. Useful regeneration with known and acceptable levels of accuracy coupled with a cost-effective tradeoff should be sought. He also observes that regenerative recording may be very difficult to achieve with systems containing unpredictable program interrupts and mass auxiliary storage that is continually being modified.

Head (1964) speaks about the data-logging problem in which input is logged as it is received in order to be able to duplicate errors by repeating the conditions that caused the error. He realizes, though, that complex operating systems may prohibit the exact reproduction of events. The idea of recording the state of the machine at various times in order to attempt an exact reproduction by reinitializing to a specific time does not occur to him. Head's data logging is essentially the same concept as regenerative recording.

9-3-2 Applications

There are only three applications of regenerative recording known to the author. They are significantly different from each other with respect to intent and design. The earliest one, for SAGE, was designed to regenerate an entire air defense system; the second, EXDAMS, was intended to reproduce the operation of a single program. The third, for ADEPT, regenerated the behavior of an entire time-sharing system. All will be described in detail.

Sage. The Semi-Automatic Ground Environment system was designed to support the continental air defense of the United States. It is a large, distributed, real-time system and is the earliest (1950's) system of that size to have been developed. Its recording and reduction capabilities have been extensively described by Sackman (1967). The input to the SAGE computer consists of tabular and pictorial displays describing the air-traffic situation and ancillary air defense information, together with messages from other components of the SAGE network.

The software structure is a large number of programs operating in a fixed sequence with each running to completion before the next is initiated. The input and output data are generated at essentially random times, but are transferred between the core memory and its hardware I/O devices only at fixed and predetermined points in the program cycle. Many of the programs and some of the data are stored on drums to be read into core when required. The data base has a tabular structure with all component tables and items being defined in a central dictionary (known as a "compool").

The purpose of the regenerative recording design in SAGE was to reproduce the behavior of an entire SAGE computer site within the SAGE network. It was partially developed by Black (1960), fully developed by Munson (1963), and applied to various operational problems by Sackman (1964).

To accomplish this goal, all of the inputs to a computer had to be recorded and time tagged. This task was relatively simple because the input is gathered into hardware buffers by the hardware itself. The input data are transferred to core memory and made available to the software only at a limited number of specified points within the program system cycle. The time tag was set to the time that the data were transferred to memory and not the time they entered the hardware buffers. The input data were then written onto tape for storage during the time that compute-bound programs were operating. This enabled channel time to be overlapped with CPU time. Since the SAGE computer has only one I/O channel, and I/O is always pre-scheduled, there were no unexpected I/O interference problems. The only significant CPU time degradation was caused by the time required to transfer a word from memory to the channel. It was possible to complete all necessary output while compute-bound programs were operating, thus avoiding a delay waiting for a buffer to be emptied. As the system load increased, the volume of data increased, but this did not increase recording overhead as the compute-bound programs operated for longer periods. The published figures indicate that the system was slowed by no more than 2 percent.

The initial state of the system was defined as the total contents of core memory. The initial state was recorded whenever recording was turned on and, thereafter, every ten minutes. This required a dump operation that halted computer operations for 8 seconds. The purpose of such frequent initialization recordings is to allow the user to select only that portion of the recorded operation of interest for the regeneration phase. Control of the recording was exercised through start and stop actions at a console.

The playback mechanism was also straightforward. At the point at which the data would have been read from the hardware buffers, the prerecorded data were read instead. The operational programs had no way of recognizing the difference. Minimal changes to the control program were required.

The fidelity of the playback was not perfect, although it was sufficient for the experiments. There was some variation of program outputs in regenerative reruns as compared to the original run. This is to be expected with a computer clock accurate to only 1/32 second and some artifact from the additional code. A schematic picture of SAGE regenerative recording is portrayed in Fig. 9-2.

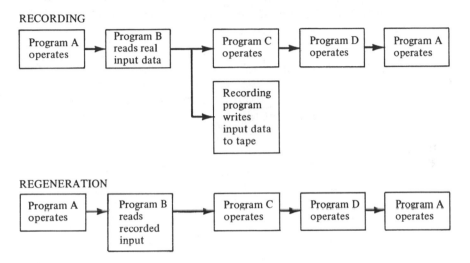

Figure 9–2.   Schematic representation of SAGE regenerative recording.

The recorded data and regenerative capability were used for several exploratory studies and experiments (Sackman, 1963). These are now described to provide some empirical evidence of the technique's utility:

1. A newer version of the SAGE system programs was compared to an older one to determine subprogram and overall operating times. A recording of the older version was played back with both versions. During the regeneration, a special recording program measured the timings. By holding all factors constant, including an entire air battle involving over 6000 switch actions taken by military operators, and varying only the SAGE program version, a rigorous timing comparison was made.

2. In a second experiment the regenerative function was used to compare the effectiveness of three different switch-processing systems. Total system inputs and most of the operational program were held

constant with the exception of the program constituting the independent variable.

3. The third study examined the switch actions taken by military operators during a multisite SAGE test. The data constituted a sample of 58,000 operator actions and were derived from the recording tapes produced at the individual SAGE sites. They provided the basis for establishing a variety of switch action norms derived from a credible user environment. Note that there was no need to regenerate to obtain these data; they were stripped off the recording tapes.

4. The fourth study involved dynamic instruction counting to develop statistical norms of how frequently single instructions and certain strings of instructions dynamically occur in the SAGE program. The data were derived from a regenerative run of a SAGE site available from a library of test tapes.

All of these experiments and studies were derived from a single set of recording tapes generated during a multisite SAGE exercise. They demonstrate both the range of use to which the regenerative recording technique has been put and the capability of regenerative recording as an economical omnibus experimental vehicle for a variety of investigations derived from a single test effort.

EXDAMS. *EX*tendable *D*ebugging *A*nd *M*onitoring *S*ystem is a debugging system for source level programs (Balzer, 1969). The source program is analyzed, instrumented, monitored and has necessary information stored on a recording tape. Subsequently, the debugging routines can retrieve information from the recording tape and prepare a variety of debugging aids.

Recording. The recording component of EXDAMS consists of static and dynamic portions. The source language program is analyzed prior to the run to determine its structure and obtain a symbol table. This defines the initial state of the program. Then instrumentation is inserted into the program in the form of debugging statements. These additional statements are compiled with the program.

The dynamic recording occurs when the program is operated. At this time the debugging statements will be activated and will pass relevant information to the recording routine. This information consists of the values of the variables on the left-hand side of assignment statements, the direction taken in IF statements, the direction taken at the end of DO-LOOPS, and the point from which a GOTO or CALL was issued. At the completion of the run, the recording tape will contain sufficient structural and operating information about the program to enable its behavior to be regenerated.

Regeneration. The regeneration portion of EXDAMS includes a library of interactive debugging aids, all of which use common retrieval routines to obtain data from the recording tape. These debugging aids are quite extensive, providing both static and dynamic information. The static aids essentially produce listings of the data or program space. The dynamic aids provide a motion picture display of the value change in variables or the flow through the program code. The user may control the regenerative execution time and can direct that movement in time be either backward or forward. The EXDAMS implementation of regenerative recording is not intended to reproduce the machine level operation of the program, but is designed to reproduce the effect of each source language statement in the program. It can associate any value with the source statement that produced it, and can associate any source statement with all the values it produces. This degree of sophisitcation is accomplished at a sacrifice of the real-time characteristics of the program. The extent of the instrumentation adds much artifact to the original operation of the program. The playback is actually interpretative, thereby obviating any possibility of real-time duplication.

ADEPT. The application of regenerative recording to time-sharing systems was experimentally investigated by the author (1970). A prototype regenerative recording vehicle was built for the ADEPT time-sharing system and its performance—in terms of the extent to which the regenerated system duplicated the original system's behavior, and the degree to which iterative regenerations exhibited the same behavior—was measured.

Motivation for this study came from the many advantages to the development and study of time-sharing systems that a regenerative recording vehicle would provide should it prove feasible. These advantages include:

- Testing. Unexpected errors that are due to subtle software bugs would be captured for offline debugging.
- Analysis. Permitting reruns of a complex system so that iterative analysis of an identical system operation may be performed.

- Low artifact measurement. Recording the original data needed for the regeneration requires very little time artifact. Measurement of the original or the regenerated system would very likely require much time. However, during the regeneration of a system, time has a somewhat artificial quality. The system's operation is controlled by the playback component; thus, the operation can be logically stopped and then resumed without any distortion to its behavior.
- Study of users and their programs. Since the users' behavior may be inferred from the recorded terminal input, and the users' programs' operation can be regenerated, regenerative recording becomes an omnibus data collection tool for this area of investigation.

The ADEPT time-sharing system was designed to support a variety of users and tasks on a medium-size computer. This general purpose system operates on an IBM 360/50 computer, includes a variety of hardware devices, and supports up to ten simultaneous users plus background operations. It has been described in detail by Linde, et al. (1969).

Recording. The only input selected for recording was from the interactive terminals (the time that the input was received was also recorded.) This included the interrupt condition from the multiplexor channel, the hardware status information, and the actual input data. Input is received from the terminals even when data are being transmitted to them. This input is the interrupt condition and hardware status occurring at the completion of the write. The initial state was defined at the point where the system had been loaded and was initialized but had not yet received its first input from an interactive terminal.

Regeneration. To regenerate the system's behavior, the system was loaded and initialized. At the time that the original inputs would have been received, the recorded inputs were instead played back to the system. The clock-interrupt capability of the computer was used to control playback timing. The major difficulty in the regeneration was caused by the coarseness of the computer's clock. It was accurate to only 16-2/3 milliseconds. The differences between the recording and playback programs caused additional problems. The results of the experiments showed that the only differences between the system's output were those calculations that depended on the exact value of the real-time clock. The operating system's behavior differed as evidenced by the slight variation between the sequence in which different jobs were scheduled. Repeated regeneration runs also showed variations of these factors between each other. However, the regeneration's validity and reliability were remarkably successful, considering the crudeness of the prototype.

9-3-3 Comparison of the Regenerative Recording Implementations

The immediate and most significant difference between the implementations is the goal of each. EXDAMS was directed at a single source language program. There was no attempt to retain the real-time properties of the program. However, because of the control exercised in the recording, the playback was otherwise guaranteed to have complete fidelity. In SAGE and ADEPT the goal was to provide complete regeneration of the entire system including all program interactions, all data base changes, and to retain the real time characteristics of the subject system. The more detailed recording and regeneration within EXDAMS could be subsumed under the system directed implementation of SAGE and ADEPT by exercising sufficient control during the regeneration so that an individual program could be analyzed at the convenience of the user.

There is an additional significant increase in the complexity and difficulty of regeneration from SAGE to ADEPT. This is the increased randomness of the input and the increased dependence upon time. First, the time-sharing system is event-driven, thus minimizing the system's knowledge of its future behavior. Demands come from a large domain; the object or user programs are continually changing; the combination of programs is random; and the rate of input is the function of a random variable. Therefore, the system must be constructed to respond in a manner determined by the events which are allowed to drive it. Second, the system is dependent on real time. It typically monitors the amount of elapsed time consumed by object programs, and uses the resultant information to change the operating priority of the programs, thereby changing the operation of the entire system. Third, the system is highly time dependent at the micro-time scale. If an interrupt affecting the queuing priority should occur one instruction cycle after the associated job's queue status is checked by the scheduler, the operation of the program may be delayed. Fourth, the regeneration is responsible for the behavior of programs that may not even exist when the technique is designed, or of which the investigator has no knowledge during the recording operation. In the previous implementations, the recording was applied to a known program and to a well-defined system. And last, the regeneration is attempting to reproduce the behavior of a complex body of software known as an operating system, which is trying to allocate a variety of resources to a continually changing set of demands while being bombarded by interrupts that create new demands and new priority configurations.

EXDAMS incorporates a sophisticated data reduction and analysis package as an integral part of its regeneration component. This is lacking in SAGE, which requires separate special-purpose recording and reduction tools to extract information from the regeneration. An ideal regeneration recording package would couple system-based recording with a regeneration capability that could rerun the system in an analysis mode and select individual programs and portions of the data base for detailed study.

A detailed comparison of the regenerative recording implementations is presented in Table 9-1.

9-4 THE REGENERATIVE RECORDING OF TIME-SHARING SYSTEMS

This section describes the application of regenerative recording to time-sharing systems. Previous applications have dealt with single programs and real-time, cyclic systems. The characteristic of time-sharing systems that make regenerative recording difficult, the utility of the application, pitfalls, and an experimental prototype are described.

9-4-1 Complexity of the Problem

The application of regenerative recording to time-sharing systems derives its interest and uniqueness from the dynamic operational characteristics of a time-sharing system as compared to the only other known applications of regenerative recording. The simplest application, EXDAMS (Balzer, 1969), was directed at a single-object program running under the control of an operating system. There was an implicit assumption in this design that the behavior of the object program would not be dependent on time, and that input data need be available only when called for by the object program. The application of regenerative recording to a network of real-time computers supporting an air defense system (Sackman, 1967) presented an increase in complexity. The application successfully regenerated a complete system of programs rather than just one program. In addition, the system was time dependent on a macro level. It was a cyclic system with a period in the several-second range, and it was aware if program cycles were consuming a disproportionate amount of time. However, the count of operating cycles was the key timing element instead of the elapsed or real time.

A summary of these increasing degrees of complexity is presented in Fig. 9-3.

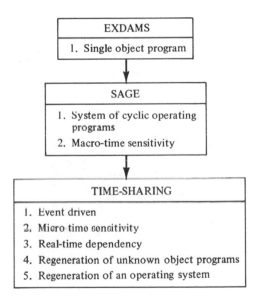

Figure 9-3.   Complexity of regenerative recording environments.

Thus, we see that the regenerative recording of time-sharing systems must deal with a larger set of unknown and poorly controlled variables, and with a system that has a significantly greater dependence on the sequence and timing of events than the earlier implementations.

Table 9-1. Comparison of Regenerative Recording Implementations

FACTOR	ADEPT	SAGE	EXDAMS
1. Goal	System regeneration.	System regeneration.	Program and statement regeneration.
2. Definition of Initial State	The state of the system after it has been loaded and initialized.	The contents of core memory and swappable drum memory. Includes all programs and data base of system.	A program model consisting of structural information and symbol table, the original source language program.
3. Purpose of Recording	To collect all "command" input to the system; i.e., user input.	To collect all input to the system.	To collect all input to the program, to each variable, and to detect all changes in program control.
4. Requirements for Recording	Instrumentation at the system level.	Instrumentation at the system level.	Preanalysis of object program, instrumentation of object program.
5. Effect of Recording	Slight increase in system overhead. No serious disruption of real-time characteristics of system.	Slight increase in system overhead. No serious disruption of real-time characteristics of system.	Elimination of real-time characteristics of program due to volume of instrumentation.
6. Technique of Recording	Write the input onto a recording tape.	Write the input data onto a recording tape while a compute-bound program is operating.	Between each statement that the program executes, branch to a data collection program to store data into a buffer. When the buffer is full, transfer it to a recording tape.
7. Content of Recording	All input from the interactive terminals. Time tags on the data.	All data that are input to the software via a hardware device. Time tags on the data.	The change of each variable. Source of executed GOTO and CALL statements. A true-false indicator for IF . . . THEN . . . ELSE statements.

Table 9-1. Comparison of Regenerative Recording Implementations (Cont'd.)

FACTOR	ADEPT	SAGE	EXDAMS
8. Purpose of Regeneration	To reproduce the exact system behavior as defined by the output to the terminals, timing relationships, and software interaction.	To reproduce the exact system behavior as defined by the output, timing relationships, and software interaction.	To reproduce the exact program behavior as defined by the output and sequential statement program flow.
9. Accuracy of Regeneration	Variations due to program being scheduled in slightly different order, and computations that involved the clock differed.	Only slight variations between original and regenerated run due to unavoidable timing discrepancies.	The regeneration produced a replication of the original program's output. No duplication of the real time characteristics.
10. Techniques of Regeneration	Reload the system and initialize it. The recording mechanism is replaced by a playback mechanism.	Reset the computer to an initial state. Let the system operate in real time, satisfying all requests for input with the recorded input.	Operate the program interpretively based on the initial state and the recorded dynamic operation data.
11. Utility of Regeneration	Requires a separate recording and reduction package for any use to be made of the regenerated run. However, with the proper support program, can analyze at the system, program, or data base levels.	Requires a separate recording and reduction package for any use to be made of the regenerated run. However, with the proper support program, can analyze at the system, program, or data base levels.	The regeneration package includes the reduction tools required to use the regenerated run. These include dynamic traces of the program space and data spaces backwards and forwards in time. Provision is made to add additional reduction routines in a simple manner.

9-4-2 Benefits of a Regenerative Recording Capability for Time-Sharing Systems

A regenerative recording capability for a time-sharing system provides a significantly increased capability in the realms of testing, analysis, and research. Note that this technique does not generate data or measurements of the subject system. Instead, it facilitates the extraction of the data by providing iterative testing, controlled reproduction, and a minimization of measurement artifact. A measurement capability is still required to extract data from the regenerated system's operation. These points are discussed in the following paragraphs and are summarized in Fig. 9-4.

- Program and System Testing
- System Analysis
- Experimental Research
- Artifact-Free Measurement
- User Studies
- Operating System Studies

Figure 9-4. Potential benefits of a regenerative recording capability for time-sharing systems.

Testing. The testing of a software complex's programs for correctness can be characterized as a search for the unexpected—the unknown but assumed errors. A major difficulty arises from this search when an unexpected error is uncovered and the programmer is unprepared to analyze it, especially when the error does not manifest itself until many instruction operations beyond the original incorrect operation. If the software's operation could be recorded in such a way that it could be played back, error and all, then the programmer could be prepared for the unexpected and could rapidly decide upon, and apply, a debugging strategy. Further, improved strategies could be devised, if necessary, with every confidence that the error would be reproducible on demand.

Analysis. The analysis of time-sharing systems has been generally characterized by much exploratory investigation. This results from the lack of commonly accepted measures of performance and from the relative uniqueness of each system. The resultant mode of analysis is to run a number of pilot tests in an attempt to determine the relevant measures. There are two difficulties with this approach. The first is that conclusions drawn from different populations as a result of the different systems' runs have a lowered reliability. The second difficulty is the prime computer time required to collect data from many separate runs. (The reason all potentially useful data are not collected at once is insufficient foreknowledge and measurement artifact.) A regenerative recording capability resolves these difficulties by permitting reruns of the same system test, each time collecting a different set of data. The correlation of these data to each other is valid as they all come from the system run. Note that the rerun cost is reduced since the rerun may occur in nonprime computer time with no additional service degradation and without the attendant costs of real users and operating facilities.

Research. Experimental research of time-sharing systems is an almost unknown endeavor. This is not because of the investigator's lack of skill, but rather to a lack of sophistication in the tools he uses. The basic tenet of experimental investigation is to obtain sufficient control of the subject problem (experiment) so as to vary only those variables of interest and thus observe the resultant effect. This has been achieved with analytic and discrete-state simulation models and with live systems operating in a repeatable benchmark mode. To achieve similar control of the real world nonbenchmark operation of a time-sharing system, we need a regenerative recording capability. After the real-world operation has been recorded, the regenerations may be treated as controlled experiments by modifying only the variables of interest and comparing the results to the original or other experimental runs. Mutations (controlled changes) may be made in both the software and the input data. Some examples of these are: modifications to the scheduling algorithm, parameter changes to resource allocation algorithms, effect of improved coding for a key program, and changes in user response time and changes in user input. Regenerative recording provides the controlled environment to make scientific experimentation feasible, but it does not provide the tools for constructing the experiment, collecting data, or analyzing the data.

Artifact-Free Measurement. Any software-based instrumentation, or measurement tool, causes some time artifact in the system being measured. In practice, this time artifact is the severest artifact with which the measurement analyst must cope. Its effect is to make the data less reliable and to limit the amount of data that can be collected. Regenerative recording provides an escape from this problem. During the regeneration of a system, time has a somewhat artificial quality. Since the rate of input is under the control of the playback component and the system's operation can be logically stopped, pauses can be made in the regenerated operation of the system. This assumes that the software and hardware clocks can be recorded at the moment of pause and then be reset to that same value upon system continuation. The measurement artifact is eliminated by directing the measurements at the regenerated system, and then forcing the regenerated system to logically pause while the measurement code is executing. The time required for measurement then becomes transparent to the system. This opens up a whole new realm of measurement and analysis possibilities. For example, the regenerated system could be forced to run in short continuous increments so that dynamic graphs could be produced; the investigator could view in slow motion the changes that take place in the system states; dynamic operation graphs could be "backed up" and restarted from an intermediate point for review of a particularly interesting portion; selected segments could be time controlled for slow-motion study, allowing the remaining operations to proceed faster than the original by deleting all idle time. Some of these ideas were implemented by Balzer (1969) in his EXDAMS project. Others are similar to work that has been done with simulation vehicles. The vital contribution of regenerative recording in this area is the capability to reproduce the original system's behavior despite many temporal interruptions in the regenerated run.

Study of Users and Their Programs. The capability of regenerating the behavior of many users and their programs naturally suggests the application of regenerative recording as an omnibus data collection tool for this area of investigation. Data can be collected about the content of user responses, response time, object program operational characteristics, and use of the system's command and utility functions. Furthermore, this data can be collected selectively by specifying the regeneration of a subset of the recorded users.

Study of Operating Systems. An operating system is a complex collection of programs for managing the system resources over a wide domain of demands and for serving as an interface between the user and the hardware. This software is typically event driven, highly time dependent and operationally best described with dynamic or stochastic methods. All of these factors make the study of operating-system behavior under real-world conditions very difficult, yet the central importance of the operating system to the effectiveness of the entire system's operation makes its study crucial. If regenerative recording can indeed reproduce such a complex behavior, then it could contribute significantly to the study of time-sharing operating systems.

9-4-3 Inherent Limitations

The goal of regenerative recording is to reproduce the behavior of the software portion of the digital computer system. The behavior of each instruction that was executed in the original run is to be duplicated and the same sequence of instructions is to be executed. A close examination of the requirements for regenerative recording discloses the unsettling fact that perfectly accurate regeneration is probably not technically feasible. The reasons for this are discussed in the following paragraphs.

Completely accurate regeneration of a system requires a timing facility that operates at the instruction execution frequency. Since the input to the system is signaled by interrupts which were originally accepted by the system at random points in its operation, we must somehow tag the recorded interrupt in order to know when to play it back. A time tag may be used which specifies the time from some standard point (e.g., system initialization) at which the interrupt originally occurred. Alternatively, the tag may be a count of the number of instructions executed since a reference point. The latter technique not only requires special hardware, but, if the regenerated system were at all inexact in its reproduction, would make the counter mechanism inaccurate. The time-tagging idea requires no special hardware other than a high resolution clock, yet it suffers from the fact that clocks are not very accurate (Koster, 1969). Time tagging does offer a limited feedback mechanism for overcoming the effects of inaccurate regeneration. If the regenerated system should begin operating faster than the original, the interrupts would not be played back until the original time, thus delaying the system. This does not work when the regenerated system begins to operate slower.

The study of controlled changes to a system nullifies the concept of completely accurate regeneration. The mutations may cause the system to deviate sufficiently from its original behavior so that a change occurs in its sequence of states that determines when input will be meaningfully accepted. In this case, the recorded input must have a logical tag associated with it so that the playback control may recognize when it is acceptable to the system. For example, the interrupt for a read command cannot be played back before the read command itself has been issued by the regenerated system. There is a trickier question of realism of the playback. In the operation of a changed regeneration there may be relatively large periods of time in which an input datum would be logically acceptable. However, it would not be realistic to play it back during most of this time period. The timing of the playback should correspond to the original or to realistic delays of the input device, such as human response time or the rotational delay of a storage device.

It is apparent, in any case, that the problem of playing back the interrupts at the correct time is crucial for accurate regeneration, and poses a major technical obstacle.

Another significant hindrance to accurate reproduction is uncontrolled variation in hardware components. A minimum hardware configuration for regeneration is the CPU and core memory. However, this is often not sufficient and/or feasible. For example, in a swapping system the regeneration should include the swapping process. This will result in regeneration distortions due to uncontrollable variation in the rotational delay of the secondary storage device such as a drum. Since this delay probably has a certain amount of random variation, a synchronization procedure would not be very effective. The effect of uncontrolled variation is to modify the behavior of the regenerated system in the amount of time the system is delayed while waiting for hardware-dependent operations to conclude. Other examples of this problem are the disc-head positioning and rotational delay, and tape acceleration times.

There are two forms of artifact that create additional roadblocks to accurate regeneration. These are the time and logical artifacts caused by the regeneration code. Time is required to read the recorded data from its storage device, to access the recorded data, and to distribute the data to the appropriate input processing routines. Although the total amount of time required for this is approximately the same as the amount required for recording (the same amount of data must be transferred and processed), the amount of time will not be identical, nor will the operations necessarily occur at the same point in the system's operation. The logical artifact results from the different operations required for recording and regeneration. The recording code must intercept the input interrupts at the point where they enter the system, whereas the playback control is activated as a result of a time-control interrupt by the normal interrupt-handling procedures. Thus, this artifact, which appears to be inescapable with software regeneration and recording, sets another limit on the accuracy of the reproduction.

There are a number of second-order problems which must be considered. The most interesting and formidable problem is the regeneration of a program that depends on real time as one of its controlling, or input, parameters. A program may depend on time in a number of ways. It could periodically monitor the clock time, it could ask the operating system to schedule it at certain intervals, and it could create its own time by executing some countable process in a manner that made it aware of the passage of time. Such programs may depend on this time awareness to determine the actions it will take. One class of action, seriously disrupting the regeneration, would be a change in the expected inputs. The new expectations could not be satisfied by the recorded inputs, thus terminating further operation of the program.

The uncontrolled variation discussed earlier also affects the cross reliability between identical regeneration runs. Programs will be scheduled in a different order, output will be produced in a different order, and input will be expected at different times. The operating system will definitely evince different behavior on each regeneration run as may the object programs. Thus, because of practical reasons, the behavior of certain kinds of programs may not be reproducible, and the attempt to iteratively regenerate identical behavior may not be successful.

The artifacts induced into the original system operation by software recording components must be analyzed to provide assurance that the system is not being distorted significantly from its normal operation. (Note that this is not as important in regeneration because that artifact is almost identical to the recording artifact, and we expect to reproduce the effect of the recording artifact.) There are several kinds of artifacts induced by the recording requirements:

Time Artifact: Processing and channel time necessary to collect the input and transfer it to a storage medium.
Space Artifact: The space required for the code and buffer areas and secondary storage areas.

Logical Artifact: The change in operation required to intercept the input at the earliest possible moment after it enters the system, and the extra operation of transferring the data to a secondary storage device.

Operational Artifact: The recording must be initiated under manual control.

9-4-4 Operational Problems in the Implementation

There are several important questions that must be resolved when designing a regenerative recording capability for a time-sharing system. These problems have a direct bearing on the accuracy, utility and feasibility of the implementation.

Hardware versus Software. Both hardware and software techniques can be used to record and play back the input. A tape recorder attached to a dial-in terminal can pick up the terminal's output signal. The playback is achieved by feeding the tape recorder's loudspeaker output into the modem. This technique would be significantly more difficult if applied to high-speed devices or channels.

Software may be used to record the input when it enters the core memory of the computer. This software is activated by the input generated interrupts.

There are advantages and disadvantages to both these techniques other than the implementation difficulties. The hardware technique does impose little, if any, artifact on the system's operation, whereas the software, as discussed in the previous section, imposes a variety of artifacts. There is more inherent control of the regeneration with the software technique. The input rate may be increased or decreased and the contents may be modified for special purposes. The hardware playback would not permit this without special purpose communication facilities and associated software to provide a feedback control over the speed of the playback device.

Hardware techniques require that the equipment receiving the recorded data must not have any transient errors. For when a receiving device gets an error reply, it normally repeats the request for input. Since the original run did not contain a second transmission, there would be no simple way for the playback device to know whether to repeat the last recorded input.

Extent of Regeneration. The range of the system's behavior that is regenerated can vary from the very small software component (a single object program), to larger software components (all object programs, the operating system alone or with object programs), to include hardware devices (channels, reader/punch, printer, discs, tapes, etc.). The range selected will be only partially dependent on the end use; the more important considerations are the problems imposed by certain ranges. For instance, if the disc units are not to be included in the regeneration, then (1) their content must be kept unchanged during normal use until after the regeneration insofar as any files are required during the regeneration run, and (2) there can be no creation of new files or modification of existing files by the original regeneration run in order that the regenerated programs will be assured of the same input. On the other hand, if the disc units are to be part of the regeneration, then all input from the disc, including interrupts, must be recorded so that during the regeneration run the discs can be logically disconnected and the recorded disc data read from the recording tape. This results in a more complex regenerative recording implementation with a requirement to manage large volumes of data, but with increased flexibility for file regeneration.

Regeneration that includes the operation of hardware must be able to handle random hardware failures. The previous section discussed this problem.

These examples demonstrate how the range of desired regeneration will impose a variety of constraints and problems on the final implementation.

Initial State. The initial state of the time-sharing system is the system state at the time that recording and regeneration begin. All input is recorded after the initial state is established It is assumed, as one of the conditions for regenerative recording, that the system can be set to a state that is identical with that when the recording began. This state represents the content of all software and data that have any effect at all on the operation of the regenerated system.

The initial state can be defined as a function of logical and temporal variables. The basic component of the initial state is the hardware. Since the hardware cannot actually be "recorded," the hardware must not change between the original run and the regenerations. The remainder of the decisions about the initial state's contents deal with the software and files. If the initial state is defined at the time of system load, then the system master tape must be "recorded." If the initial state is defined at some point after system load, then there must be a way to reconstruct the system to the point defined as the initial state. This may be done by allowing the system to operate in a highly controlled mode up to the point of the defined initial state, and then to perform the recording and regeneration. It could also be achieved by recording the contents of the entire system at the time of the defined initial state. This may require the recording of all core memory, the registers, swap storage, and perhaps part of the files. This can be a burdensome, if not infeasible, task. However, it offers greater flexibility since the system may be regenerated from any of a number of points (assuming initial-state recordings are made at periodic intervals) instead of just from the first initial state.

Recording the contents of the files as part of the initial state is optional. If the files are recorded in the initial state, then the file-storage mechanisms must be reinitialized to contain these same files. This can create bookkeeping problems because of duplicate file names—the original, if it still exists, and the regenerated file. Ideally, we would want a restricted file-storage device for storage of the re-generated files. To avoid including the files in the initial state, the individual records can be recorded at the time they are requested by a program. Then, in the regeneration, whenever a record is to be read from the file, it is furnished from the recording instead. This tech-nique limits the regeneration to requesting the same files in the same order as the original run. For study of controlled system changes, where a different sequence of events may occur, this technique of recording the input records may prove too limiting.

Regeneration Control. The extent to which the user desires to control the regeneration is an influencing factor on the overall design. If the sole goal of the regeneration is to study the original perfor-mance of the system, then the only capability to be assured is that the playback process will provide the inputs to the system in their original order. However, if the goal is to study controlled changes, then provision must be made to provide inputs in any order, as they are requested. This is best achieved for interactive-terminal playback by recording all terminal inputs on separate logical channels, one channel for each terminal. Then the regenerated system may schedule terminals at different priorities with assurance that the input received will be dependent solely on the recorded terminal user's behavior and not on the order that the input was originally received with respect to all the terminals. To facilitate the study of program changes that in-clude file access, the entire file must be made available to the regen-eration so the program may request records from any file in any order.

Another form of regeneration control is the capability of starting the regeneration at preselected points in the total recorded time period to allow the study of periods of interest selected from a long recording. To permit this control, recording of all core, swap storage, and possibly the file storage at each of the preselected times must be feasible in order to define a number of initial states at which regeneration can commence.

A number of other questions deal with the utility of the regeneration and affect the amount of information that may be extracted. Selective regeneration allows us to delete some of the input from the system; for instance, the deletion of all input from a specified subset of terminals. Accelerated regeneration refers to a reduction in the amount of real time required to regenerate the original run. This may be accomplished by deleting all idle time in the regenerated run. Delayed regeneration slows down the regenerated run by inserting temporary halts at points of interest in the regenerated operation. This is used to provide a window into the operation of the system, or to make the system operate in apparent slow motion so that dynamic graphs and charts representing a component's behavior may be observed at human viewing speeds. Extensions of the regeneration control to allow online and dynamic insertion of probes, selection, acceleration, delay, requesting a variety of analysis aids such as the automatic tracking of selected variables' values, and dynamic graphing of a selected component's operation all should be considered in the design of the regenerative recording facility.

9-4-5 The ADEPT Regenerative Recording Implementation

Background. A prototype regenerative recording vehicle was successfully implemented for the ADEPT time-sharing system by the author (1970). It was used to quantitatively evaluate the feasibility, validity, and reliability of time-sharing system regeneration.

The ADEPT time-sharing system (Linde, et al., 1969) supports a variety of users and tasks on a medium-size computer. It operates on an IBM 360/50 computer, includes a variety of hardware devices, and supports up to ten simultaneous users plus background operations. The hardware configuration consists of a 256K byte memory, single CPU, drum for swapping, three selector channels, one multiplexor channel, card reader/punch, printer, and a variety of discs, tapes, and interactive terminals. The hardware configuration most effectively supports programs with large file and channel requirements, and moderate core and processor requirements. Only one user resides in core at a time; i.e., there is no multiprogrammed operation. There are several levels of job priorities that are determined by dynamic program characteristics.

Studies were made of the regeneration's validity (reproduction of the original system's operation) and reliability (similarity between iterative regenerations). The regenerated run was modified by deleting input, deleting all idle time and thereby decreasing the regeneration's elapsed time, and halting the regeneration at random times to take dumps.

Design of the Regenerative Recording Implementation:

Hardware versus Software. Both hardware and software mechanisms for recording and playing back the input were considered. The software direction was chosen because of the relative ease of modifying the resultant recording and playback "machine," and to eliminate the problem of random errors in the transmission hardware that would have ruined the regeneration.

Input Selection. The only input selected for recording was from the interactive terminals. This includes the interrupt condition from the multiplexor channel, the hardware status information, and the actual input data. Note that for output to the terminal the only information to be recorded is the interrupt and status data. This design excludes recording input from the tapes, discs, drum, printer, card reader/punch, and the operator's terminal [a special terminal (IBM 1052) that communicates directly with the operating system].

Initial State. The initial state was defined to be at the point where the system is initialized and is awaiting its first input from a terminal. This requires that the system master tape, corrections, and files be preserved for the regeneration runs.

Constraints. A number of restrictions were imposed on original system operation in order to reduce the complexity of the project and conform to the limitations imposed by the input and initial state design. Only hard copy terminals were used (IBM 2741 and Teletype model 33) in order to obtain hard copy output during the recording run. No tapes or demountable disc packs were used because of the human delay time involved in mounting and preparing them. The card/reader and punch were not used because of the possible effects of variations in the mechanical delays and possibility of mechanical failures. The printer was not used in order to make it available for the regenerated output (discussed in a following paragraph). Certain file operations involving generation of new files without subsequent deletion, reading a record that is to be rewritten, and extending or moving files, are prohibited.

Swapping. The swapping operation which involves data transfer between drum and core is allowed to proceed normally. There was no attempt to synchronize the drum position with the processor's operation.

Playback Timing. The time that the recorded interrupts are to be played back to the regenerated run is determined by the computer clock. The original inputs are time tagged with the value of the computer clock when they are recorded. The regenerated run will have its clock set to the same value as at recording initialization. Interrupts from the clock are used to signal the playback. Since the clock on the 360/50 is accurate to only 16-2/3 milliseconds, the time of the playback of the inputs may be inaccurate by as much as 16-2/3 ms. This represents a significant source of possible regeneration error.

Measurement. The measurement is accomplished by comparing the interactive terminal output of the original to the regenerated runs and searching for certain factors. As noted already, hard copy of both is available. A further aid is the time tagging of all output in both the original and regenerated runs. This is accomplished by modifying the terminal output program to add to each line of output the computer maintained time.

This design does not appear to seriously handicap the realism of the regeneration experiments, as the major system components (the resident executive, nonresident executive, and the user programs) are able to operate, and the major system functions (swapping, scheduling, resource allocation, program loading and execution, command language operations, and file manipulation) are exercised.

Input/Output State. It was previously noted that the regeneration will not be completely accurate, primarily because of unavoidable artifact and the low resolution of the playback clock (16-2/3 ms). This inaccuracy suggests that the following critical problem could occur. If the sole criterion for playing back the input is a comparison of the recorded time with the regenerated time, then a recorded input (i.e., an interrupt) may be played back before it is expected by the regenerated program operation which issues the I/O instructions. This sequence of events would cause the input to be discarded by the program, thereby making the playback irrevocably asynchronous with the regenerated operation. The effect is, at a minimum, to cause one terminal to be deleted from the regeneration; and at worst, to abort the entire regeneration.

An additional element of control information had to be defined to avoid this problem. This additional element is called the input/output state. The executive program that interfaces with the multiplexor channel, and thence the terminals, was modified to note the hardware activity of each terminal. This activity was defined as the I/O state of the terminal. The possible values reflect the command issued to the terminals. For example, some of the values are:

> read has been issued
> write has been issued
> sense command has been issued
> terminate the previous command
> terminal is inactive

This I/O state is dynamically maintained by both the original and regenerated program operations. When an input is recorded during the original run, the I/O state value of the associated terminal is recorded also. When the playback is scheduled, the input will be delayed until the associated terminal's I/O state is set to the originally recorded value. Thus, the playback is controlled by two parameters. An input will not be played back before it originally occurred (the regenerated time is equal to or later than the recorded time), and the regenerated terminal is prepared for the input (identical I/O states).

These general design principles can be graphically portrayed. Figure 9-5 contains a simplified description of the ADEPT time-sharing system.

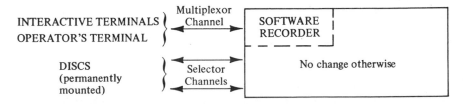

Figure 9-5. Simplified description of the ADEPT time-sharing system.

The content of the box on the right is the portion of the system of interest to the regeneration studies. We would like to record all input to the box and then logically disconnect the channels for regeneration. It was concluded earlier that this was expensive and not required for the basic experiments. Therefore, we have considered the system when recording the original run to appear as in Fig 9-6. Certain hardware components have been deleted and a special software recording machine has been added.

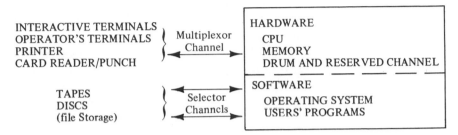

Figure 9-6.   ADEPT system logical configuration for recording.

Since we are completely playing back the interactive terminals, there is no need for them in the regeneration configuration. Figure 9-7 portrays this and, in addition, shows the replacement of the recording mechanism with the playback mechanism.

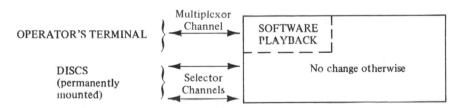

Figure 9-7.   ADEPT system logical configuration for regeneration.

The recording mechanism requires a secondary storage device to retain the possibly voluminous data. This device is not shown in Figs. 9-6 and 9-7. There was a choice between the drum, tapes, and discs for the storage device. The drum was discarded because it lacked permanence between runs. Tape acceleration time is much less than disc average access time. This makes tape a better choice of recording for the small core buffer sizes that were available. Thus, one tape drive was reserved for recording and playback purposes. The required

I/O bypassed the ADEPT system file maintenance programs to minimize physical distortion of the file cataloging scheme.

During the regeneration, output that would normally be routed to the interactive terminals was sent to the printer for hard copy availability. All printer I/O was done with direct code to eliminate the overhead associated with the normal printer control system programs, and to permit overlap between the CPU's regenerated behavior and the printer's operation. The printer is not shown in Fig. 9-5 because its use is transparent to the regenerated system.

The operator's terminal remained attached to the system and was operational during the recording and regenerating runs. Its operation was neither recorded nor regenerated because the operator's terminal plays a unique role in communicating with the system for debugging and operations management purposes. Use of the terminal does not cause the creation of a new job. Instead, it inputs to the system initialization program and to a special resident debugging program. To facilitate debugging and, as it fortuitously happened, to experiment with delayed recording, the operator's terminal was operationally retained.

Experimental Design. The idea of performing experiments on a computer system is foreign to most system designers. Typically, complex software products are evaluated only in response to observed problems or given nothing more than an operational shakedown. It is important to evaluate these products under controlled scientific conditions; i.e., to develop experiments for the evaluation process. This approach is followed here with the definition of hypotheses, controlled laboratory conditions for the experiments, sufficient data collection to obtain the requisite experimental data and thorough analysis of the data by using statistical techniques.

Hypotheses. Three major hypotheses were tested in this series of experiments, dealing with the feasibility of regeneration and the possibility of extending it for greater utility.

Validity of the Regeneration. It has been hypothesized that the regenerative recording technique is capable of reproducing the behavior of the operating system and user program software. This presumption has been shown to be pragmatically infeasible. Therefore, measures of reproducibility must be defined that will test the hypothesis in a statistical manner.

Reliability of the Regeneration. To use the regeneration for iterative studies there must be assurance that each of the iterations will produce the same results. Therefore, the second hypothesis is that the regeneration runs based on the same recording are reliable in the sense that each will operate the same. Again, because of uncontrollable playback variation, this hypothesis must be judged on a statistical basis.

Extensions of the Regeneration. Previous discussions have proposed that the regeneration can be modified to facilitate its utility in solving problems. This hypothesis states that the regeneration can be accelerated (operated faster than in the original run), delayed (interrupted at arbitrary points to take measurements), and be made selective (delete input not of interest). The degree to which this hypothesis is satisfied will also be determined statistically.

Definition of Measures. Formal measures were defined to test the hypotheses. These measures should indicate the degree to which the regeneration reproduces the original system's behavior. The selected measures all depend on an analysis of the output to the interactive terminals. From this output it is assumed we can infer meaningful information about the behavior of the regenerated software because of the typically highly interactive nature of a time-sharing system.

Reproduction of Output Measure. This measure determines whether the regenerated system can reproduce the original output to the terminals. The assumption is that if the output, or response, to the user is identical to the original, then the user programs or user-called system programs were regenerated properly. There are clearly exceptions to this such as when a program is also sending output to a nonterminal device. In this case the output to the nonterminal device may differ in the regenerated runs with no change in the terminal output.

The measure is implemented by collecting all hard copy output from the runs and comparing them manually to find and categorize discrepancies. The measure may be presented quantitatively as the percentage of logically incorrect lines over the total number of lines that should have been printed.

Sequential Reproduction of Output Measure. The previous measure provides insight into the correct regeneration of users' programs and user-called system programs, but does not provide any information into the operating system behavior. One means of inferring information about the operating system considers the order in which it scheduled the user programs that initiated the terminal output. By examining the sequence with which lines were output to all the terminals, we can estimate the ability of the regeneration to reproduce the scheduling characteristics of the operating system.

This measure is implemented by manually collecting all terminal output from the runs that are to be compared. Since these output lines had been time-tagged by the regenerative recording modification, it is a relatively easy job to determine the order in which the output was generated by the system. The sequence used as the basis for comparison is that of the original run.

A mean difference is used as a quantitative measure. Each line in a regenerated run is assigned two numbers. One is the original sequence number for that line; the other is the regenerated sequence number. The difference of these numbers averaged over all the lines is the measure of sequential reproduction.

Synchronous Reproduction of Output Measure. The previous measures give no indication of the time distortions that occur in regeneration. These distortions may be due to artifact, programs being executed in a sequence different from the original, programs receiving different queue priorities, or deliberately induced changes to the regeneration. The sequential reproduction measure is sensitive to some of these problems. An even more sensitive indicator is a comparison of the times of the output of different regenerations and the original run. Essentially, this measure characterizes the real-time reproducibility of the regeneration.

This synchronous reproduction measure is implemented by using the time tags that had been included in all the terminal output of the original and regenerated runs. This time tag is as accurate as the computer clock (16-2/3 ms). Manual analysis of the output enables us to associate each line with the original and regenerated time at which it was produced. The measure is made quantitative by computing the mean difference between the original and regenerated times for all lines in a run.

In both the synchronous and sequential measures, the basis for comparison is the operation of the original run. This provides simple cross comparisons between different regenerations, using the mean differences. While it does not directly compare two regenerated runs, it is adequate for statistical analysis.

With the aid of these three measures, it is possible to experiment with the regenerative recording hypotheses. Each of these measures provides insight and quantitative values for the basic tests of the validity and reliability of regenerative recording, and for determining the effect of the extensions on validity and reliability.

The Recording Environment. The recording run which generated the input for the regeneration experiments was produced according to these criteria:

1. The same recording was used for all the regeneration experiments. This allowed comparisons to be made among the individual regenerations. Of particular interest was a comparison of the regeneration extensions to the unmodified regeneration.

2. The original recorded system operation was to be highly interactive in terms of the user tasks. This assures adequate input for the recording and playback functions, and provides sufficient data for the measurements (the measurements being based on the terminal output lines).

3. The user tasks for the recording run were to cover the range of normal user operations on the ADEPT time-sharing system.

4. The user-initiated program could not attempt to execute those system functions for which the regenerative recording prototype was not prepared.

5. The test length had to be of sufficient duration to allow a user to interact meaningfully with the system, but should not be so great that a large amount of computer time would be required for running the experiments.

6. Several terminals should be in use simultaneously to make credible the claim for regeneration of multiple users and to adequately stress the operating system with competing requests for service.

The run that was recorded consumed about 11 minutes and incorporated five users, each working separately and simultaneously on a different terminal. The terminal types were IBM 2741s and Model 33 Teletypes. Each user initiated the following activity:

User A: The ADEPT system's command language was exercised. A total of 23 system commands were input to perform functions that included determining the status of the hardware, files, and other users' jobs; to load, start, and quit programs; and to log in and out of the system. Illegal commands were included.

User B: Exercised the interactive debugging commands. A program was loaded and executed. Then it was "debugged" with the debugging capabilities of breaking, dumping, modifying, and restarting a program.

User C: Interacted with the system in a highly interactive, question-answer mode that was representative of such applications as computer-assisted instruction and information retrieval. The program actually used was the COUCH (Vetter, 1970) program which asks questions in an attempt to psychoanalyze the patient (user). Responses from the user are in natural English.

User D: A symbolic file was selectively printed onto the terminal by a system utility program. This represents the activity of a file editing procedure.

User E: A program was assembled by the online assembler. The input to, and output from, the assembler were disc files. This activity was representative of a compute- and file-bound operation that occurs quite frequently in a time-sharing environment.

In summary, a wide variety of user applications were run in a time-sharing mode to provide a realistic load on the system and give credibility to the regeneration experiments. The applications included exercising the command language, debugging, file editing, conversational interaction, program assembly, file access, and an occasional heavy CPU load. These activities, in turn, stimulated the major system functions such as swapping, scheduling, resource allocation, file activity, excessive CPU demand, and terminal activity.

A statistical summary was made of the recording tape to provide a quantitative estimate of the system activity as it concerned the recording and playback functions. The key figures are the number of interrupts that occurred (581) and their average frequency (0.86 per second). This represents the load on the recording and playback mechanisms. It is very low compared to any normal measurement (recording) application. Assuming that each interrupt required as much as 1 millisecond average time for collection and recording, the time artifact is only about 0.01 percent, an insignificant amount. The number of bytes required for each interrupt is about 50. At the average interrupt rate, this represents an average data-recording rate · of 43 bytes per second. This is a very low rate and one that causes little problem for a recording mechanism.

A crude significance measure of the recorded data can be made. (Remember, the only reason for the recording is to regenerate the system's behavior.) Assuming that the average instruction execution time on the 360/50 is 5 microseconds, and the CPU is executing instructions all the time, then each word (4 bytes) of recorded data results in the regeneration of 18,000 instructions. This is a high order of information retrieval efficiency. Sackman (1967) estimates the equivalent ratio for the SAGE system regeneration to be 1 to 100.

The Validity Experiment Design. The regeneration was initiated by loading the ADEPT system into the computer with the modifications for regeneration, preparing the recording tape, typing the regeneration command, and allowing the regeneration to proceed. All terminals that had been turned on when the original run was made were turned on in the regeneration to allow the system initialization to proceed as normal and to assure that the regeneration initialization would occur at the same logical point as the recording initialization. The output that is normally directed at the terminals was routed to the printer. No human interaction at the terminals was allowed while the system was regenerating. This process was repeated three times to acquire data from three regenerations for statistical analysis.

The regenerated output was compared, line by line, against the original output for all three runs to determine the reproducibility measure. Each line of the regenerated output was sequence numbered and the mean differences of these sequence numbers with the original were computed to produce the sequential reproduction measure. Then the time tags of corresponding regenerated and original lines were compared to determine their mean difference, yielding the synchronous reproduction measure.

The Reliability Experiment Design. The reliability experiment used the data collected for the validity experiment. However, it compared the data between the individual regenerations to determine whether separate regeneration runs resulted in the same operation of the system. The data was statistically analyzed to determine the probability that each run came from the same population.

These basic analyses of validity and reliability served as standards against which to evaluate the regeneration extensions.

The Regeneration Extensions Experiment Design:

Selective Regeneration. This technique is designed to select from the recorded input specific terminals of interest to be played back. It will result in the regeneration of only a portion of the original user jobs and the original operating system behavior. To accomplish this, a modification was required to the playback routine to ignore all input associated with one or more terminals. The terminal numbers were input to the system at load time.

The regenerated system was initiated in the same manner as described for the first experiment, with the addition of the modifications to the correction deck and the terminal numbers.

Two terminals' input were deleted from the regenerated run. The activities they represented were the command language and the file editing. Thus, regeneration was reduced to three users from the original five. The regenerated run was repeated to obtain two sets of data. It was analyzed in terms of validity and reliability with the three basic measures.

Accelerated Regeneration. The purpose of this technique is to reduce the amount of real time required to execute the regeneration. This may be accomplished in theory by deleting all the idle time in the regenerated run. Two implementations were proposed. One deletes the time constraint of the playback. That is, an interrupt will be played back as soon as the I/O state is set to an appropriate value. This simulates zero terminal and user response time. The second method is to modify the scheduler program to detect the condition of no user ready to operate; i.e., an idle condition. Upon detection, the software clock is updated to the time of the next recorded interrupt. When the playback mechanism checks the time to determine whether the interrupt should be played back, it will be satisfied and the regeneration will continue.

Both of these methods were implemented and tested. The regenerations were initiated in the normal method with additions to the correction deck for the modifications. The elapsed real time was manually measured. Their comparative success in terms of validity and reliability was determined by using the three basic measures.

Delayed Regeneration. This experiment determined whether a regeneration run could be temporarily stopped by both manual and automatic intervention to examine the contents of core memory. This would normally be used to support debugging, measurement, and dynamic analysis.

The experiment began by initiating the regeneration in the normal manner. Shortly after the regeneration was operating, the system was manually interrupted by depressing the interrupt button on the computer console, upon which control transferred to the basic executive debugging program. This program saves the value of the software clock so that at completion of its activity it can reactivate the system as if no interruption had occurred. The purpose of BXBUG is to provide debugging aids at the operating system level. The major aids provided are a breakpoint, core dump, and core modification capability. In the experiment, a breakpoint was inserted into a program that operated frequently. Whenever the breakpoint was executed, normal operation of the system ceased and the debugging program regained control. Core dumps were taken before releasing control back to the operating system. Occasionally, the interrupt button would be depressed to cause interruptions at arbitrary points in the system and dumps would also be taken.

Two regenerated runs were made. The delaying activities were:

	Test 1	Test 2
Breakpoint generated delays	18	19
Manually generated delays	4	2
Core dumps	11	12

The results of these experiments were analyzed in the same manner as the others.

Results of the Experiments:

Content Reproduction Measure. All of the experiments were able to reproduce the program behavior leading to the same terminal directed output. The only discrepancies are calculations that depend on the passage of real time and/or the exact contents of the computer clock. It can be concluded that this regenerative recording implementation is sufficient for regenerating and studying the behavior of user programs.

Sequential Reproduction Measure. Refer to Fig. 9-8. The best sequential regeneration is achieved by the selective extension. All lines are reproduced in the same sequence in both tests. This is probably due to the reduced system load which minimizes the effect of random errors on the scheduling process. Both the unmodified and the delayed regeneration have very small discrepancies. The accelerated "clock reset" regeneration has about three times as many lines out of sequence as the unmodified run, and the absolute mean and standard deviation also increase proportionately. The "time constraint deletion" acceleration is by far the worst with half the lines out of sequence. This is about fifteen times higher than the unmodified run.

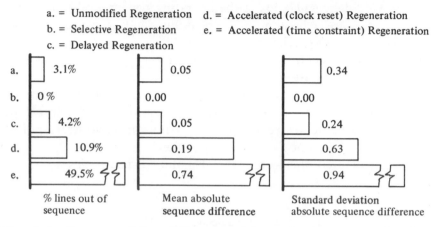

<table>
<tr><td>a. = Unmodified Regeneration</td><td>d. = Accelerated (clock reset) Regeneration</td></tr>
<tr><td>b. = Selective Regeneration</td><td>e. = Accelerated (time constraint) Regeneration</td></tr>
<tr><td>c. = Delayed Regeneration</td><td></td></tr>
</table>

	% lines out of sequence	Mean absolute sequence difference	Standard deviation absolute sequence difference
a.	3.1%	0.05	0.34
b.	0 %	0.00	0.00
c.	4.2%	0.05	0.24
d.	10.9%	0.19	0.63
e.	49.5%	0.74	0.94

Figure 9-8. Summary of the validity sequential reproduction measures for all experiments.

It appears that the sequence reproduction measure can be kept to 10 percent or less with regular and extended forms of regeneration, and a low load encourages better regeneration. These performance bounds are important considerations when the regeneration is to be used for analysis of scheduling strategies of the operating system. It is important to be able to duplicate the sequence in which programs are initiated in order to make realistic comparisons between different strategies.

Synchronous Reproduction Measure. Refer to Fig. 9-9. Note that "time constraint deletion" acceleration data is omitted since it is invalid. The regenerated system operates at about the same speed as the original system. There is no extreme slowing or speeding noticeable in these tests. This is shown by the mean time difference which is always less than 1 second. The unmodified, selective, and delayed regeneration all operate slightly faster while the accelerated runs operate slightly slower. There is no apparent reason for this. If the regenerated system tended to operate slower (for instance, because of

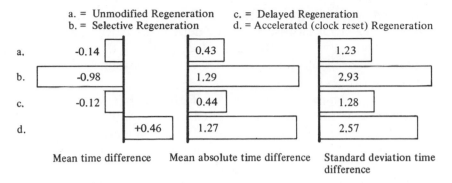

Figure 9-9.   Summary of the validity synchronous reproduction measures for all experiments (time in second units).

extra playback overhead), there would have been no way to detect it, since the idle time would have absorbed the delay. It is interesting to note that the accelerated regeneration, which presumably has no idle time, does run slower.

The mean absolute time difference is the actual average discrepancy between the original and the regenerated output. This value varies threefold among the different tests. The accelerated regeneration, which shows a large discrepancy in the sequential reproduction measure, also has a large time discrepancy of 1.27 seconds with a standard deviation of 2.57 seconds. Interestingly, the selective regeneration, which has no discrepancy in the sequential reproduction measure, has the largest time discrepancy. This indicates that the two measures may be independent of one another. The probable reason for this large time discrepancy is that the load reduction caused by the selection allows programs to operate sooner than in the original run. This idea is supported by the large negative mean time difference. The delayed regeneration most closely matches the unmodified regeneration in both measures.

The standard deviations of the time differences, ranging from 1 to 3 seconds, indicate the typical range of error in the time reproduction. These values provide a guide as to the degree with which the operating system behavior is being regenerated. Clearly, with time differences in the second range, the micro behavior of the operating system programs is not being accurately reproduced.

Reliability:

Content Reproduction Measure. The only difference between duplicate regenerations are the time-dependent calculations. Otherwise, the output was exactly duplicated, implying that experimental reliability is available for studying the functional behavior of programs.

Sequential Reproduction Measure. Refer to Fig. 9-10. Note that the accelerated "time constraint deleted" test is omitted because only one run was made. The hypothesis that the sequential reproduction differences between identical regenerations does not represent different system operations was tested. A chi square test on the number of differences was used. The results vary widely. The selective regeneration and accelerated regeneration results do not reject the hypothesis. The delayed regeneration produces a marginal result of 0.10. The unmodified regeneration rejects the hypothesis. This rejection occurred because one of the three runs has a much larger number of differences than the others.

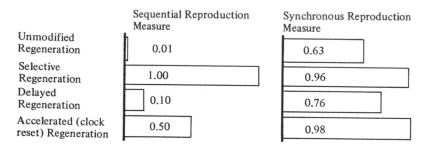

Figure 9-10.   Summaries of the reliability probability for the sequential and synchronous measures for all experiments.

There is not necessarily a direct correlation between the validity and reliability of the sequential reproduction measures. The unmodified regeneration has a high sequential validity but a very low sequential reliability. The other regenerations show mixed relationships. The validity and reliability measures appear to represent different characteristics of the playback mechanism.

The significance of these results relates to the application of the regeneration. Studies that make use of the sequential output measure to determine the effect of changes to the system may have little confidence that the observed results are caused by the induced changes and not by random fluctuations.

Synchronous Reproduction Measure. Refer to Fig. 9-10. Note that the accelerated "time constraint deleted" test is omitted because its time measures are not valid. The hypothesis that the mean time reproduction differences between identical regenerations does not represent different system operations was tested. An analysis of variance could not reject this hypothesis. The computed probabilities are presented in Fig. 9-10. The lowest is 0.63 and the highest is 0.98. It is interesting to note that the experiments with the worst synchronous time validity have the best reliability. The reason for this is not clear.

There does not seem to be any significant relationship between the sequential and synchronous reliability. This suggests that the two measures are independent, and that in this regeneration implementation the synchronous measures are better indices for studying the effects of changes to the regenerated system.

9-4-6 Experimental Conclusions

These experiments attempted to determine the feasibility of the regenerative recording of a time-sharing system. The emphasis was on the ability to recreate the exact software behavior. No investigation of the regeneration of program mutations was conducted.

These experiments demonstrated that the regeneration of a time-sharing system is feasible. The degree of reproducibility was quantitatively measured and expressed as a statistical value. It was shown that regeneration of functional program behavior—the macro system operation is not a difficult process. The operating system can be made to perform its functions of allocating and scheduling system resources, and activating user programs; the user programs can similarly be made to repeat their functions.

The regeneration of the exact software operation at the instruction level is only partially successful. It can be inferred that the user programs execute the same sequence of instructions because they reproduce the same output. However, the instruction sequence of the operating system is not duplicated as indicated by the variance in the sequence and time that the user programs' output is produced.

These results demonstrate the basic strengths of this implementation and set standards for measuring the success of future regenerative recording projects. This is an important by-product of this research, for only with a detailed statement of methods and quantitative analysis of results can future work be intelligently guided and evaluated.

These experiments establish evaluative criteria, measures, and measurements for studying a regenerative recording implementation. The *evaluative criteria* are the statements of validity and reliability. The first asks whether the regeneration can reproduce the original system behavior, and the second whether the regeneration's results can be reproduced in order to support experimentation. The *measures* used as inputs to these evaluative criteria are the ability to reproduce the terminal output, to reproduce the terminal output sequence, and to reproduce the time of the terminal output. The first of these determines whether the user programs operate correctly; the other two are an indication of the operating system behavior. The *measurement* is made by time tagging and saving all the output from the original and regenerated runs, and then manually comparing them. These measures and measurement techniques are fairly simple and somewhat coarse. However, they are capable of distinguishing between the effects of different experiments, and the measures appear to be independent of each other. In a more accurate regeneration implementation these measures and measurement techniques might not provide sufficient resolution. The measures do have immediate deficiencies—they will not detect regenerated variance in the use of the CPU or channels if this usage is not closely related to, and has an effect on, terminal output.

9-4-7 Directions for Research

Future research and development work in regenerative recording can continue along four different lines:

1. Extend the technique to include the recording and regeneration of files located on high-speed I/O devices. This capability is required for a complete and useful regenerative recording implementation.
2. Develop methods for improving the validity and reliability of regenerations. This includes determining the practical limits of these factors and designing control mechanisms to assure that the regeneration never gets out of phase by more than a predetermined amount.

3. Add a mutation capability to the regeneration. The ability to modify programs and stimulate their behavior with pre-recorded input is an important capability for system verification and experimentation. This application of regeneration will produce a host of new problems.
4. To make a regenerative recording implementation a useful tool for the system designer, developer, and investigator, a variety of utility extensions must be built onto it. These include such items as the ability to start the regeneration at different times in the system operation, independent activation of measurement tools during a regeneration, and dynamic data and program tracing features.

REFERENCES

Balzer, R. M., EXDAMS—Extendable Debugging and Monitoring System, *Proceedings of AFIPS Spring Joint Computer Conference,* Montvale, N. J., AFIPS Press, 1969, 567–580.

Black, A. J., "SAVDAT" (Save Input Data), A Routine to Save Live Input Data in Simulator Tape Format," FN GS–151, System Development Corporation, Santa Monica, Calif., July 1960.

Head, R. V., *Real-Time Business Systems,* New York, Holt, Rinehart & Winston, Inc., 1964.

Karush, A. D., "The Regenerative Recording of Time-Sharing Systems," Master's Thesis, University of California at Los Angeles, June 1970.

Koster, R., "Low Level Self-Measurement in Computers," UCLA-10P14-84, Report No. 69-57, University of California at Los Angeles, October 1969.

Linde, R. R., C. Weissman, C. Fox, "The ADEPT-50 Time-Sharing System," *Proceedings of the 1969 Fall Joint Computer Conference,* Montvale, N. J., AFIPS Press, 39–51.

Sackman, H., *Computers, System Science, and Evolving Society,* New York, John Wiley & Sons, Inc., 1967.

———, "Regenerative Recording in Man-Machine Digital Systems," *Proceedings, National Winter Convention on Military Electronics,* Chapter 16, February 1964, 14–19.

Sackman, H., and J. Munson, "The Investigation of Computer Operating Time and System Capacity for Man-Machine Digital Systems," SP-1462, System Development Corporation, Santa Monica, Calif., November 1963.

Van Horn, E. C., "Three Criteria for Designing Computing Systems to Facilitate Debugging," *Communications of the ACM,* Vol. 11, No. 5, May 1968. 360–365.

Vetter, C., "Dr. Otto Matic, I Presume," *Playboy,* April 1970.

10

INTERACTIVE DATA REDUCTION IN PLANNING

S. G. Swerdlow

Abstract

Alternative design features in interactive data reduction systems are studied by examining several systems discussed in the literature. Essential factors involved in those designs are extracted by cross comparing the systems. A rating is made of the importance of these factors in the context of interactive data reduction in support of planning. Low-level interactions among them are considered. The detailed ratings are presented in a series of tables. General aspects of these tables are discussed in the text.

Overall conclusions arrived at are: First, that interactive data reduction is most useful as a tool for playing with data or models. This means examining the underlying structure to determine the most likely hypothesis that the data can support or reject. The heavy computing required for testing the hypothesis should be performed offline. Second, identification of the user class for which the system is being designed is the most critical factor in design decisions. This conclusion implies that a general purpose system may not be desirable. Third, some advanced features which the ultimate user class may not require will have to be implemented in order to support program development.

366

10-1 INTRODUCTION

Data reduction includes data organization and data analysis. It is difficult to specify a desirable data reduction system for an application when the nature of the data and its uses are not specified. Further, it is probably impossible to develop a "general-purpose" data reduction system because of the sensitivity of the implementation to so many factors.

The size of the data base influences the type of algorithm that can be used, especially at the boundary between maintaining the data in core, and having to overlay I/O processing. Also, the organization of the data base determines how the data must be retrieved for any given inquiry. This includes questions such as which data must be sorted, what indices have to be searched or updated, and the number of passes which may be required to converge toward satisfactory solutions. If a particular data item occurs in more than one data file, the maintenance problem is increased. That data item may have to be changed in all or some nonsingular subsets of those files. A cross-reference file or inverted list directory may have to be implemented to keep track of all occurrences of a given data item. Knowledge of the ways in which the data will be accessed is a prerequisite to designing the index structure used. This knowledge is necessary both to avoid superfluous index entries, and to avoid omitting necessary entries. This study is devoted primarily to examining interactive data reduction systems and determining the design choices that have to be made for various system objectives.

10-2 CURRENT INTERACTIVE DATA REDUCTION SYSTEMS

10-2-1 Console Oriented Model Building

An interactive statistical modeling tool is discussed in Schatzoff's paper on "Console Oriented Model Building" (1965). To provide a frame of reference, Schatzoff begins by listing six steps characterizing scientific method (see Fig. 10-1). He then makes two observations. First, the process is essentially iterative. Second, the computer is used mainly to perform the computation required at step 4. The proposed system is designed to involve the computer more extensively in steps 2 through 5, and to facilitate iteration through the entire process. The proposed system flow is outlined in Fig. 10-2. Note that

```
1. Formulate problem

2. Construct model

3. Test model

4. Form inferences based on
   performance of model

5. Test "solution"

6. Implement "solution"
```

Figure 10-1. Steps comprising scientific method (from Schatzoff, 1965).

parenthesized numbers adjacent to procedure blocks refer to process steps in Fig. 10-1 for which the procedure step provides the greatest assistance.

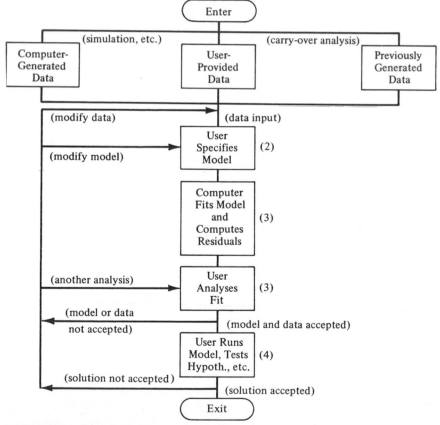

Figure 10-2. System flow for console oriented model building (from Schatzoff, 1965).

The article contains excellent short descriptions of several statistical techniques useful in steps 2 and 3. References are given for more detailed discussions, and a sample terminal session is provided in the appendix. The system is designed so that addition of new statistical procedures is relatively easy. The level of interaction reaches only to the point of providing control information for what are essentially batch procedures. However, much can be accomplished at this level by breaking procedures into small units and allowing the user to change his approach at any control point. The system does not discuss any graphic capability. The type of service performed would provide a useful complement to a graphics system such as DISPLAY-70 (discussed later).

10-2-2   Automatic Off-Line Multivariate Data Analysis

An interactive system for examining multivariate data is discussed in an article by Sebestyn entitled "Automatic Off-Line Multivariate Data Analysis" (1966). The system is designed to interactively study experimental data generated offline. Three techniques for pattern recognition in multivariate data are discussed: irreducible error, degree of disjointness, and information theoretic measures (e.g., entropy). These techniques would be used to partition the data sets into their sources of origin.

The emphasis of the article is on mathematical techniques. However, it does provide an instructive demonstration of how to take advantage of the interactive mode. For example, the analyst has the opportunity to monitor the convergence of the technique as it is being applied and to modify it as necessary. As in the previous system, the approach involves a combination of online and offline features to optimize the contributions of each to the total data reduction process.

10-2-3   TRACE

The TRACE system (Shure, et al., 1967) resembles the Schatzoff system (1965) in organization and purpose. A control program and a library of application programs are provided. All entries to and returns from the application programs flow through the control program. The analyst explores the data by using TRACE, and it is expected that this exploratory period would provide insights into the best methods of analysis.

The library available under TRACE differs from the library in Schatzoff's system. Schatzoff is oriented almost exclusively toward regression and analysis of variance. TRACE has a broader library overall, but is much less sophisticated in regard to regression and analysis of variance; its emphasis is on classification. The TRACE system is the most versatile of those reviewed with respect to handling the underlying data base. A dictionary containing label and format information is formed for each separate data base, thus permitting great flexibility in acceptance of source data in any format. It also permits incremental construction of the data base. Variables and values within variables may be changed, added, or deleted.

The user communicates with TRACE in its own simplified language. This permits greater flexibility than those systems which allow the user only to select from a list of pre-edited options. It is assumed, however, that the user is relatively sophisticated in statistical analysis and in TRACE.

10-2-4 IDEA

The IDEA system (Press and Rogers, 1967) is an extension of the TRACE system. While TRACE is employed to manipulate the data base, IDEA is used to "search heuristically for regions which are well fit by a simple model in which the dependent variable in that region is assumed to be constant with random error." It outputs a classification tree as it proceeds.

The intent of the system is similar to that of Sebestyn (1966), but the mathematical techniques are quite different. IDEA prompts the user at the decision points, enabling him to take advantage of his pattern recognition skills and his own heuristics to develop the classification tree. The system described in the article did not contain graphics; however, mention was made of adding graphics in the future.

10-2-5 MAP

The MAP system described by Kaplow, et al. (1966) is an interactive mathematical analysis system which provides access to a library of mathematical programs through an interpretive command monitor. It is implemented on the Project MAC CTSS system. The user class consists mainly of upper-division and graduate physics students who are relatively sophisticated in mathematics and relatively unsophisticated in programming. The system design goal is to allow the user to perform the same type of analysis he would perform without the computer, but with the computer taking over the computational burden while the user still controls the flow of the analysis.

MAP takes advantage of the online environment to interact with the user. Incomplete or ambiguous problem specifications cause MAP to request the missing information or a clarification. An estimate of standard error is included, when it can be computed, as standard output with computed values. Parameter specifications outside the function domain are flagged. Implementing an interactive capability such as that offered by MAP is feasible for applications in which the types of questions, errors, and information required can be anticipated. That is, the MAP system is feasible for use in relatively well-structured interactive environments.

MAP contains several other advanced system features which are not widely implemented. Among these are capabilities for saving command sequences, and for adding assembly-language subroutines to the library. The ability to save command sequences allows the user to develop an analysis procedure for a given problem and then reuse it; the dialogue may be modified at any point while it is being reused. The individually written subroutines are allowed to call any of the standard system subroutines; access is usually limited to the math library. Editing problems and user-system communication are greatly simplified for the programmer by the availability of system routines for these functions.

10-2-6 Graphic Displays

The system described by Miller (1969) is designed to be used by a business manager in planning and evaluating alternatives. The method is to allow the manager to display the current situation as a set of graphs and then determine, through changes in the graphs, the effects resulting from some set of changes in the assumptions. Miller believes that quick response to the "what if" type of question answerable by the system will enhance small group discussions between managers by providing answers to spontaneous questions. It will also aid the manager as he privately attempts to develop a position on a given question before having to take a public stand.

Underlying the system's graphic component is a mathematical

model of the application area. This model is individually programmed for application area, inventory, product development, etc. Since the user is not expected to be highly sophisticated in mathematics and statistics, the system display programs must be written to anticipate the questions that the manager or planner will be most likely to ask; this is done separately for each application area. The system's approach is feasible for well-structured problems, as is the case with the MAP system previously discussed.

Miller includes an outline (see Fig. 10-3) of the programming stages involved in developing such a system and estimates—somewhat optimistically—the programming effort required. A detailed example of the use of the system is also presented, clearly demonstrating the system's strengths.

1. Develop basic graphic capabilities:

   Initiate plot routine.
   Plot lines.
   Display alphanumeric characters.
   Accept light-pen detects.
   Enter typewriter data.

2. Develop general utility package:

   Draw graph axes.
   Label graph axes.
   Draw multiple graphs.
   Write table of contents.
   Write instructional panels.
   Write table formats.

3. Develop specific applications:

   Formulate planning and market strategies, market assumptions, distribution demands.

   Monitor planning and marketing strategies, budget operations; signal deviations from existing plans.

   Test hypotheses and predictions, including competitors' interaction with existing plans.

Figure 10–3. Procedural steps in interactive graphic planning (adapted from Miller, 1969).

10-2-7 DISPLAY-70

The DISPLAY-70 system described by Lickhalter (1969) is designed as a general-purpose graphics system that can be useful to managers and planners in much the same manner as the graphics system discussed by Miller. In contrast to the latter system, however, DISPLAY-70 does not use a model of the application area. This means that the user must be somewhat more sophisticated in mathematical-statistical analysis, although a high degree of sophistication is not expected.

Table 10-1.   Graphic Capabilities Versus System Features

CAPABILITY		S1	S2	S3	S4	S5	S6	S7
A.	Plotting	N	N	N	N	N	Y	Y
	1. Curve fit						N	N
	2. Plot overlay						N	Y
	3. Automatic scaling						Y	Y
	4. Manual scaling						Y	Y
	5. Function plots						Y	N
	6. Raw data plots						N	Y
	7. Smoothing						—	—
	8. Line plots						Y	Y
	9. Histograms						—	Y
	10. Regression fits						—	Y
	11. Regression fits						—	Y
	12. Residuals						—	Y
	13. Scrolling						N	N
	14. Measures and plot overlay						Y	Y
	15. Display face formatting						N	N
		S1	S2	S3	S4	S5	S6	S7
B.	Trees	N	N	N	Y	N	N	N
	1. Generation from grammar				N			
	2. Generation from directions				Y			
	3. Scanning				Y			
	4. Assigning measures to nodes				Y			
	5. Incremental construction				Y			
C.	Geometric Structures	N	N	N	N	N	N	N
D.	Moving Picture (Simulated system in action)	N	N	N	N	N	N	N

Legend: *System Identifier Codes*

S1 = Schatzoff   S5 = Kaplow
S2 = Sebestyn   S6 = Miller
S3 = Shure   S7 = Lickhalter
S4 = Rogers   Y = Yes; N = No

At each decision point, the user is presented a list of possibilities from which he makes his selection. The construction of such a list implies that the developers of DISPLAY-70 believe they can anticipate the most frequently used sequences of analysis, as in Kaplow's MAP system.

The graphs are generated from a previously prepared data base. Scatter plots, regression lines, and other displays are formed from the vectors in that base. The user can look at his data from various points of view, using DISPLAY-70 in the manner indicated. Current analysis capability is limited essentially to descriptive statistics. Future models are planned for more sophisticated data reduction.

10-3 INTERACTIVE DATA ANALYSIS

Each of the seven systems reviewed in the preceding section had its particular strengths and weaknesses. Essentially, each system required consideration of a different aspect of man-machine interaction in data reduction. However, the aspects considered did not exhaust the list of potential factors. A more inclusive list (no claim of completeness is expressed or implied) is presented in Tables 10-1, 10-2, and 10-3, where the projections of the reviewed systems on the listed factors are shown. The following subsections consider various characteristics of interactive data reduction based on those factors.

10-3-1 Response Time

Response time should be acceptable to the needs of the user, which often means that the computing load must be light. Therefore, the interactive systems which employ externally generated data are oriented toward data exploration. The intent is to allow the user to explore and play with his data so that he can decide on some optimal set of analysis to be performed offline. Indeed, he may find an online data-editing scheme very useful. The systems which do not use externally generated data are oriented toward allowing the user to play with some mathematical model. These systems can perform a great deal more computation than the others because it is faster to generate data internally than to retrieve it from an external file. All non-data-driven systems considered here used a mathematical model. However, it is obvious that a graphic system driven by a process or event model would be a desirable addition.

Table 10-2.   Data Base Capability Versus System Features

CAPABILITY	S1	S2	S3	S4	S5	S6	S7
A. Incremental Data Base Construction	Y	N	Y	Y	Y	Y	Y
1. Add, delete, modify values	Y		Y	Y	Y	Y	N
2. Add, delete, modify relations	N		Y	Y	N	Y	Y
B. Associative Retrieval	N	N	N	N	N	N	N
C. Dictionary	N	N	N	N	Y	Y	Y
D. Access to "Non-Standard" Files	Y	N	N	N	N	N	Y

Table 10-3.   Level of Interaction Versus System Features

CAPABILITY	S1	S2	S3	S4	S5	S6	S7
A. Access to Math-Stat Library	Y	N	Y	Y	Y	Y	Y
1. Standard functions built in	Y		Y	Y	Y	Y	Y
2. Ability to add functions	Y		N	N	Y	N	Y
B. Procedure Monitoring	N		N				
1. Convergence		Y		Y	Y	N	N
2. Trace		Y		Y	–	Y	Y
C. Procedure Specification	N	N	N	N	Y	N	N
1. Select sequence of steps for repeated application							
D. Communication							
1. Select next step only from list of valid options	Y	Y	N	Y	N	N	Y
2. Explanations of procedures, syntax any time	N	N	N	N	N	N	Y
3. Warnings about numerical analysis or statistical problems	N	Y	N	N	Y	N	N
4. Standard default output includes estimate of statistical error	N	Y	N	N	Y	N	N
5. Language syntax	N	N	Y	?	N	N	N
E. Output							
1. Formatting	N	N	N	N	N	N	N
2. Hard copy	Y	Y	Y	Y	Y	N	N
3. CRT	N	N	N	N	N	Y	Y

10-3-2 Math-Stat Library

The nature of the mathematical-statistical library available to the user is largely a function of the anticipated user class and the personal prejudices of the system designer. The range and scope of available statistical procedures is vast—selection of "best" procedures is half the battle. In terms of flexibility, the low end of the scale is represented by the graphics system presented by Miller (1969). This system is aimed at the mathematically naive business manager. With the incumbent model, it presents a canned set of operations which is redesigned along with the design of every new model. No access to a library is allowed. The other end of the flexibility scale is represented by MAP, which is oriented towards the mathematically sophisticated physics student. The system's main function is to provide access to an extensive open-ended math library. The user is entirely responsible for planning and conducting each analysis.

Libraries differ in contents as well as size. MAP contains primarily analytical procedures, such as numerical integration-differentiation and Fourier transforms. None of these procedures would be found in the TRACE library, which, instead, contains routines for means, medians, correlations, and t-tests. (TRACE's expected user class consists of statisticians.)

The nature of the library can be considered in yet another way. Is the library fixed from the user's point of view? In TRACE, it is; but in MAP, it is not. The MAP user can add his own routines, which can call MAP system routines. This type of facility is directed toward a user population which is sophisticated in programming as well as in mathematics; it is assumed that system designers would be members of such a class.

10-3-3 Man-Machine Communication

Syntactically, the design of the language used in man-machine communication ranges from a simple algebraic parser to parameter-list format (control-card format), to a multiple-choice option list. The use of an algebraic parser occurs in more flexible systems—those systems which anticipate more sophisticated users. The flow of the analysis is more completely under the control of the user in such cases. In general, the user is not protected from applying analysis to data which does not satisfy the assumption under which it applies.

Nor is he helped in determining what might or might not be useful. He accepts the responsibility for open-end analysis and sacrifices system prompting in order to acquire the power to solve the problem in the way he sees fit.

The parameter-list format is intermediate with respect to power, "responsibility," and help. In an option-list system, the user has no power to perform an analysis sequence not anticipated by the designer. However, he is relieved of the responsibility of attempting a technique where it does not apply. He is given a great deal of help in deciding what could be useful—indeed, in a well-designed system, he is given a multiple-choice test with more than one correct answer. Systems of this type must anticipate user requests in order to design the option list, which implies that they have some model of the "typical" user. This also implies a high level of expertise in the application area in order to develop the set of equations making up the math model.

10-3-4 Diagnostics

The nature and level of diagnostics generated by the reviewed systems vary considerably. An option-list system such as DISPLAY-70 has no need for response format diagnostics. The other systems, however, should edit for format and legality. The most extensive diagnostics would be required for the algebraic parser. Numerical and functional diagnostics are required in every system and are crucial in a system which accepts externally generated data. Any such system should also include a data-editing function and, if possible, should force the use of that function as its first step. Systems which generate their data internally from an application model have no need for this type of diagnostic procedure. However, once the user is allowed to modify parameters, a need is created. One example of a model-driven system in which the user can modify parameters is discussed by Miller (1969). The MAP system provides the most extensive numerical diagnostics and automatically provides estimates of standard error where such a value can be computed.

10-3-5 Continued Sessions

The ability to save work from one session to the next includes the ability to save intermediate values. Model-driven systems generally do not have this ability, and data-driven systems may not have it (e.g., DISPLAY-70). The ability to save intermediate values and retrieve them later implies the ability to name them, which requires the maintenance of a runtime dictionary. An example of a system with this capability is TRACE. In addition to saving intermediate data values, it is desirable to save procedure steps. This corresponds roughly to catalogued procedures in the IBM operating system (OS). Such a capability allows the user to develop an involved analysis on one set of data which can be used again as new sets are acquired, thus saving many hours of terminal time. The only system reviewed which has this capability is MAP.

10-3-6   Graphic Capability

Of the seven systems reviewed, only the last two—DISPLAY-70 and Miller's graphic displays—had an extensive graphic capability. However, this may be the most significant factor involved in selling such a system to a naive user class. The members of that user class typically believe they understand graphs in contrast to complex numerical operations. Indeed, graphs can present more information, more economically, than tables or statistical measures. Insight into data can be provided by a simple graph, which might be difficult or impossible to convey in any other manner. Nevertheless, graphs are not sufficient for extended and detailed analysis, and the earlier systems reviewed survived with a weak graphic capability or none at all.

10-4   PLANNING APPLICATIONS

The preceding section discussed the various design choices and the factors determining them. In this section, an attempt is made to fit those design choices over the factors which apply in a planning system. A difficulty arises in that the planning system, in which the data reduction system must fit, is not yet specified. As a consequence, the following discussion is both tentative and general.

Two factor spaces apply. The first is the user factor space. The second is the level of planning and planning method factor space.

The user factor space contains these classes of users: (1) system design team, (2) system measurement and evaluation team, and (3) planning team. The characteristics of the first two teams can be anticipated. For the sake of argument, they will be classified as sophisticated users, both in programming and in math-stat. The characteristics of the planning team cannot be anticipated, only the possibilities. These possibilities are: general management, planning staff, operational (line) management. Again, for the sake of argument, we will assume a general manager is naive and the planning staffs and operational

		System Designers	Measurement Evaluation	Planning Management Staff	
Data Source					
1.	External	R	R	U	U
2.	Model	U	U	U	U
Library					
1.	Fixed—no access	NA	NA	U	U
2.	Fixed—with access	–	U	U	U
3.	Expandable with access	R	U	U	U
4.	Math-oriented	R	U	U	U
5.	Stat-oriented	R	R	U	U
Interactive Language					
1.	Algebraic	U	U	U	U
2.	Parameter	R	R	U	R
3.	Option List	NA	NA	U	U
Control of Analysis					
1.	User responsibility	R	R	U	U
2.	System prompt	–	U	U	U
3.	System control	NA	NA	U	U
Diagnostics					
1.	Format	R	R	U	U
2.	Function	R	R	U	U
Develop Analysis Procedures					
1.	Save intermediate values (dictionary)	R	U	U	U
2.	Save procedure steps	U	U	U	U
Graphics					
1.	Extensive	U	U	U	U
2.	Moderate	U	U	U	U

LEGEND: R = Required   NA = Not Acceptable

U = Useful   – = does not apply

Figure 10-4. Design choices as a function of user class.

management are sophisticated in math-stat, but not in programming.

The design choices made as a function of user class are presented in Fig. 10-4. The following comments apply. The system designers are the first users and the measurement-evaluation team the second. This means that the sophisticated capabilities such as access to a library, diagnostics, and catalogued procedures will, to some extent, have to be

		Normative	Strategic	Tactical	Operational
Data Source					
1.	External	–	U	R	R
2.	Model	U	U	U	U
Library					
1.	Fixed–no access	U	U	U	U
2.	Fixed–with access	U	U	U	U
3.	Expandable with access	U	U	U	U
4.	Math-oriented	U	U	U	U
5.	Stat-oriented	U	U	U	U
Interactive Language					
1.	Algebraic	U	U	U	U
2.	Parameter	U	U	U	U
3.	Option list	U	U	U	U
Control of Analysis					
1.	User responsibility	U	U	U	U
2.	System prompt	U	U	U	U
3.	System control	U	U	U	U
Diagnostics					
1.	Format	U	U	U	U
2.	Function	U	U	R	R
Develop Analysis Procedures					
1.	Save intermediate values (dictionary)	U	U	U	U
2.	Save procedure steps	U	U	U	U
Graphics					
1.	Extensive	U	U	U	U
2.	Moderate	R	R	U	U

LEGEND: R = Required   NA = Not Acceptable

　　　　　U = Useful   – = does not apply

Figure 10-5.   Design choices as a function of planning level.

	Dialectical Delphi	Tree Search	Modeling	PERT
Data Source				
1. External	R	U	U	U
2. Model	NA	U	U	U
Library				
1. Fixed—no access	U	U	NA	U
2. Fixed—with access	U	U	NA	U
3. Expandable with access	U	U	R	U
4. Math-oriented	U	U	R	U
5. Stat-oriented	U	U	R	U
Interactive Language				
1. Algebraic	U	U	NA	U
2. Parameter	U	U	NA	U
3. Option list	U	U	NA	U
Control of Analysis				
1. User responsibility	U	U	R	U
2. System prompt	U	U	U	U
3. System control	U	U	U	U
Diagnostics				
1. Format	U	U	U	U
2. Function	U	U	R	R
Develop Analysis Procedures				
1. Save intermediate values (dictionary)	U	U	R	U
2. Save procedure steps	U	U	R	U
Graphics				
1. Extensive	U	U	U	U
2. Moderate	U	U	U	U

LEGEND: R = Required   NA = Not Acceptable

U = Useful   − = does not apply

Figure 10–6.   Design choices as a function of a planning method.

developed first. Failure to do so will result in extended system development time. This is the phenomenon of bootstrapping. The sophisticated facilities may not be required by the third class of users; however, that does not mean they should be removed from the system. A better choice is made by adding another face to the system. The individual user then sees the particular face that most suits him. A conflict does arise, however, in allocating the scarce resources of time and manpower. The system library cannot be extensively developed without sufficient time to complete the instructional panels required for the option lists. A PERT system may be required for planning the specific development sequence.

The level of planning and planning method space is more involved. Design choices as a function of planning level are displayed in Fig. 10-5. Design choices as a function of planning method are displayed in Fig. 10-6. The following comments apply.

A data reduction system can be designed for a fixed planning level or method. Design choices which reflect a requirement for flexibility now become optional. The choices the analyst would make are anticipated and built into the system. The library contains exactly those functions which will be required. Control of the analysis is taken over by the system up to the level of an option list. There is no need to develop new procedures. However, the more powerful features never become unacceptable as long as they coexist with the tutorial ones. The resulting figures reflect this in that almost every cell is marked U (useful).

In Fig. 10-5 there are essentially four exceptions. External data will not be available in the case of normative planning; therefore, that cell is marked not applicable. In contrast, external data describing the real world is considered necessary for tactical and operational planning, and these cells are marked required. It is assumed that catastrophic functional diagnostics must always be supplied. An R in a function diagnostic call is then interpreted as a requirement for measures of convergence and standard error. Tactical and operational, planning, at the implementation level where money is expended, require those measures. Moderate graphics are marked as required for normative and strategic planning because at these levels the user is looking for insight. Insight is probably more effectively derived from graphs than from tables.

Figure 10-6 has essentially two exceptions and one special case. The dialectical techniques are based on the interchange of opinion between humans. A model would have to incorporate a set of fixed opinions. This is not equivalent; hence, the only data available in this case is external. The comment concerning function diagnostics in operational planning now applies to PERT.

The special case is modeling. The market and choice scales do not apply. Modeling implies the ability to build and manipulate a model. None of the language choices presented is sufficient for this task. A more extensive and general purpose programming language would be required. The user is building the model; hence, he requires the ability to analyze it in the most general way. This is reflected in the library and control of analysis blocks. The requirements for analysis development procedures are imposed by the need to incrementally build and analyze the model.

A study of Figs. 10-4, 10-5, and 10-6 indicates that design choices are mostly a function of user class. However, certain exogenous factors can be the determining factors in any given instance (e.g., modeling in Fig. 10-6).

10-5 SUMMARY AND CONCLUSIONS

The above review of alternative design choices for interactive data analysis systems leads to these key conclusions:

- Interactive data reduction is probably most useful as a tool for exploring and playing with data or models, as opposed to standardized analysis of experimental data.
- Perhaps the most critical factor in system design decisions is identification of target user classes and representative data problems.
- It may be economical over the long run to develop some advanced features not used by the ultimate users in order to enhance system development.

REFERENCES

Kaplow, R., J. Brackett, and S. Strong, "Man-Machine Communications in On-Line Mathematical Analysis," *Proceedings of the FJCC*, Vol. 29, 1966, 456–477.

Lickhalter, R. A., "Display-70: An Interactive Data Analysis System for Management Decision," SP-3457, System Development Corporation, Santa Monica, Calif., December 1969.

Miller, I. M., "Computer Graphics for Decision Making," *Harvard Business Review,* November-December 1969, 121–132.

Press, L. I., and M. S. Rogers, "IDEA–A Conversational, Heuristic Program for Inductive Data Exploration and Analysis," *Proceedings of the ACM,* 1967, 35–40.

Schatzoff, M., "Console Oriented Model Building," *ACM 20th National Conference Proceedings,* 1965, 354–374.

Sebestyn, George S., "Automatic Off-Line Multivariate Data Analysis," *Proceedings of the FJCC,* 1966, 685–694.

Shure, G. H., R. J. Meeker, and W. H. Moore, Jr., "TRACE Time-Shared Routines for Analysis, Calssification and Evaluation," *AFIPS Conference Proceedings, SJCC,* Vol. 30, 1967, 525.

INDEX